PARIS CONCEALED

PARIS CONCEALED

MASKS IN THE CITY OF LIGHT

James H. Johnson

THE UNIVERSITY OF CHICAGO PRESS
CHICAGO AND LONDON

The University of Chicago Press, Chicago 60637
The University of Chicago Press, Ltd., London

Published 2025
Printed in the United States of America

34 33 32 31 30 29 28 27 26 25 1 2 3 4 5

ISBN-13: 978-0-226-83646-1 (cloth)
ISBN-13: 978-0-226-83647-8 (e-book)
DOI: https://doi.org/10.7208/chicago/9780226836478.001.0001

Library of Congress Cataloging-in-Publication Data

Names: Johnson, James H., 1960–, author.
Title: Paris concealed : masks in the city of light / James H. Johnson.
Description: Chicago : The University of Chicago Press, 2025. | Includes bibliographical references and index.
Identifiers: LCCN 2024025401 | ISBN 9780226836461 (cloth) | ISBN 9780226836478 (ebook)
Subjects: LCSH: Masks—France—History. | Masks—Symbolic aspects—France. | Masks—Political aspects—France. | Masks—Social aspects—France. | Self (Philosophy)—France. | Self-presentation—France—History. | Masks in art—History. | BISAC: HISTORY / Social History | HISTORY / Europe / France
Classification: LCC GT1748.F8 J65 2025 | DDC 391.4/340944361—dc23/eng/20240712
LC record available at https://lccn.loc.gov/2024025401

♾ This paper meets the requirements of ANSI/NISO Z39.48-1992 (Permanence of Paper).

To Christopher Ricks and to the memory of Roger Shattuck

Contents

Preface

This book recounts the history of identity in terms of how people have concealed it. It is a history of masks in a wide sense of the word, from the physical object that covers the face to the diversions and distortions of speech, dress, and behavior. Festive and formal masks, as well as comic, dramatic, and carnivalesque masks, are part of this story. A larger part treats the invisible masks of pretense, delusion, fraud, and self-deceit. Whatever protection or advantage masking may provide, it also reveals something about the masker and the larger context. This, too, is the subject of *Paris Concealed*: to understand the range of possible selves, and the limits of imaginable selves, by looking at the ways people have concealed themselves.

I told the first part of this story in *Venice Incognito*. Travelers came to the famous carnival city expecting to see roles reversed and the social order suspended under cover of the mask. What they found instead was a city whose residents wore masks for six months of the year, not principally for celebration but to smooth transactions in public among a vastly unequal population. Seventeenth- and eighteenth-century Venetians watched plays and listened to operas in masks. They visited cafés, shopped in markets, and strolled near San Marco in masks. Foreign princes attended learned societies at which all were masked. Patricians and diplomats were compelled by law to wear masks at formal receptions.

Venetian masks went beyond the white hardened pasteboard that covered their faces. In a society that punished religious doubt and political dissent, writers recommended "honest dissembling," a partial truth that concealed more than it revealed. Moralists who esteemed an open heart invoked allegorical masks to condemn deceit. In art and literature, the mask could mean prudence or self-preservation. Women gained a measure of freedom when they donned a veil and stepped outside by themselves. Beggars whose identities were known wore masks to save face. In Venice, masks protected identities without always hiding them. Their fictive anonymity guarded status and preserved distance in an unchanging hierarchy. Here, most masks were conservative.

The 250-year span of *Paris Concealed* contains a wide array of masks both seen and unseen. In the time of Louis XIV, unaccompanied women wore masks to maintain their privacy in public. Dancers in ballets and operas wore masks to shroud individual expression and draw attention to the language of movement and gesture. When Italian troupes brought commedia dell'arte to the French public, their masks remained a fixture on the stage for decades. Masks were expected in carnival celebrations both on the streets and in royal and commercial balls. Elsewhere, context turned them into a mortal risk. Impersonating an aristocrat was a capital crime in early modern France, as was cross-dressing. In 1698, when a man was hanged in Montpellier for having forged noble letters, banners reading *Notorious Fraud* lined his route to execution. When an escaped convict in the early 1800s assumed the identity of a count, by contrast, and worked his way to the top of the military order, his exact crime was not clear. Aristocratic titles now had no legal status and he had proved his worth on the battlefield.

Only in the nineteenth century did Parisians in substantial numbers engage in the riotous scenes we usually associate with carnival. In the public balls of the 1830s and '40s, to wear a mask was to imagine other identities. It served as both inspiration and incitement. Parisians covered their faces and denounced elites, defaced emblems of authority, and fought with police. In the long history of masking, this moment was an exception. In earlier courtly and commercial balls, masks seldom assured anonymity, and the social order was rarely threatened. In the 1860s and '70s, masking receded and the public lost interest in most carnival celebrations. Nearing the *fin de siècle*, when the unconscious loomed as a place of unknown urges, unmasking was the path to one's truest self.

The range of masking is wide, with differences both evident and subtle. A physical mask, for instance, is not a disguise. It frustrates full deceit. Its physicality—in paper, plaster, pasteboard, or cloth—announces concealment and limits any ruse. Disguise, by contrast, is in essence deceptive. False hair, an artificial mustache or beard, misleading clothes, an altered walk or voice: these are the raw materials of disguise, whose aim is to pass unnoticed. Physical masks conceal identity in a visible way. Disguise asserts an identity—a *false* identity—by concealing its concealment. Only when disguise is discovered does its mask become known.

Beyond disguise, acts of dissembling, deceit, insincerity, and hypocrisy may also play a part in crafting identities. Particular settings have made one or another of these masks especially dangerous or appealing. Courtiers' guides described the flattery needed to succeed at Versailles as honorable. Critics later condemned such "politeness" as duplicity and called it the particular vice of monarchy. "The man of the world is complete in his mask," Jean-Jacques Rousseau wrote in a typical denunciation. "What he is, is nothing. What he appears to be is everything for him."[1] During the French Revolution, the fear of masked traitors haunted patriots and fueled the Reign of Terror.

The connection between masks and identity is ancient. The Romans called Greek tragic and comic masks a *persona* from their ability to amplify actors' voices (*personare,* "to sound through"). In ancient Rome, to be a person carried legal status, which was denied to women and slaves. The anthropologist Marcel Mauss cites a still older use of the word among ancient Etruscans. Here, too, it could mean both mask and person. Mauss traces the path of modern selfhood through the *personae* of the ancient stoics, early Christian theology, Germanic and Saxon law, and the Protestant Reformation. He credits Latin and Greek moralists with endowing its legal standing with moral intent. Mauss describes this as "a sense of being conscious, independent, autonomous, free, and responsible." "Moral conscience," he continues, "introduces consciousness into the juridical conception of law."[2] Etymologically, historically, and philosophically, every person is a persona: someone who plays a role.

Since Mauss, the nature and contours of selfhood have been the subject of a growing body of work. The philosopher Charles Taylor writes of intense subjectivity, inner depth, and radical reflexivity in characterizing the modern self, finding its precedents in Augustine, Montaigne, and Rousseau. The historian Jerrold Seigel describes inwardness in similar terms but accords a greater role to social and cultural settings. His way of imagining selfhood is in three dimensions: the corporeal, relational, and reflective. The first acknowledges the body's needs, urges, and dispositions as a part of self-knowledge and understanding. The second sees the individual within networks of communities, each with its own idioms, values, and assumptions. The third understands the self as active in its own creation as it embraces, orders, and revises particular beliefs and commitments.[3]

A central theme of *Paris Concealed* is the emergence of this singular, autonomous, and capaciously introspective self. In pivotal moments, its facets are explicit: when the writer Stendhal fears that readers will grow weary of the incessant *I's* and *me's* in his autobiography; when the philosopher Victor Cousin exhorts his pupils to become masters of their own heroic and unfettered *moi*; and when, late in the nineteenth century, the nationalist writer Maurice Barrès describes the unconscious as an immense reservoir of inherited racial habits, loyalties, and hatreds. In the long history of selfhood and the particular ways people have fashioned their identities, masking and unmasking have been central.

This book aims to keep the large changes in selfhood and identity present as it moves through widely varied settings. Its diverse sources reflect the many sites and types of masking. These include manuals of etiquette and civility, moral and political treatises, plays, novels, and paintings, and criminal and military proceedings. At all times, I have tried to put the lived experience of individuals at the center of this story. Only by considering the particular choices of past lives can we grasp the range of possible selves they might have imagined.

While masks in their many forms are universal, their role in the history of France is especially revealing. From Louis XIV to the *fin de siècle*, successive political and social regimes affected how individuals understood their own identity and the degree to which they could change it: from a static view that defined identity by birth, to the disruptions of wealthy commoners buying titles of nobility, to the revolutionary credo of advancement by merit, to nineteenth-century claims, however unrealized, of universal equality. As the means of self-creation shifted, so, too, did the aims of self-concealment. The book ends at the threshold of the twentieth century. A legacy of this moment—the conviction that authentic selfhood entails unmasking one's truest nature—remains with us today.

Paris Concealed has five chronological sections, each named for a sphere in which the mask was most salient. *Status* presents the court and its gradations of rank, which generated powerful motives for dissembling. *Society* narrates the spread of courtly politesse and its fierce condemnation as false. *The Body* outlines new techniques for reading others by their anatomy at a time when traditional markers of identity were disappearing. *Politics* describes settings in which carnival and masked balls threatened revolution. *The Psyche* conveys the anxieties of modernity, when awareness of the unconscious turned the mask inward and knowing one's true self became both urgent and uncertain.

The mask still figures in our understanding of identity. From the early modern period to the present, it has gone from being a tool for advancement or protection in a largely static hierarchy, to a means of auditioning other roles or positions, to standing as an obstacle, goad, or inspiration for realizing who we truly are. One of the aims of this book is to suspend modern assumptions about masks to see the many ways they have functioned in the past. Making sense of our identity today—of what we choose to conceal or reveal to others and ourselves—is also part of this story.

PART ONE

Statust

First Promotion of Knights of the Order of Saint-Louis, François Maron (Art Resource)

If someone should try to strip away the costumes and makeup from the actors performing a play on the stage and to display them to the spectators in their own natural appearance, wouldn't he ruin the whole play? Wouldn't all the spectators be right to throw rocks at such a madman and drive him out of the theater? . . . This deception, this disguise, is the very thing that holds the attention of the spectators. Now the whole life of mortal men, what is it but a sort of play?

—ERASMUS, *Praise of Folly* (1511)

One never judges things by what they are but by the persons they concern.

—LOUIS DE ROUVROY, duc de Saint-Simon, *Memoirs* (1691–1723)

1
Mutual Delusion

BEHIND THE MASK

The duc de La Rochefoucauld's declining years witnessed the sorry end to a life of fierce pride. Estranged from the court, discredited for his role in conspiring against the monarchy, and physically wrecked from fighting royal troops, he was a relic from another age. Long hobbled by gout, by forty he was altogether lame. Believing his days were numbered, he retreated from society, composed a last will and testament, and made plans to cede the title of duke and peer to his son. His afflictions included double pneumonia, failing eyesight, a chronic cough, and bloody spittle. A friend wrote of him: "He has no hope of walking. He craves to be carried into other houses or taken outside in a carriage for a change of air."[1]

The misery was unremitting, but his mind, fed by books, writing, and conversation, still teemed. Living near the Seine in a mansion belonging to his uncle, he received visitors there or was borne in an upholstered chair to the home of Mme de Lafayette, just beyond the Luxembourg Palace. On good days they sat in her garden with some of the age's most distinguished thinkers, including the playwrights Corneille, Racine, and Molière, the philosopher Pascal, the poet Boileau, and the fabulist La Fontaine.

Writers read from their plays and poems, those with news from the court related triumphs or humiliations, and the theologically minded spoke of human corruption and God's grace. For La Rochefoucauld, the gatherings were an oasis. He knew that the center of power and prestige lay elsewhere. Roughly a dozen miles due east, workers were completing work on the palace of Versailles, the site of royal hunts, receptions, parties, and performances.

Watching from a distance, La Rochefoucauld felt both resentment and relief. Of the many in his day to describe deceit, no one was better suited.

FIGURE 1.1. *François VI, duc de La Rochefoucauld*, anon. (Bridgeman Images)

As the scion of an ancient line, he had access to the highest levels of royal power. When he challenged it, he suffered its most severe reprisals. His fate captures the domestication of France's nobility more generally. When Louis XIV was born, La Rochefoucauld was twenty-four. Ten years later, he was at the center of the Fronde, the aristocracy's last great resistance to absolutism. Imprisoned in the Bastille, shunned from court, and stripped of his positions, he was the victim of brute force as well as court ceremony. While the costs of these defeats were considerable, they were not what he dwelled on in the last decades of his life. The things he pondered were instead more intimate and abstract.

La Rochefoucauld is renowned for a work that lays bare human hypocrisy in a sequence of unsparing declarations. *Reflections, or Sentences and*

Moral Maxims is the age's most damning catalog of deceit, combining the crystalline prose of French classicism with the cold precision of a pathologist. Its central figure is the mask, which humans use to conceal their impulses from one another and themselves. Sincerity, it declares, is a ruse to win the trust of others. Chastity is mere submission to necessity. Friendship is transactional. "Love" is a desire to control. An anonymous introduction to the first edition grasps the counterfeit quality of all virtuous things. Morality, it reads, is a fiction by agreement.[2] The book's immediate reception, equal parts interest and indignation, matches the same anxious response that has greeted the work ever since. Rousseau dismissed it as a "sad book" without appeal to decent people. For Nietzsche, it was formative.[3]

The *Maxims* bears evidence of a historic turning point as the contest between nobles and royals began to shift decisively in favor of the king. Writing in his fifties, La Rochefoucauld recorded not only the psychological mastery of Louis XIV in manipulating the realm's most powerful elites but the willingness of men like him to accept servility if it meant royal favor. His insights extended beyond the moment to expose universal truths about human nature. Vanity and self-interest, he concluded, were at the root of every action. Humans are innate actors, ready to please their audience if it will bring them profit. On the book's frontispiece, a smirking Cupid has unmasked the philosopher Seneca to reveal a face creased in anger. Behind the Stoic's serene front is churning agitation. The message is clear: every seeming virtue is a mask.

La Rochefoucauld spoke from experience. As a young man, he embodied the legendary qualities of the ancient aristocracy. Known as the prince de Marcillac before his father's death, he held high esteem in Louis XIII's court. In his teens, he was a regular visitor to ballets and balls at the Louvre palace. He strolled in royal promenades, hunted, fenced, and danced. He watched solemnly as the king rose from bed. He paid elaborate court to the young Queen Anne, an infatuation that brought trust and common cause before curdling into disappointment and blame. The king addressed his father as "my cousin." While the family's peerage was not especially old, their aristocratic bloodline was. Some claimed that young Marcillac was of the twenty-first generation; others traced the line to Roman Gaul.[4]

Marcillac was proud and headstrong. He was recklessly ambitious, extravagant in his love affairs, and scalding in his enmity. Whatever polish he had did not come naturally. With dark eyes, thick brows, a fleshy mouth, and flowing hair, he looked the part but was awkward, moody, and often insecure. He was quick to take offense and slow to forgive. Those in power knew he could be manipulated by the promise of titles or positions. When rewards failed to materialize, his response could be explosive. Married at

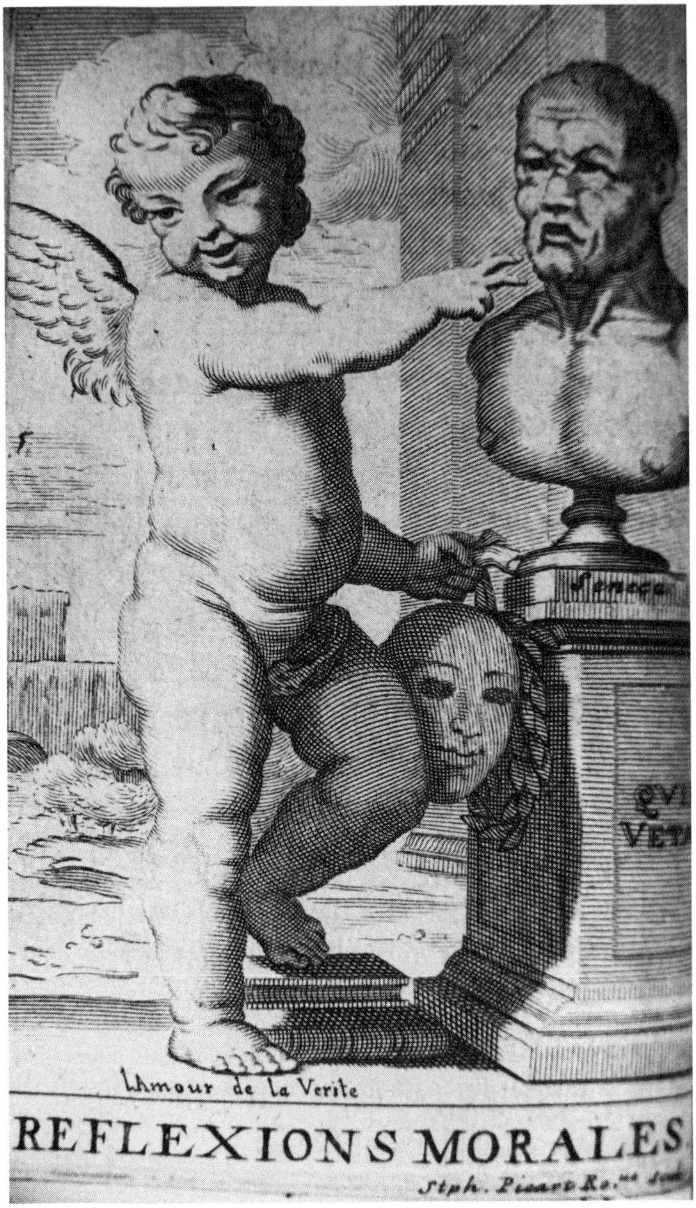

FIGURE 1.2. Frontispiece, La Rochefoucauld, *Reflections, or Sentences and Moral Maxims* (courtesy of Houghton Library, Harvard University [François, duc de La Rochefoucauld, *Réflexions; ou Sentences et maximes morales*; *FC6 L3273M665])

fourteen to a cousin still younger, he fathered eight legitimate children. The son he had with his lover Mme de Longueville was much better known. Born during the Fronde, the baby they named Charles-Paris was paraded through the capital's streets as a symbol of defiance to the monarchy.

Louis XIV was still a child when the Regency's chief minister Mazarin pushed France's aristocracy into open revolt. At Louis XIII's death in 1643, powerful nobles saw an opportunity to reverse the king's drive toward absolutism. Acting as Regent, Queen Anne drew close to Mazarin and embraced a hard line against the rebellion. Former allies and intimates, including Marcillac, suddenly found themselves compromised. His fawning messages to the queen were answered with silence or cold reproach. When she refused him a ceremonial court honor in 1648, he cast his lot with the revolt.

A rebel council led by members of the Parlement of Paris selected the prince de Conti as Paris commander and assigned Marcillac a partial lieutenant generalship. In the three waves of fighting across the next four years, Marcillac was almost killed on two occasions. In 1649, he led nearly one thousand cavalrymen in a charge against royal troops. Fighting from the ground after his horse was killed beneath him, he lunged at a royal officer, piercing his horse's thigh. The officer shot him in the throat. In the second wave, the newly named duc de La Rochefoucauld transformed a funeral for his father into an armed gathering of nearly three thousand rebels. Welcomed by a sympathetic populace in Bordeaux, the contingent defended the city against attacks before its eventual surrender.

Facing royal troops near the Bastille two years later, La Rochefoucauld was struck at close range. A musket ball entered the corner of one eye and exited just beneath the other. A valet helped his son carry him through the streets, drawing crowds of onlookers. Aristocrats on both sides died in this final battle, which ended the rebellion. The fourteen-year-old Louis XIV offered La Rochefoucauld clemency in exchange for a pledge of loyalty. When he refused, he was stripped of his titles and declared guilty of *lèse-majesté*, the highest offense against a sovereign.[5] To avoid arrest, he fled to Holland.

To a later age, the affront that pushed Marcillac to join in the Fronde seems trivial. His wife did not possess the *droit du tabouret*, the right to sit on a backless stool in the presence of the queen. For his part, Marcillac was forbidden to enter the palace courtyard of the Louvre in a carriage. He was instead forced to walk. Traditionally such rights were accorded only to nobles who met two conditions, both of which Marcillac lacked. Because his father was still living at the time, he had not yet inherited the title of duke. Title or not, he was not a blood relative to the king. His intimacy with Queen Anne gave him cause to believe that he would be an exception, and more than once she had seemed to agree. When his name did not appear on the list granting privileges, Marcillac was incensed. Mazarin told him in humiliating terms that his reaction was inexcusable.

The screed he wrote in response bears the same dark view of calculation and deceit that pervades his later writing. The decision to keep the *Apology of M. le prince de Marcillac* private likely spared his beheading. Its tangled reasoning foreshadows the convolutions of pride and self-interest that he exposes in the *Maxims*. The raw candor of this "apology," which unabashedly defends personal ambition, is startling. The source of its passion—dishonor before other courtiers—was the vulnerability Louis XIV would exploit to secure his own dominance of the nobility. It begins with a cold acknowledgment:

> I do not presume to have sufficient virtue to claim that I would have hated Cardinal Mazarin if he had loved me. Perhaps he would have done things in my interest that would have obscured to me the many acts he has committed against the state. Perhaps then a cowardly shame would have caused me to die for an unworthy cause, drawn inexorably by obligation.[6]

The nineteenth-century philosopher Victor Cousin, who discovered this document during research for a biography of the duchesse de Longueville, comments on its exclusive concern for the author's wounded pride. "The mask is lifted. We are no longer onstage, we are in the wings."[7]

To see behind the mask is the main task of the *Maxims*, whose central theme is the gulf between seeming and being. The book describes two inescapable drives—*amour propre* and self-interest—as responsible for duplicity. *Amour propre* encompasses various terms: vanity, self-delight, pride. It "sees, senses, hears, imagines, distrusts, penetrates, and intuits all." As Jean Starobinski writes, "Under a thousand masks is a single face," that of *amour propre*. As for self-interest, La Rochefoucauld is clear that one's own gratification and advancement provide a far stronger motivation than any allegiance to the good.[8] The *Maxims* details the strategic emphases, embellishments, and omissions meant to tilt daily encounters to one's own benefit. The compass of such "glory" testifies to vanity's cunning. "In all professions," La Rochefoucauld writes, "each person affects an aspect and exterior intended to show what he wishes others to believe."[9] Even at an early age, children mimic the speech and manners of others, and in every such imitation there is something "false and uncertain" as they adopt "a spirit other than their own."[10] They soon understand that pleasing others—peers, parents, strangers—will advance their interest.

La Rochefoucauld employs analogies from the stage. The qualities that generate trust also define gifted actors, he writes, since every sentiment has its particular gesture, bearing, and tone. Credibility depends more on consistency than sincerity. We praise people or embrace their tastes to gain favor, and we stay silent when a word might diminish us in their eyes. This extends to identity, which for La Rochefoucauld derives from three qualities: birth status, talent, and reputation. Falseness enters when one takes on airs untrue to these features. "Consider the many magistrates who fruitlessly mimic the gestures of the Chancellor, or ordinary women who give themselves the airs of a duchess."[11]

To be successful in society therefore requires self-knowledge coupled with a convincing enactment of the words and gestures that match one's inborn nature. As La Rochefoucauld writes, "A particular tone suits the standing and talents of each person: one always goes wrong when one abandons this for some other tone. One must endeavor to know which of these is natural to us, never to stray from it, and to perfect it as much as possible."[12] This public performance of identity is an outside-in kind of calculation: based on your abilities, birth, and reputation, you must do all you can to learn your role and embody it. Authenticity or sincere self-expression is not applicable. Acting is inevitable, preferably the kind that elicits the loudest applause.

La Rochefoucauld concedes that some may live honestly and still retain their integrity. He does not equate this with virtue, however. *Honnêteté*—a word endlessly parsed as a guide to true noble conduct—was for La Rochefoucauld a clear-eyed acknowledgment of pervasive human corruption, most of all in oneself. "Those with false honesty disguise their defects to others and themselves. Those truly honest know their defects perfectly and admit to them."[13] This claim, from the last edition of the *Maxims* published in his lifetime, stands in stark contrast with the *Apology* he wrote almost thirty years earlier. The defiant arrogance of his youth had by now mellowed into a rueful realism. Among elites, surviving the currents of power meant accepting society's transactional nature. For La Rochefoucauld, the insincerity this involved—an awareness of one's own falseness and the insincerity of others—was characteristic.

> If men wished to excel solely on the strength of their talents and fulfillment of their duties, there would be nothing false in their taste or conduct. They would show themselves as they are, would judge things by their own lights, and would attach themselves to them by reason.

The delusion they prefer instead is mutual. "Humans would not live long in society if they were not the dupes of one another."[14]

La Rochefoucauld casts such corruption as rooted in human nature. It is not surprising that he counted among his acquaintances Pascal and the theologian Jacques Esprit, who both embraced Augustinian views of sin. Most of all, however, it was his understanding of the court's hierarchy of birth and status that shaped La Rochefoucauld's account of mutual delusion. The court's necessary vigilance—the need to please by tactical agreement and others' perpetual scrutiny—implied dependence and an unpredictable parceling of rewards. At court, there was good reason to be a willing dupe.

Indeed, when his son reached a marriageable age and wished to make a name for himself, La Rochefoucauld ceded principle to necessity. After years of making no serious attempt to gain entrance to Louis XIV's court, he pledged loyalty to the king and yielded his title so his son could appear in full dignity. The new duke was named Grand Master of the King's Wardrobe and Master of the Hunt, and he went on to marry the daughter of the king's war minister Louvois. The aged patriarch, never forgiven by Louis XIV for his rebellion thirty years earlier, was treated with demeaning solicitude and made to feign interest in the least remarkable aspects of courtly life, which Louis XIV knew he could force him to do.

The full flowering of this dynamic was yet to come. Two years after La Rochefoucauld's death in 1680, as Versailles became the official seat of Louis XIV's administration, the king invited the realm's most powerful nobles to make it their permanent residence. The presence of ceremony in every aspect of daily life, with each ritual an apportionment of obligation and reward, provided abundant occasions for calculations of self-interest. La Rochefoucauld's *Maxims* is an exceptionally lucid articulation of what Versailles's new residents would soon learn through experience.

STAGE PRESENCE

In the masquerade balls of Louis XIV's Versailles, it was fashionable to wear a wax mask of one's face under a more ornate carnival mask. The surprise came late in the evening, when you unmasked yourself to reveal the second, lifelike mask. The false face was faithful enough to fool people for an instant, and then the shock brought laughter. On one memorable occasion, wax masks from the previous year's carnival had been kept and stored, and costumers had the idea to use them again. Most were in decent shape, but the wax on two of the masks worn by a pair of noble officers had turned cloudy. Efforts to fix them were unsuccessful, but the officers wore them anyway. When they pulled off their carnival masks, people gasped. They looked like death. This proved prescient: several months later, both were killed on the battlefield.[15]

At Versailles, the idea of a wax mask that doubled one's features was apt year-round. The best courtiers' faces were themselves a strategic facsimile, an adaptation that outsiders were well suited to describe. As the private tutor of a spoiled young aristocrat, the writer Jean de La Bruyère, born of solid bourgeois stock, spent much of his time watching courtiers' habits. "A man who knows the court is a master of his gestures, of his eyes, of his face," he writes. "He is profound, impenetrable; he conceals bad turns, smiles at his enemies, curbs his impulses, disguises his passions, denies his heart, and speaks and acts against his own wishes."[16] To succeed at court entailed consummate self-control. It meant knowing when to feign, dissemble, or divert. It also required discerning what others might be concealing.

La Bruyère's *The Characters, or Manners of the Age* (1688) combines vivid portraits with commentary ranging from several pages to a single stinging epigram. The principal theme of the chapter "On the Court" is deceit: in love, anger, and admiration; through words, actions, and omissions; and of oneself and others. Its images are evocative. The court is a hardened, polished marble edifice. The courtier is a watch whose gears and springs are finely concealed, revealing only the smooth circuit of its hands. His existence is an unending game of chess, serious and melancholy. Courtly life is a drama whose scenes and characters remain always the same, played by different actors.[17]

An inheritance from his uncle allowed La Bruyère to buy a lifetime position as treasurer general in Caen, where he stayed two months before accepting the prince de Condé's offer to become a preceptor to the family. He taught geography, history, mythology, and philosophy to the Condé's teenaged grandson, whose favorite pastime was insulting others. Judging from his spirited writing, La Bruyère relished the assignment. Those who have seen the court, he writes, have also seen what is "most beautiful, most ornate, and most specious" in society. At court, everyone is *petit*, petty. The sentiment that unites courtiers is not fellow-feeling, he continues, but wounded pride. Without Versailles, the critic Sainte-Beuve later wrote, La Bruyère "would have been as a hunter with . . . no big game who must settle for a paltry hare he comes across in the field."[18] At the court, he found his prey.

For all its brio and bite, *The Characters* holds itself at a distance from particular people and events. Its characters remain caricatures, however sharply drawn. Their given names—Glycère, Émire, Eutimème, Aronce, and the like—are fanciful. An acute sense of psychology nevertheless informs most descriptions. A once-favored courtier, for instance, now frowns less, listens more readily, and displays an open face. La Bruyère's commentary is unsparing. "Such are the small resources man has within him. It takes a disgrace or humiliation to make him more humane, more tender, less savage, more honest."[19]

Despite the book's detachment, disillusionment colors its pages. Its critical stance earned the author powerful enemies. The *Mercure galant* echoed the resentment of some who felt targeted by his portraits, and his entry into the Académie Française was loudly opposed by those who believed that his writing slighted noble ideals. An epigram was left on academy members' desks before his induction:

> As Alcippus mounts these august steps
> We ask, Why call him hero?
> It is because our number forty
> Contains as well a zero.[20]

La Bruyère's acceptance speech was preceded by two introductions that offered little in the way of praise, and the speech itself was met with silence. Within three years, he was dead. His observation that those who had seen the court had also seen society concludes with a corollary. "Those who despise the court, having seen it, also despise society."[21]

Louis de Rouvroy, duc de Saint-Simon, also spent his life describing the polished facade of Versailles. By the time of Louis XIV's death in 1715, Saint-Simon's sprawling, living history had begun to take shape. Completed thirty-five years later, it is remembered most for the texture of courtly life it conjures in its essential sameness, month after month, decade after decade. Where La Bruyère offered abstraction and commentary, Saint-Simon provided chronicle and incident, and unlike the former, Saint-Simon named names. Combining a novelist's eye for the particular with an architect's grasp of the whole, he offers a sweeping narrative through innumerable dazzling set pieces. In the thirty-two years the work chronicles—from Saint-Simon's entry into the military in 1691 to his 1723 withdrawal from the court in disgrace—more than 10,000 individuals are named. The most recent edition runs to more than 13,000 pages.

Saint-Simon's work is cast as tragedy, depicting Louis XIV's reign as a terrible fall masked by blinding grandeur. It chronicles the substitution of empty honors for ancient noble rights, as the ennobled and newly rich replaced aristocratic administrators and a cloying luxury distracted the powerful from their growing irrelevance. Despite his status as an insider, Saint-Simon is unsparing in his judgment of the king, whose rule, he believed, was dangerous and unsustainable. Just after Louis XIV's death, Saint-Simon's chief lament was over the opportunities the king had squandered. "I was seized with bitterness over the loss of a prince who was born for the happiness of France and all of Europe."[22]

FIGURE 1.3. Louis de Rouvroy, duc de Saint-Simon, Jean-Baptiste van Loo (Alamy)

Saint-Simon's themes are not always evident in the daily scenes he takes such pains to portray. These include elaborate processions, protocols of seating and standing, inflections of address, and refinements of gesture, tone, and expression. Such details, from the numberless balls, receptions, concerts, masses, and meals he describes, are part of the encompassing calamity. Until the seventeenth century, a strong tradition in legend had identified the French aristocratic spirit with fierce, self-defining pride. Rather than conform to others' codes of conduct, nobles derived virtue from the duty to be worthy of one's own blood. Louis XIV's project was to break this resistance to any standard but their own.

Over time, the king smoothed the rough core of aristocratic diffidence through ceremonies of grace and distinction. The prestige that came with such luster was considerable, but the cost, political emasculation, was long-lasting. Rituals were invented that both flattered and abased, often explicitly. Women of quality were given the privilege to kiss the hem of blood princesses' dresses, for instance, and the duty of the king's "Official Chair-Bearer," entrusted to two uniformed noblemen, was to carry and maintain the royal toilet seat.[23] By enveloping the daily lives of nobles in ceremonies of courtesy, the king embedded hierarchy into their every action. Participation implied a readiness, real or feigned, to accept his authority.

This staged submission had its practical side. In veiling belligerence among rivals, the rituals tempered violence. "At court you will find many who raise their hat but would as soon remove your head, and who bow before you but would rather break your legs," writes the Spaniard Antonio de Guevara in *Contempt at Court*, a book that circulated in sixteenth- and early seventeenth-century France. The historian Robert Muchembled cites examples of the "art of indirection"—toasts invoking titles rather than names, say—intended to steer encounters among unequals away from confrontation. Such rituals "transformed the blusterer into a genteel, fashionable person and the shady noble into an exquisite companion."[24]

Louis XIV did not invent such displays, but he extended and elaborated them as a means of rule that blanketed every waking moment at Versailles. They announced and enforced rank. Just below the king were the "sons of France." Below them were the "grandsons of France," and, below them, the "princes of the blood," after which came Saint-Simon's rank of duke and peer.[25] Detailed genealogies were kept and consulted for ceremonies involving Versailles's residents, as the ancientness of noble lineage governed all formal proceedings. During Louis XIV's long reign, notions of hierarchy hardened, particularly among those with a stake in its maintenance. An influential writer repeated the certainty that inequality reigned among aristocrats "just as we see in stars and angels, among whom there are spirits yet more noble and excellent than others." Everyday details strengthened the hierarchy. These extended to who stood or sat in the king's presence, who watched him rise or retire, and who was required to remove their hat in his presence. They governed the quality of fabric one wore and the adornment of one's carriage and retinue.[26]

The structure was explicit even in the upper echelons. When the king or queen stood, all stood. When either sat, the "sons of France" as well as princesses and duchesses could also sit, although only on a tabouret. Exceptions were made for meals and entertainments. When the king was absent, those with tabouret rights could sit in a seat with a back before lesser nobility. When lesser nobles were presented, they were permitted to "kiss" one of the king's daughters, whose proffered cheek ought not actually be touched. Each time the king took the Eucharist, he would name the two most senior dukes in attendance to help lift the fabric from a small table beneath the altar. If a "son of France" was present, he alone did so.[27]

The king's ability to praise or damn with the merest shrug or glance ensured adherence to these codes. His rages, though rare, were fearsome, and their unpredictability kept everyone on edge. At one royal dinner, Mme de Torcy, the daughter of Louis XIV's foreign secretary Arnauld de Pomponne, inadvertently took the seat of the duchesse de Duras. The king remained silent for the rest of the meal, which, as Saint-Simon writes, "rendered everyone present intensely alert." At last Louis spoke to declare that he had been witness to such great insolence that he was unable to eat. Blame fell on both women: on the "*petite bourgeoise* daughter of Pomponne" (the family had been ennobled a mere one hundred years earlier) and the culpably reticent duchess. Failing to demand an honor to which one was entitled, his majesty thundered, was to withhold it from the king himself.[28]

Beyond one's particular standing by birth, another order prevailed, the changeable hierarchy of opinion. Unlike ancientness of lineage, status was fluid, contingent on the esteem of others. To read Saint-Simon's *Memoirs* is to witness limitless strategies for advancement, assault, and self-protection. To rise in status required pleasing those whose stock was high and whose judgment could elevate or destroy reputations. "One never judges things by what they are," Saint-Simon wrote, "but by the persons they concern."[29] By definition, such arbiters enjoyed the king's favor.

The sociologist Norbert Elias describes how the structure of Louis XIV's rule generated specific patterns of thought and behavior among courtiers enmeshed in perpetual battles for prestige. One person's rise implied another's fall. Rituals of etiquette were "a ghostly *perpetuum mobile*," Elias writes, inescapable and often unwillingly borne. Such rituals of the "great world"—*le monde*—were the very constituents of identity.

> Each individual was hypersensitive to the slightest change in the mechanism, stood watch over the existing order, attentive to the finest nuances, unless he happened to be trying to change it to his own advantage.[30]

The fluidity of status required constant adjustments in behavior toward others. It also raised skills of observation to an art. It's no wonder that Saint-Simon's *Memoirs* refers so often to the theater. Allies conspire "backstage." Diplomats perform "comedies" with false trails and misleading subplots. All became actors, dispensing careful words and gestures to keep their true thoughts safely hidden.[31]

At court, appearances mattered most. For all but the highest blood princes and princesses, the art of seeming prevailed over who one was or what one had done. This is why so many of Saint-Simon's vignettes include the reactions of a voracious public. The first scene of consequence in the *Memoirs* describes the king's grand coup of marrying one of his bastard daughters to his nephew, the timid young duc de Chartres, who would become Regent for the child Louis XV twenty-two years later. In Saint-Simon's dramatic telling, Louis XIV commands the trembling fifteen-year-old to dress in her finest clothes and wait outside his apartment. She fears she is about to be rebuked for some unknown fault. "I was there within moments," Saint-Simon exults.

> People had gathered in small groups, and their faces showed great astonishment. . . . Madame [the duc de Chartres's mother] paced in the gallery . . . holding a handkerchief, weeping without restraint, speaking loudly, and gesticulating, the very portrait of Ceres after the rape of Proserpina now pleading furiously with Jupiter to bring her daughter back.[32]

Such was the theater of Versailles. Judging the landscape well, pleasing the favored and smiling indifferently on the rest, finding protectors among those who might help, and helping those who could be useful: these things were necessary, but success also required an effective execution. Performing one's role with preternatural grace and self-possession was essential.

When the stage machinery showed, the audience responded with cruel delight. Saint-Simon reports that the son of a respected officer first visited Versailles on the evening of a formal ball and was asked if he knew how to dance, to which he responded with misplaced confidence. He soon lost the rhythm and awkwardly tried to improvise. He leaned too far to one side and then raised his arms too high, prompting "laughter that turned into loud guffaws, which, despite the respect expected with the king in attendance—who was himself trying hard not to laugh—finally degenerated into jeering."

The youth returned the next night. He approached the king to apologize and promised that his dancing would be better. An early stumble brought fresh jeers and mocking applause, which spread throughout the hall as he continued. "There was laughter from every side, including the king, and it came in great explosions. I know of no one who has ever endured anything like this," Saint-Simon writes. He did not show himself again at Versailles. He joined Dauphin's Regiment and was killed in battle before he married. "He possessed great honor and courage," Saint-Simon comments. "This was unfortunate."[33]

Such glee betrays insecurity, a vulnerability covered by condescension. The fear of ridicule pervaded most moments at Versailles, especially when the king was present. Judging from the distance of more than a century, the writer Germaine de Staël grasped a connection between this fear and the elegance that defined life at Versailles. The subtler the distinctions of an unequal society, she wrote, the more exactly they must be understood and respected. For those who populate such settings, the greatest misfortune is ridicule. In the seventeenth century, avoiding missteps stifled originality, but it also sharpened the senses. The young man's performance was enough to give anyone nightmares.[34]

HARDENED AND HIGHLY POLISHED

Politesse, whose etymological root is in *polish*, smoothed relations and maintained harmony among selfish and untrusting courtiers. It served to soften dissent through sweet phrases, convey esteem with a glance or nod, and praise a rival or correct a subordinate. However willing and gracious, it did not often stem from generosity. When wielded well, it also served to protect. Politeness, the skill of knowing when to speak and when to remain silent, when to advance and when to recede, preserved appearances. It was the court's most common means of concealment.

La Bruyère's vignettes of life at court came near the end of a century in which books on politeness appeared from both secular and religious writers.[35] Widely read and applied, they exercised their own subtle influence in the domestication of French nobles. Most tied politeness to moral virtue, and many held that genteel manners came naturally to the highly born. From the earliest works, however, an anxious tension is present. In hierarchies of status maintained by opinion, the polish needed to advance requires some level of dissembling, which compromised aristocratic honor. Most authors were aware of the dilemma of reconciling new courtly demands with these older ideals and did their awkward best to reconcile the two.

The first such book to draw a large readership was Nicolas Faret's *The Decent Man, or The Art of Pleasing at Court* (1630), which went through eight editions in thirty years. While Faret acknowledges that non-nobles might also benefit from the book, its audience is mostly aristocratic. The popular classes, he notes, have little occasion to advance beyond their station, whereas if elites fail to learn the art of pleasing others, "each day will bring a thousand opportunities for shame and embarrassment."[36] *The Decent Man* lays out its advice in short chapters that are by turns lofty, didactic, practical, and confiding. Its topics span questions of character, ethics, history, dress, and manners, with sections on liberality, greed, obedience, impertinence, vanity, and despair. Its aim is to cultivate elegance, offering guidance on to how to choose friends, resist gamblers, select clothes, and moderate one's voice when speaking to ladies. A portrait of the perfect courtier emerges. While merit must be this courtier's foundation, Faret writes, only moral values will earn the good opinion of the *grands,* honest men, and decent ladies.[37]

These values depend on self-mastery. For the courtier, this requires softening one's ambition to appear subservient. One must measure one's words and hide one's passions. One must show no bitterness, obstinance, or scorn. One should demonstrate humility whenever necessary, never seem wiser than others, and be neither too earnest nor too familiar. Not least, one should aggressively pursue access to the powerful but never let it show. To conquer others' affection, Faret concluded, we must first command our own.[38]

Faret's handbook is in a literary tradition that praised the qualities of the *honnête homme,* a principled and urbane man whose humanistic learning kept him squarely in the world but not quite of it. The French title makes the connection explicit: *L'Honneste homme. Ou, l'Art de plaire à la court.* Being an "honest man" had not always involved the art of pleasing at court. Earlier ideals of *honnêteté* had drawn from both ancient and modern sources, folding the wisdom of classical virtue into the convictions of the present. The detachment of Michel de Montaigne, who chronicled his own roving thoughts in the seclusion of his study, was one such example. A firm rejection of dissembling runs through his essays. "Of the mask and appearance we must not make a real essence, nor of what is foreign what is our very own," Montaigne writes. "A generous heart," he observes, "is eager to reveal its innermost depths."[39]

Because its sources were independent of courtly requirements, *honnêteté* resisted artifice and insincerity, assuming instead that one's outer expression flowed naturally from one's inner being. Pierre Bardin's 1632 *Lyceum,* for instance, draws a distinction between the *honnête homme* and the worldly man. For Bardin, the decent man proceeds with an "open face," indifferent to his reputation and ever willing to serve others. Flattery, which Bardin calls "concealed fraud," is altogether unworthy and forbidden.[40]

One sign of the growing incompatibility of traditional *honnêteté* and courtly ideals was the ease with which court observers embraced artifice, flattery, and insincerity. Eustache du Refuge was among the earliest writers to publish instructions for courtiers, writing under the reign of Louis XIII. His 1616 *Treatise on the Court* is uncommonly direct, with language that is both more vivid and more calculating than others of the genre. The aim of a man at court is "to control all others," Refuge asserts. One should walk "with the bridle in hand." Others' faithlessness requires "warfare with the eyes." Refuge is direct about the need for concealment. "While dissembling is necessary to all kinds of persons," he writes, "it is especially essential to a man who wishes to advance at court."[41]

Refuge lays out a framework that seems to constrain its abuse. He repeatedly uses the words *dissimuler* and *dissimulation*, which contemporary readers understood to designate a limited kind of secrecy. To dissemble was to hide one's thoughts by withholding the full truth. Its mask was prudent and perhaps defensive, but it was not deceitful. This is in contrast to the words' close cousins, *simuler* and *simulation*, which went beyond concealment to indicate deliberate falsehood, a disguising of the truth. To Refuge, simulation entails greater risk than dissimulation, since it can invite the suspicion of others.[42]

Yet his *Treatise* does not sustain the distinction. There are three categories of dissembling, Refuge writes: our silence (not revealing what might harm others), our appearance (concealing our passions, both positive and negative), and our words. The third category admits falsehood, so long as the intent is noble and contains no harm or deceit. "Provided the aim is worthy," Refuge concludes, "and the lie harms no one while profiting someone, one may permit oneself."[43] Others provided their own version of how a decent man might be justified in shading the truth. For Nicolas Faret, the path from *honnêteté* to something on the far side of flattery was continuous. The courtier must be "accommodating" and "susceptible to several forms." He should learn to sympathize with the wishes of the great, even when they require acting against his own inclinations. "If he wishes, and if his generosity is not offended, he will know to feign and disguise. When one expedient fails, his mind will be calm and quick enough to invent a thousand others to produce what he wants."[44]

Just how accommodating might the courtier be? Having first faulted flattery as "a mask of devotion," Faret admits that excess praise has its place. Courtiers "may incline toward flattery above all if the goal is good." His example—how to win the affections of a lady whose beauty is imperfect—implies selflessness in its apparent chivalry. She will have "no defect" that the suitor cannot "disguise through some form of sweetening." If her complexion is dark, he will praise the famous beauties of antiquity. If her hair is red, he will praise the taste of Italians. If she is too thin, he will praise her agility, and if she is too plump, he will declare her the equal of an Amazon. With this, Faret's "honest man" acquires his prized self-mastery. He has become a perfect prevaricator.

When Faret's *Decent Man* appeared in 1630, the original ideals of *honnêteté* were already under threat by the dynamic at court. Forty-one years later, when Antoine de Courtin's *New Treatise on Civility as Exercised in France by Honest Persons* was published, they were scarcely recognizable.

Between 1671 and 1730, the *New Treatise* appeared in thirty editions. Its instructions are exacting and go well beyond the general accounts of its predecessors. Courtin recommends sitting at an angle when in the company of eminent men rather than facing them directly. An indirect gaze, he writes, conveys the greatest respect. If a superior sneezes, reverently remove your hat. It is not enough to refrain from turning one's back when joining or leaving the company of eminent persons: the truly civilized always enter and exit a room facing their portrait as well. Occasions to display cultivation abound. In the presence of a superior, sit in the chair closest to the door. Never wear a hat in a room with a bed. When bowing, take pains not to bump heads.[45]

A century earlier, Erasmus had sought to teach the habits of cleanliness, manners, and public decency in his groundbreaking book *Civility for Boys*. The uprightness of one's behavior, he wrote, grew naturally from the heart's virtues. Courtin's treatise reversed these terms. One should remember to match one's actions with earnest intentions, it advises. In other words, one should try to be as good as one seems. If one would rather not kneel at church from "lack of devotion, weakness, or laziness," kneel nevertheless, lest others notice. As regards offering praise or compliments, Courtin sets a loose standard. "It is not a matter of knowing whether one is speaking the truth each time one praises another. It is enough to believe one is doing so. Then it is not a lie."[46] The distinction provides an easy path to deceit without the need for self-scrutiny, a comfortable response to the demands of the moment.

Courtin's defense of the strategic fib is striking. "If we can persuade the person to whom we are speaking that we ourselves are persuaded of his merit, the compliment becomes sincere and obliging, even when the person knows in his heart that it is false."[47] This dance of deceit and collusion is complex. Both are aware of the other's mask, but each has a reason to accept the fiction. One doubts his own flattering words but contrives to believe their truth, which absolves him of mendacity. The other suspects him to be insincere, but the praise is welcome. At court, the equivocation of such *obliging* words is a benefit to each. The inferior speaks praise as if he means it, and the superior hears it as if it's true. La Rochefoucauld knew the mutual delusion all too well.

READING MINDS

Honesty suffered over the course of the seventeenth century, as increasingly refined rituals at court caused the rift between appearance and reality to widen. Politeness was both necessary and ethically dubious. Its smooth words and gestures signaled distinction. Associations of the word *civility* thus shifted from the inclusive ideal of Erasmus to the exclusive domain of elites. Its practice was no longer merely a sign of eminence. It became a means of discrimination. "Peasants lack *civilité*," reads an excerpt from a 1690 dictionary. "Peasants are not as *civilized* as townspeople, just as townspeople are not as *civilized* as courtiers."[48]

By the end of the century, the term had also assumed connotations of hypocrisy and self-interest. The *honnête homme* was increasingly old-fashioned: saluted, perhaps, but not especially esteemed. Some, moreover, had begun to identify the court's duplicitous civility with the rituals of fine society more generally, an association that would grow widespread in the next century. Criticism came from both religious and secular quarters. "Civility is nothing other than a continual commerce of ingenious lies meant for mutual deception," declared Esprit Flechier in a funeral oration for the duc de Montausier, who had served as the dauphin's tutor. The words are bracing, given the occasion. In society, Flechier stated in another sermon, "one calls vices virtue in order to cover one's own faults and makes an art of fooling others while also being fooled. This is *honnêteté*, this is worldly *politesse*."[49] The marquise de Sablé, whose *Maxims* appeared in 1678, put it even better:

> When the nobles hope to make others believe that they have some great quality they do not possess, it is dangerous to show that we are not convinced. When we deprive them of the hope of deceiving the world, we deprive them also of the desire to perform worthy acts in conformity with the role they are playing.[50]

For those living at Versailles, the refinement of politeness prompted ever greater vigilance and self-control. Nicolas Faret gave precise instructions for maintaining "perfection in the movements of the face." It was to be serene at all times, pleasant, accommodating, and suffused with kindness. Beware of your eyes, the soul's portal, he continued, which risk exposing us to those who seek to know our secrets. Hands, too, must be controlled: "they are able to speak on their own."[51] By the century's end, such affectations drew mocking responses. "Men of the court no longer know what to do with themselves," declares a book in the style of La Bruyère's *Characters*. "Their feet and hands are mere instruments of propriety, rather than indispensable appendages. It is only to show refinement that they exist at all."[52]

A prolific Jesuit writer named Morvan de Bellegarde voiced exasperation. The "gait, gestures, words, winks, and squints" of polite society's members are all planned, he wrote. "It is as if they were always onstage."

The anxiety was nevertheless real. Life at court was a perpetual audition. "No faux pas goes unnoticed," Jean de La Chétardie warned his young readers in 1684, adding that all must assume that those who watch "will not fail to profit from our errors."[53]

The ability to turn one's face into a mask brought with it a heightened awareness that others were doing the same. For La Bruyère, virtually any gesture, however slight, would reward analysis. Everything signified: how one entered or left a room, how one sat or stood, the words and tone one chose. The courtier's complete education therefore included careful study in penetrating appearances. The chevalier de Méré, who defended traditional ideas of *honnêteté* when others had begun to abandon them, held that the true *honnête homme* could always grasp the designs of others, however well concealed. "All that moves in the heart and mind leaves a clearly discernible imprint on the face and the person."[54]

Scientific and artistic thinking encouraged these convictions. Marin Cureau de La Chambre was a member of the Académie Française and personal physician to Louis XIII and Louis XIV. In 1659, he published *The Art of Knowing Men*, a massive work suffused with the quiet confidence of one engaged in discovery. In an age when public faces are "ordinarily masked," La Chambre announces, this new science will reveal "the inner reaches of the heart." A window on the chest—the Renaissance-era symbolic image for transparent virtue—is no longer needed. Nature herself offers a view of private intentions, written on the face and body "in clear and visible characters."[55]

Physiognomy's roots lie in antiquity. A work called *Physiognomonica*, attributed to Aristotle, linked dispositions such as strength, weakness, brilliance, and stupidity to particular physical features. The book was a standard reference in the seventeenth century and beyond. In France, the appeal of a science that claimed to read intentions from physical traits would wax and wane in the coming two centuries, with each resurgence tied to social change and the anxieties it produced.[56] Its urgency for Louis XIV's contemporaries was clear. Physiognomy is "a guide for conduct in civil life," La Chambre writes. It counsels how and when one should speak and act, recommending the best tone and manner for any particular circumstance. It is a tool in choosing mentors, allies, friends, and servants. To the knowledgeable, it uncovers "hidden designs, secret actions, and the unknown authors of events." "No dissembling is too deep for its penetration, no veil too hidden for its removal."[57] The frontispiece of *The Art of Knowing Men* offers a vivid rendering, with La Chambre in his study taking careful note of a bust before him while a pair outside formalize an agreement before witnesses.

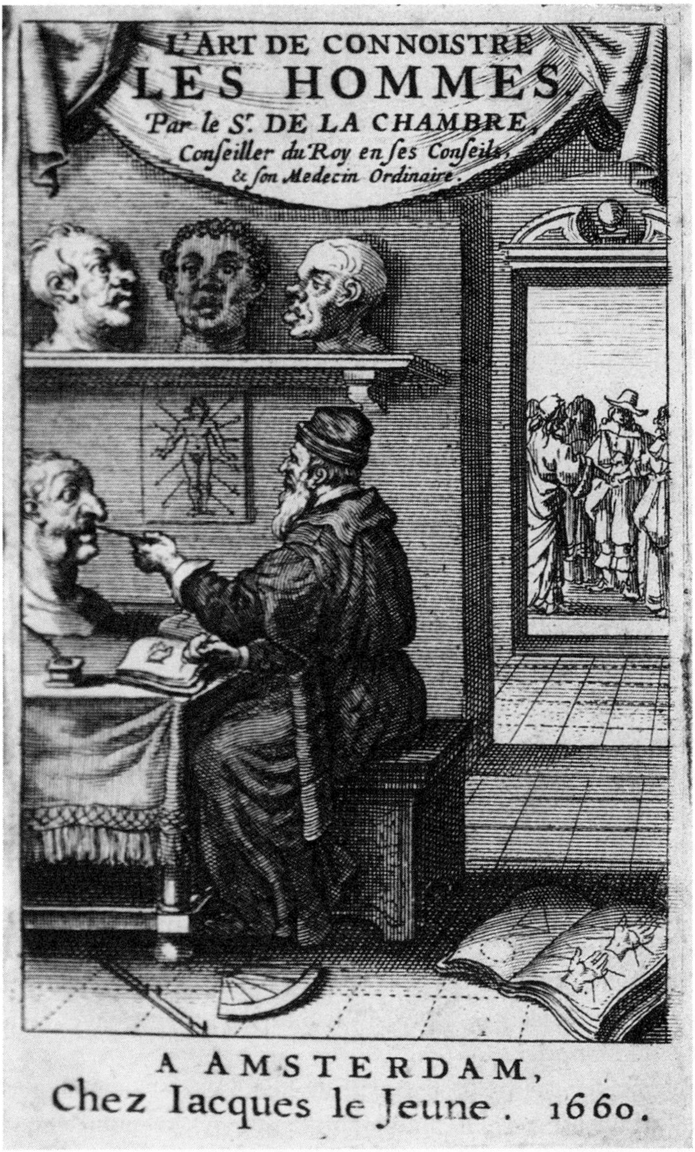

FIGURE 1.4. Frontispiece, Marin Cureau de La Chambre, *The Art of Knowing Men* (courtesy of Harvard Medical Library Collection, Center for the History of Medicine in the Francis A. Countway Library, Harvard University [Marin Cureau de La Chambre, *L'Art de connoistre les hommes*; FC6 L1168659a])

La Chambre lists the signs by which inner dispositions are known. Details of the face and voice and the body's overall build and features are fundamental. Degrees of beauty and ugliness are pertinent, as are the tint and quality of skin. The head is most revealing—the eyes in particular—with the forehead, nose, and mouth following in order of importance. Next comes the build of the chest and shoulders, the arms and legs, and the belly. Extensive lists of specific elements of temperament follow. These include the passions known to humans, the natural and moral sources of their inclinations, the true character of men and women, the vices and virtues, and the humors. La Chambre's colorful inventory of human types, each familiar to the physiognomist, could populate a stage comedy:

> The Idiot, The Extravagant, The Affable, The Hypocrite, The Pious, The Rustic, The Drunk, The Enemy, The Liar-by-Words, The Liar-by-Actions, The Forgiving, The Truthful, The Persevering, The Player, The Hunter, The Miser, The Sage, The Fool, The Ingrate, The Presumptuous, The Pusillanimous.[58]

In this scheme, a round face is a sign of malice. Dark eyes reveal timidity and, if large, inconstancy. Heavy lips indicate prying curiosity into the affairs of others and perhaps avarice and dishonesty. A long bony neck indicates a gossip, and a fleshy throat signals poor judgment. Among men, a square forehead, enlarged nose, and large chin point to grandeur, courage, and magnanimity. Among women, white teeth, small ears, and firm middling breasts indicate gentleness, innocence, and reserve.[59]

Despite its meticulous groundwork, the book's great promise—the means of reading the character and intentions of others—remains unrealized. Nearing the four-hundredth page, the reader learns that it will take nine more volumes to impart this knowledge. The crucial eighth volume was to be called *A Treatise on Dissimulation and the Means of Its Disclosure.* At the time of his death in 1669, La Chambre had completed only the second, *On the Character of the Passions.*

The hope persisted. Charles Le Brun, Louis XIV's "First Painter" who dominated the art world in the last third of the seventeenth century, was an avid reader of Cureau de La Chambre. Le Brun was invested in physiognomy and read extensively in human anatomy and philosophy to understand the effects of emotion on the body.[60] He detailed his findings in a 1688 lecture before the French Royal Academy of Painting and Sculpture. In it, he pointed to small details that revealed inner feeling. He described muscles that revealed joy, sorrow, cruelty, and pain and detailed postures expressing esteem, veneration, fear, or jealousy. He demonstrated each with illustrations. Eyebrows rise with the "gentlest and mildest" emotions. They

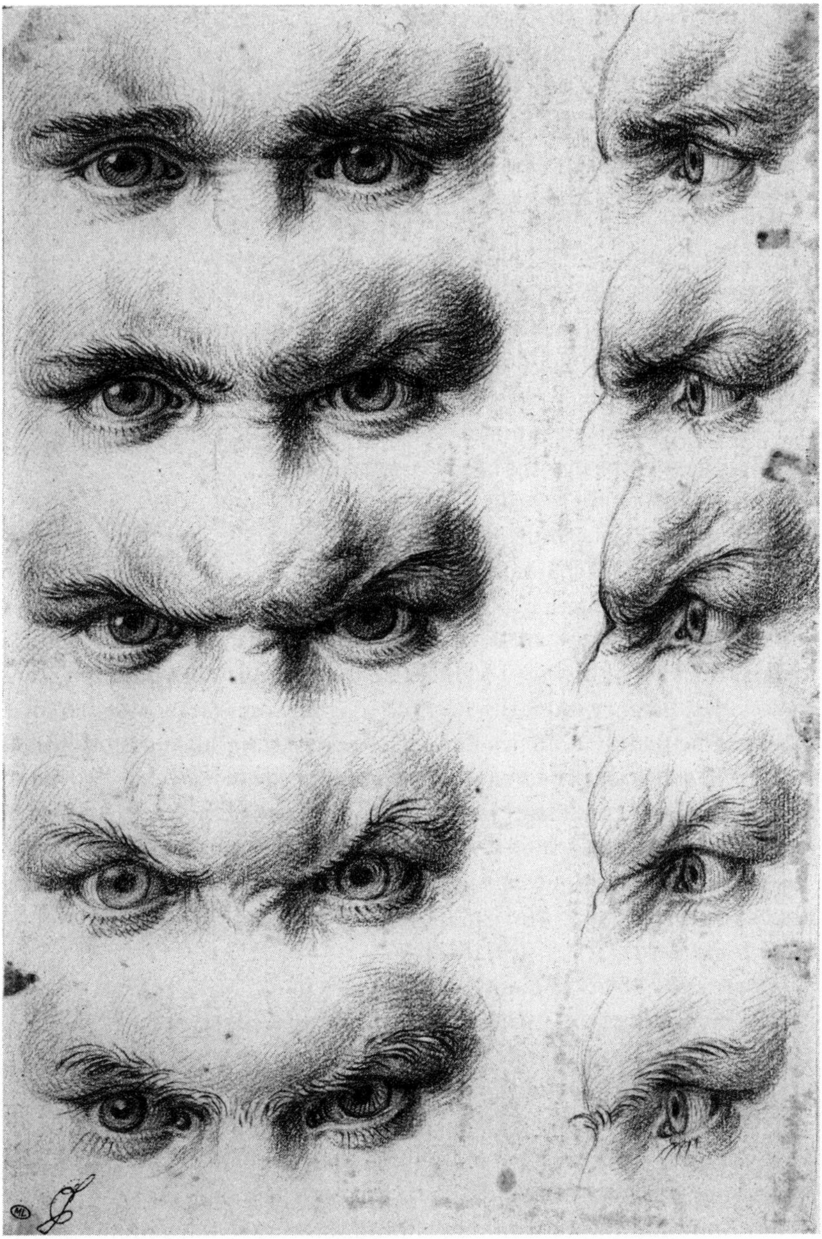

FIGURE 1.5. *Eyebrows*, Charles le Brun (Art Resource)

turn downward with the "cruelest and most violent" passions. In esteem, they thrust forward above the eyes, their inner ends depressed and the outer ends slightly raised. In scorn, the inner ends are drawn toward the nose with their outer edge more sharply raised. In fear, the pupil is bright and restless, while in jealousy it is hidden under low brows, watching as if ablaze.[61]

Le Brun was especially drawn to the resemblances he found between human types and animals. No explanatory text survives, but his drawings point to affinities and nudge viewers to form their own assessment. Next to an eagle, a man's aquiline nose intimates sharp fierceness. The boar and his human double, with their dull gaze and bristling hair, suggest brutishness. Alongside a fleshy pig's snout, Le Brun has written the word "gluttony," and "bestial" appears next to the nostrils. In other sketches, he has written "cruelty" next to the mouths of a lion and lynx.[62]

These projects are revealing in what they say about the age. Courtly society produced the burning desire to read minds, and physiognomy promised a key. Saint-Simon's *Memoirs* are marked by this same hope. His descriptions contain precise accounts of their characters' gait, voice, and identifying features, often with comparisons to animals. Nicolas Desmarets, the king's Director of Finances, was "a boar sunk so deep in his wallow that he knew virtually nothing of what went on outside his own sphere." The maréchal d'Huxelles, a climber who was ostentatious in his flattery, had a "sour physiognomy": tall and obese, with a dragging step, tiny eyes, and a florid face, "he resembled a vicious beef merchant."[63] By contrast, the duc de Chaulnes, a military officer and ambassador to Rome, was admired for his integrity. He had the "corpulence, thickness, weightiness, and physiognomy of an ox," his solidity serving as moral ballast for his quick mind.[64]

A particular object of Saint-Simon's scorn in the *Memoirs* is Achille de Harlay, president of the Paris parlement, who played the decisive role in a major conflict between Louis XIV and the high court aristocracy. By Saint-Simon's reckoning, Harlay's influence in legitimating the king's bastard children was venal and unscrupulous: the "greatest wound the peerage could have received, which was first leprous and then became a cancer." Harlay's appearance was eloquent. His face was hard and diamond-shaped. His eyes were vulture-like ("they seemed to devour objects and penetrate walls"), and his sharp nose was like a raptor's beak.

> His entire exterior was constrained, awkward, affected: the hypocritical odor, the false and cynical carriage, the slow and deep reverences. He

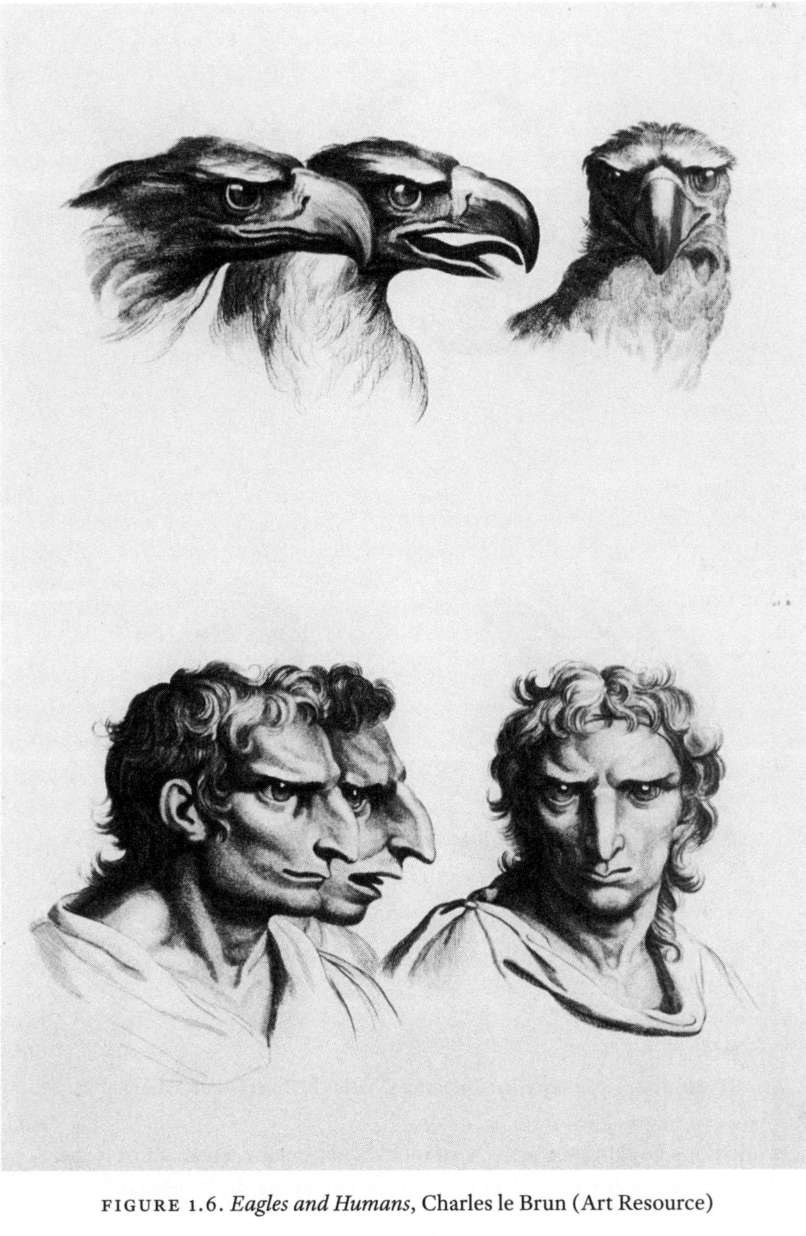

FIGURE 1.6. *Eagles and Humans,* Charles le Brun (Art Resource)

FIGURE 1.7. *Boars and Humans*, Charles le Brun (Art Resource)

went along hugging the walls with rehearsed phrases and an air of respect, through which shone insolence, audacity, contempt, and derision.[65]

These descriptions were consistent with Saint-Simon's vocation as the court's most astute observer. His principal task, schooled by a lifetime of observation, was to see beyond appearances. The very conception of his life's work, undertaken in an environment of disguised intentions, carried this aim. Nearing the end of his vast chronicle, Saint-Simon reflected on its purpose. The resulting essay, which serves as a preface to the *Memoirs*, is "To Know. Whether it is Permitted to Write and to Read History, Particularly of One's Own Time." The value of history, it begins, is not in accumulating facts and events. Its goal instead is ethical. We write history so readers might become more virtuous.

The first step in writing a truly ethical history is to penetrate concealment: "to uncover the interests, vices, virtues, passions, hatreds, alliances, and every other tributary, central or secondary, that feed faction and intrigue." To write such a history is to dwell in the midst of one's subjects, "within the secret of all that is present." What does such access reveal? For Saint-Simon, who spent thirty-five years writing about Louis XIV's Versailles, it was "a story of extreme passion and vice, the revelation of vast criminal intent and great shameful vistas." History, he concludes, is "the unmasking of many who would otherwise have kept their esteem."[66]

These observations shaped the advice Saint-Simon gave to Philippe d'Orléans as the court prepared for the death of Louis XIV. Saint-Simon had long been close to the king's nephew, who would soon become Regent. He shared his hope that the monarchy could regain its former status. In place of a court whose members were puffed up and powerless, Saint-Simon urged an older model in which the reigning order was ancient and the king ruled alongside, rather than over, *grands seigneurs*. He counseled d'Orléans to rely more on trust than intimidation, to mind only large matters, and to leave for others the minutiae that Louis XIV had craved to know. In his account of their conversations, a single emphatic imperative stands out. "Strip away appearances, which are so often found to be deceitful. If scrutiny counsels you to probe further, do so with care and precision. If you find nothing, beware nevertheless. Stand guard against the bitter shame of being fooled."[67]

A lifetime of vigilance had led him to this imperative. It was therefore a supreme humiliation when, shortly after urging this advice on the Regent, Saint-Simon fell victim to a ruse that nearly destroyed his reputation. Seeing Saint-Simon's standing with d'Orléans as an obstacle to his own rise, Adrien-Maurice, duc de Noailles, engineered a maneuver to bring about his friend's downfall. The two had long been allies, which made the betrayal especially sharp. Noailles first circulated a proposal for protocol at the king's funeral that was deliberately insulting to nobles below the peerage and then reported that Saint-Simon was its author. The outrage was explosive. When the deceit was discovered, Noailles was justly blamed, but Saint-Simon's bitterness remained. He would publicly insult Noailles at every opportunity, keeping his foul play conspicuous.

A kind of resolution replayed the final years of La Rochefoucauld's life nearly fifty years before. The Regent's sudden death had ended Saint-Simon's access to power. He and his wife moved to Paris, where they were "dead to the world," with an unmarried son who lacked all "credit and consideration." Now a fixture in the court of the young Louis XV, Noailles's reputation soared. When his niece became a widow at age nineteen, he saw a means of mending things. Saint-Simon's wife, who grasped what the marriage would mean for their son, persuaded him. Complex negotiations brought the two families together. Noailles made a show of stooping to clasp Saint-Simon beneath his shoulders, an act of exaggerated humility. Breathing with difficulty and speaking with a tremor, Saint-Simon answered in few words to Noailles's expressions of joy and withdrew. On arriving home, he felt such revulsion that he had himself bled.[68]

The similar fates of La Rochefoucauld and Saint-Simon, both expert in penetrating courtly deceit and equally subject to its allure, illustrate the effects of hierarchy on truth and transparency. Each wrote from experience, recording what its dynamic revealed about human nature, individual choice, and the management of public affairs. Its defining quality was concealment as a means of advancement, just as its penetration was a necessary skill for survival. In the coming decades, sanctioned inequality and the spread of courtly manners throughout society would propagate this dynamic. While less personal than in the day of La Rochefoucauld and Saint-Simon, the concealment they described, similarly exposed by philosophers and social critics, would question the very foundations of politics and society.

2
Formality and Farce

THE MASK'S LIBERTIES

The court's polished gestures and hollow praise were not the only means of concealment to result from the seventeenth century's social structure. Physical masks also flourished. They were in fact worn more widely in the 1600s than at any other time. Masks appeared in the streets and parks, on horseback and in carriages, in private balls at court and for celebrations in noble homes, on the stage, and of course during carnival. Judged by later centuries' standards, their associations are surprising, which ranged from a sign of Satan's work to a proud assertion of women's independence. Depending on the occasion, masks were formal, comic, discreet, or boorishly intrusive. Concealment was not always their intent.

During Louis XIV's reign, foreign visitors noted the many women who wore masks in public, a tradition dating back over a century. The most common mask, made of pasteboard and covered in black velvet or satin, was oval. Women held it in place by clenching a button with their teeth, which made speaking impossible. Some wielded it like a fan, by turns holding and withdrawing it. This mask was called a *loup* ("wolf"), so named for the fright it supposedly gave children. Women also wore the *mimi* in public. These were half masks of fabric or pasteboard that concealed only the eyes. Modeled on Italian actors' masks, the *mimi* was widespread at balls. A variant was the domino, a *mimi* with a light cloth attached to its base that covered the nose and mouth.[1]

Seventeenth-century images of women in a *loup* or *mimi* often feature sumptuous dress. The less privileged also wore masks. An Italian who visited France marveled at the liberty they granted women in public markets or when visiting family and friends unescorted. His description suggests fine taste but not necessarily wealth. "A light, black-velvet mask on the face, a black scarf held fast by ribbons of the same color, fairly simple clothing, and a pair of elegant slippers: such is the typical *toilette* of these French wives."[2]

Initially worn by elites in the Renaissance, the *loup* persisted into the eighteenth century. Women wore it in public spaces and at receptions and weddings. Masked women were common on the *Cours la Reine,* a stylish walkway along the Seine. Motives ranged from reserve to brazen independence. Antoine Furetière's 1690 *Universal Dictionary* observes that women had made use of masks "for some time." Its definition keeps to the humbler motives. The *loup* is "the cover that women of a certain status place over their faces to guard against sunburn or in modesty so as to be less seen."[3]

A bantering book from the previous century offers other reasons. *Two New Dialogues in the French Language, Italianized and Otherwise Disguised* (1578) helps date when the practice began. Women have recently begun to make use of this "subtle and sophisticated invention," Philausone tells his friend Celtophile. Masked wives will now be free to defy their husbands, he says. "I know well the kind of headache you speak of," Celtophile replies. "Migraine engendered by jealousy." An anonymous English work voiced the same anxiety. "With a Black-velvet Visor they go sometimes to church as to a Ball or Play, unknown to *God* and their *Husbands*."[4]

Perhaps husbands truly feared the prospect of a masked wife, but the *loup* was more typically worn for the privacy it offered, whether or not it concealed identity. Women's masks certainly could, and did, disguise, but a more common purpose was to maintain psychological distance where physical distance was lacking.[5] They granted women a degree of freedom otherwise absent. Some were surely impelled by modesty. Others wore a mask to avoid the appearance of immodesty, which is not the same. Everyone was aware of barefaced women who strolled alone and looked men in the eye.[6]

Mme de Sévigné was wearing a mask when she watched the disgraced minister Fouquet enter a Paris prison. Catherine Meurdrac de la Guette describes wearing a mask when she traveled alone, including when she rode her horse through Paris streets. In 1683, Jean-Baptiste Colbert, Louis XIV's Finance Minister, reported to the lieutenant general of police that a high magistrate's wife had recently been seen wearing a mask in church, an impious practice, he added, that the king opposed.[7] A mean-spirited satire on supposed female vice by the poet Boileau mocks the mask of a noblewoman whose gambling has sent her family into poverty:

> Shall I describe her stockings so riddled with holes,
> Her revolting slippers soled and resoled,
> And her hair from which hangs, at the end of a string,
> An old peeling mask just as hideous as she?

A telling note appeared in the 1713 edition of these poems, which was first published nine years before: "Most women at the time wore a mask made of black velvet whenever they went out."[8]

Masks also played a part in sinister deeds. Marie Marguerite Monvoisin, daughter of the convicted sorceress La Voisin, gave riveting testimony in the scandalous Affair of the Poisons. Marie's mother had been in contact with Louis XIV's mistress Mme de Montespan to devise ways to bind the king's affections. She described the toads, moles, and red slugs her mother had boiled for potions and recounted the black masses with naked women she had staged by candlelight. Mme de Montespan still wasn't satisfied, so La Voisin arranged for a fellow witch to prepare a powder. At their rendezvous outside the Petits-Pères convent in Paris, the witch lifted her *loup*, spat on the ground, and passed over the precious philter.[9] That a witch could don a mask and fear no suspicion is a measure of how common it was.

The fashionable *loup* was worn in a wider context of condemnation. Claude Noirot, a judge from Langres, fiercely denounced all forms of masking. In *The Origins of Masks* (1609), he wrote that masks "hide and confine the hallowed dwelling of the intellect." He objected to women's makeup for the same reason. Its colors and paints give women "an alien face," clothed in "shameless and impiety."[10] Jean Savaron, a magistrate and historian, published his *Treatise against Masks* in the same decade. He notes that the word itself had roots in the underworld. In Italy's Piedmont and Ligurian dialects, *masca* meant sorceress, with an even more ancient pre-Indo-European layer meaning soot or smut. According to Savaron, these origins carried associations that confirmed his conviction that masks were demonic. The horrific acts they inspired were no surprise. "How many thefts, assassinations, parricides, murders, rapes, and acts of adultery have been committed by those in masks!"[11]

Legislation regulating masks evokes the crimes they were said to encourage. A royal ordinance from 1399, for instance, aimed to reduce murder and theft by forbidding persons from "wearing a false face." In the sixteenth century, regional parlements issued orders banning masks, including a 1508 order in Rouen that forbade the possession, sale, or purchase of "false faces, noses, beards, or other kinds of disguise." A 1514 royal edict banned Paris shops from selling masks and called for them to be burned in public bonfires.[12]

The steady flow of prohibitions suggests the practice persisted. An edict from François I was regularly reissued in the seventeenth and eighteenth centuries that prohibited masked and armed groups from traveling through towns, cities, forests, woods, and villages.[13] Nicolas de La Mare's *Treatise on the Police*, compiled during Louis XIV's reign, includes royal edicts forbidding maskers from carrying "swords, canes, or other weapons." The law was needed, de La Mare notes, among those "whom the mask renders equal in appearance but are often of very different ranks."[14] A disguised commoner with a sword was not only dangerous: it usurped social privilege.

Behind these laws is the disruptive presence of carnival. Condemnations of its impiety in sermons, tracts, and books had been consistent since the Middle Ages. Some recalled that the first mask was worn by Satan, who came to Adam and Eve in the guise of a serpent. A mask disfigured man, made in the image of God. One author drew from St. Augustine's sermons to make his point about carnival. Is there anything more shameful to humans, Augustine had asked, than to take the form of a goat or deer?[15] The anonymous *Layman's Letter to his Friend on the Lawlessness of Carnival* denounces the holiday itself as blasphemous. Its every element is corrupt, including "frenzied dances," "lascivious postures," "dishonest songs," and "illicit encounters." There is no license untried: "libertines rule these ghastly days." Fathers and sons become shameless gluttons. Mothers dress as their daughters and glory in the same disgraceful pleasures. Church decrees in the seventeenth century forbade clergy from wearing masks and prohibited them from appearing in the company of maskers. Regulations from local councils forbade church officials from attending masquerades and balls under threat of excommunication.[16]

Carnival traditions in early modern France were often rowdy. During carnival, masked bands in and around Paris interrupted marriage and baptismal celebrations in charivaris that laced festivity with menace. Maskers descended on outdoor feasts bearing muskets, pistols, and fireworks. They muscled their way into private homes, burned effigies, and called out curses and insulting names, claiming the right to dance whether their partner wished to or not. An ordinance from the 1740s condemns the "supposed custom" of maskers to thrust their way into such gatherings to "inflict violence on caterers, their wives and children, and the servers."[17] A Parisian's journal recounts François I and his entourage careening through the city on horseback in masks and motley costumes, stopping in various households "to mock and play." Contemporaries describe the king's grandson Henry III crashing weddings and invading family feasts of the high aristocracy. He did so masked, dressed as a woman, and surrounded by his *mignons,* also masked. In carnival 1584, they rode through the streets claiming to be merchants, priests, and lawyers, lashing pedestrians and committing "a thousand acts of insolence."[18]

Was Louis XIV aware of the royal precedent when he and a masked entourage tried to force their way into a private ball during carnival? Nicolas

Potier de Novion, president of the Paris parlement, was with his family and guests when the king and three carriages of masked revelers appeared near midnight. When guards refused them entrance, a dozen maskers brandished swords, lit firebrands, and tried to set the front door on fire. The king's celebrated war minister Louvois lowered his mask and confided to Novion that he was "the least of the company here." Novion grasped what this meant and "corrected his misstep." The others kept their incognito and stayed late eating, drinking, and dancing.[19]

An eyewitness account places the episode in the late 1670s, when Louis XIV was in his forties. In 1683, Colbert signed a royal order condemning disturbances caused by masked persons who force their way into private assemblies waving swords. It begins by stating that His Majesty has "been informed of the disorders caused in several places in Paris by masked persons who, wishing to enter gathering-places, have forced open their doors holding swords and committing other egregious acts."[20] The king knew whereof he spoke.

By comparison with the renowned celebrations of Venice, Paris was a relative latecomer to carnival revelry with its masks and costumes. Jean Savaron's 1608 denunciation of masks, for instance, which catalogs every instance of their perfidy, makes no mention of carnival. The country's bloody religious wars and the battles of the Fronde probably made its celebrations unthinkable. By the end of the century, however, its spirit was on full display. Carnival officially began on January 7, the *Fête des Rois* or Epiphany, which marked the three kings' visit to the baby Jesus. It was during carnival's last three days that large numbers of Parisians donned costumes and a mask. Thousands came out on Mardi Gras. The principal rendezvous of coaches, carriages, and maskers on foot was the Saint-Antoine quarter of Paris, a popular district whose chaos attracted wealthy revelers. Its Mardi Gras procession featured displays ranging from wagons bearing prizewinning livestock to sumptuous floats.

For many years, the holiday's high point featured a gift from the Venetian ambassador Alvise Mocenigo. Six horses and their masked coachman drew an immense gondola on wheels through the densely settled neighborhood. In its center was a conch shell that reached to the street lamps to form a kind of amphitheater. Seated inside were twenty musicians who played festive music. In advance of the float rode masked and mounted gentlemen outfitted in the dress of ten different nations.[21]

The journalist Jean Loret, a contemporary of Louis XIV, provides an exuberant rhyming account of Paris carnival in the 1650s. Four thousand maskers appear on Fat Tuesday in the rue Saint-Antoine, he writes, engaged in three thousand different masquerades: Amazons, shepherds, peasants, and fishwives; Albanians, Spaniards, and Indians; holy men, courtesans, Gorgons, clowns, and princes. Some wear pearls, silks, and brilliant satins. Others wear tatters, soiled fabric, or rough canvas. Children chase carriages, maskers pass on horseback, "singers serenade," and "violins violinize." The amount of food the popular classes provide is staggering.

> This one holds a fattened rooster
> That one has a cask of mustard
> This one brings a shank of ham,
> This one bread, and that one jam,
> Between two plates, three piping omelets,
> . . .
> Here are salads, here is fruit,
> Here is broth, and here is soup,
> Here is rice, here is cheese,
> Here's the salt, and here's the sweets.[22]

Good-Time Roger, one of the boozy revelers in a pamphlet called *Essential Advice for Present Affairs*, shares a confession. "I won't disguise it. You know full well that I've been drinking, and I don't just sip. There aren't any of you who wouldn't do the same. . . . So let's get drunk together on Mardi Gras. We'll gorge ourselves, laugh, make war on misery, and kill nothing or no one but gloom, an innocent murder!"[23]

Such scenes continued during Louis XIV's reign and beyond, mixing elites with the lower orders in predictably chaotic abundance. In his 1727

FIGURE 2.1. *Paris Carnival Scene*, anon. (Musée Carnavalet)

travelogue *Paris Sojourn*, the German lawyer Joachim Nemeitz describes carnival as a series of celebrations beginning just after New Year's and ending on Mardi Gras. It is "the Golden Age of Paris," Nemeitz writes. "Here, everything is permitted, and the stranger the mask, the more it is admired." Nemeitz describes masks of every fashion, age, and country. He saw men in women's dresses and women in men's trousers. By his telling, the city's public and private balls drew a wide range. Most began around midnight. Some limited who entered, while others "closed the door to no one who was masked."

Nemeitz relates what he saw. A pair of young lovers forbidden to meet by their parents come masked. An unknowing husband tries to seduce his own wife. A brash gallant approaches a stranger, who, removing her mask, reveals that she is "of the highest extraction."[24] Absent from this and other accounts is the abandon later associated with carnival. True, men dressed as women and women as men, a practice harshly punished outside of the season. But there is little evidence of the violence that marked carnival just before the French Revolution or the political threats it posed in the 1830s and '40s. For much of the eighteenth century, carnival's misrule consisted chiefly of feasting and drunkenness.

LICENSE WITHOUT DISORDER

The seventeenth century's proliferation of masks was a product of its hierarchy. Carnival masks loosened the hierarchy's hold, but they rarely overturned it. An indication of the mask's limited powers to subvert was that a lady "of the highest extraction," as witnessed by Joachim Nemeitz, unmasked and identified herself to the brash gallant. Before 1789, this same scene was repeated often during carnival by indignant elites. Rather than a means of escaping hierarchy, and even less of effacing or inverting it, masks were adaptations to a power structure rooted in inequality.

That one's place in this order rested in part on the opinions of others made strategic concealment essential. The invisible masks of courtiers were perhaps hierarchy's purest expression: their very masks were masked. What was never fully concealed was the underlying order. Those in superior positions were expected to display their distinction at all times. Consider the ire the duchesse de Duras earned from Louis XIV for failing to demand her due honor when an inferior usurped her seat. Covering the face did not suspend such privilege.

Between New Year's 1700 and Ash Wednesday, there were fifteen courtly masquerades and another two dozen private balls at Versailles. People marveled at the "infinite" number of masks. Those who danced, danced masked. Musicians played and singers sang masked. Masked spectators watched masked actors perform short scenes and plays. Courtiers sipped warm chocolate and sweet wine and ate pastries, fruits, and jellies with their masks on. "We enjoyed it tremendously," Saint-Simon writes of the marathon, "and went three weeks without seeing daylight." The marquis de Dangeau said that recovering from such pleasure could be difficult.[25]

Courtly masquerades, which punctuated the winter months at Versailles, featured a stunning array of costumes. Participants took note of what those close to the king wore. The duc d'Orléans, Louis XIV's brother, regularly dressed as a woman. Queen Maria Theresa sometimes came as a lawyer. Her thirty-nine-year-old son, the *Grand Dauphin,* once came dressed in children's clothes and was led about by his "tutor," a relative of the king's first mistress, who wore professorial robes. France's future Regent, the duc de Chartres, cross-dressed as the tutor's wife. Queen Henrietta Maria of England, sister to the late Louis XIII and again in France after Charles I's beheading, was a Bohemian girl.

Organizers sometimes announced themes for the balls in advance. When the theme was *Don Quixote,* the *Grand Dauphin* was Sancho Panza. When it was the Turkish court, the marquis d'Antin—the son of Madame de Montespan, the king's second mistress—was the Grand Sultan, with a menagerie and slaves. One night the theme was faux poverty, with soiled masks and tattered rags; on another it was pastoral, with milkmaids, shepherds, and shepherdesses. "We came as peasant girls," Madame de Montpensier writes, "in low-necked dresses whose yellow sleeves and ruffs matched the country style of the provinces, although to be honest our fabric was of a slightly better quality than theirs. My entire body was draped with pearls and diamonds." On occasion, the theme was the gardens of Versailles, and costumers did their eccentric best to imitate fountains, statues, and trees.[26]

A series of masked balls in 1700 honored the fourteen-year-old Marie-Adélaïde of Savoy shortly after her marriage to the king's grandson Louis Bourbon, the *Petit Dauphin.* Her appearances featured one splendid costume after another. She was a magician, an *Américaine,* a sultan's wife, and—only in the masquerade, alas—a queen. Marie-Adélaïde was the honoree of the grandest masked ball of the season, hosted in early February by Chancellor Phélypeaux and his wife at their mansion near the palace. There were theatrical scenes, dancing, and indoor booths with delicacies from across Europe. Crowds gathered outside while guards checked lists to keep interlopers out. Only "persons of distinction" were allowed entry.[27]

It's easy to imagine such balls as a breeding ground for intrigue, with the mask's anonymity a cover for what could never be done in the open. In fact, given the court's hierarchies of birth and status, true disguise was rarely sustained. Protocol required those attending alone to unmask and identify themselves at the door. When maskers came in a group, one of the members had to unmask, give his name, and identify each of the others. The pool of guests—by and large the same people who populated the court by day—was restricted. At smaller, private balls, guards admitted "only the most worthy persons of the court."[28] Familiarity with the aggregate made identifying individuals part of the fun: by a voice or laugh, a certain way of walking or dancing, or a recognizable physique. At court, masks did not reliably hide identities. Accounts of masked dancing in letters and memoirs often include dancers' names. Stories of bad behavior usually identify both the culprit and victim.

Many chose costumes in keeping with their rank, which operated as a marker even with the face covered. Some masked themselves but did not wear a costume. The duc de Luynes noted that ambassadors, foreign ministers, and certain court officials often came in their "accustomed attire." An author in the early 1700s recommended the practice for high nobility more generally, lest they be mistaken. "When they wish to go incognito, it is prudent for a prince and great lords to mask themselves nobly in a way that will always distinguish them from those who are common, so as not to be exposed to incidents that might otherwise arise."[29] The operative word *incognito* was an import from Italy, where it described identities known but not acknowledged. Not all who were masked wished to be unrecognized.[30]

The balls' unreliable anonymity made for some embarrassing scenes. On Mardi Gras 1664, Cardinal Maldaquin, in a red gown and masked, was pushing his way through a thick crowd when he suddenly broke free and fell flat, revealing his nakedness beneath the robes. Everyone knew who it was and roared with laughter. Another priest, selected to officiate at Versailles in its Ash Wednesday mass, was spotted at a Mardi Gras ball the night before, "saying and doing the most filthy things." It was not the first offense. The honor was revoked, along with a promised bishopric. More commonly, maskers undertook to guard their cover for as long as they could before acquaintances gradually worked out who was who. The duc d'Enghien was charmed by a woman who spoke sweetly to him at a ball; he eventually realized he was talking to Madame, sister-in-law to the king.[31]

The court's clubbish intimacy gave pranksters a unique opportunity for cruelty. A man appeared in the midst of a ball at Versailles wrapped in an immense cloak, with four wax faces attached to a false head held high on a pole. Each face was recognizable, and all came from ancient families. He went straight to a woman whose attentions toward the comte d'Évreux, one of the four, had fed rumors. Coming close, he bowed and danced, keeping Évreux's face fixed on hers. The room fell silent and some stood on benches to watch. Given her status, no one dared to laugh.[32] A similar scene stripped of all subtlety unfolded when a costumer entered wearing a headdress of antlers. He spotted the duc de Luxembourg—"perhaps the only man in France unaware of his wife's conduct," writes Saint-Simon—and gestured elaborate greetings to him and his wife. The laughter was malicious and explosive, and when the king joined in, the jeers grew raucous.[33]

Disguise was possible at courtly balls, but its limits were known and enforced. Over the course of a ball that the king also attended, for instance, the *Petit Dauphin* changed costumes several times to keep others guessing. As the duc d'Uzès offered candies to the marquis de Lassay—both of them titled but tainted, one from a family of Protestants and the other known as a rampant seducer—the dauphin suddenly appeared and struck the duke's hand, scattering the sweets. Uzès gave the masker a slap, Louis returned the blow, and Uzès replied with a kick in the royal backside. The dauphin unmasked himself, to the horror of Uzès. Such blunders reminded ball-goers that masks provided no immunity. Beyond such individual unmasking, all also knew that the king or queen could at any moment command all present to remove their masks. This was not uncommon.[34]

The risk of offending the highly placed prompted Antoine de Courtin to urge prudence toward those in masks. "One must demonstrate yet greater correctness to maskers than to others, since those wearing masks often deserve not merely civility but also our esteem." It was uncivil to touch the mask of another person, Courtin continued, and unthinkable to remove it. The dancing-master Pierre Rameau echoed this advice. "One should demonstrate particular honor to those in masks, for quite often the disguise covers persons of the first rank."[35] In Louis XIV's courtly balls, masks did not give license to adopt alternate identities or inhabit other roles. Their function was instead to loosen, slightly and temporarily, the constraining rituals of unquestioned hierarchy.

The disposition of the hall made it clear that this was still the court. Whenever Louis XIV was present, he sat in an armchair at the head of the room. The prescribed arrangement of seats for his kin and courtiers remained as it was at formal balls, with his sons and daughters seated alongside him. Ladies of the high aristocracy sat on either side of the room, and their husbands stood behind them. In the masked ball for Marie-Adélaïde at the Chancellor's mansion, there were three armchairs at the front of the ballroom, where the king's brother Monsieur, his wife Madame, and the young duchess sat. Behind them was a row of tabourets for those ladies permitted to sit.[36] The visible map of power displayed on other occasions reigned here as well.

Masquerades nevertheless offered a measure of freedom. The respite is evident when set against the scripted rigors of the court's *bals*

FIGURE 2.2. *Formal Ball at Versailles*, anon. (Bibliothèque nationale de France)

réglés—"ordered balls"—which were frequent at Versailles. These formal balls attracted elites from Paris, the provinces, and foreign countries, who joined courtiers to celebrate royal betrothals, weddings, births, military triumphs, and diplomatic openings. Handwritten invitations urged guests to come in their "richest, most fitting attire." Men wore dazzling coats embroidered with gold and silver brocade, and women's dresses were heavy with jewels.[37] The balls began when the king stood, an act that brought all present to their feet. Couples made their formal reverence two-by-two, and the king then led them in a series of dances. The branle was first, followed by a gavotte and a courante. The king danced the first minuet alone with the queen or first princess, who then selected a gentleman of royal blood to succeed them. The relay continued until all members of the royal family had danced. The king then sat, which all others could now do as well.

Ritual shaped the dancers' every move. Gentlemen who danced saluted the king with a deep bow before turning to the queen or first princess. A complex pair of matching bows executed in time with the music initiated each couple's dance, and a different sequence of bows ended it.[38] As with much else at court, each nuance conveyed distinction. Invitations to dance were issued with a wordless bow. Any woman who declined an invitation was obliged to decline all others. Hats were removed with the right hand before each bow unless the couple was side by side, when they were removed with the left. Such stateliness could be hard to bear. "In addition to its solemnity," a writer complained of the balls, "one should also note its confounding formality, its cold repetition of dances, its inflexible rules established for maintaining order in such gatherings, its silence, its constraints, and the idleness of those who do not dance."[39]

Masquerades weren't so much an inversion of Versailles's formal balls as their blurred double. A common interpretation is that the court's masked balls suspended hierarchy. More typically, their concealment was a fiction embraced by consent. Social distinctions were usually known and seldom neglected. When identities were unknown, courtiers advanced with care. When ball-goers tweaked the wrong masker, they were embarrassed and sometimes contrite. The duc d'Enghien mentions seeing Monsieur at a ball "in a mask, pretending not to be known."[40] This was a necessary complement to the court's mutual delusion, a dynamic according to which courtiers acted as if its unseen masks did not exist while knowing that they did. At masquerades, most acted as if masks hid identities when they did not.

Both fictions furnished acceptable terms on which unequals could interact. "One stands where one wishes," d'Enghien wrote of the balls, "one speaks to whomever one chooses, and one acts as if all were equal." The effect was "liberty without disorder." He understood that the balls' enjoyment did not depend on keeping one's identity disguised. He continued: "If one wants to be known one is, and, if one does not want to, one is not."[41]

The relief from court ritual that masks granted was real but far from total. The boundaries that separated teasing from impudence and impudence from insult depended largely on the mood and rank of recipients. Masking was a particular kind of fiction, which could suddenly end with a command from the monarch or an affronted worthy. Versailles's balls were nevertheless a release from the court's demands. Their masks eased the feeling that someone was always watching and taking note. To judge by their popularity, the relief was welcome. "Since the invention of balls with masks," the duc d'Enghien wrote in a 1665 letter, "no one can bear the others, which do not even come close."[42] This was a curious kind of cover, introducing uncertainty though not always disguise. To note that masks did not confer immunity is somewhat beside the point. These maskers were not inclined to test their limits.

PLAYING FOR LAUGHS

One way to describe Louis XIV's reign is that it took all the joy out of laughter. There were no jesters at Versailles. The delight of palace courtiers, according to Colin Jones in his history of the smile, was "disdainful," "bitter," "ambiguous," "proud," "knowing," or "ironic."[43] Laughter at Versailles was calculated and strategic, and it usually came at someone's expense. This, too, was the consequence of fierce competition for status, expressed in the most personal of terms. Derision proclaims a loser.

When Louis XIV was still a boy, the laughter of the realm was Rabelaisian. Amusements brought full-throated glee. An especially brutal version had reigned during the Fronde. An anonymous flood of "Mazarinades"—short pamphlets with scathing gibes against the cardinal—gushed from printers' workshops into the streets. Their wit ranged from silly to taunting to vicious. In *Mazarin's Farewell Ballet Danced before the King and Regent Queen Mother*, the minister is a tooth-extractor, hawker of knickknacks, and promoter of a healing balm made of mites' eyes, snails' kidneys, and the blood and tears of the people. *Mazarin, A Pole for Mardi Gras*, mixes mockery with violence. The minister talks to himself as he flees Paris. *They'll grill my guts in the marketplace. They'll dangle me from a pitchfork. Here's my disguise, a plush green robe to hide my scrawny member!*[44]

An anonymous Mazarinade attributed to the playwright Paul Scarron managed to be both jokey and savage:

> Buggering bugger, buggered bugger
> Bugger in plumes and bugger in stubble
> Bugger of boys and bugger of sheep
> Bugger of all to the highest degree
> He buggers the small and buggers the great
> This bugger is now sodomizing the State.

> . . .
> We'll cut them off, poor Jules,
> First one and then the other,
> You'll be a Cardinal mutilated,
> A Cardinal detesticulated.[45]

Such was the comic climate in the half century before Louis XIV's birth: insulting, brutal, and explicitly political.

The theatrical equivalent of this brand of humor was farce. Among its originators was a small troupe run by Robert Guérin, who took the name Gros Guillaume. Fat William led with the belly, which was said to precede him by two steps. He wore two belts, one arounld his waist and the other below his ample breasts. With his face covered in flour, Fat William was a slow-moving clown, mixing silliness with teary sentiment. He was known to suffer from kidney stones, which brought still greater hilarity. At strategic moments, he blew flour on other actors' faces. When he was eighty, he was arrested for mimicking a magistrate a little too faithfully. Two others joined Fat William in performances. Gurgling Gautier was rail-thin with long, straight hair, a pointed beard, black heels, and doublet. He played a "tragic" old man, posing as a scholar, merchant, lawyer, and sometimes king. Limber as a marionette and known for his bad singing, he always wore a mask. Turlupin, full of fire and wit—by turns a seducer, prude, valet, tyrant, and conspirator—was fluent and attractive. He, too, played masked. The trio's regular theater was an unused tennis court in the Latin Quarter, where they drew crowds of students.[46]

Their break came when the premier French theatrical troupe, led by Valleran le Conte, complained to Louis XIII's chief minister Richelieu that their performances were unauthorized. Le Conte held the lease in the city's earliest theater, the Hôtel de Bourgogne, where the *Comédiens du Roy* would one day premiere the classics of Corneille and Racine. Richelieu responded by summoning the three farceurs to perform, which they did with gusto. Dazzled by what he saw, Richelieu ordered le Conte to open the theater to the trio, where the two troupes performed on alternate nights.[47]

The masks that Turlupin, Gurgling Gautier, and Fat William wore had their counterpart in a new dramatic genre from Italy. Commedia dell'arte, originating in Padua in the 1540s, had initially come to France as a private entertainment for princes and monarchs. After 1600, it was increasingly available to the public. The first commedia company to perform in Paris

FIGURE 2.3. *Fat William*, anon. (Bibliothèque nationale de France)

was *I Gelosi*, led by the renowned Arlecchino Tristano Martinelli. In France, the generic name Comédie Italienne soon caught on. Private journal entries by the royal secretary Pierre de l'Estoile capture some of the dangerous allure of this unscripted genre, which reputedly drew bigger crowds than the best preachers of Paris. "These comedies teach filth, promote adultery,

FIGURE 2.4. *Gurgling Gautier*, anon. (Bibliothèque nationale de France)

and educate Parisian youths of both sexes in debauchery," a contemporary complained.[48]

Commedia performances were irregular before midcentury, when an Italian troupe settled permanently in France. The Fronde had made short work of efforts to house a troupe in Paris. The best Italian players were nevertheless known. In 1640, the celebrated Scaramouche Tiberio Fiorilli lifted the tiny Louis XIV, two years old and bawling, onto his lap. Fiorilli was confident he could divert the baby. The royal infant stopped crying, began to laugh, and then defecated all over Fiorilli's hands and clothes, to the raucous delight of all.[49] Twenty-one years later, the young monarch named

FIGURE 2.5. *Turlupin*, anon. (Bibliothèque nationale de France)

a group of Italians led by Domenico Biancolelli the "King's Troupe" and granted it an annual pension of 16,000 livres. This was the highest subvention of any royal company and three times what Molière's actors received. Until its abrupt banishment at the end of the century, the Comédie Italienne was a regular presence in Paris.

The plays' basic elements stayed true to commedia tradition with its stock characters, familiar costumes, and reliable pranks. The recipe was simple, with whimsy, wordplay, and buffoonery, but it was not the Rabelaisian fare of an earlier age. Now under the king's direct authority, the company was outlandish but seldom vicious or political. The changes mark a key moment in the effort to tame the anarchic humor of Mazarinades. The historian Sara Beam describes its impetus in political terms in her book *Laughing Matters*. "The gradual demise of satirical farce was not the product of absolutism," she concludes, "but one of its central constituents."[50]

In Italy, commedia's outdoor performances drew spectators from the popular classes, who responded with rowdy approval. In France, ticketed performances in theaters meant that audiences were mostly well-to-do.[51] The king's early support and the cachet it carried drew elites, which meant that most who came to commedia also knew Corneille and Molière. Despite the atmosphere of money and the presence of more elevated tastes, performers still knew what brought the loudest laughs.

The masks these actors wore produced a style of acting that relied on every part of the body except the face for expression. A classic work on commedia dell'arte from 1927 describes their effect on spectators. Modern audiences are accustomed to watching a performer's face to the exclusion of the body, its author Constantin Mic observes. Cover the face and we suddenly become aware of movement and gesture. Then something magical occurs.

> Thanks to the work of our imagination, as the actor moves, the mask's fixity disappears before our eyes. He slips free of its immobility. . . . Taking advantage of the mask's features, he conveys to it a new power of expression—a force, a character—which the large hall requires, and which a mere face, however enhanced with makeup, could never attain.[52]

Spectators affirmed the view. The movement and postures of a renowned eighteenth-century Arlequin, one reviewer wrote, are "so true and so expressive that one could see, so to speak, the expression of his physiognomy through his black mask."[53]

On this point commedia masks resembled the serious masks of ballet. From the founding of the *Académie Royale de Danse* in 1661, most performers danced masked. The practice served the intent of dramatic spectacles at court and on operatic stages, which was the artistic expression of dignity, grace, and controlled passion. Dancers' masks, the same simple oval that women wore in public, transformed mortals into gods and other mythical beings. Contemporaries described their effect as displacing emotion from the face to the body. Was this why, after dancing masked at court for the last time at age twenty-five in *Carnaval de Benserade*, Louis XIV never again covered his face?[54]

One hundred years later, the ballet master Jean-Georges Noverre launched an effort to remove masks from dancers' faces. He acknowledged the reasons for their remarkable longevity. Some still insist that the mask carries an air of nobility, he wrote: it does not hide the dancers' eyes, they say; one sees the passions that move them. "Nature cannot approve of this coarse practice," he responded. A contemporary of Rousseau, Noverre spoke for many who prized sincerity and declared a readiness to be moved. Masks hide true sentiment, he claimed. "Whatever eclipses and degrades must be condemned by enlightened Artists."[55]

Seventeenth-century audiences, by contrast, were fully fluent in strategies of concealment, and they grasped the necessity of masks. Whether at court or watching commedia, these spectators were attuned to the details of voice, posture, gesture, and movement.[56] Arlequin makes the point colorfully in *The Fountain of Wisdom*, a comedy from 1694. "The distance from persona to person is no farther than from my mask to my face, or from my costume to my skin," he observes, before delivering the sting. "Anyone can see that in Paris actors aren't the only ones acting."[57]

CLOSE TO THE BONE

For playwrights, the variety of masks in the theater and beyond provided a rich opening for comedy. The masks of elites were a tempting subject, since they were particularly skilled in dissembling. It was also dangerous, since elites dominated audiences. Might authors find a way to make such spectators' vanity a subject for laughter without stirring resentment?

The Liar, a work by the tragic playwright Pierre Corneille, casts a pitiless light on aristocratic deceit. An arrogant young aristocrat named Dorante arrives in Paris fresh from the provinces. Having quit the study of law, he is full of bluster and ready to cut a figure. He hires a servant and declares his intention to impress women. When an elegant lady named Clarice, strolling with her friend in the Tuileries, stumbles just in front of him, he sees his chance. Dorante offers an arm, declares himself unworthy, and professes his love. Flattery soon turns to falsehood. He is an officer from an ancient noble line just back from the German wars, he tells her. No major battle has been won without him. His lies continue, not only to Clarice, but to his father, his friends, and the woman he eventually marries, Clarice's friend Lucrèce.

First performed in 1642, *The Liar* comes from the middle of Corneille's career. Its register is altogether different from his masterpieces *Le Cid*, *Horace*, and *Cinna*. Its characters are shallow, its plot implausible, and its action dominated by Dorante's blatant ambition. Its language, however, is unfailingly beautiful, especially when the liar speaks. Corneille himself pointed to the man's charm.[58] Judged more than three hundred years after its premiere, the play seems a clear indictment of the courtly polish that bent the truth out of self-interest. Dorante's deceit is shameless and undetected, and in the end he wins a wife. Wouldn't Corneille's audiences, denizens of the court and high society, see themselves unmasked and mocked? By all accounts, they loved it.

The height of the play's popularity came during Louis XIV's reign, when it was staged 172 times, including thirteen performances at Versailles.[59] Over the next century and a half, commentators wrote regularly about *The Liar* and its companion, *A Sequel to The Liar*. Voltaire reported that by his day some of its lines had become proverbs. This is one he cites:

> "*I spoke the truth.*" When a liar says it,
> It leaves his lips and loses credit.[60]

The play's significance grew as its portrayal of noble hypocrisy became ever more relevant.

Dorante's deceit begins before Clarice's stumble. He asks his servant Cliton how he looks as a chevalier, hoping that no "stench of books" has stayed with him. His opening words betray an anxious regard for appearances.

> One learns to form a fashionable face,
> And now it is my turn to learn.

When Cliton frowns on his lies, Dorante is vicious ("Shut up, you wretch!") and boasts of his remarkable talent.

> Heaven grants this grace to choice few persons,
> Which demands wit, dispatch, vigilance, and recall.
> Be disputatious with no one, and show even less shame.

Near the end, as others prepare for the wedding, Cliton is alone. His words make explicit the play's cynical conclusion, which rewards Dorante's deceit.

> Few could know how to dodge with such grace.
> So for all who thought he could not escape,
> Study well this rare example: you, too, can learn to lie.[61]

Why did *The Liar,* which puts the worst construction on politeness and leaves aristocratic honor in shreds, draw such a following among Louis XIV's contemporaries? The play's full title is *Le Menteur, comédie,* and Dorante's servant Cliton was played by a clown. The actor spoke in a whining voice and covered his face with flour in tribute to Fat William. Dorante's venerable father Géronte, who calls his son a fraud, also wore a clown's mask.[62] What Voltaire and others read as social commentary was to its contemporaries mere farce.

How could such a silly play have a serious message? After his death, an account reputedly by Molière surfaced that praised Corneille for having shown him what comedy could do. Jean Pocquelin was twenty-two when *The Liar* premiered. He had just defied his father by abandoning his studies for the stage. He joined with nine others, assumed the name Molière, and called their new venture the Illustrious Theater.

> I really wanted to write, but I did not know what to write. My ideas were confused. This was the work that focused them. Its dialogue showed me how honest men talked. . . . The cold-blooded manner in which [Dorante] delivered his falsehoods clarified how to create a character. . . . Without *The Liar,* I would have surely done some farces . . . but I would never have written *The Misanthrope.*[63]

Writing in the nineteenth century, the critic Jean-François La Harpe echoed the sentiment. In *The Liar,* he wrote, French audiences saw for the first time a conversation among *honnêtes gens.*[64] This was not a compliment. If Corneille wished to plant a subversive seed deep enough to stay dormant for a time, this was the way to do it. *The Liar* is a serious play masked as farce.

Voltaire understood the kinship between Corneille's Dorante and the iconic characters from Molière's maturity: the impostor Tartuffe, the misanthrope Alceste, and the tone-deaf Monsieur Jourdain. "In a time that knew only romanesque adventure and *turlupinades,* Corneille put morality on the stage," he wrote. "It is inconceivable that the inimitable Molière could have seen this play without at once grasping the genre's prodigious superiority over all others and devoting himself to it wholeheartedly." Molière saw his work in the moral terms Voltaire described. In the preface to *Tartuffe*, he wrote: "It is a heavy blow against iniquity to turn its carriers into a laughing-stock." He also knew to be careful. "Such people will gladly endure rebuke, but they cannot bear to be mocked. They are willing to be malicious but refuse to be ridiculed."[65]

From the start, Molière's comedies were coherent, integrated, and fully finished scripts. In this regard, they differed substantially from slapstick farce and Italian commedia. Yet in look and feel, they share much with these predecessors. A farceur named Fat René played the title role in Molière's comedy *Barbouillé's Suspicions* with flour on his face. Molière himself wore a mask as Mascarille in *The Blunderer*. Commedia's more consequential legacy is less conspicuous. In his mature works, Molière transformed the facile plot device of disguise into barefaced hypocrisy. Instead of the melodramatic intrigue familiar in commedia, Molière offered a more refined imposture: the pretense of elites consumed by vanity. It did not require great distortion to make the portrayal comic.[66]

Two of Molière's best-known plays, *The Bourgeois Gentleman* and *The Misanthrope*, provide ample opportunities for derision. In *The Bourgeois Gentleman*, Monsieur Jourdain is the son of a merchant, now improbably rich, who has the means to live nobly. He has neither taste nor discernment and is oblivious to the fact that those who fawn on him are exploiting his naivety. He is the worst kind of courtier, both gullible and oblivious. In *The Misanthrope*, the wretched Alceste knows all about the treacherous currents of flattery and broadcasts his disgust openly. Each is ill suited for society, Jourdain out of blindness to how others see him and Alceste fully aware of his own unpleasantness. Both are outsiders, a grave fault in the court's small world.

Molière sets their folly within the web of esteem and reciprocity. The very things Jourdain finds wondrous draw scorn from Alceste. Jourdain marvels to his wife at the honor of lending vast sums to a courtier who once spoke to the king. "He calls me a friend and treats me as an equal." He is thrilled by the attention he draws, surprised by how kind others are to him, and speechless before strangers' elaborate displays of respect. Alceste, by contrast, denounces every human kindness. "Everywhere I look I see nothing but craven flattery, injustice, interest, betrayal, and deceit." "Everyone regurgitates praise."[67]

Donneau de Visé, a playwright and critic, was an early detractor of Molière who grew convinced of his gifts. He read *The Misanthrope* and, with Molière's approval, drew up a preface that appeared in the play's first edition. In it, he salutes the playwright for choosing a cynic to speak against the manners of the century. Alceste, he writes, is "laughable without being ridiculous."[68] Visé noticed something else about the play.

> It makes honest folk laugh without the tedious and vulgar jokes we're accustomed to seeing in comedies. To me, jokes of this nature are more amusing, even if the laughter is not as loud. They amuse us more—appeal to us more, I think—and make us laugh more continuously within ourselves.[69]

The interior laughter Visé describes does not come from Fat William's tears or Arlequin's silly gibes. Neither is it the derision seen at court. *The Misanthrope* works on another register. Its humor is less blatant and more private, with the suggestion that its true target might be oneself. To expose iniquity to ridicule in this way was both familiar and shrewdly new. It provided spectators with suitable prey for their courtier's laughter—a bludgeon it shared with commedia dell'arte—while also baiting them with something subtler. That Molière managed to do this within the comic conventions of the age is a measure of his genius. He exposed *le monde* by giving them someone to jeer.

In mid-May 1697, more than three decades after the Comédie Italienne had settled in Paris as the "King's Troupe," actors arrived at the Hôtel de Bourgogne to find its doors blocked by heavy steel bars. On the king's orders, all future performances by the company were canceled, its performers' pay abruptly stopped, and theater personnel given six weeks to leave the city. No protest or appeal would be heard.[70] The apparent cause was a play called *The False Prude,* which some took as a reference to Louis XIV's pious consort Mme de Maintenon. Its mockery was reputed to be unsparing.

Since its early years, when the silliness of Fat William and Gurgling Gautier reigned, the troupe had shed their masks and exchanged improvisation for French scripts. The company introduced more elaborate effects. Fountains spouted wine, characters crash-landed on the stage clinging to plywood eagles, and tables heaped with food magically rose up and out of sight.[71] The boisterous tone of early commedia turned more acerbic as comedy came to reside more in words than in the body. A mean-spirited tone appeared, one closer to the pointed laughter of Versailles. In *Divorce,* Arlequin speculates with the king of China about Isabelle's age: "Let's see her teeth," he says. In *The Lucky Man,* he gives commands to another woman: "Head up! Walk! Trot!" Whereas earlier comedies had featured young women who were protected by fathers or guardians, the women in two plays from the late 1680s, *The Swindled Merchant* and *Colombine, A Woman Avenged,* are abandoned and resort to violence, deceit, and illicit sexual relations.[72]

If these changes reduced the quotient of slapstick, they enlarged the capacity for critique. Arlequin's absurd transformations gave way to recognizable schemes. In *The Failure*, he games the system to move up in society, bending the truth, deceiving his creditors, and staying one step ahead of the law. In this play, Arlequin calls himself Monsieur Persillet. He decides that the surest way to status—which means acquiring a mansion, marrying his daughter to a prince, and buying a noble title for his son—is to declare bankruptcy. He only needs a million *livres*. His lawyer tells him it will be simple: falsify your financial records, let drop some impressive names, touch up a last will, and lenders will flock to help. The charade convinces three bankers, who lend him the money.

This being commedia, the florid manners of an upstart who apes nobility are laughably crass. Yet Monsieur Persillet, modeled on the many wealthy commoners who purchased nobility in these years, is not ridiculous. The comedy instead celebrates the success of self-interest. With the purchase of a splendid hôtel on the Place Royale and a venal office for his son, Persillet's bankruptcy is complete, but it's no less useful. The bankers agree to a tiny fraction of their losses, he keeps the mansion, and his son acquires a title. A prince appears, recognizes Persillet's obvious virtue, and marries his daughter. Whereas Molière had targeted the malicious, peevish, and vain, *The Failure* presents its truth straight. With audacity, strategic lying, and the right amount of capital, a man can transform his roots. Appearances are deceptive, but only briefly. They soon remake reality.[73]

This was the context for the demise of the Comédie Italienne, which was both sudden and portentous. The public response was bafflement. Perhaps the king was genuinely offended by the troupe's indecent words and gestures, although such things were not new. Perhaps he truly meant to purify Paris and the court of impiety. Or perhaps, given the crown's desperate need for money, it was a way to trim the royal budget.[74] Whatever the particular reason, it seems clear that the king was looking for a way to close the theater. Since the early happy days when Louis XIV had laughed with the Italian players, much had changed for both comedy and the king. Plays in the company's last decade had moved in the direction of Molière's humor and were now far from its earlier improvised slapstick. Comedy could now carry social and political content. Based more on ideas than antics, they cut close to the bone.

In one telling respect, *The False Prude* was a sign of things to come. It was one of just six plays since 1650 that had the word *false* in its title. Between 1700 and 1775, this number jumped to thirty-one, with many singling out a character's counterfeit identity as its subject. These included *The False Man of Honor*, two *False Scholars*, and *The False Lord*. In the coming years, awareness of all manner of insincerity would intensify, from the empty rituals of elites to the climbers who changed their names to hide their roots. The knowledge of such untruths was widespread, an indication of the extent of concealment said to pervade society. Unmasking would gain momentum in the coming century, not only in the theater. Denouncing insincerity in all its forms, eighteenth-century unmaskers imagined a world in which the expression of true thoughts and genuine feeling might be the basis of a new social order.

3
Crises of Identity

SUPPOSITIONS TRUE AND FALSE

In the spring of 1699, a sailor appeared in the port city of Toulon who claimed to be the heir of an exiled noble family. He said he was the eldest son of Scipion de Caille, a Calvinist who had fled France for Switzerland to escape persecution. The sailor described his own Catholic convictions, which had caused bitter quarrels. In his teens, his father had beaten him and locked him in their home. After much hardship, he had at last reached France and was ready to claim his family's inheritance.

The sailor described his path to Toulon. He had escaped his family nine years before, was kidnapped in Savoy, and was forced to serve in the army. He was seized as a war prisoner and brought to France, where he served in the royal navy and a provincial militia. He was working as a guard in the home of an officer in Nice when his eyes fell on a silver vase that bore the Caille coat of arms. It was a treasured heirloom, seized and sold when his family left the country. "I instantly dissolved into tears," he recalled. That was the moment he decided to claim his inheritance.[1]

Scipion le Brun de Castellane, seigneur de Caille et de Rougon, was living with his wife and three children in a southern French village called Manosque when Louis XIV revoked the Edict of Nantes. The edict, which allowed Protestants to worship freely, had kept an uneasy peace between Catholics and members of the Reformed Church for nearly a century. With its 1685 revocation, Protestants were subject to persecution and arrest. Waves of emigration followed, and whatever property and possessions emigrants left behind went to Catholic relatives or, if unclaimed, to the State.

Caille was a widower when he took his family to Switzerland. He went with his mother, his two daughters, and his only son, a slight, fair-haired twenty-one-year-old. Most family documents were lost, including his children's birth records. The substantial annual income of 12,000 livres from his lands and a mansion in Provence went to his widow's Catholic sister, Anne le Gouche. In 1696, his son Issac suddenly fell ill and died. He was a serious young man whose studies had spanned the law, letters, mathematics, and theology. When his aunt Anne le Gouche received news of the death, she donated the mansion and land in France he was meant to inherit to a charity in his memory. It became a home for indigent women.

The official who heard the sailor's tale in Toulon was Jean-Louis de Vauvré, a highly placed official. He had served in the realm's major ports, including Rochefort, Le Havre, and Dunkerque. Through his patron Jean-Baptiste Colbert, he had direct access to the king. Vauvré spoke regularly with the sailor for three months and quietly informed himself about the Caille family. In June at the cathedral of Toulon, flanked by three Jesuits and Vauvré, the sailor renounced Calvinism and returned to the Catholic Church.

By now, Vauvré had learned things that cast doubt on the man's claims. He called himself André, not Isaac. He said his mother's name was Susanne rather than Judith, the name of Scipion's wife. He said he was born in 1676, not 1664, the date of Isaac's birth. When Vauvré received a detailed letter from Caille describing his son's death three years earlier, he received approval from the king to arrest the sailor on charges of imposture. "The intention of His Majesty," came the terse reply from Versailles, "is that this case be heard by the accustomed magistrates and that the accused be subject to the punishment his imposture merits."[2] This meant death by hanging.

For Pierre Mêge, the false Isaac de Caille, imposture came easily. The son of a jailed counterfeiter, he had moved from one enterprise to the next, earning his bread as a sheep shearer, seller of cures, bandit, beggar, condiment maker, and now sailor. He was a "latter-day Proteus," as one attorney put it.[3] He was heavyset and coarse in speech and manner. He could neither read nor write. He floundered in the first interrogation after his arrest, unable to say what his father looked like or describe his sisters. He claimed to have four siblings, not two. He could not identify where the family had lived in Manosque or say much about their home in Lausanne. When pressed about family names and dates, he improvised. His father had never spoken about his late wife, he said. He had no idea when he was born, he insisted, and his father had always called him André.[4]

In his first formal hearing, the sailor refused to speak. This left the magistrates with no choice but to order a full trial, to be held in Aix-en-Provence before the Parlement of Provence. Isaac's aunt Anne le Gouche had news and knew about the man. Her husband André Rolland was an attorney who had argued cases before the Grenoble parlement. Together they joined the suit charging Mêge with "supposition of name and person," the crime more commonly known as imposture.[5]

In French law, imposture fell under the broad category of *Faux*, "the false." The designation was substantially similar to *Fraude*, "a ruse employed to deceive," and *Dol*, "any misleading ruse, plot, or malign plan meant to harm another."[6] *Faux* encompassed many offenses, ranging from fabricating counterfeit coins, falsifying contracts, and altering church records to forgery and lying under oath. Legal scholars described its damage as threefold: it was an offense against God, the author of all truth; against society, whose foundation is good faith; and against particular individuals, whose life, honor, or wealth has been harmed. It could be active or passive, involving alteration ("making things appear to be other than they are") or suppression ("disguising the truth when one is obliged to make it known").[7] Supposition—the fraudulent substitution of another person or thing for the true article—involved both.

Penalties for supposition with malicious intent were harsh. When a youth in 1691 was discovered to have forged his father's consent to marry, he was banished from France for life. When a man falsely assumed the title of bailiff in 1727, he was forced to stand in the stocks for three days and then exiled. In 1710, when a presumed priest who had celebrated mass in a village church for four years was found to be a simple schoolteacher, he was made to beg forgiveness for his sacrilege. The hand that had administered the host was then severed, and he was burned alive.[8]

From a modern perspective, the course and outcome of Mêge's trial, which began in 1700, defy belief. By every description, Pierre Mêge's appearance, intellect, and demeanor were the stark opposites of Isaac de Caille's. The testimony he gave was reckless and far-fetched. He identified Anne le Gouche as his French aunt and charged that she and her husband Rolland were secret Calvinists. Since his arrest, he said, Rolland had tried to kill him by poison and assassins, falsified documents against him, and bribed witnesses. His attorney accompanied these claims with a series of suits accusing Rolland of fraud, slander, and attempted murder. His extraordinary self-possession was convincing. Public interest grew, and the sailor won over many who were once skeptical.

His attorney reminded the court that his French relatives had a financial interest in lying. Villagers in Manosque hadn't seen him in fifteen years, he observed, so it was no surprise that some former neighbors didn't recognize him. As for his father's claims of his supposed death, how could a fanatical Protestant be believed? Wouldn't he, too, lie to punish his son's betrayal? Mêge's attorney drove these points home. The man had been "oppressed by the hatred of heretics" and cursed "by the cruelty of his own kin."[9]

When the court allowed the sailor to visit Manosque, Rougon, and

Caille—villages where Isaac had lived growing up—people stood along his path to shout their support. A loyal son had defied his father, many said, embraced the true Church, and returned home to claim his land. Over one hundred people swore under oath that he was Isaac de Caille. Parlement worked slowly, receiving fresh correspondence from Switzerland, reviewing the few family records that could be found, and weighing villagers' testimony. Over a seven-year period, from 1699 to 1706, magistrates in Aix devoted more than fifty sessions to the case.

In mid-July 1706, news came that magistrates had reached a decision. The streets near the courthouse filled before sunrise, and merchants closed their shops. By a vote of twelve to nine, the court declared the sailor "truly to be Isaac le Brun de Castellane, the son of Scipion le Brun de Castellane, sieur de Caille & Rougon, and Judith le Gouche." Cheers greeted the verdict, and shouts rose when each magistrate left the building. The court secretary was borne home on a chair with a train of happy followers. Anne le Gouche and her husband Rolland were ordered to pay all expenses for the proceedings, a crushing sum. The most prominent witnesses against Mêge—who included a miller, dovecote keeper, priest, and prior—were arrested for perjury and had their possessions seized.[10]

Three weeks later, the newly proclaimed Isaac le Brun de Castellane married a local physician's daughter named Madeleine Serry. The court awarded him ownership of all Caille income and property still in France, including the home for indigent women. He turned its residents out and, with his new wife Madeleine, took possession of the estate. To mark his victory, he commissioned an engraving of himself in full noble dignity. It bears the words *Isaac le Brun de Castellane, Seigneur de Caille de Rougon, 37 years of age in 1707*. An accompanying poem affirms his resolve.

> Since my youngest days, my steadfastness
> Has seen me through Fate's whims.
> Some wished to strip me of my honored birth
> And prove that I was dead.
> But Heaven, protector of the innocent and weak,
> Has led me through the storm to my safe port.[11]

CAPITAL CRIMES

Forty years before Pierre Mêge inherited the Caille property, a trial in the same Aix courtroom brought a starkly different outcome. A person claiming to be Esprit Adaoust was declared an impostor and hanged. The outline of events is simple: a young man leaves home, someone purporting to be him

FIGURE 3.1. *The False Seigneur de Caille de Rougon*, anon. (Picryl)

returns years later, locals take sides, and the court pronounces judgment. Unlike the absent Caille clan, the Adaoust family was present and active in the prosecution. Unlike the lengthy investigation of Mêge, proceedings in the Adaoust case were rushed. And in contrast to the exacting procedure for Mêge, basic protocol was ignored.

The man who called himself Adaoust was accused by a family substantially different from the one Esprit had left more than two decades before. In the intervening years, the patriarch Sauveur had steered Esprit's older brother Barthélémy into a career as legal secretary. Barthélémy's two sons Laurent and Barthélémy fils became attorneys and now held positions in the Royal Chancellery of Provence and Bureau of Finances. Esprit's wife Angélique Ardouïne, believing her husband was dead, married a notary named Pena, who also worked in royal administration. The couple had three children. The Adaoust family was on the rise.

Esprit had married Angélique twenty-one years before his flight, a union arranged by their fathers. Things quickly soured. The couple quarreled endlessly, agreed to a two-year separation, and then resumed hostilities. A baby died the day it was born, and Esprit left Provence for Paris, arriving on New Year's Day 1632.[12] Here he either survived or died of the plague. During the trial, three men close to the Adaoust family—a priest, surgeon, and merchant of Aix—all testified that they had been present at his death.

Eleven years later, the man calling himself Esprit Adaoust arrived at a first cousin's home near Aix. He later testified that his cousin and father had welcomed him with tears. He told them about his illness in Paris, he said, where he spent six months between life and death. He then joined the light cavalry of the duc d'Orléans and fought in Flanders, Piedmont, Naples, and the German states. He went to Madrid, where he was arrested for stealing a mule. To avoid bringing shame to the Adaoust name, he had called himself Mounier.

Word of a man who claimed to be Esprit soon spread. Within days of coming to Aix, he was attacked in the street by Angélique's husband and several other men, who dragged him to jail. A trial was convened that very day. He had no defense counsel. Thirteen witnesses testified against him, all claiming to have known the true Adaoust. No relative—not his father, nor Angélique, nor his sisters, brothers, or cousin—took the stand. That evening, two strangers appeared in his cell and told him they believed and supported him. They then coached him to say things that were later turned against him. One of them was a relative of Matthieu Pena, Angélique's husband. The next day, the Provence parlement declared him guilty of supposition. He was sentenced to five years' hard labor in the galleys and forbidden on the threat of death from ever again using the name Adaoust.[13]

Five years later, the man returned to Aix still insisting he was Esprit. He was instantly arrested for using the name. The complaint pronounced him "foolhardy and extravagant" in a "ludicrous pursuit to surpass nature itself." The plaintiffs were Angélique and Matthieu Pena, Esprit's nephews Laurent and Barthélémy, and his younger brother Antoine, who had come into

Esprit's inheritance when he disappeared.[14] Laurent and Barthélémy had good reason to defend their family's honor. Not long after the execution, Barthélémy moved to the Bureau of Finances as *Conseiller et Avocat du Roi.* Four years later, the brothers purchased letters of nobility for themselves and their posterity.[15]

In late April 1664, the Parlement of Provence again declared the man who claimed to be Esprit Adaoust guilty of supposition of name and person. He was hanged the same day. According to the verdict, he had wished "to strip the rightful heirs of their father's estate and usurp the position of a legitimate husband, question the status of this husband's marriage, and trouble the lives of his children."[16]

BODY OF EVIDENCE

After the illiterate sailor Pierre Mêge was declared by the Parlement of Aix to be Isaac de Caille, Anne le Gouche and André Rolland hired an attorney named Louis de la Blinière to appeal the decision. The ruling had stripped them of an inheritance, awarded the family's country manor to Mêge, and brought them to the brink of bankruptcy. Blinière was twenty-six years old, tenacious, and not afraid of risk. His entry into the legal profession had coincided with the new century. When the verdict came six years later stripping Pierre Mêge of his false name and title, Blinière spoke of it as a rare victory of reason over passion, prejudice, and ignorance.

Acting against the advice of André Rolland, who had faulted the Provence parlement on procedure, Blinière took the high-stakes path of appealing directly to the King's Privy Council on grounds of *iniquité évidente*, the miscarriage of justice. The body granted the appeal, owing to two letters that had arrived since the initial verdict. One was from civic magistrates in Bern asking the king himself to review Isaac's death certificate. The other was from Pierre de La Closure, a French diplomat in Geneva who had personal knowledge of Isaac's death.[17]

When the Parlement of Paris took up the case in 1710, it had been almost twelve years since Pierre Mêge first appeared in Toulon to claim his inheritance. With the Privy Council's decision, Mêge was stripped of his estate and forced to return what remained of the Caille wealth and possessions to Isaac's French relatives. He was then transported to Paris and put into custody. It would be another two years before the case was heard.[18] The same attorney who had represented Mêge before the Parlement of Provence, a lawyer named Sylvain, was once again called to defend him. He rehearsed the evidence that had convinced magistrates in the first trial, which drew from the sworn testimony of nearly 600 witnesses. Of these, 110 had been sure that the man was Caille and 139 had insisted that he was Mêge. The other 351 were uncertain.[19]

In the absence of reliable documents, Sylvain argued, the central question turned on memory. Isaac's father Scipion de Caille was now dead. The same risks as a Protestant that had kept him from returning to France to testify earlier now deterred his daughters. The only descriptions of Isaac's manner and features the Paris judges heard were therefore based on impressions dating back twenty-five years.

Sylvain turned what looked like a fatal weakness—the fact that his client looked nothing like Isaac de Caille—into a plausible strength. He relentlessly attacked the credibility of those closest to Isaac and turned the focus away from obvious holes in Mêge's account. It was a reasonable strategy in an age that knew nothing of fingerprints, medical records, or genetic analysis. Reason is misleading, he warned, memories are distorted, and human judgment is fallible.

Sylvain presented women who claimed to have nursed Isaac as a baby. They spoke of his rheumy eyes and spindly legs, of accidents, injuries, and scars, and of the resemblance he bore to his late mother. One swore on her soul that this was Caille, and another said her heart had leapt to see him after so long. Some wept. Sylvain quoted testimony from twelve former neighbors, friends, and schoolmates, as well as servants from the Caille household.[20] A portrait gradually emerged, which, the lawyer admitted, was unflattering. Isaac de Caille was "ugly and unpleasant," he said. His cheeks were sunken, and his teeth were diseased and discolored. His face and back were laced with scars. A growth on one knee had been lanced three times, and a bad foot made him limp. Sylvain was unsparing. Caille was illiterate, vulgar, and rash, and he had neither honesty nor good judgment. "He looked like a peasant and had the gait of a fool."[21]

Yet for all its unpleasantness, Sylvain claimed, this portrait was believable, whereas the descriptions offered by Caille's relatives were not. By their account, Isaac de Caille had beautiful eyes, a sculpted nose, and a fine complexion. He was fit, his manners were correct, and his morals were pure. Conversation came easily to him, and he showed delicacy in matters of taste. He was a veritable scholar, at home in a library, a master of mathematics, and fluent in the mysteries of grace and free will. "What a beautiful portrait," Sylvain announced, shading his words with sarcasm, "perfect for a novel."[22]

From this, Sylvain drew his conclusions. The Caille family had obviously created an image that looked nothing like Isaac in order to have him executed as an impostor. By becoming Calvinists, they had betrayed their country. Was it so hard to see that they would also betray their kin for returning to the Catholic Church? What you see before you, Sylvain told the Paris judges, is humanity as it is. You have never seen the son of M. de Caille, he continued; you do not know that he is not this man. "From this it follows," he concluded, "that the accused is the original source of the true portrait, and the man named as Caille by ten thousand people is incontestably the true Caille."[23]

The judges responded with a remarkable request, ordering an exhaustive physical description of the accused. On a February day in 1712, a team of three Paris physicians, assembled by Dr. François Vernage of the city's Faculté de Médecine, spent nine hours inspecting Mêge's body. The doctors measured his height from the top of his head to his bottom of his heels, first along the front of his body and then along his back. They measured the distance from his hairline to his big toe, first on the right foot and then on the left. They measured each leg, the length of his nose, and the circumference of his skull.

They noted every identifying feature. He was swarthy with ruddy undertones. His face was oval, and his chin more sharp than round. One tooth was broken off at its roots, and five others were missing. The left nostril opened wider than the right. The left armpit had less hair than the right. His breasts were unnaturally low. The right testicle was tiny and withered, while the left testicle, plump and better conditioned, was lodged high in the fold of the groin. His penis, although very small, was without blemish or extrusion. The doctors' sheer meticulousness is dazzling, as if exactitude could settle identity. It was akin to transcribing a language no one knew. The exam indeed matched one of two verbal portraits judges heard, but it did nothing to answer which was correct. Those who recognized Mêge as Caille had described a Caille that matched Mêge, which made the exercise circular.[24]

The attorney Blinière began by observing where one or another trait was missing from witness accounts, singling out the scar beneath his ear, his low-slung breasts, and his malformed testicle. He resisted Sylvain's language of portraiture and cast memory as unreliable. He relied instead on dogged research and verifiable fact. He unearthed a journal from the Caille family with the names of five of Isaac's wet nurses, none of whom was among those Sylvain had called to testify. He questioned the credibility of villagers who had insisted that the soldier was Caille: twenty were beggars and sixty more were illiterate peasants. These are the "miserable poor," he said, "whose mind and faculties of reason have been neither schooled nor strengthened through study."[25]

Of those who had remembered Caille as a slim, bookish youth, on the other hand, two-thirds were educated. These included attorneys, priests, and students who had been in school with him. Blinière produced service records from Pierre Mêge's tours in the navy long before he claimed to be

Caille that perfectly matched the traits doctors had detailed. "What he undertook with a deceitful heart," Blinière declared, turning the physical examination against Mêge, "is now destroyed by his body. However he tries, he can efface neither Nature or his own roots."[26]

There was additional devastating testimony from a witness who did not appear in the first trial: Honorade Venelle, Pierre Mêge's wife. She had stayed silent, but when Mêge came into wealth and married a rich doctor's daughter, she stormed out of seclusion. Armed with notarized documents attesting to their fourteen-year marriage, she had demanded a meeting with officials of the Parlement of Provence. Expecting a hearing, she was instead charged with having falsified the documents. Threatened with arrest, she went into hiding.[27]

Blinière had learned about Venelle as he was preparing the appeal, and he followed the trail of documents. He spoke to her friends and family, identified witnesses to the marriage, and found legal transactions in the couple's name. The testimony he presented was potent. Venelle had been afraid to testify in Aix, he said, since speaking against her husband would have meant his certain death. Defending him as Caille, on the other hand, would have made her an accomplice. She was happy that the verdict had spared him, but within two weeks he was remarried. This, she said, was blasphemy against her own promise before God.[28]

The Paris parlement's verdict was a wholesale reversal of the earlier decision: the false Caille was in truth Pierre Mêge. His marriage to Madeleine Serry, who was now pregnant, was declared null. He and his legal wife, Honorade Venelle, would remain separated. He was ordered to pay court costs as well as damages to the Caille family in France. The principle of double jeopardy spared him execution, but he was returned to prison on a charge of bigamy, which was also a capital crime. Pierre Mêge died in his cell at the Conciergerie awaiting trial.[29]

For Louis de la Blinière, it was not surprising that a man like Mêge would go to such lengths to prove a false identity. Its dangerous plausibility was a recurring theme in the attorney's remarks. He dwelled on the power of doubt and the errancy of human judgment. Our beliefs, urges, and desires are what actually guide us, he explained, and in most cases they lead us away from the truth. Resemblance draws the imagination. Recognition is "a weary kind of knowledge" and more often turns to other grounds for support, including deference, hatred, friendship, fear, and hope. The case of Martin Guerre, Blinière said, affirms the peril. The imagination is "seduced, altered, and corrupted by false and misleading images."[30]

Blinière's analytical approach carried the day. "Our goal," he stated, "is to render this reasoning reasonable."[31] Given its peculiar circumstances, with family documents dispersed, close relatives unable to testify, and a disposition among many to doubt the words of Protestants, judges in the case might have been subject to the sway of appearances. Blinière's words, which circled back again and again to "the lights of reason and justice," also bore a wider relevance. For his generation, questions about aristocratic identity were pressing as they had never been before.

Gayot de Pitavel, the chronicler of Pierre Mêge's trials, ends his long account with the words of an unnamed woman who had followed the proceedings and shared her thoughts about it in writing. Her tone ranges from astonishment to outrage to high irony. What a shame that this man's brilliant ruse failed after his first victory in Aix, she writes, a verdict that brought him riches, land, and status. "And in the bargain, he got rid of a bothersome woman. What a clever secret for husbands who are tired of their wife-unto-death!" She continues:

> I'll admit, I'm a mere woman, which means I have only half the intellect of you men. . . . But however much you wish to raise men above women, you will never persuade me that a Senate of Women would exchange our own good sense for the good sense of men. Nature gives us ours, and it is never obstructed by erudition.[32]

The point was different from la Blinière's earnest pleas for reason. For this writer, common sense was more sensible than lawyers' reckoning. For her, the future promised more fumbling uncertainty. If truth is singular, she writes, its principles should be unchanging; they should lead to the same conclusions. "Yet it was utterly hidden from one parlement and revealed to the other: a subject for profound reflection! I will say no more." For this observer, the larger context of a nation thoroughly familiar with falsehood was relevant. "On a certain level, we have to admire the impudence and effrontery of the impostor, who chose for the stage of his comedy a country in which one can be so easily be duped."[33] The fact that Mêge was successful at least for a time suggests that many others—those with the wits, money, or connections—might succeed for their whole lives.

HARSH JUSTICE

Laurent and Barthélémy Adaoust were among a legion of ambitious men now making their way into the nobility as attorneys in royal courts, officials in financial and administrative offices, and titled secretaries for the king. The money they paid for their positions as lawyers, financiers, and royal officials—the so-called *noblesse de robe*—helped fund Louis XIV's growing administrative state. It also brought them the full prestige and privilege that accrued to France's aristocracy. The most valuable possession was outright ennoblement transmissible to posterity. In other cases, nobility became hereditary after a determinate period of time, and in still others it ended with its purchaser's death. Prices varied accordingly.

Ennoblement brought considerable benefits. It exempted its possessors from the commoners' tax of the *taille* as well as fees levied on non-noble fief-holders. It conveyed the right to carry a sword, to hunt, and to stand bareheaded before the king. It allowed members to possess family arms and display its escutcheon on carriages and residences. When accused of crimes, its members were tried by courts established uniquely for aristocrats. They could not be whipped as a judicial punishment, and in capital crimes they were beheaded instead of hanged.[34] In theory, the king granted ennoblement in return for services, but in practice it was often a simple transaction. Louis XIV praised the merit and moral excellence of his new nobles, but he also drew attention to their wealth, which, as he announced in a 1696 edict, "gives aid to troops who defend the state." A writer in the next century was more explicit: men are like coins on which the master of the mint stamps whatever denomination he sees fit.[35]

A larger group gained nobility through venality, the purchase of office or position. French monarchs had first employed the practice to raise funds in the twelfth century. Until the 1520s, fewer than twenty offices were sold in a given year. In 1600, some 15,000 men purchased venal posts. Within forty years, there were 45,000. Growth continued to accelerate. When Louis XIV assumed the throne in 1643, there were fifty-nine King's Secretaries, one of the few venal positions that conferred nobility outright. Twelve years later, there were more than 500. Louis XIV extended heritable nobility to a broad range of officeholders, including officials of the realm's sovereign courts and financial tribunals. He granted the status to designated classes of attorneys, auditors, clerks, procurators, and military officers. By the end of his reign, venality accounted for every major office in the judicial hierarchy and most of the realm's financial positions.[36]

By elevating administrators who invested in the king and his success, the sale of offices weakened the sway of blood aristocrats. The consequence was a deliberate restructuring of France's elites. By one estimate, only one-twentieth of all French nobles in 1660 could trace their ancestry to the Middle Ages.[37] The process widened the gap between rich and poor nobles, a dynamic that usually favored the recently ennobled. It also introduced a degree of social mobility into a hierarchy that had been by and large static.

This did not mean that integration was always easy. Rancor from old blood was formidable, and defenders of French tradition lamented what they called a debasement.[38] Complaints targeted new nobles' ignorance and ostentation. A common charge was that they confused wealth with honor. "Where to begin?" reads a blast from the early 1700s. "You have emerged from the basest, most vile source. What admiration you deserve! We know that eagles beget eagles, but to see toads give birth to leopards and tigers is a veritable prodigy of nature." A blunt declaration concludes the harangue: nobility is won by blood shed over generations and never by the stroke of a pen.[39]

As alarming as ennoblement was for blood aristocrats and the values they claimed to embody, usurpation also surged in the seventeenth century. Included among crimes of *Faux*, usurpation was "the seizure of another's wealth, dignity or status by ruse or violence." This typically described misdemeanors of the well-to-do, whose punishment, usually in the form of fines, was relatively lenient. A noble son might usurp his father's title by claiming it before his death. The younger branch of a noble family might usurp the rights of an older branch while its members still lived. A seigneur might usurp the title of baron, count, or marquis without royal permission or decorate his family coat of arms with undeserved insignia. Commoners with means who bought the land of a defunct noble line might usurp its manorial name.[40]

Over the course of the seventeenth century, a more serious kind of usurpation also appeared. Commoners increasingly assumed an aristocratic style of living to usurp noble identity itself. Earlier monarchs knew of and had attempted to police scattered instances of families falsely asserting aristocratic roots, although their numbers were contained. During the rule of Louis XIV, the number of usurping families steadily grew.[41] The contours of these transformations, which typically occurred over three or four generations, were similar. A merchant's or skilled artisan's son marries the daughter of a local notable; their son, better off than his grandfather, marries into the family of a low-ranking official; a notation appears in a property transaction or baptismal record that falsely reports the family's aristocratic status; it is duly copied into later records. A descendant, now living as a landed seigneur or working as a finance official or magistrate, responds to the king's call to share family records with examining officials, who confirm his nobility.

Such journeys could lead to high office and esteem. A lowborn merchant in Colmars identified himself as noble in his daughter's 1576 wedding contract, and in 1676 a royal act certified the nobility of his grandson, the seigneur du Cartier, de Prads, Blégier, and Chanolles. In Marseilles, the great-grandson of a merchant acquired noble fiefs, served as a military officer, called himself a seigneur, and was certified as noble. In 1668, a gentleman in the King's Chamber was declared noble 150 years after a forebear, the son of an inspector in the Arles fish market, began studying law.[42]

Under sustained pressure from sword and robe nobles, Louis XIV launched a series of high-profile investigations into usurpation that began early in his reign and continued well beyond his death. Officials announced plans to assemble a single volume for the royal library bearing the family names, arms, and dwellings of every true aristocrat. In 1666, commissioners fanned out through the provinces to corroborate clear cases and question suspected usurpers. They reviewed records for inconsistencies in spelling, inspected stamps and seals, and compared signatures. They also took testimony from local notables eager to relate the fraudulent claims or actions of their neighbors.

Suspended in the 1670s, the search resumed to great fanfare in 1696, the same year Louis XIV put 500 new titles of nobility up for sale. Nothing was worthier of the realm's glory, the king announced, than the end of this abuse. A single fraudulent document could now condemn usurpers. The hunt lurched forward in fits and starts, accelerating in 1703, substantially slowing in 1718, and ending definitively in 1729. "From this point, no one spoke more of the investigations," the eighteenth-century legal scholar Pierre Jean Guyot noted, "although they were needed more than ever." Just who was and wasn't noble was becoming less and less clear. "Usurpers showed no restraint," Guyot wrote.

> False nobles and the ennobled rushed to assume titles of elevated and powerful lords, indeed of those very high and very powerful. . . . Persons well known to be commoners, unsatisfied with the simple status of gentleman, presented themselves as marquis, counts, barons, and viscounts, claiming the titles in the papers they presented.[43]

To a large extent, the king himself had produced this crisis of identity in the pursuit of greater control and glory. The incoherence of his approach—staging elaborate means to honor noble distinctiveness at the very time he diluted it—contributed to the wider circle of social dissembling. The combined effects of ennoblement, venal offices, and usurpation brought unprecedented numbers into the aristocracy. Many grasped with unease—although some, too, with complicit satisfaction—that noble identity rested more and more on appearances.

The trials of the men who claimed to be Esprit Adaoust and Isaac de Caille, bookends to Louis XIV's rule, were each touched by this dynamic. There was no precedent in Roman or Church law for execution in such cases, a fact that the judge Jean de Coras had noted in writing about the false Martin Guerre. He could find no instance of capital punishment for imposture in French history. The death of the man who insisted he was Esprit Adaoust may well have been the first such execution in France. Another came in 1698, when a man named Martel was executed in Montpellier for having forged noble letters.[44] Had Mêge been found guilty in his first trial eight years later, he, too, would have been hanged.

This new threat of death for the crime of imposture was a response to the wider crisis of identity. Changes in the economy and social structure, precipitated by the king's massive military and domestic spending, had plunged the aristocracy into a period of soul-searching about what it was to be noble. To ancient families, the newly ennobled were undeserving interlopers. Nobles both new and old viewed usurpers with contempt. In such conditions, the appeal of exacting harsh justice for real and imagined impostors makes sense. It left no doubt about the privileged order's seeming commitment to an immemorial hierarchy. That the ennobled and aspiring had no true claim to old blood did not prevent them from endorsing the prosecution of impostors. Given the eagerness of Laurent and Barthélémy Adaoust to convict a man who may well have been their own uncle, it probably fed the appetite.

CROSS-PURPOSES

Alongside imposture and usurpation, the crime of *Faux* included one additional category of concealment: cross-dressing. In his late eighteenth-century *Treatise on Criminal Justice*, Daniel Jousse cited the words of a jurist from the 1500s to denounce any attempt to "disguise oneself and change one's sex in order to deceive other persons." His contemporary Muyart de Vouglans defined women in men's clothes, or men in women's, as supposition of person achieved by disguise.[45] Their authority was scriptural. "The woman shall not wear that which pertaineth unto a man, neither shall a man put on a woman's garment: for all that do so are an abomination unto the Lord thy God" (Deuteronomy 22:5).

Punishment for offenders was severe. In 1566, a woman living near Blois was executed for having passed as a man. She worked for nine years as a winemaker and stable boy and had married a woman. Four years later, a woman near Bordeaux received the death penalty for posing as a man and marrying her employer's daughter. When the sentence was reduced on appeal, she was stripped to a thin shirt, forced to beg pardon, and paraded through town with a rope around her neck. She was then publicly flogged. In these two cases, the punishment owed more to the sins alleged—"crimes against nature" and "shameful vice"—than to the clothing worn. Prostitutes who dressed as men to slip into taverns, barracks, or monasteries were merely stripped naked, whipped, and put on humiliating public display.[46]

Arrests of men in women's clothes occurred most often when they disguised themselves to escape prison or gain clandestine access to lovers. In most cases, the punishment fell far short of what women suffered for dressing as men. There were comically absurd cases, as when Jean-Gabriel de Montempuis, a professor of theology and canon at Notre-Dame, put on his grandmother's clothes to attend the Comédie-Française. The explanation he gave to police was that he had hoped to go unrecognized as a religious man at the theater. Instead, he was spotted by the gleeful parterre, lustily cheered, and led out of the theater by guards. The humiliation spread in the form of mocking songs:

> They spotted Montempuis
> In garments of Bo Peep;
> But it's useless for a wolf to don
> The clothing of a sheep.
>
> The more she made her faces
> The more the parterre leered;
> "I see," cried one, "the traces
> Of a razor and a beard."[47]

Montempuis's farce was replayed in a tragic register in the same years in Toulouse. Pierre-Aymond Dumoret, born to a prominent attorney in that city's parlement, was convinced from childhood of being a woman born into the body of a man. From youth, Dumoret dressed in women's clothes, eventually preferring a simple green-and-white taffeta smock, which reached to the knees. Dumoret fashioned breasts from crushed flax and wore a corset lined with metal to compress the waist. Pierre-Aymond went by Mademoiselle Rosete and grew enraged when addressed as Dumoret. She was buried in what she wore at the time of her death: a smock, a necklace, pendant earrings, and a ring.[48]

Mlle Rosete's existence was unsettled. She studied theology, earned a degree in law, and taught for a time at a Catholic girls' school in Toulouse, where she was harassed by jeering children whenever she appeared in public. Strangers mocked her, and acquaintances considered her mad. After several months, she stopped teaching and returned home to the village of Bagnères. Her father, hoping to cure her, forced her to do physical exercises fit only for a man. He deputized her as judge to hear local disputes, which she did for three years. Crowds gathered to watch the neighbor they knew as Pierre-Aymond settle cases as she sat under an elm tree. Her insistence that she was a woman and wished only to spin and to sew led to violent arguments with her father, who eventually evicted her from the house with a pistol.

She attended mass regularly, sometimes carrying a bobbin and spindle, and was met with hostility from religious officials who called her presence corrupting. Priests drove her away, but she persisted in attending. One Easter Sunday, an almoner named Jaula chased her out of the church and sent a band of children after her. She traveled alone to Agen and Cahors. On the road, she was beaten by military officers who were "offended to find a man who wished to be a woman."[49] She eventually returned and lived as a recluse. Efforts to scrub away stubble left her face bloodied. A crude attempt at self-emasculation, which involved severe binding and animal skins superimposed to resemble female pudenda, likely contributed to her death in 1725 at age forty-seven.

Mlle de Rosete's story survives because of an attempt by villagers to claim her inheritance. Jaula the almoner, working with two brothers-in-law and a local judge, worked up a last will and testament transferring her family's wealth and property to them, which they brought to her deathbed. She signed it unwittingly. When a blood relative learned of it, he filed suit with the Parlement of Toulouse on the grounds that, having lived, dressed, and acted as a woman, Dumoret was demonstrably insane. The court agreed.[50]

The magistrates' reasoning is powerful testimony to how unthinkable Mlle Rosete's professed identity was to them and their contemporaries. Pierre-Aymond Dumoret defied the biblical injunction laid out in Deuteronomy, the judges wrote. Witnesses described the blasphemy of his having received communion as a woman. For a man in his right mind to commit such crimes before God and human justice was punishable by death, the magistrates continued, but Dumoret was innocent. "Why? Because he was in a state of dementia, and one cannot sin when one does not have the use of reason."[51] Dumoret was "worse than a beast," the court wrote. He had "neither reason, nor instinct, nor sentiment."[52] The inheritance stayed in the family.

Mlle Rosete's sad life stands in stark contrast to the colorful reputation of the abbé de Choisy, a priest of the same generation known to posterity as an ostentatiously public cross-dresser. Thanks to a well-executed ruse in the eighteenth century and a steady stream of books and articles ever since, two unsigned manuscripts left at his death, now published as *Memoirs of the Abbé de Choisy Dressed as a Woman*, are now widely assumed to be his autobiography. The modern view that Choisy lived openly and was tolerated as a man in women's dresses is in fact improbable on many counts. That the tales thought to describe Choisy's life are works of fiction, however, does not deny them a certain element of truth. Choisy confided to others the appeal of dressing as a woman. His stories were an imagined autobiography. The impulse typified identities in the seventeenth century, when dreams were often checked by larger forces that forbade them.

François-Timoléon de Choisy was born six years after Louis XIV and outlived the king by a decade, dying one year before Mlle Rosete. He belonged to a family that in three generations had pulled itself up from the wine trade to the high judiciary. From the cradle, he was accustomed to privilege. His father was one of Louis XIII's *Conseillers d'État*, and his mother was in Queen Anne's inner circle. At the height of her influence, Mme de Choisy was granted audiences with Louis XIV.[53]

Choisy's early life was profligate. After squandering his inheritance at the gambling table, a near-fatal illness brought a dramatic conversion. He became a priest, was assigned to an abbey, and began to write, producing biographies of David and Solomon, dialogues on divine grace and the immortality of the soul, and an eleven-volume history of the Church. He participated in a papal conclave and joined the French mission to bring Catholicism to Siam. The short accounts of illustrative lives he published as *Pious and Moral Histories* were widely read. His erudition earned him election to the Académie Française at age forty-two.[54]

Choisy is best known for the posthumous *Memoirs of the Abbé de Choisy Dressed as a Woman*. At his death, Choisy's papers went to his nephew and literary executor, the marquis d'Argenson. Set in the 1660s and written in the first person, its male narrator describes his mother dressing him in girls' clothes as a child, a practice he continued as a teenaged actor in Bordeaux and later in Paris and the countryside. The habit, the narrator writes, was "impossible to break."[55] The narrator of the manuscript, who first calls herself Mme de Sancy and later the comtesse des Barres, is supremely self-assured. Her open and exuberant cross-dressing is welcomed by all, including the duc de La Rochefoucauld, Mme de Lafayette, the archbishop of Paris, and a large number of priests, curates, and confessors who recognize and praise her. She distributes alms in dresses among the working-class poor of Paris and hosts dinner parties for local notables near her country house in Bourges. She attends balls and the theater in dresses and strolls in the Tuileries gardens and along the *Cours la Reine*. One night she shares a box at the Paris Opera with Louis XIV's firstborn, the eight-year-old dauphin, who declares that she is as pretty as an angel.[56]

Mme de Sancy also attends mass each Sunday at the Paris church of Saint-Médard. Her reception by clergy and parishioners differs dramatically from the hostility Mlle Rosete faced. Here, a priest praises her wardrobe and the warden arranges for her to sit where all can see and admire her. At the opera, she wears a white dress adorned with golden flowers, black satin trim, and pink ribbons. At an intimate dinner party, she wears two white slips to keep her warm beneath a blue damask dress and silver silk bodice. "Now that I was wearing dresses, I no longer wore drawers. I believed myself truly to be a woman."[57]

Since the eighteenth century, readers have both condemned and celebrated the singular story of a cross-dressing priest. In a 1779 oration before the Académie Française that became part of the institution's official history, Jean Le Rond d'Alembert deplored Choisy's "strange and blameworthy" tastes. In the nineteenth century, Sainte-Beuve wrote: "His life resembles a play . . . and in each of his roles he was natural, serious, and sincere, at once playful and pleased." The critic Jacques Lacan described Choisy as "utterly at ease in his perversion from start to finish."[58]

The tales of Sancy and Barres are more likely works of fiction, which gave shape to what Choisy imagined, talked about, and likely acted on in private. Among the letters and published work by his contemporaries, including those of La Rochefoucauld and Mme de Lafyette, there is no reference to Choisy dressing as a woman. Saint-Simon writes about Choisy but says nothing about a taste for women's clothes, in contrast to his account of the dresses and debauchery of the abbé d'Entragues.[59] Artists identified in the manuscripts as having painted portraits of Mme de Sancy have no such works in their inventories, and an estate that the comtesse des Barres recounts having owned in Bourges never existed.[60]

How then did Choisy become known as the age's most famous cross-dresser? The bizarre publication history of his manuscripts suggests foul play. In 1735, eleven years after his death, *The History of Madame la Comtesse des Barres* appeared anonymously in French with an Antwerp imprint.[61] It was republished the following year with a Brussels imprint. Seven years later, an anonymous biography appeared called *The Life of Monsieur l'Abbé de Choisy of the Académie Française*. It asserts that *The History of Madame la Comtesse des Barres* was a true account of Choisy's early life, written by Choisy himself.

The Life of Monsieur l'Abbé de Choisy begins with an extraordinary preface. An unnamed editor states that a friend brought him the manuscript after a nobleman, lost in the woods and needing shelter for the night, caught sight of his château. The friend fed and lodged him. The guest was gone before sunup, leaving behind a bundle of pages, which the editor has now published. This "biography" closely follows the 1735 *History of Madame la Comtesse des Barres* but is now told in the third person, with Choisy named as the man who dressed as a woman. Lurid sexual details remain, as do its lavish accounts of clothing. Choisy's actual life continues seamlessly from where the *History* ends, with his gambling and conversion, his travels, and a bibliography that includes, among its many religious works, *The History of Madame la Comtesse des Barres.*

The "biography" is admiring and censorious in ways that both build credibility and arouse indignation. It praises the aristocratic stranger's exacting research and condemns Choisy's dress and actions. The clear aim of the "biography," its editor concludes, is to "inspire a love of truth and a horror of vice."[62] When d'Alembert invoked Choisy three decades later in his speech at the Académie Française, he repeated the language and the tone of this book, giving authority to a narrative that has now become accepted as fact. The 1735 *History of Madame la Comtesse des Barres* circulated widely in the eighteenth century. The Sancy manuscript was first published in 1839, with Choisy named as its author. Twenty-three years later, the two works were joined in print to become *Memoirs of the Abbé de Choisy Dressed as a Woman.* Since then, editions of the book have appeared regularly.

Choisy's modern biographer Van der Cruysse attributes the "biography" to the cleric Pierre-Joseph d'Olivet, an acquaintance of Choisy who was elected to the Académie Française in 1723.[63] In his memoirs, the marquis d'Argenson writes that Olivet stole the Barres manuscript from his collection, along with Choisy's manuscript history of Louis XIV, which he published without Argenson's permission.[64] He wonders what might have motivated Olivet to do so. Choisy considered him a friend, and a year before Olivet's death, Choisy delivered a warm speech marking his entry into the Académie Française.

Argenson's memoirs also relate conversations with Choisy, who spoke fondly of his dissolute youth and an attraction to wearing dresses. They describe Choisy's "strange contradictions," his "unspeakable delight" in recalling his past, and his lifelong inability "to think as a man."[65] If Choisy spoke this freely with his other friends, the priest Olivet may have wished to demean his memory. He certainly had the temperament. When the poet Alexis Piron was elected to the Académie Française, Olivet torpedoed his candidacy by sending Piron's pornographic poem *Ode to Priapus* to a contact at court with instructions to deliver it to the king. Louis XV annulled his election, and the seat went to the naturalist Buffon.[66]

What to make of Argenson's report of Choisy's taste for dresses? It was probably true. When *The History of Madame la Comtesse des Barres* appeared, Argenson likely concluded that the book was indeed an autobiography. It was Argenson who wrote at the top of these manuscripts "Adventures of the abbé de choisy, dressed as a woman." Yet there are grounds to doubt his conclusion. In December 1724, just two months after

Choisy's death, the writer Jean de Valincour eulogized his late colleague at the Académie Française by contrasting his moral integrity with that of "licentious authors" who spend their old age writing about "the excesses of their youth."[67] Had Choisy truly been the extravagant public cross-dresser his narrator recounts, the tribute would be unthinkable. Valincour's words described Choisy's reputation until the appearance of Olivet's biography two decades later. Whatever the motive, Olivet's calculation that the book would bring strong discredit to Choisy, at least in the short term, was right.

The Choisy of Argenson's memoirs was garrulous, proud, open, and unembarrassed about his desires. That he lived his fantasies in writing was significant and, given his status today, enduring. His story reveals a larger truth about him and his contemporaries. In the seventeenth century, the gap between lived and imagined identities could be considerable.

IDENTITIES IN THE SEVENTEENTH CENTURY

In his book *Aristocratic Experience and the Origins of Modern Culture*, the historian Jonathan Dewald isolates elements of emergent individuality among seventeenth-century nobles. The contexts he explores include family relationships and passionate friendships, literary and autobiographical accounts of powerful emotions, and settings in which the ambitious might rise in position and status. In each case, Dewald locates expressions of an independent self as "real, important, and complicated." The view challenges any simple notion that a single shared identity characterized elites. Dewald points to the place of concealment in constructing and preserving these individual identities. "Nobles interpreted even the long-standing relations of local politics in terms of repeated betrayals and disguises," he writes. "Ultimately, so Machiavellian a view of civic life made the individual seem more real than the community."[68]

The practiced insincerity of elites shaped a selfhood that was at once intentional and shallow. Its necessary dissembling navigated hierarchy but resisted being defined by it. A lifetime of playacting intended to hide authentic responses loosened the obligation to one's own words. For the chevalier de Méré, an astute observer of the century's indirection, the pervasive figure of performance licensed a more forgiving standard of honesty: "It is not without value to consider what one does as theater and to imagine oneself as a dramatic character. This thought prevents one from taking things too much to heart and consequently brings a freedom of word and action that one lacks when one is disturbed by worry and concern."[69]

The writers Jean-Claude Courtine and Claudine Haroche describe this experience as a splitting of the self. Their book *A History of the Face* demonstrates how facial expression has been influenced historically by large cultural forces, including at Versailles. "To govern the self through detachment is a kind of mastery that amounts to *treating oneself as an other*, from above, from afar," they write. This is "a distancing of the self by calculation rather than negligence."[70] In the terms of de Méré, courtiers were both actor and audience. They were participants who watched themselves perform.

Those who lived at court were keenly aware of the gulf between genuine feeling and performance. Whether inspired by fear or ambition, dissembling enlarged and made explicit an inner sphere of self-evaluation. For Jean de la Chétardie, the author of *Instructions for a Young Seigneur*, this private realm of judgment was an internal governor that managed interactions. It is not enough to be "secretive, circumspect, cautious, assiduous, and flattering," he writes. "These qualities, although essential, will not be useful if one's judgment does not know how to adapt them to the occasion."[71] To extend the analogy with theater, the self, in addition to being actor and audience, was also director. Rather than an integrated whole, selfhood was partitioned in ways that drew attention to one's individuality, which circumstances counseled concealing. The philosopher Pascal understood this.

> I am not obligated to respect you because you are a duke, but it is necessary that I salute you. If you are a duke and a decent man, I will render what I owe to the one and the other of these qualities. . . . But if you should be a duke but not a decent man, I would still do justice to you, for in observing the exterior duties that the human order has attached to your birth, I will not fail to maintain toward you the inner scorn that your baseness of spirit deserves.[72]

Versions of this reasoning appeared across society in the masks its structure generated. At court, polite words and rituals eased relations among rivals and gave supplicants an opening to those with greater power. In markets, churches, and public promenades, they granted women a measure of freedom by asserting a meekness that they may not have felt. In the respite of masquerades, they permitted a freer mingling through token or temporary anonymity that could be revoked at any moment. In each case, their conservatism stands in sharp contrast to the common view today, which associates the mask with concealing or remaking identities. In the seventeenth century, it more often protected and preserved them.

What to make of those whose crimes were classed as *Faux*? Weren't the choices of Mlle Rosete, the impostor Mêge, and the imagined lives of Choisy an effort to remake identities? The capacity to think of themselves in a rank or gender outside the given order was indeed notable when most others considered identity to be God-given and immutable. Yet these are not clear cases of changing an identity. Pierre Mêge did not try to mimic Isaac's habits or master his gait or speech. He pretended no mastery of law or theology. He prevailed in the first trial because witnesses insisted that his own traits—swarthy, scarred, illiterate—were the traits of Isaac. Apart from claiming the name and title of another man with fraudulent intent, Mêge did little to fashion a new self.

Many have of course intended disguise, from the false Martin Guerre to the countless burglars, lovers, runaways, and spies whose false features or misleading clothes were strategic. Few, however, acted from a conviction that identity itself could be changed. For Mlle Rosete, the impulse to dress as a woman was to express a true identity, not to hide or transform it. Insofar as the abbé de Choisy actually dressed as a woman, and assuming his narrator's reasons for doing so were a rough reflection of his own, his motives included an avowed incapacity to "think like a man."[73] Mlle Rosete and the abbé de Choisy display a kind of self-fashioning, but it falls short of the sense that selfhood was mutable. Few believed that they had the capacity to redefine their identity. Those who tried were often mocked, denounced, or arrested.

By the end of the century, climbers like the Adaoust brothers and the thousands of others who joined noble ranks through merit, purchase, or fraud had put severe strain on the view that identity was fixed. The fiction of noble blood on which their privilege rested produced still more masks. It was again the philosopher Pascal who grasped this most subtly. His *Three Discourses on the Condition of the Great* was first offered as instruction to the duc de Luynes's only son. The boy would go on to become a decorated officer, a duke and peer of France, and adviser to Louis XIV. He was fourteen when Pascal recounted the fable to him.

A king has been lost in a storm at sea, and a man who resembles him is washed up on shore. Its inhabitants mistake him for their ruler. He knows that he must now assume the role. You have no more rights by virtue of yourself or your nature than this man, Pascal tells the boy. A string of contingencies, he explains—of visits, chance encounters, words spoken or omitted that led to one particular marriage over another—has produced a title conferred by convention. Your soul and body are the same whether you are a boatman or a duke. Nothing innate attaches you to one or another condition.

> The people who admire you do not know this secret. They believe that nobility is real greatness and consider the great to be of a nature different from

> the others. Do not reveal this error to them, if you prefer; but neither abuse your own superior position through insolence. Above all do not deceive yourself by believing that your being has something higher in it than that of others.[74]

For Pascal, authority resides in appearances: in the square caps and wide robes of magistrates, in doctors' gowns and slippers, and in the pomp that surrounds the king. Without these, their possessors' power would vanish. The wise understand this but refrain from unmasking themselves or others, because they know that order requires hierarchy. Understanding behind appearances—what Pascal called the *pensée de derrière*—advises a knowing acceptance of concealment. "The populace honors persons of high birth. The half-adept scorn them, saying that their birth is not a personal superiority but an accident. The fully adept honor them, not by thinking as the populace but by the *pensée de derrière*."[75]

Pascal's fable attests to the unsettled state of a social order declared divine but widely known to be open to those wealthy, well connected, or cunning enough to advance. Many others with high ambitions but few prospects did not have to read Pascal to know that the newly ennobled were playing a role. The century revealed glimpses of what it might be to change one's condition, but it also enforced strict limits on what one could attain. What was absent in the age of Louis XIV were the social and economic structures to act on such hopes.

PART TWO

Society

Reading of Voltaire's Tragedy "Orphelin de la Chine,"
Anicet Charles Gabriel Lemonnier (Art Resource)

The man of the world is complete in his mask. What he is, is nothing. What he appears to be is everything for him.

—JEAN-JACQUES ROUSSEAU, *Émile, or Education* (1763)

The difference between you and me, said Monsieur ***, is that you say to every masker, "I recognize you," whereas I leave them with the hope of having fooled me. This is why society finds me preferable to you. It is a ball in which you have destroyed others' interests and your own amusement.

—NICOLAS CHAMFORT, *Maxims, Thoughts, Characteristics, and Anecdotes* (1796)

4
To the Truthful World

HISTORIES OF THE HEART

In an early play by Marivaux, Silvia is wandering in the forest with her fiancé Arlequin when she catches the eye of the prince. He decides he must have her. Silvia and Arlequin are country folk, giddy and in love, and when court officials appear with a promise of special treatment they are dazzled. The prince disguises himself, pays his own humble court to Silvia, and promises a conniving woman named Flaminia a fortune if she will assist him. Each turn in what follows is played with malicious precision. Flaminia pricks Silvia's pride by repeating the harsh words other women have said about her. Courtiers tell her she deserves a better man than Arlequin. The prince uses noble titles to coerce Arlequin into marrying Flaminia, who has no affection for him. His own wedding with Silvia follows.

If *Double Infidelity* is a comedy, its tone is dark. Practitioners of the court's fine manners have their way with two innocents, who stand no chance. Part of the shock is its gratuitousness: the prince is not an especially bad person, and he sees the injustice he has done to Arlequin. The work's casual manipulation and Silvia's acquiescence are what make it so unsettling. "Frankly speaking," a character remarks in a 1950 play by Jean Anouilh, *Double Infidelity* is "the elegant and graceful story of a crime."[1]

Pierre Carlet de Chamblain de Marivaux was born just after the Sun King installed himself at Versailles. He grew up familiar with—but not party to—the court. His early work, which includes *Double Infidelity*, was for an Italian troupe in the commedia tradition that had come to France just after Louis XIV's death. In his journalism, Marivaux assumed the voice of outsiders—a city ambler, a destitute sage, a philosopher alone in his study—to offer his bracing observations. His two best-known novels, *The Life of Marianne* and *The Peasant Parvenu*, offer a view of elite culture through the eyes of two would-be initiates, an orphan of uncertain birth and a clever peasant determined to rise. His plays, prose, and fiction describe events as if from a distance, tracing the path of feeling in a world steeped in falsehood.

In each genre, Marivaux's subject is not the court per se, but the diffusion of its manners in society. That its dynamic of mutual delusion could prevail far from Versailles was an endless source of fascination. His settings range from the private sphere to politics and the social order. The mask, both physical and figurative, is a constant presence in his plays, essays, and fiction. Across its many expressions, Marivaux poses a single overarching question: how to distinguish appearance from reality.

A tale from one of his news sheets depicts the ease with which people hide their intentions. *Journey to the Truthful World* is the first-person account of a land whose inhabitants resemble the French in every way but one: they are incapable of concealment. Try as they might, their astonished visitor discovers, they live with "their souls uncovered."[2] The story begins when its narrator discovers an affair between his lover and best friend. After a duel that leaves his friend in a pool of blood, he leaves Paris. On a ship, he meets a man who produces a thick, copiously annotated book called *The History of the Human Heart*. The narrator studies the book on their journey, and when they reach land he is stunned by what he sees. Everyone he knew in France is here, too, but their character and words are strangely different.

At an elegant reception, a twenty-year-old tells a lady three times her age that her dress would look much better on someone younger. The woman replies that only one thing could mar such a ravishing dress: seeing it on an ugly twenty-year-old. A woman flatters the wife of a judge about to hear a case involving her family and then mocks her for believing such flattery. The judge's wife quickly contradicts her: the compliments are fully deserved, she says, and vows to speak to her husband.[3] So goes his every encounter. He recognizes an officer he knows, but instead of his accustomed reserve, the officer boasts about his virility and luscious fiancée. He proposes a game to prove his fiancée's devotion. He will tell her flattering stories about the visitor, who, he instructs, must flirt with her in return. She will remain unmoved, he says. At dinner, the woman speaks to him.

> You are from Paris, you have seen the court, you come from a world of refined tastes. You must have brought pleasure to many beautiful women. . . . It would flatter me to excite you, too, in this land—to inspire an adventure.

She removes a glove and toys with a piece of embroidery. Her hand is soft and moves nimbly. She watches him watch her.

Early in his account the narrator makes a claim that carries some mystery. "I do not mean to suggest that these people said exactly what I have written. Their candor is not in their words—I almost forgot to say this—but in their turns of phrase, the feel of their speech, their tone, their gestures, even their gaze. These are the things that contain and declare their thoughts so forthrightly. The spoken word is never as clear as this."[4]

He and his companion approach a city that is the double of Paris and come upon a house that is the very image of his own. His cook and groom are drunk. Everyone is singing and laughing. A stranger has his arm around the servant girl's waist. They see their master and are aghast. The groom is not with his dying father and has pocketed the pay his master sent for a replacement. The servant is not sick and has spent his money sent for medicine on liquor instead.[5] This city is not a duplicate, but rather Paris, and the country they visited after three weeks at sea was France. *The History of the Human Heart*, the wise man explains, has taught you "to know men and penetrate the mask that covers them."[6] The traveler had absorbed the book's lessons on the sea voyage without noticing. He is now capable of hearing past words to grasp intentions, mastering the language of the body, watching faces, weighing phrases, and judging tones. Such is the education to salve a bitter heart. The wise man warns him against misanthropy. You now inhibit the Truthful World, he tells the narrator, a world wholly different from our own: you will see these things for the rest of your life.

The language of masking saturated discourse in the eighteenth century, identifying falsity in words, emotions, friendships, clothes, and the urbanity of Paris itself. Reformers tried to recover civility's moral roots to uncouple it from falsehood, but such efforts did little to alter its discrediting connection with the court. The distrust was related to what Jean-Jacques Rousseau would denounce so powerfully later in the century: the steady intrusion of a corrupting civilization. The association of refinement with insincerity was one of the enduring legacies of Louis XIV's Versailles.

For Marivaux, the source of insincerity is vanity. A searing sketch in a news sheet he called *The French Spectator* narrates its decisive role in disenchantment. A seventeen-year-old boy is in love with a beautiful girl. She is the sum of all grace and virtue, seemingly unaware of her effect on others. They are walking in a wood, he sees that she has dropped a glove, and he doubles back to retrieve it. When he returns, she is gazing at herself in a mirror, rehearsing every expression that has so entranced him. Humiliated, he tells her that he has just seen the Opera's backstage: "I will still be amused but much less moved."[7] For Marivaux, vanity in solitude feeds envy and delusion, whereas in society it fuels pride and hypocrisy. Among men, its most common expression is infidelity. Among women, it is coquetry. "A woman who is not a coquette," he writes, "is no longer a woman."[8]

From the distance of three centuries, the statement, coupled with the lad's disenchantment, sounds misogynistic, and it may well be. But a response that Marivaux gives in the voice of a clear-thinking woman confounds any simple judgment.

> Tyrants that you are (so say such women to us), if our *coquetterie* is a flaw, whom must we accuse but men? Have you given us any resources other than the miserable task of pleasing you? We are cruel, you say. And you dare to accuse us? . . . Are we not your prisoners and you our jailors? In such a state, what remains to us but artifice? . . . Our "coquettishness" constitutes the sum of our wealth. We have no other fortune but to find favor in your eyes.[9]

Change "coquettishness" to flattery and replace "men" with the higher ranks of French society, and you have an eloquent description of how inequality produces masks.

Marivaux's depictions of vanity in society are astute. When a *petit noble* is in the company of a *grand*, he arranges his face, stands more erect, and swells "like a toad who longs to be as big as a bull." When a provincial *femme de qualité* appears before the lowborn, her tone grows brusque, her bearing turns rigid, and her step becomes precise. Marivaux calls such postures accidental graces: acquired ways of speaking, standing, and moving taught in childhood by vain parents. In maturity, they are consciously polished. Accidental graces are attractive to the young, Marivaux writes, intimidating to the populace, and ridiculous to the reasonable. They are also inimitable by the bourgeoisie, he concludes, which does not stop its members from trying.[10]

Marivaux sees this dynamic in all stations of society. An indigent philosopher watches from a window as pedestrians bow to a nobleman they do not know. "It is not he they are saluting, but his privilege," the philosopher reflects. Content in his room with his books and cheap wine, the philosopher watches with amused scorn. The commoners may resent the aristocrat's disdain, but they covet his prerogatives still more. Modesty is "a mask so fine that it is easily mistaken for the face."[11]

Questions of identity are central themes in Marivaux's novels *The Life of Marianne* and *The Peasant Parvenu*. Despite his relentless unmasking, the thrust of the works is not to expose hierarchy as unfounded. In addition to accidental graces, humans also possess essential defining qualities "that are with us, that are within us, that are ourselves."[12] The protagonists of his novels, Marianne and Jacob, go far in mastering a noble air. Their craving to please comes naturally, and their proximity to power channels its expression in all the familiar ways. They mingle in elite circles, but their entry is not assured. Over the course of each work, Marivaux keeps open the question of whether the essential qualities of an aristocrat can be mastered by an impostor.

Marianne is two years old at the start of the novel, when robbers attack the coach carrying her and other travelers. She and a frightened cleric who flees the scene are the only survivors. Two victims remain unidentified, a young, beautiful, and stylishly dressed woman who bears all the marks of nobility and a chambermaid who looks to be around forty. One of them is the child's mother, but no one knows which. A village priest entrusts the girl to a simple woman to raise, with whom she lives for fifteen years before the woman's sudden death leaves Marianne alone once more. She makes her way to Paris, where a laundress takes her in. Before long, she is noticed by a benefactor, who squeezes her hand, gives her fine clothes, and urges her to be less formal with him. Reflecting on her new wardrobe, she concludes that the gifts are appropriate. She merits his attention and has incurred no obligation.[13]

In *The Peasant Parvenu*, Jacob has a clearer understanding of his own motives. He has come to Paris as the servant of a great noble. Following his master's death, he trades his humble clothes for stockings, gloves, a suit, and a hat. He is a quick learner. Mme la Présidente, a magistrate's wife, offers to help him find a position. She is worldly and well connected, telling Jacob he has a fine complexion for a country boy. When he asks permission to kiss her hand, she blushes, but not very much. "It was not she that I loved," he admits. "It was her rank, which was considerably higher than mine."[14] Jacob marries a Parisian and adopts the surname of la Vallée. His sentimental education proceeds—"a schooling in softness, sensuality, corruption, and, as a result, feeling"—when an aristocratic lady receives him in her rooms, dangles a slender leg, and lets a slipper drop. He returns to his wife dizzy with self-love ("a vanity that made me happy") and showers affection on her. "Mme de la Vallée had never before seen me so loving, nor so liberal with my caresses."[15] The ecstasy of it all keeps him from asking whether his words are sincere.

Both novels are unfinished, but the two characters' paths are sufficiently clear to suggest that identity for Marivaux does not consist in simply perfecting one's performance. In *The Peasant Parvenu*'s opening pages, Jacob observes that the truth of one's identity takes its revenge "however much you try to disguise it."[16] Until the book's closing pages, his rise has been steady. A word from an aristocratic lover has won him an audience at

Versailles and the assurance of a position. He meets the comte d'Orsan, who believes he is a young nobleman worthy of support. At the Comédie-Française, d'Orsan presents him to his friends, who are all titled aristocrats.

Now among them, Jacob's confidence suddenly fails, and his smooth exterior begins to crack. He is awkward and self-conscious—like a "smuggler" or a "freak"—and feels shamefully out of place, searching in vain to adopt the right face. "I had jumped too fast," he admits. "I had become a monsieur without acquiring the most basic preparation. I feared that they could read it in my looks, that this particular monsieur was only a Jacob." He hears himself voice platitudes and watches himself perform the same stilted bow to each man. Their laughter is a humiliation. The book's final paragraph begins: "The play was a tragedy."[17]

The novel's ending is abrupt, but its action is not unresolved. Jacob's impressive ascent has hit a barrier that his dexterity cannot surmount. The sting is sharp, yet his response, consistent with his temperament throughout, is neither grief nor resentment. He is easily flattered and often selfish but never presumptuous. His happiest moment in the novel comes when he decides to skip the trysts and visits that have paved his rise and instead spend the morning at home with his wife, content with her tenderness. He savors his good fortune. He sits, stands, surveys his possessions, smiles at his furniture, calls to his cook, and then, taking it all in, admires himself in his robe and slippers.

"Imagine that!" he exclaims. "Jacob, in a robe and slippers. Only when I looked at myself as Jacob did I find such unexpected delight in all these trappings. It was to Jacob alone that M. de la Vallée had brought such joy."[18] Marivaux creates a wide scope for this self-made man, a token of what was becoming increasingly possible for those with initiative, wit, and good fortune. All things considered, Jacob's life is not a tragedy.

With each new step in Marianne's rise, by contrast, a private conviction seems confirmed. Her earliest memories assure her that she was no ordinary child. She was sweet and playful, Marianne says of herself. Her manner was refined, her spirit was lively, and her face "foretold beautiful features," a promise, she writes, that has been fulfilled.[19] As a young woman, she feels revulsion at the idea of working as a servant and is humiliated when forced to accept charity. When a commoner grazes her ungloved hand, she feels sudden disgrace. "Where did I get such discrimination?" she asks. "Was it in my blood?"[20] For her protector Mme de Miran, the evidence is clear. Marianne's lucid mind, her qualities of soul, and her noble bearing speak for themselves. "What I observe owes nothing to her exposure to society or education," Miran says. "It must be in her blood."[21] That Marianne does not find comfort in the pleasures Jacob feels is of course no proof of noble birth. In Marivaux's universe, the quotient of self-deceit is universally high. Marianne's presumed nobility is provisional knowledge, but it is enough to confer an assurance that Jacob lacks. Without omitting her own displays of vanity, Marivaux gives Marianne a natural authenticity that differs from the grandiose gestures of other characters.

Such unadorned civility is for Marivaux a measure of true nobility, which forms the foundation of sincere politeness. Marianne describes conversation among the friends of a gracious aristocrat as without cleverness or exclusion. Having once regarded society's codes as "an utterly unknown science," she registers surprise at finding nothing unkind in the attitudes of this circle. Its members are unaffected, welcoming, and accommodating.[22] For Marivaux, true sincerity makes hierarchy bearable. Deference, gratitude, and generosity acknowledge moral equality without denying social difference.

How do such harmonious scenes accord with the ugliness of *Journey to the Truthful World* or the indigent philosopher's scoffing cynicism? Any number of Marivaux's works contain characters who are clear-eyed about duplicity. They name it for what it is, a fiction that most are happy to employ. In Marivaux's play *The Island of Reason*, the humble Fontignac takes advantage of an enchanted isle to speak his thoughts with impunity. "Let yourself be duped by my words," he says to a haughty superior, "and I'll act as though I am persuaded by yours. . . . Let me lull you to sleep so that I may slit your throat at leisure."[23] This version of mutual delusion has no courtly polish.

Marivaux's world teems with such concealment, yet he resists denunciation. His sociability is without illusions but remains fully intact. His friend d'Alembert wrote that in company Marivaux was much more attentive to others' tone, gestures, and turns of phrase than to their actual words. "He sought only what they wished to say and often discovered subtleties that even those speaking were unaware of."[24] Marivaux's indigent philosopher comes closer to his creator's temperament than the disenchanted narrator of *Journey to the Truthful World*. Conscious of the pretense surrounding him, he responds with laughter and more wine. "Leave others in peace, suffer them with virtue, and forgive them their vanity," he says in *The French Spectator*. "You must live with others."[25]

For Marivaux, living with others did not require a pure heart. Sincere politeness is a matter of living *as if*, a mode content with the surface of things and aware that the truth is not always what it seems. What is true about others' false phrases might also be said of their more egregious vices, namely that some good may come from countenancing duplicity. "As deplorable as it is, hypocrisy serves the general order of things," Marivaux writes in *The*

Philosopher's Study. "A man who loves virtue inspires ten others who are not at all virtuous to act as if they were."[26] This was a version of what Mme Sablé had written half a century before: to call out others' untruths deprives them of the opportunity to live up to the role they are playing. The difference was that Marivaux now spoke of not only courtiers but the general population, too.[27]

POLITE SOCIETY

An engraving from 1700 by Nicolas Guérard shows the many masks a person might wear. The woman wears masks of modesty, compassion, gentleness, and devotion, and the man wears masks of justice, candor, and honor. She holds a sheet reading "Sympathetic Tears." His reads "Friendly Laughter." Emblems affixed to her dress outline the public virtues of a proper lady (ceremony, civility, a composed countenance, reverence), and those on his suit sketch the solid virtues of a decent man (compliments, offers of service, pledges of friendship, open arms). Time, who "uncovers all," has the last word, but the verses that frame the image make any revelations uncertain. The poem at the top ends:

> Our masks fool everyone
> And will themselves bear witness
> When time makes known
> That in all things we are nothing less
> Than that which we seem to be.

And at the bottom:

> However disguised one may be
> No one wishes to appear so.

Marivaux's central theme of seeing beyond appearances resonated throughout the eighteenth century. The spread of fine manners meant that civility was no longer the exclusive domain of elites. The hierarchy defined by dress also began to blur, as fashions once limited to the rich grew more abundant and affordable. In a society still premised on immutable orders, the response among its defenders was a resort to the language of imposture, usurpation, and masquerade, as if to speak or dress out of station was itself a crime of *Faux*. A 1704 guide to the city of Paris gives a foretaste of still greater dissonance to come. The appeal of courtly manners is widespread, reports its British author with astonishment, and teachers have begun to

FIGURE 4.1. *Universal Masquerade*, anon. (Bibliothèque nationale de France)

offer courses in civility. "It is practis'd with a great deal of Grace among Persons of Quality. The Citizens pretend to it, but *affectedly*; and the common People come off with it *grossly*."[28]

An influential guide to comportment from early in the century was by the priest sainted for his work among the poor, Jean-Baptiste de La Salle.

His 1703 *Rules of Decorum and Christian Civility* was intended for pupils in the Schools of the Christian Brothers, which he founded. It remained in print well into the nineteenth century, reaching a readership far beyond its original audience.[29] La Salle aimed to "rechristianize" civility, which he believed had lost its ethical center in courtly ceremonies and manuals. The aim of civility, La Salle wrote, was to bring the inward person into conformity with one's words and actions. The elaborate manners of courtiers, in other words, were an empty shell.

La Salle's meticulous instructions provide a glimpse of the pupils he hoped to improve. One is not to fidget, slouch, lean, or sway; not to roll one's eyes, wrinkle one's brows, or puff one's cheeks; not to go burrowing in one's nose or pass wind. Chapter by chapter, the civilized child takes shape. There are sections on cleanliness, posture, and diction, advice on what to wear on which occasions and when to doff a hat or gloves, and descriptions of entertainments deemed honest and dishonest. Sections on dining include advice on how to set and remove plates and cutlery, how to eat bread, fruit, sauces, and jellies, and how to show respect to superiors when drinking wine. ("If one is obliged to respond to a person of a higher status while he raises his glass to his mouth, one should wait until he has finished drinking to continue one's words.")[30]

The book's concluding chapters provide advice on visiting those of superior status, including how to deliver compliments, which should not be prepared in advance. They must instead flow from one's heart "in a manner that is natural, without affectation or the appearance of study." Words of praise must never exceed the merit described, "so that the modesty of the one who speaks and of the one who receives it is not harmed."[31] This was the Christian's response to mutual delusion.

The Rules of Decorum and other books on civility attained wide circulation. Most guides were less concerned about sincerity than La Salle. By the end of the eighteenth century, they reached many thousands of readers. These included provincial nobles, urban readers, well-to-do professionals, and the aspiring young. As the forms and phrases of civility spread beyond Versailles, its exclusive refinement lost some of its luster, at least among its original carriers. The author of *Reflections on the Ridiculous*, for example, complained that the lowborn had become tiresome with their rote politeness: city dwellers, provincials, and pedants "encumber every doorway with interminable arguments about who shall enter last." Such people viewed civility as a skill to be learned rather than the natural result of blood and milieu.[32] The same complaint was heard decades later. "Only among the petty bourgeois are those pointless ceremonies and customs practiced, which they still take for *civilities*. This is tedious to people accustomed to society."[33] The greater attentiveness to comportment brought a shift in character, from a marker of noble prestige to a set of bourgeois habits. In the process, the words and acts that had once conveyed exclusivity became common.

Most books on civility urged readers to adjust their speech to the rank of their interlocutor, which meant that the association of fine manners with deceit persisted. Of the twelve examples illustrating the word *civilité* in the 1743 *Dictionnaire de Trévoux*, seven were disapproving. "*Civilité* is a certain jargon that men have established to hide the bad sentiments they have for one another (Charles de Saint-Évremond)," one entry reads. "It is quite difficult to distinguish flattery from *civilité* in society's politeness (Madeleine de Scudéry)," reads another.[34]

A 1731 miscellany called *The Gleaner* described a well-to-do Parisian trained in politeness as "prostituting" his esteem to everyone he encountered, whether they were gentlemen or fools. "His sincere air, the foundation of his personal merit, is a mask he uses to disguise his essential hidden flaws."[35] Writing in Diderot's *Encyclopédie*, the chevalier de Jaucourt made a similar observation. "Without necessarily emanating from the heart, politeness and civility maintain appearances, making men seem on the outside what they should be on the inside."[36] Despite efforts to align civility with uprightness, many believed that its worst features remained.

Others were unbothered. Voltaire considered the spread of civility an attribute of national glory: the French, he wrote, are "the most sociable and most polite people on earth."[37] If the concord it produced did not create actual community, so be it. Just as at court, politeness in society was a means of channeling rivalries and deflecting confrontation. Late in the century, Louis-Sébastien Mercier wrote that civility permitted a heterogeneous population to exist more or less peaceably. "The man who lives in society, and in a society whose ranks are unequal and functions overlap, soon grasps that there must be a supplement to law, which is politeness. Politeness brings a kind of equality and asserts a reserve of goodwill."[38] The word choice is telling: to *assert* goodwill is something short of feeling it. The *Dictionary of Manners*, published in 1773, expressed the same view with more bite. "Harmony: An art of societies that have little cohesion and much calculation, perhaps existing perfectly only where there is indifference and politeness."[39]

The eighteenth century's democratization of dress brought both unease and approbation. For over two centuries, legislation on clothes had asserted the identity of rank and person by prescribing garments, fabrics, and adornments according to position. A decree from the early sixteenth century had made distinction explicit: all non-nobles were prohibited from imitating nobility "either in their style or in their clothes." Statutes expressed the expectation that each would dress "in one's own guise."[40] Decrees of 1561 and 1563, for instance, forbade non-noble women from wearing pearls or jeweled bracelets. Footmen, servants, and artisans were forbidden to wear anything made of silk. Other non-nobles were permitted silk but only in undergarments or the inside lining of sleeves.[41]

Nobles were known by their sword and clerics by their long robe and tonsure. Tradition and successive statutes elaborated additional features. Clerics of the four minor orders wore a surplice or long white robe, subdeacons a maniple, deacons a stole, and priests a chasuble. Bishops wore a miter, glove, and ring; cardinals wore a hat or bonnet and scarlet robe. Among nobles, princes wore a special cloak, knights had spurs and gilded harnesses, and simple gentlemen bore their family coat of arms. Particular hoods and headgear identified attorneys, doctors, and licentiates. Magistrates, attorneys, and administrators wore either long or short robes in crimson, violet, or black, depending on their position. Social command entailed knowing the significance of such details. They signaled whether to speak or stay silent, what title and form of address to use, whether to stand or stay seated, whether to bow (and if so how low), and how to enter and exit the room.[42]

In 1675, the Paris *prévôt* alerted the head of police that precious fabrics were now seen among non-nobles, "including even those of somewhat middling status." An anonymous work described butchers' wives in satin kerchiefs and peddlers' daughters in expensive new dresses in the Luxembourg gardens: it was becoming difficult to distinguish "a duchess from a bookseller, a marquise from a spice-seller, and a countess from a meat-seller." A marquise in a fictive dialogue near the end of the century responds with stiffening pride about bourgeois women seen at the theater in gowns resembling her own: "One now permits them to dress as we do, but however much they try to copy us, they will never have the refined air of women at court."[43]

There is hyperbole in such reports. In the seventeenth century, few merchants' wives risked being mistaken for duchesses. The concern was nevertheless real. By 1700, the ordered hierarchy of dress was coming apart, and by midcentury it was effectively gone.[44] "In Paris, all is in confusion," a journalist announced. "Leisured artisans and rich merchants have left their estate."[45] A public slip embarrassed the marquis de Mirabeau when he mistook a worker for an aristocrat. On a Sunday stroll, he found himself alongside a man in a black suit and powered wig. "I fell all over myself offering compliments," he relates. The man introduced himself as a blacksmith's assistant. "Everyone has become a Monsieur," he grumbled.[46]

The historian of dress Philippe Perrot describes this shift as "an imperceptible movement from the prestige of 'being' toward that of 'having,' from that of 'grandeur' toward that of 'possession.'" By the end of the century, tailors, printers, and booksellers were carrying swords with impunity. Nobles, meantime, had begun to appear without them. According to Perrot, this inversion revealed to contemporaries the contingency of hierarchy.[47] The wide availability of once rare fabrics helps account for this shift. Greater domestic production drove down prices of women's and men's wardrobes and permitted seasonal variations. Lighter cloth appeared and was available to women of all classes. Those with means wore silk regardless of their rank, and high-quality cotton fabric replaced the expensive broadcloth once used for mantles, skirts, and waistcoats. New patterns and colors were marketed to emphasize personal choice. Men wore vests with floral patterns, stripes, and zigzags, and women dressed in gowns dyed in vividly named shades, including "queen's hair," "king's eyes," "bull's blood," "Paris mud," and "goose scat."[48]

In 1770, a typical noble family spent one hundred times more than working-class families on clothes and linens, but only ten times more than bourgeois households. This meant that the wealthiest commoners could make themselves largely indistinguishable from nobles. Clothing was the most public sign of a commercial revolution that brought clocks, books, canes, crockery, umbrellas, fans, and snuffboxes into the homes of the lowly.[49] What industry made possible, the allure of distinction made appealing. A serial publication at midcentury announced that fashion "makes a gentleman of the merchant and a merchant of the workingman." Household inventories of middle- and lower-class Parisians reveal that those owning gold watches rose from 5 percent of the population in 1725 to 55 percent in 1785.[50]

This transformation in appearances prompted the language of disguise. A small book from the 1780s with the message that luxury was the ruin of morality recalled a time when differences in dress distinguished the magistrate from the soldier and the worker from the merchant. No more, writes its author. "I would eagerly compare society today to a spectacle or perpetual ball, in which each wishes to hide all evidence of his status, disguising and masking himself as well as he can."[51]

SINCERELY CIVIL

When intellectuals in the eighteenth century took up the topic of truth-telling and deceit, they wrote on a level of abstraction far removed from the things that made many so uneasy. They nonetheless shared certain reference points in considering how a society of orders affected its members' self-presentation. They, too, wrote about how hierarchy and fine manners shaped everyday life in thought and action. Whereas others had treated dissembling as a matter of individual ethics, these thinkers widened the frame to consider the effects of governing institutions. By the middle of the century, what was formerly a concern of conscience had assumed the contours of a sweeping political critique.

The century's preeminent political philosopher, the baron de Montesquieu, was among the first to write systematically about the relationship between dishonesty and France's ruling structures. In *The Spirit of the Laws*, politeness falls under the topic "Of Education in Monarchies." The education Montesquieu has in mind occurs not in colleges or academies but in "the school of that thing we call *honor*." The discussion is part of a larger analysis of the ways particular forms of government generate values that define a population. In republics, probity must necessarily prevail. In aristocracies, moderation is the ruling principle. In monarchies, honor influences subjects' behavior, motives, and beliefs, shaping words and actions according to three large convictions: one's merits must have a particular nobility, one's morals a particular directness, and one's manners a particular politeness.[52]

How does honor become the animating principle of monarchy? Given the dynamics of court and its necessary hierarchy, the common good is best served by personal ambition. Acts of heroism or self-sacrifice win favor from the monarch, praise from elites, and admiration from the people. Montesquieu is mindful of the iniquities that may also flow from this pursuit of glory. These include pride, flattery, treachery, contempt for duty, and scorn for the truth: the very things politeness hides. In the name of honor, Montesquieu observes, monarchies produce both moral transgression and the means to conceal it. Reputation—the elevation of appearance over essence—is what matters most. Actions are worthy not because they are good but because they are praised. Veracity is valued not for the love of truth but for the credibility it confers.

Vanity is central to Montesquieu's critique of politeness. To be polite and treated with politeness is a public affirmation that "one is of the court and deserves to be there." Through fine manners, he writes, people assure themselves that they are not among the baseborn. This is why Montesquieu believed it was so difficult for people to be virtuous. Pride is of course present in republics, too, but the civic equality among those who govern themselves reduces incentives for flattery and deceit.[53]

Widely read in France and throughout Europe, *The Spirit of the Laws* was condemned by civic and religious authorities for its apparent cultural relativism. In 1751, it was placed on the Church's Index of Prohibited Books for passages deemed critical of religion and its institutions.[54] That same year, one of Montesquieu's friends published a book that drew similar connections between deceit and France's governing order. Charles Duclos's wide-ranging *Considerations on the Century's Morals and Manners* was an immense success, going through fifteen editions before the century's end.[55] Duclos was a celebrated member of the Republic of Letters when he wrote the book, having just been elected to the Académie Française and named successor to Voltaire as Historiographer of France. As a regular dinner companion of the king's mistress Mme de Pompadour, he had friends in high circles. He was also a fixture at the Café Procope, where he spent hours with Diderot, d'Alembert, Helvétius, and other Enlightenment writers.

Duclos's path to distinction was not straight. The son of a merchant from Brittany, he maintained an outsider's irreverence throughout his career. His *History of Louis XI* was banned for the claim that piety in a queen was a sign of political irrelevance. He also wrote that powerful men fear intellectuals the way thieves are afraid of street lamps.[56] Quentin de La Tour's sparkling portrait of the man with its level gaze and hint of a smile conveys something of his mischief. Duclos wrote histories, commentaries on language and orthography, the libretto to an opera, and two racy novels ostensibly meant to warn readers of the corruptions of the age. One of the novels, the *Confessions of Count* ***, was pivotal in at least one regard: his friend Rousseau credited its spirit and title as inspiration for his own *Confessions*.

The central theme of Duclos's *Considerations* is how a nation grown wealthy, comfortable, and proudly dishonest might be reformed. The opening pages provide a stark portrait of its main subject, France's elites, who live in opulence and are led only by pleasure and self-interest. They are passionate about ephemeral things, fickle in their affections, and indifferent to any true human connections. Their conversation is lively but cold, their friends are as soon forgotten as embraced, and to them shame is unknown. Such is the state of the ruling class, Duclos asserts, from whom any moral sense is absent. To repair the age's selfishness, Duclos proposes "sensitivity of soul," a capacity for feeling that encompasses more than the intellect. This sensitivity is endowed with inward depth, emotional rather than calculating, and generous instead of self-seeking. For Duclos, the capacity to feel is itself a moral attribute. It is the foundation for honest human relations.

> Sensitive souls have a fuller existence than other people: good and evil are compounded in their experience. They possess an additional advantage for society, which is to be persuaded of truths of which the intellect is merely

FIGURE 4.2. *Charles Duclos*, Maurice-Quentin de La Tour (Art Resource)

> convinced. . . . Intellect can and should impart rectitude, but sensitivity prepares one for virtue.

From such sensitivity grows "a love for humanity."[57]

For Duclos, the corruptions of the age stemmed from the particular history of France's aristocracy. There was a time, he writes, when the *grand seigneur* upheld a moral law that encompassed both virtue and duty. Honor was elective and therefore inviolate. But because this ethical autonomy—a virtue that was self-defined, self-enforced, and accountable chiefly to oneself—was tied to the nobility's political status, it was subject to greater forces. The coming of Louis XIV's absolutism destroyed this ancient virtue by corrupting its moral independence. What resulted, Duclos writes, was a tainted legacy that debased its carriers and drew scorn from all others.

Honor today is therefore little more than concern over where one stands in the pecking order of status, Duclos writes. Pettiness has replaced grandeur. Insincerity prevails and is preferred. "It is judged right in general," he observes, "that the obliging things men say to one another are not words of truth. On these occasions they are the dupes of one another." What may sound ironic is in fact meant straight: "Deceit carries respect where the truth would be insulting. It is humiliating to know that one is thought poorly of." Such was the extent of nobles' self-flattering illusions. For these reasons, Duclos believed that reform could not come from France's aristocracy. Instead he calls for those "of whatever profession" to be the bearers of a regenerated set of morals and manners, which will restore truly human relations to society. He identifies the carriers of the new morality as patriots and citizens.[58]

Who are these patriot-citizens destined to reform a wayward population? Despite Duclos's bracing words about noble values, he makes clear that he is not out to undermine the social order. He hopes instead that true honor can once again prevail. It is also evident that non-nobles are essential to the reform. The historian Jay M. Smith, who has written much about the cultivation of national feeling in the eighteenth century, describes Duclos's position as "a middle road between a patriotism based on the moral equality of all virtuous citizens and a patriotism defined by the moral excellence of a few."[59]

For Duclos, the way to reform, whether led by nobles or commoners, is through sympathy. To see oneself in others is to grasp the mutual obligations that bind a community. The consequence for Duclos's contemporaries would be a redefined politeness in which one's words are the faithful record of one's intentions. Duclos points to the utility of these refashioned social relations and affirms that what is good for society is also good for each of its members.

Duclos's refashioning of politeness as the alignment of sentiment, word, and intention was consistent with other voices at midcentury. François-Joseph Toussaint, the son of a cobbler who became an attorney for the Parlement of Paris, also envisioned a new civility that elevated sincerity. In his book *On Morals and Manners*, Toussaint offers a virtuous gloss on Marivaux's *Journey to the Truthful World*. "Transport yourself to an imaginary world in which you may assume that words are at all times the faithful expression of thought and sentiment. Here you can live without suspicion or distrust, and where plots, imposture, ruse, guile, treachery, betrayal, and treason are absent. What delicious commerce there is among these people, what a happy place!"[60]

Toussaint looked beyond France's nobility to describe those who would populate such a place. The consequence was a systematic dismantling of aristocratic ideals. The vicious, he writes, have distorted language to hide their depravity. Their honor is mostly vengeance, their nobility raw ambition, and their bravery a kind of savageness. Toussaint clearly found a following with this vision of renewed social relations. Between the book's appearance and the French Revolution, *On Morals and Manners* went through thirty-two editions. The journalist Barbier reported that a single copy might pass through fifty hands.[61]

Despite their potent critique of aristocratic mores, Duclos and Toussaint still embraced the place of politeness. This was in keeping with their overall moderation. Neither imagined a society without hierarchy. Their recognition that nobles could not be agents of reform in morals and manners was nevertheless essential. The virtues their vision of politeness embodied were recognizably bourgeois. Duclos put it well: "Politeness without deceit, candor without rudeness, consideration without baseness, deference without flattery, respect without coercion, and, above all, a heart filled with kindness. This is the sociable man, the citizen par excellence."[62]

TRANSPARENCY AND ITS CRITICS

Three months before Duclos's *Considerations* appeared, Jean-Jacques Rousseau landed an essay in the nation's leading literary journal with a message that would define his life and legacy. An aspiring but unpublished author, no longer young, and discouraged by a series of failures and false starts, Rousseau had chanced upon the announcement of an essay competition in the *Mercure de France*. He had the newspaper with him as he walked to visit his friend Diderot, who was in prison outside Paris for work deemed heretical. In Rousseau's telling, the instant he read the topic—whether the progress of the arts and sciences had improved human morality—he became another man. His heart raced, searing thoughts flashed through his mind, he went numb as if drunk, and a torrent of tears soaked his vest. He suddenly saw the truth of society: the acts and institutions of humans' own devising have made us untrue to ourselves and one another.[63]

Rousseau's revelation was the *fiat lux* of his own creation story. His entry won the competition. Its later publication as *Discourse on the Arts and Sciences* laid out a vision he continued to develop over the next two and a half decades. In a public letter addressed to the archbishop of Paris a dozen years later, Rousseau provided an account of what prompted the central idea of this seminal essay. Its terms reveal the same preoccupation that Marivaux, Montesquieu, and Duclos held. "I watched others act and listened to them speak. Then, having noticed that their actions did not resemble their words, I sought the reason for this disparity, and I discovered that reality and appearance were for them two things as different as acting and speaking, this second difference being the cause of the first."[64]

Rousseau's *Discourse on the Arts and Sciences* was the first of a series of works spanning fiction, philosophy, autobiography, and political thought that sought to narrow the gap between essence and appearance. Where writers before him had singled out speech, conduct, or governing structures as sources of insincerity, Rousseau accused civilization itself. The arts and sciences have spread flowers across civilization's chains, he wrote. They have schooled societies in depravity and called it refinement. The essay smolders with Rousseau's trademark indignation. Civility commands, propriety dictates, and all are forced into the same unfeeling mold. Society's skewed values reward elegance and wit over kindness and magnanimity. It counsels the distrust of friends and a fear of intimacy. Under its "deceitful veil of politeness" lurks resentment, hatred, and betrayal.[65]

In his next major work, Rousseau provided a mythic account of civilization's origins, which made the mask a permanent condition. This story of the Fall, which describes the roots of human inequality, is an unredeemed tragedy. Rousseau conjures a mythic scene for the truth it carries. Originally solitary, humans later clustered in families and sought mutual aid in communities. Small societies appeared. Gathered in front of huts, some sang and danced, and spectators praised the most skillful, clever, or attractive. The moment marked a fateful change. To observe others being judged is an apprenticeship in dissembling. This is the origin of vanity, as well as contempt, shame, and envy. It was "the first step toward inequality," Rousseau writes in *Discourse on the Origin and Foundations of Inequality*, "and, at the same time, toward vice."[66]

This malign foundation, reinforced by inborn differences, gave rise to a whole series of unjust institutions. As formerly free populations became enmeshed in mutual needs, duties, and services, occasions to profit by manipulating appearances grew. Ambition, Rousseau writes in this second discourse, often wears a "mask of benevolence": amid so much learning and politeness, "we possess nothing but a deceitful and frivolous exterior."[67]

Rousseau offered the path to a more truthful world in *Émile*, a book that describes the imagined education of a boy from infancy to adulthood with no other guide than nature. Émile is an orphan, although Rousseau thinks of him as the son of noble parents. The child, he says, will be protected against all prejudice. In the fiction, the tutor and his pupil live in the country. Émile is his own master. Punishments are rare, and for many years there are no books. Rousseau is confident that his simplicity will set him apart. There is no disparity between his words and actions. Rousseau draws a stark contrast between this innocence and products of society. "The man of the world is complete in his mask," he writes. "What he is, is nothing. What he appears to be is everything for him."[68]

Émile will move through the world with serenity, satisfaction, and none of the self-love that feeds vanity. Ignorant of conventional politeness, he is without the means to feign sentiments he doesn't feel. "True politeness," Rousseau writes, "consists in showing benevolence to others. It shows itself naturally in one who possesses it. Those without it are forced to make an art of its semblance." Here Rousseau joins Duclos and Toussaint in aligning intentions with words and transferring its carriers from sophisticates to the sincere. In fact, Rousseau inserts a passage from Duclos's *Considerations* as commentary on Émile's development. "Instead of being artificial to please, it will suffice to be good; instead of being false to flatter others' weaknesses, it will suffice to be forgiving."[69]

Rousseau claimed to live in the same sincere state as Émile. In the books and correspondence of his later years, he increasingly equated concealment with iniquity and considered transparency—the thoroughgoing identity of essence and appearance—an ideal for life. Jean Starobinski's masterful book on the subject, *Jean-Jacques Rousseau, Transparency and Obstruction*, opens with a series of recurring oppositions in Rousseau's work that align with the title's two poles: good and evil, the righteous and the wicked, nature and society, humans and their gods, man and himself.[70] Rousseau probed this last pair in his late set of dialogues, *Rousseau, Judge of Jean-Jacques*. To set man and himself as opposites conveys the magnitude of self-deception that Rousseau believed civilization had sown. Here he describes having achieved the kind of openness nurtured in the pupil Émile. "His heart," Rousseau writes of Jean-Jacques, "*transparent as crystal*, can hide nothing of what goes on inside. Every emotion is transmitted to his eyes and face."[71] He confides much the same to readers of his *Confessions*: "I would like in some way to render my soul transparent to the reader's eye."[72]

Starobinski notes that Rousseau's means to transparency was self-scrutiny. Living honestly with others, he believed, required a genuine unmasking of the self. What made this possible was the conviction that one could strip oneself of all of society's perversions and accretions. In *Rousseau, Judge of Jean-Jacques*, the subjective, passionate Jean-Jacques questions the rational Rousseau. As in the *Confessions*, such moments of sincerity aim to show an identity between feeling and expression. This interior voyage was for Rousseau a truer, more natural state. The inner depth it implied would be embraced and enlarged by a generation of Romantics seeking inspiration from within.[73]

Throughout his work, Rousseau provides instances of transparency. The close society of friends he describes in the novel *Julie, or The New Heloise* portrays relationships in which the feelings of each are known to all.[74] *The Social Contract* is a political blueprint for a society analogous to this condition. Here, the crucial step toward eliminating the veil hiding humans from themselves and one another is a vow of common identity: the mutual sacrifice of all individual rights to the whole. The result is a version of transparency writ large. "Each of us places his person and all his power under the supreme direction of the general will; and we receive as one each member as an indivisible part of the whole."[75]

Not all were sanguine about living in such sincerity. In the wake of Rousseau's prizewinning essay, a series of poems, speeches, and letters appeared in the *Mercure* that took issue with its claims. The text of an address by a professor of mathematics and history, for instance, defended politeness in its benefits to society. Civilization compels the wicked to disguise their vices, he argued, which makes them more aware of their flaws. "The obligation to copy virtue ceaselessly will at last render them virtuous." The professor targeted Rousseau's avowed closeness to nature. "Being a rustic does not prevent disguise."[76] Another essay objected to Rousseau's foundational myth. "We were long ago disabused of a fanciful Golden Age," it begins. "In all places, barbarism has preceded the establishment of societies." The selfishness and vice of that barbaric age is still present, but the masks of politeness fortunately keep much of it unseen. "Our hearts are not perfect enough to show themselves unveiled."[77]

A pamphlet called *Masks*, attributed to Gabriel-François Coyer, was vivid in its dim view of transparency. It alternates between sarcasm and scorn. Calling himself a patriot, Coyer declares it his duty to praise, exalt, and immortalize the refined manners of the nation. He proceeds to trace a scathing path through the masked ball of society, detailing universal falseness. The magnanimous man with an affable tone, who smiles, encourages, and offers to help you, has his own agenda: do not trust him. The natural features of a woman without makeup are a mask more damnable than any amount of rouge: it leads men to believe she's honest. A financier's lavish table has made his son an officer and his daughter a marquise: they mask vulgarity, theft, and native stupidity.

After expressing similar disdain for the hypocrisy of physicians, courtiers, climbers, and a titled young *seigneur* ("let us laud his red heels"), Coyer moves on to inanimate things. These, too, reveal the vanity of their possessors. Golden andirons and sugared fruit are hollow efforts to impress. Seasoned pâtés, fowl, and fish laid out for guests are more versions of the mask. The intent of such vitriol is hard to identify. Is it a hectic endorsement of Rousseau? A mocking send-up of his words? Even bookstore owners engage in disguise, Coyer writes, "masking and recycling wretched old works with impressive new titles . . . filling the space on display tables with the caustic jeremiads of J. J. and literary lampoons." The seeming reference to Jean-Jacques stands without comment. The work ends with a final encompassing reproach. "We pass our whole life in a mask. It conceals the most esteemed, attends all transactions, and serves on every important occasion. What we wear to balls is but a facsimile of our true mask."[78]

5
Festivity and Its Limits

TO CHARM AND BE CHARMED

The wide range of references to masks in the eighteenth century was a sign of unease. Rousseau's denunciations were in line with a series of particular claims, acts, and objects called false, from the vain displays of fish and fowl Coyer evoked, to the jarring sight of rich clothes among the humble classes, to the masks of "Sympathetic Tears" and "Friendly Laughter" in Guérard's engraving. In 1768, the marquis de Mirabeau asserted that the learning and urbanity of civilization itself was a "mask of virtue and not its true face."[1] While not every reference had its roots in the court, its continued associations with duplicity echoed throughout society. The references spread even as the object receded. Women no longer wore masks in markets, churches, or public parks, and actors and dancers performed barefaced.

In two notable settings, masks remained abundant: in the commercial masked balls now open to the public, and in the last days of carnival. Throughout the eighteenth century, the character of public balls was much as it had been in the masquerades of Versailles. Genuine role reversals were rare, there was little effort to assert new identities or subvert accustomed roles, and the social order was not suspended. Carnival was another matter. In the last third of the century, violence spread and was often directed against elites. Political protests were common, often with menacing undertones. This stark difference reveals two important realities: the continuing influence of courtly culture in formal settings and the bitter resentment it stirred in the street.

Just months after the death of Louis XIV, the duc d'Orléans, Regent to the five-year-old heir, signed an order establishing the country's first commercial masked balls. Masked balls reemerged after the Revolution to continue for most of the nineteenth century. With time, dozens of masked balls both large and small would appear throughout Paris, where scenes of dull routine alternated with sexual provocation, political violence, and ecstatic drunken communion. Eighteenth-century balls fell somewhere between the controlled affairs of the seventeenth century and the wild glee of the 1830s and '40s. Their larger and more varied public made these balls less predictable than masquerades at court, but the rich setting and willingness of elites to assert their rights kept the tone more or less orderly. Late in the century, the mood began to shift. Social distrust was more evident, irreverence grew more pointed, and the monarchy itself endured gentle mockery. Louis XV attended regularly and choreographed his appearances to bask in the crowds' delight, while Louis XVI, known for his early bedtime, came exactly once.[2] Marie-Antoinette, by contrast, came often, which did nothing to quell rumors about what she did while he slept.

Public masked balls were part of the shift in aristocratic culture from Versailles to Paris. With Louis XIV's death, the court's allure waned. His successors showed little interest in the Sun King's spectacles, and the nobility itself was growing more diverse. The Regent Orléans, who lived in Paris and favored the capital's new entertainments, gave authorization in 1715 for balls on Mondays, Wednesdays, and Saturdays from January until Lent. Between early November and Advent, they were offered only on Sundays. The Opera claimed a monopoly, so no other Paris establishment could hold balls. All who bought a ticket were admitted as long as they were masked.[3]

Maskers gathered in the main hall of the Opera, known formally as the Académie Royale de Musique, which adjoined the Palais-Royal. The royal affiliation ensured luxury, and maskers basked in the sovereign's reflected glory. Sumptuous fabrics adorned the hall's boxes, which ball-goers could rent by the evening or season. They held eight, ten, or twelve people. Branching chandeliers dangled from the ceiling from cords of silk and gold braid. Other candleholders were affixed to walls and columns, with oil lamps and lanterns flickering in the wings and walkways, which were lined with statues of Mercury, Momus, and the muses.

A complex system of winches raised a false floor to the height of the stage for balls, producing an uninterrupted parquet from wall to wall. Mirrors on the back of the stage created the illusion of a vast enclosure and doubled the sight of maskers moving in the dim light. At either end of the hall sat fifteen masked musicians, who played in alternation. In its center was a buffet piled high with sweets and fruit. There was dancing, but the number of those talking and circulating was usually greater. Masked balls opened at eleven at night and closed the next morning at six.[4]

The balls' profits were dwarfed by opera revenues, but their income was still solid. Attendance was strongest after New Year's, with a surge in the week before Lent. Late-fall maskers numbered only in the hundreds. In the days before Mardi Gras, attendance could reach 2,000.[5] With the price of tickets set at six livres, an amount that equaled fifteen large loaves of bread and met or exceeded the most expensive seats at the Comédie-Française, most maskers were well-to-do. Many in the early years had been regulars at the balls of Versailles. The Regent, who relished entering the hall directly from his palace, came twice in the inaugural season's first week. Five years later, when the eleven-year-old Louis XV first set foot in the hall, only members of his immediate entourage were admitted. He left at midnight, when the public could enter, but even then all maskers were obliged to identify themselves before entering.[6]

To judge by lyrics published one year after the opening, the mood in these early years was gay, gallant, and slightly precious.

> This fertile destination
> Is Cupid's land of love.
> All is made for delight,
> And the secret is simple.
> There are one thousand ways
> To charm and be charmed.[7]

The *Mercure galant*, which carried the poem, offered advice on proper conduct: (1) Your mask should be audacious, if not insolent; (2) You should commit a half-dozen tart phrases to memory and be ready to deliver one at any moment; and (3) You should make a declaration of love to someone you do not know.[8] For the Heidelberg-born Madame, mother of the Regent, this so-called land of Cupid was a euphemism for the indecencies about to be unleashed on her grandson. "I learned yesterday that my son and Mme d'Orléans have permitted the duc de Chartres to go to this accursed *bal de l'Opéra*, a shameless place," she wrote in a letter. "It will be the physical and moral ruin of this child, who, until now, has been so pious. To go there and to go to a brothel are one and the same thing."[9] Another set of verses targeted the Regent and his tastes, which gave some substance to her fears:

> How sad that the Regent of France
> Stages scenes that elicit such shame.
> He spends all his time at balls with the dancers,
> Defaming the family name.[10]

Despite ordinances forbidding violence, insults, and indecency, tempers sometimes flared in the crowded hall.[11] A fight broke out when the grandson of a farmer general tried to pull the mask off an official from the Châtelet law courts. When their insults turned to blows, guards moved in, and both were sent to the Bastille for showing "lack of respect for the Opera hall, which belongs to the king." Another night, a violinist from the orchestra called an artillery officer names in a corridor outside the hall, and the officer responded with kicks and punches. The two spent three days in jail.[12]

An encounter in the Opera ball's first season had more serious consequences. The duc de Richelieu, who made little secret of his libertine ways, had been accused of spreading rumors about the comtesse de Gacé and certain noblemen. Verses circulated calling Richelieu a gossip and hypocrite. When the countess's husband taunted him with these lyrics at the ball, Richelieu demanded a duel. In the street outside, he sliced the arm of Gacé, who opened a gash across Richelieu's stomach. They were arrested and spent five months in the Bastille.[13] On Mardi Gras a year later, two masked men fought a duel outside the hall. The one disguised as a woman was killed. When his companion seized his sword for revenge, she, too, was killed. Both bodies were displayed in costume at the Châtelet morgue.[14]

Despite such scenes, vignettes from police reports, memoirs, and newspapers describe a spirited if mostly controlled mass. Unsuspecting husbands flirt with their wives. A mislaid love letter signed in blood is found on the floor and read aloud theatrically. A group of maskers comprising three kings, an "impious woman," and the spirit of poetry enter, limp, stagger, and fall down in a heap. On the same day that ten initiates are announced for the *Ordre du Saint Esprit*—the monarchy's highest distinction—ten maskers appear with its identifying blue ribbon dangling from freakishly long noses. Their medallions read *Chevalier des Ordres du Roi*, a pun that turns order into disorder. Six maskers carry another masked man into the hall on a stretcher, set him down, and leave, which causes great shock when the mask is eventually lifted to reveal a corpse.[15]

Early in his reign, the idea of circulating among the masses was appealing to Louis XV, who attended balls regularly. Stories of visits in which he was said to have gone unrecognized circulated widely, and reported sightings proliferated. Near midnight on *lundi gras* 1737, with the court lodged at the Château de La Muette on the edge of Paris, he recruited nine gentlemen as escorts and set out for the ball. At the rue Saint-Nicaise, he ordered the carriage to stop and alighted wearing a blue robe and pink mask. He and several masked attendants walked the rest of the way. When they entered the hall, the king radiated delight, especially when revelers jostled him. When he left, he paid a boy in the street to clean his boots and sat down on a wine crate to wait for his carriage.[16]

In his later appearances, the pretense of anonymity gave way to knowing encounters. Louis XV came twice in January 1739, spending one of the visits unmasked in the royal box between two princesses. He was "charming, lustrous, confident, and gallant," the marquis d'Argenson reported. A masker wondered loudly if someone should call out, "Your Majesty, let's see your hands!," a line that wags in the parterre regularly shouted to torment priests during operas.[17] When the king dropped plans to attend another ball, he sent the duc de Noailles to stand in for him, with instructions to do all he could to pass for royalty. Disguised as a disguised Louis XV, Noailles was convincing, stirring astonishment when he let a lady take his arm and led her on a full circuit of the hall. Cardinal Fleury, Louis's First Minister, fretted that the act had compromised the king's dignity. "I am pleased by it," Louis remarked coldly before turning his back on the minister. "He did exactly as I asked."[18] In her memoirs, Henriette Campan described the ease with which Louis XV donned a mask, gathered his masked guards, and plunged into the crowd. He spoke to hairdressers, merchants, and tailors. Campan adds that he also learned a good many vulgar expressions.[19]

The masked balls that Louis XV staged at Versailles were less formal than the stately affairs of Louis XIV, principally in the large number of Parisians they drew.[20] Masks were mandatory, but all were required to identify themselves as they entered.[21] Costumes were encouraged, but many still wore identifying clothes. These included ministers, officers of the court, and ambassadors.[22] Louis XV's dress was often conspicuous and at times eccentric. On one occasion, he appeared among a handful of maskers dressed as bats. He mixed freely with the crowd, avoiding those he knew and eager to listen to those he did not. He danced with strangers and was thrilled when guards once pushed him aside for blocking a passage.[23]

In 1745, the king staged a public masked ball at Versailles to celebrate his son's marriage to the Infanta Maria Teresa of Spain. Tables in the château's Grand Gallery were heaped with salmon, sole, trout, fresh fruit, and candies. Wine flowed freely. A large orchestra played as guests danced in four radiating salons. Masks were required, as was identification at the door, but as one of the attendees noted: "Those unknown could easily furnish whatever name they pleased."[24] Arrivals from Paris flooded the outer court with coaches and carriages. The crowd swelled, lines grew long, and eventually those at the door stopped taking names.

Maskers soon filled room after room. Lacking seats, six hundred guests sat on the floor outside the king's apartment. Another fifteen hundred

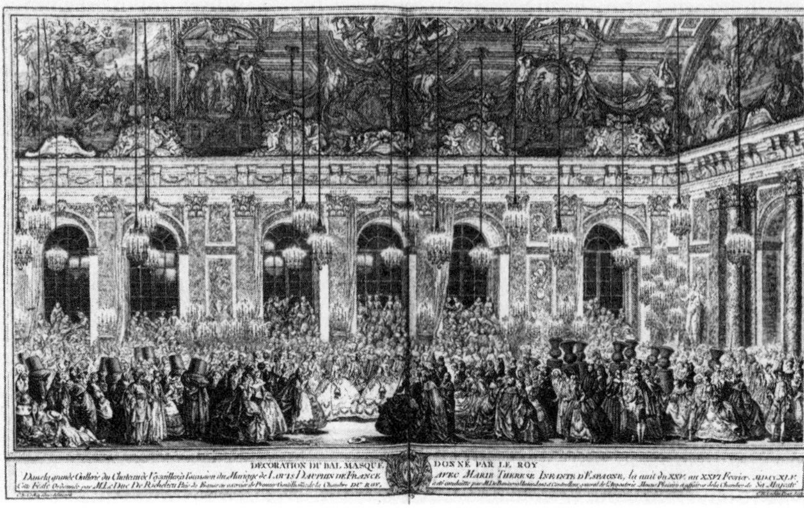

FIGURE 5.1. *Decor of a Masked Ball Given by the King*, anon. (Bibliothèque nationale de France)

maskers milled about in the packed Grand Gallery, where "one was virtually carried from one end to the other without touching the floor." The queen removed her mask early in the evening. The dauphin and dauphine eventually entered as a shepherd and shepherdess. The king, masked but known, periodically changed clothes. His most stunning costume, captured in a lavish engraving by Charles Nicolas Cochin, was as one of eight yew trees.[25] Also present were sultans, Turks in colossal turbans, Asian dignitaries, peasant girls in hoop skirts, and peasant boys in stately breeches.[26]

Opinion differed on whether a certain peasant at one of the Versailles balls was the king. The masker was seen speaking at length with the queen, who had declared a week earlier that she no longer found masks amusing. At the time, rumors circulated about a certain graceful guest the king had danced with at earlier balls. When Jeanne-Antoinette Étioles was identified, the duc de Luynes noted in his journal that she was "a flirtation, not a mistress." A bawdy poem called "The King's Beauties" that followed suggested otherwise.

The wisest dames
Would surely agree
To stay in the game.
How absurd it would be
To give up this mission
For a well-paid position.[27]

Soon the marquise de Pompadour, the title and name conferred by her lover the king, was a regular presence at the balls.[28]

Whatever pleasure Louis XV took from masked balls, he also knew that attending was good for his image. He sometimes came without guards. "It reflects well on him to have entrusted himself to his people, whose confidence he has earned," an adviser observed. His minister Argenson also understood the importance of the appearances. "All of this was done manifestly to please the public," he wrote in his memoirs. "It displays the king to his people. . . . It shows him as a king and above all as a man."[29] This was a point that Louis XVI never grasped, whose lone visit was noted. When Marie-Antoinette came, she was usually masked, rarely unrecognized, and in the company of a lady from the palace or the king's brother Artois. Her appearances fit a narrative that had begun to coalesce around the royal family, which featured a disengaged king and a queen who sought ever more titillating ways to defeat her boredom.

The loose familiarity of the mask made approaching the queen a sport. A Mme Dugas, convinced that a costumer disguised as an old woman and her smart escort were the queen and Artois, fell on her knees and begged permission to kiss the woman's hand. "Touch my heart," Dugas said, placing the lady's hand on her chest, "and know that it is not mistaken about its masters, for whom it throbs with devotion." She kissed the hand, and the couple slipped away. Some near Dugas broke into applause. "Are not all things permitted at a ball?" she asked, adding that the mask had authorized and excused her kiss.[30]

Several years later, a masker dressed as a fishwife spoke to the queen at length. She approached the royal box and called out *Antoinette!* When the queen appeared, the masker told her that everyone knew she refused to sleep with the king because he snored. This was a polite version of rumors about the royal equipment and her own tastes. The queen leaned in, and the conversation stretched to half an hour. It ended, to the shock of those who watched, with the fishwife kissing the queen's hand.[31]

An attendant reported that Marie-Antoinette enjoyed acting as though she were unknown at the balls. This was a fiction to which most were party: "By pretending not to recognize her, people could stir up some intrigue to provide her the pleasure of incognito." Others played along. The baron de Ruhlière, recognizing her in her black mask but feigning otherwise, sat down near her and proceeded to repeat gossip about the principal ladies of the court, which drew the queen's laughter.[32] The mutual pretense of disguise was what gave encounters between the high- and lowborn their thrill. Louis XVI's masked brother Monsieur, the comte de Provence, bantered with an actress, who extended the flirtation by affecting not to recognize him. "Let me test your devotion," she said. "I would like an orange. Please bring one to me." The prince complied.[33]

For every willing exchange between unequal maskers, there were at least as many rebuffs, when the more powerful declared the game over. In 1782, the duc de Chartres, a cousin to the king, was repeatedly interrupted by an unknown masker as he spoke to a woman. At last Chartres exploded with indignation, asking the masker if he had any idea who he was. "I beg your pardon, Monseigneur," the masker shot back. "You have so thoroughly unmasked yourself that I have the honor of having already recognized you." The prince was dumbstruck and called for guards to seize the man. They dove into the crowd after him, but he disappeared.[34]

More routine heckling drew similar responses. Jean-Jacques Barthélemy, a priest, archaeologist, and royal conservator of medals, was at a ball with his noble patron Choiseul when a group of maskers approached. One of them, whose lanky frame resembled Barthélemy's, wore black robes and a skullcap. He struck a pose next to Barthélemy as a companion cried out, "Who are you? What is your station? Are you a priest?" The faux Barthélemy replied: "It doesn't matter, as long as I receive my 30,000-livre income." The farce seems harmless, but Choiseul was irked enough to command the men to unmask themselves, which they refused to do.[35]

Given the readiness to taunt, take offense, or settle scores, the relative absence of major turmoil at the balls is notable. In a public ball at midcentury, an elegantly dressed woman commanded maskers on a bench to make room for her to sit. They stayed put. Lifting her mask, she announced, "I am the princesse de Conti!" "We do not recognize you," one of them replied. She sharpened her tone. "Are you persons whose company is displeasing?" "Indeed!" a masker replied, "—so displeasing that we refuse to let it get worse." There were more direct confrontations. A woman in 1768 pummeled a maskless poet in the face and shoulders as gleeful onlookers made disparaging jokes about his poetry. In 1781, a fight between two prostitutes led to a bloody sequel the next day.[36]

While eighteenth-century balls brought impertinence and acrimony, they seldom saw unbridled license. Tempers could be short, and insults could provoke isolated violence, but conflict was more typically settled civilly. A remarkable case of the mask's power to suspend protocol came when a man in a domino scuffled briefly with the king's brother Monsieur. They inched through the packed crowd, pushes turned to shoves, and the two were soon trading punches. When a guard moved to arrest them, a lady of the court materialized to inform him of one masker's "importance." The agent released his grip, and Monsieur explained: "I hit him once, and he hit me twice, which I deserved. But I would ask him next time not to push so hard."[37] Such dustups notwithstanding, regulars at the balls describe their final years as lackluster. It was the height of fashion to attend, but the experience had lost its excitement. "You must tell everyone what a good time you had," observes a book from 1781, "and repeat all the clever things you heard, and relate all the handsome proposals you received." But in truth, it continues, "you yawn, you grow bored, you chase pleasure or wit but it's gone like the wind."[38]

Revenues fell in the 1780s, fewer were interested in dancing, and the "tremendous merriment" known in former days was no longer present. The enveloping gloom of a bankrupt government, widespread crop failure, and the tremors of deep social discontent likely played a role. Louis-Sébastien Mercier, who wrote of the earlier merriment, pointed to another source. "You don't see anything in a mask that you can't see in society."[39]

In the eighteenth century's balls, whether courtly or public, the mask loosened rank and permitted encounters otherwise inconceivable. It softened barriers that segregated the baseborn from the genteel and, for some, gave direct access to royalty. It also provided face-saving security to those of whatever station who were made uncomfortable by such intimate proximity. The encounters masks allowed were rare and remarkable, but they were possible only by mutual consent, which might end at a moment's notice. Masks also encouraged many to act out of character. As the century advanced, greater numbers took the mingling masks permitted as an opportunity to approach, address, tease, and sometimes defy their social superiors, who tolerated it in varying degrees. Yet despite the irreverence and occasional violence, these masked gatherings were by and large harmonious, which was no small achievement.

While the social order was never threatened, the freedom masked balls offered was without precedent. They granted nobles and non-nobles alike a temporary pause from the rituals that policed social divisions in all other settings. Their atmosphere of regal festivity, with its food, music, and colorful costumes, encouraged companionable mingling. Among unequals, this could mean closer contact, conversation, and a kind of parity. To the extent that the balls were harmonious, this fellowship was remarkable, however temporary. Without their royal trappings, expensive tickets, and, not least, armed guards with the power to arrest, social tensions below the surface would surely have been more threatening. Just outside the Opera's doors it was another story.

BRUTAL LAUGHTER

A common view of Parisian carnival in the eighteenth century describes a raucous, merry holiday that let off steam by temporarily upending the order. David Garrioch, one of the city's foremost historians, describes carnival as "an affirmation of the fundamental unity of the urban community, a moment when the normal spatial, social, and sexual barriers came down." Its insults and mockery were genuine, he continues, but confined to "a period of general good humor."[40] In this view, the licensed disorder of carnival was in the end conservative, reaffirming traditional hierarchies by permitting a controlled release of pent-up pressure.

Before the last third of the century, the spirit of Parisian carnival was indeed largely genial, with its variety of costumes a common feature of travelers' accounts. There were clowns, ruddy fishwives, sailors with clay pipes, cart drivers, boot scrapers, and satyrs. Women wore pants, men put on dresses, and teenagers posed as babies in tow. They strolled and shambled, rode donkeys, mules, and horses, and packed themselves into various conveyances. The crowds were greatest on the Thursday, Monday, and Tuesday before Lent, when maskers in outlandish costumes moved in packs. The working-class quarter of Saint-Antoine was still the center of carnival festivity, but there were also celebrations in other parts of the city.

Costumers included the accustomed array of exotic foreigners, shepherds, and shepherdesses. Contemporaries regularly described men dressed as women and women as men, including among married couples. A 1779 poem called "Masks of the Porte Sainte-Antoine" provides a vivid account.

> Here's where they meet, as ridiculous cries
> Resound through the street from the crowd in disguise
> It's here where a herd of hilarious clowns
> Harasses the crowd with frightful sounds. . . .
> Sexes are changed: there are corsets on men
> Whose muscular chests tear the delicate lace,
> And women come dressed as hired assassins
> Though attempts to be crude are betrayed by their grace.[41]

The grounds on which cross-dressing was a crime of *Faux*—the deliberate intent to alter one's identity with an intent to deceive—was of questionable relevance in carnival. Another law targeted the season more specifically. Cross-dressing during carnival was a crime if done in order to harm, steal from, or insult another person. Such cases were not rare.[42]

The spirit of carnival in these decades was bawdy and often scatological. Children "gave rats" to passersby by slapping them with rodent-shaped pieces of fabric loaded with flour. "You've shit in your bed!" was a common cry. The crude line stuck: maskers were called *chienlits*, shit-abeds.[43] Maskers fashioned costumes to match the taunt, appearing on the streets in

FIGURE 5.2. *Masker at Porte St. Antoine*, anon. (Bibliothèque nationale de France)

white nightshirts whose seats were smeared with gobs of mustard. Others followed with sausages, using the meat to wipe off the goo and then offering it to strangers to eat. A small book prepared for carnival in 1759 set the taunt to music. "Schoolchildren" is its first poem, a derisive ten-stanza litany of dupes and bunglers, with each line ending in the same refrain: "He's shit in his bed! He's shit in his bed!" In "The Impotent Fool," Nicaise at sixty takes a wife of sixteen, who lies in his arms until he falls asleep: "*then her lover slips in without a sound.*" In "It Can Happen There," twenty-five carats convince Lucille to leave her convent for Robin; they exchange vows, all sing, all dance, her bows are deep: "*then Lucille drops three turds on the ground.*"[44]

Diarrhearama: A Mirthful and Savory Collection for Connoisseurs promised carnival diversion to "young fools" with its anecdotes, quips, scenes, and bon mots. Its humor never leaves the bathroom. A great aristocrat calls on a lady friend. Aware of his own bad breath, he cannot bring himself to speak. She nevertheless smells something, and to avenge his insulting silence she has her servants examine his drawers. "He must have let fall a certain noxious object," they report. "Send him away!" However silly, *Diarrhearama* possesses a certain kind of skill. It opens with *Crapaïre*, a twenty-eight-page parody of Voltaire's *Zaïre* in rhymed Alexandrines. Everyone in the pasha Cacadoo's seraglio has been stricken with loose bowels. Cacadoo is bereft, but all is saved by the beautiful Crapaïre, whose turds are as hard and dry as the Pasha's own.[45]

Police depositions reveal that such hilarity often provoked bloodshed. Starting in the 1760s, daily reports submitted from across the city describe mounting carnival violence in vivid detail.[46] One shocking confrontation occurred in the small hours of Mardi Gras 1764, near the Opera, where traffic was heaviest before Lent. Just after 1 a.m., five revelers on their way to the masked ball—three men and two women—approached in a coach. They were all in costume, including one in a magistrate's robe and hat. The group stopped in a café to buy masks, which they donned and returned to their coach. As traffic slowed, a speeding two-man cabriolet swerved in close to cut them off. Lashing at his horse, its driver sliced their coachman's hand and just missed his face. He struck back with his own strap. The younger man in the cab unsheathed a sword, and the coach's maskers roared out profanities: "Bastards!" "You scum!" The cab's driver jumped to the ground. "I am the count de La Tour du Pin," he shouted, "and I demand to know your names." "We're maskers!" came the reply from inside the coach. "And we don't give a goddamn whether you're a count or not. Go screw yourself!"[47]

The younger man was now hacking at the coachman's reins. Du Pin ran to the coach, threw open a door, and ordered the passengers to unmask themselves. What came instead was a pummeling. A masker leapt out of another carriage and held du Pin from behind as two maskers from the coach laid into him. A third bounded out and ran away. Du Pin's young companion now plunged into the coach, ripped open the woman's blouse, and began pulling down her skirts. He was struggling to drag her out when a man from another coach jumped aboard to tackle him. In the street, the two maskers were punching du Pin without letup as blood streamed from his head, at last throwing him facedown in the mud. A guard eventually arrived to find du Pin—Brigadier of the King's Armies and Chevalier of the Order of Saint-Louis—the prisoner of one man in a sailor suit and another dressed as a judge.

The reveler who dashed out of the carriage just before du Pin was attacked is familiar to some today. Claude-Nicolas Le Doux was already working in the ranks of royal administration, but at twenty-eight he was not yet the renowned architect he would later become. He was going to the ball with his friend Edme Thibault, a master plumber and machinist who worked in royal properties known as the *Bâtiments du roi*. Thibault had invited two of his friends to come along, Jean-Baptiste La Marque and Jeanne Masson. Although a step removed from the bureaucracy, La Marque was also close to its administration as chief of household for François-Balthazar Dangé, one of the wealthiest tax collectors in Paris. While not noble, all three men were well situated. In their own way, however modest, they each had a stake in the status quo.[48]

Returning from dinner on the Left Bank, René-François-André, comte de La Tour du Pin, was a stone's throw from his home on the rue de Richelieu when he swerved before the coach. He was forty-nine and no longer in active service, having retired eighteen years before. As commanding officer, he had won over a dozen battles. A doctor's report specified his Mardi Gras injuries: swelling across the face, severe contusions above and below the left eye, scratches on both hands, and acute swelling in the right index finger. Witnesses described his humiliation. His face was bloody, his riding coat and breeches were covered in mud, and his wig was in tatters. His gold watch chain and a jewel-studded snuffbox were gone.[49]

The two dozen men and women who gave testimony did little to clarify who was at fault. A gendarme reported hearing taunts from inside the coach before du Pin left his vehicle ("Goddamned lowlife, you dirty son of a bitch!"). The hired coach driver described being horsewhipped by du Pin. Le Doux said that du Pin burst into their carriage "like a drunken man" and furiously punched and cursed Thibault: "Tell me who you are, you bastard. Tell me who you are. I'm taking you with me." A dressmaker reported seeing du Pin's companion, an eighteen-year-old commoner named Elfebvre, dive into the coach with his sword. The bystander who seized him as he tore off Masson's clothes called the act a disgrace. A passerby saw Thibault and La Marque heave du Pin out of the carriage and beat him in the mud.[50]

At 2 a.m., battered and filthy, du Pin filed a complaint accusing Thibault, La Marque, Masson, and Le Doux of assault, declaring them agitators, accomplices, and parties to insult, malicious treatment, and violence. For their part, Thibault and La Marque filed a complaint against du Pin and Elfebvre for assault and malicious treatment.[51] The cases were heard in April by the Parlement of Paris, whose judgment was confirmed on appeal in late July. The comte du Pin was cleared of any wrongdoing. Thibault and La Marque were each ordered to pay 1,000 livres, a staggering sum that amounted to more than two years' pay for workers in their position.[52]

In the decades before 1789, what Parisians had once praised as a common and joyous celebration grew anarchic and elemental. Ceremony receded, play gave way to insult and injury, and pranks that were once largely innocent turned increasingly cruel. Violence erupted regularly, often with startling severity. Was it a lack of adequate policing, as some complained, or something more? On the eve of the Revolution, masks revealed a truth better concealed at other moments: just beneath the surface was deep animosity.

Four years after Thibault and La Marque dumped the bloodied du Pin in the street, a fifteen-year-old masker near Notre-Dame amused himself during carnival by throwing mud at the skirts of elegant ladies. One woman's husband, or relative, or possibly a stranger, responded by cracking his skull with the bulbous end of a walking stick. The boy died in the street. Three years before du Pin's humiliation, a father walking with his family on Mardi Gras near the Place des Victoires was nearly killed when a soldier burst out of the Flower Basket tavern waving a sword, insane with rage. Women in carnival masks had come into the room where he was drinking and said something tart. He chased them out of the building, and when the father moved to protect his children, the soldier cursed his wife and slashed his throat. Police arrived, arrested the soldier, and carried the bleeding man away.[53]

A fight among maskers another Mardi Gras would have been disastrous with weapons. A married couple and their friend—the man in a dress and the two women wearing pants—were stopped in the street by an acquaintance named Segard, a master tradesman. He demanded the couple pay him the money they owed. When they refused, he called the man scum and battered his head with a cane. When one of the women tried to stop him, he put her into a stranglehold, shouting, "You bitch! You whore!" As she sank her teeth into his arm, another man in women's clothes rushed to help free her. The assault wasn't over. Trailing the couple and their friend to a nearby tavern, Segard attacked the woman once more and was finally wrestled to the floor by others, who kept hold of him until police arrived.[54]

Whatever celebration carnival masks brought in these years, they also abetted brutality. Just before midnight on Mardi Gras 1772, a pair of young men in women's dresses—one a nobleman's servant, the other a vicar's valet, and both raging drunk—wandered into a lemonade seller's shop. One stumbled to the counter and vomited. When the owner went outside for help, the men attacked his pregnant wife, punching and kicking her in the belly. They were imprisoned that night in the Grand Châtelet.[55]

Several years earlier, it took four officers to control a cross-dressed man named Jean Briaudeux. He had shouted threats at passersby near the Place

Maubert before attacking a butcher he claimed had insulted him. By the time the guard arrived, Briaudeux, a physician's coachman, had ripped out clumps of the butcher's hair, torn open his cheek, and battered an eye. He continued to struggle as his captors took him to jail.[56] Elsewhere in the city, an elderly notary who stopped to help a boy lift a heavy bag was pelted with mud and rocks as another boy burst out of the bag crying, "He's shit in his bed, he's shit in his bed!"[57] In 1785, two days before Lent, a "masked bourgeois" was stabbed to death during an argument on rue St. Honoré.[58]

Sometimes the belligerence was political. Carnival responses to the so-called Maupeou coup were the most explicit. In 1772, six weeks after the royal Chancellor sparked outrage by exiling magistrates who had opposed the king's will, *chienlits* from the Saint-Antoine district paid raucous visits to three notable addresses, lingering long enough to cause alarm. One group gathered outside the home of an official who oversaw the city's auxiliary police force. Another took carriages to the Palais-Royal quarter, assembling first at the home of the Paris lieutenant general of police, Antoine de Sartine. They then went to the home of Chancellor Maupeou. The maskers dispersed peacefully, but the political thrust of their presence was clear.

Scathing songs and verses about Maupeou's orders recall the carnival Mazarinades from a century before, with the singular difference that later versions lack any levity. *Epigrams, Couplets, and Vaudevilles Relating to the 1771 Revolution* was a handwritten, roughly bound book whose small size made it easy to tuck into a pocket. One of its poems forms an acrostic.

> **M**iserable friend, worse citizen,
> **A**rdently evil, cold to all good,
> **V**ile excrement, nature's refuse,
> **P**acked with bile, fraud, and pride,
> **E**nemy to every law.
> **O**ne recognizes the portrait:
> **U**nholy traitor to France and her king.[59]

The savagery of the final lines of a twenty-two-stanza poem in the same collection called "The Chancelleries" is typical of the tone throughout.

> This is how, tracing the knife's path to your heart,
> I come to drink your blood, drop by drop,
> Brewed in a goblet of terror
> And steeped in the people's hatred.
> I will blithely mock your suffering,
> And if Louis does not exterminate you,

> Then it shall come to pass, when I open your chest,
> That I will teach you who I am.[60]

Such violent acts and threats are notable, but they were not unique to carnival. Hostility brimmed among Parisians in all seasons. The historian Arlette Farge documents daily hardships of the poor that could lead to unspeakable violence. A furniture builder's wife is attacked by a neighbor who slashes her face with a broken plate. A basket maker viciously canes a boy he finds urinating outside his shop door. Two men force their way into the apartment of an unmarried pregnant woman to beat her, calling her a whore and her partner a scoundrel. "The people settle their conflicts at once," Farge writes, "with blows from their fists and feet or with the tools of their trade."[61] Often, the brutality was against those who endured the same precarious existence.

In certain ways, the violence of eighteenth-century carnival resembles the crimes Farge records. Viciousness among costumed women and men of the popular classes is a common thread. Yet not all of their aggression was against their own kind. The pummeling of du Pin bears every sign of an attack on privilege. That the perpetrators worked in royal administration and would have had a close view of men like him makes their ferocity more personal. The menace of late-century carnival, moreover, was not always in response to individual wrongs. The masked visits to the homes of Maupeou and Sartine, for instance, touched on issues of civic and political justice. Carnival mockery more generally reached across the orders. It is a nobleman whose drawers are inspected in *Diarrhearama*, and Lucille, who embarrassed herself during the wedding dance, was a former nun. Whether in anger or jest, carnival irreverence and the mask's impunity fueled defiance from below. Its intensity showed that it was not all done in good fun.

Rétif de la Bretonne details a series of carnival scenes from the 1770s that he viewed as offenses against the social order. He describes watching maskers rob a shopkeeper as he counts the day's earnings, taunting him as they leave. He is outraged when a gang of maskers accosts a family near Les Halles, insulting three girls, robbing their father, and fleeing in raucous laughter.[62] He relates other scenes: an Arlequin and Pierrot methodically destroy street lamps with rocks; a friend's son is beaten to a pulp by maskers on Mardi Gras and requires six months to recover; a teenager, having dressed himself as a girl on Mardi Gras, is abducted and sodomized.[63] He quotes an acquaintance who comments on these events at length:

> How can we permit such sickening, disgusting filth in a civilized, well-run city! . . . . People in masks running to insult others unafraid as though

> they're unhinged! . . . Nations! Nations! There used to be nations! . . . The only nation we have is a tribe of savages.[64]

The violence and political resistance that appeared before Lent defies any sense of human community. There would be a time in the coming century when carnivalesque laughter reigned: when hierarchies were gleefully upended, the rich donned trappings of the lowly and those on the margins were empowered, and an ecstatic fleeting freedom united people of vastly different circumstances. Carnival in prerevolutionary Paris, by contrast, was much less about ritual inversion than attacking the existing order. Its license was not a preventive burst of pressure before returning to accustomed roles. Instead, it was a sign of tensions both long-standing and immediate. The violence did not depend on anonymity, and revelers' masks may or may not have disguised identities. The season was instead a pretext that turned irreverence into lawlessness. What carnival revealed was a fraying social fabric. As successive Ash Wednesdays brought an end to the revelry, the animosity persisted. An imagined pre-carnival order was not restored, in part because so much was already in flux.

IDENTITIES IN THE EIGHTEENTH CENTURY

When the nineteenth-century historian Hippolyte Taine characterized the last decades of the monarchy, he drew attention to a passion for theatricals. Marie-Antoinette's playacting at the Trianon in shepherdesses' clothes was not unique. Nobles staged scenes from stage works and improvised their own dramas. They sang songs from light opera and devised elaborate games of charades. "Near the end of the century, everyone became an actor," Taine observed. "In fact, everyone had become one already." Analogies drawn from the theater reached all ranks. Charles-Joseph de Ligne, an officer and writer known in intellectual circles, claimed that his contemporaries were better actors than the professionals. "Each day, we play kings, we play lovers, we play husbands, and we play honest people—and it is usually in this latter role that we are at our worst."[65]

Public life in Paris fed the sentiment. Theaters, promenades, salons, and cafés turned everyday encounters into small spectacles. Audiences at plays and operas watched with one eye on the stage and the other on the house to gauge their own responses by reactions of the powerful. Strollers passed judgment on one another's taste by the cut and quality of fabrics. Conversation, however refined, had its winners and losers, with triumphs and humiliations on display for all to see. However shopworn, the trope that called all the world a stage gained new significance in the public places of eighteenth-century Paris.

The pervasive place of performance was more evidence that patterns of dissembling once required at Versailles were now widespread. In many ways, the social and legal structures that had shaped seventeenth-century selfhood among elites to be at once insincere and highly intentional now described society at large. Despite gains in wealth and education among the upper ranks of commoners, the law still enforced sharp distinctions in rights and privileges between aristocrats and all others. While not the all-encompassing imperative that had once reigned at court, there was still a need to defer to the privileged, whose opinions could affect one's own fortunes. Ritualized phrases tailored to one's place in the hierarchy discouraged sincerity.

Conversation therefore stayed to the surface of things. According to the historian Philippe Perrot, the eighteenth century's inner world was largely closed off and irrelevant to one's public face. "Under the brilliant glaze of propriety, one did not look for the 'secret' soul or the 'true' personality," he writes. It wasn't so much that a private self was absent or unthinkable, but that the obstacles to expressing it were rooted in the social order. "Insofar as one does not search for the truth of the 'moi,' the other is a mystery to no one," Perrot observes. "The public remained impermeable to the private."[66]

Elements of performance defined not just daily interactions but the hierarchy itself. Across the eighteenth century, large numbers of men whose wealth came from finance, the courts, and the professions continued to enter the aristocracy, either by an ennobling position or by outright purchase. Of France's 25,000 noble families in 1789, comprising some 120,000 individuals, one-fifth had been ennobled since 1700. The royal genealogist Louis Chérin, who published a history of ennoblement and usurpation just before the Revolution, offers a startling figure. A mere one-twentieth of the families who claimed aristocratic roots in 1788 appeared in the noble register of 1666. Ennoblement accelerated in the monarchy's last years. In the decade and a half before the Revolution, 2,477 commoners received noble letters.[67]

To describe the noble order in terms of ancient blood was therefore absurd. Nobles nevertheless continued to defend their status as a race apart. Critics had their own reasons for perpetuating the myth. "In truth, there is but one Order, and that is the Nobility," Sieyès wrote in *What Is the Third Estate?* "It is a separate people, a *false* people, who, for lack of any useful attribute, can live only . . . as leeches on the lifeblood of the plants they enfeeble and deplete."[68] With its patent fiction of separateness, this was mutual delusion turned to devastating effect. Revolutionaries fueled the fiction in the *Marseillaise* when they sang of impure blood, the better to condemn this race apart.

Social change blurred traditional markers of identity beyond clothes and possessions. Alexis de Tocqueville observed that those above the masses increasingly resembled one another in habits, tastes, and pleasures.[69] Such differences grew yet smaller as traditional prohibitions barring aristocrats from "degrading" work were steadily repealed. Growing numbers of aristocrats owned or invested in capitalist ventures by producing armaments, ships, chemicals, fabrics, paper, glass, and cotton. "From this moment," the historian Guy Chaussinand-Nogaret has written, "no important difference separates noble from bourgeois. The nobleman is nothing more than a bourgeois who has succeeded."[70]

Nobles nevertheless continued to assert their superior legal status in speech, bearing, and temperament. Comparisons drawn from the theater were especially apt. "In this quest for identity," writes the historian Pierre Serna, "the spectacle of the second order, taken as a whole, was presented as social distinction; the principle of legitimacy was confirmed by daily practice." Chaussinand-Nogaret is more direct. "To be noble is to be distinct," he writes, enumerating the defining privileges on exhibit in everyday life. "It exists in one's way of appearing."[71] In a population growing more similar, such displays rankled. One hundred years earlier, concealing one's thoughts and covering one's face had protected identities at court and in masquerades. Now masks were used to challenge a system whose claims of fixed identities looked increasingly arbitrary.[72] Ball patrons ribbed, taunted, and sometimes insulted elites. Men dressed as women and women as men, a mockery of laws that condemned cross-dressing. During carnival, resentment among maskers could be explosive.

Against this backdrop, a powerful countercurrent emerged that challenged fundamental assumptions. Sentimentalism, the conviction that sincerity was virtuous and that sympathetic tears were the sign of an open heart, affected all ranks. With the authority of both science and philosophy, sentimentalism aligned emotion with moral virtue to shape a new view of community.[73] Its effects were far-reaching for the individual and society. Private experience, until now largely extraneous to one's social identity, assumed a prominent place in culture, politics, and the public sphere.

At midcentury, Charles Duclos had proposed sensitivity of soul as a corrective for the shallow insincerity of elites, who he said lacked any ethical sense. On the eve of the Revolution, great numbers readily expressed their feelings without shame. Audiences wept openly at the Opera, painters depicted tender and tumultuous domestic scenes, and friends pledged trembling vows of fidelity. For those so inclined, this public self was not impermeable to the private: the truth of the "moi" was at once more capacious and less calculating. Vulnerability, guarded against in court society with the very muscles of the face, could be a virtue.

Rousseau's displays of sincerity were essential to sentimentalism's spread. His books, which used personal feeling to claim intimate kinship with others, were a model for the public expression of private thoughts. Readers responded with hundreds of letters, describing to him their tears of tenderness and grief, the sweet simplicity of nature, and the need above all to share such sentiments with other open-hearted people. A Protestant minister wrote to him: "No, Monsieur, I can no longer keep quiet. You have overwhelmed my soul. It is full to bursting, and I must share its torment with you."[74]

The posthumous reverence for Rousseau gives some indication of sentimentalism's reach. Two years after his death, subscribers to a volume of songs called *Consolations for the Miseries of My Life* included Benjamin Franklin, the princesse de Lamballe, and Marie-Antoinette. *Refreshment for the Sensitive Man*, a best-selling series launched in 1783, ran to seventy-two monthly installments, providing a full six years of selfless love, joyous reunions, and wrongdoers moved to reform.[75] Such emotional expansiveness spread through the culture late in the century, altering the grounds for assessing oneself and others. One's essential identity came to rest less on status than on intent.[76] With the locus of truth now shifting from public authority to private sentiment, earlier claims of a prevailing falseness in society took on new relevance. Since the middle of the century, writers, critics, and political philosophers had called for unmasking. The appeal now assumed a decisive new stage, with the project not only individual but institutional.

6
Unmasking the Heart

SERIOUS FUN

As legislators built the institutions of liberty in the early months of the Revolution, carnival became unrecognizable. The first Mardi Gras after the Bastille fell reflected the new mood. The press reported calm, and the season's accustomed mischief and extravagance were absent. Only two public dances were held in the capital in the weeks before Lent. Each was advertised pointedly as an *unmasked ball.* Elsewhere, no masks were seen, "the people having sensed," as one journalist wrote in the newspaper *Révolutions de Paris,* "the absurdity of this monstrous custom." Another reported that "the fun of carnival this year was all serious." Disapproval of the tradition was widespread. Jean-Paul Marat described the season as a "festival for slave peoples," whose degrading license was the opposite of liberty.[1]

Two events that year convey how fundamentally the Revolution changed the most ingrained customs, including the people's pleasures. The first was a solemn ceremony in the vaulting spaces of Notre-Dame. Announcing the hope that citizens would forget the "masquerades, orgies, and madness that took place on this day in years past," Paris officials orchestrated an event that was to be repeated and refined by festival planners in the years to come. Citizens would be actors in a grand spectacle of self-celebration. "The locale, the clothes, the speeches, even the order of events must carry within their seeming confusion the imprint of fraternity and patriotism."[2]

On the morning of Mardi Gras, crowds gathered on the Champs-Élysées. General Lafayette reviewed the National Guard, and the procession made its way to the cathedral, where a corps of cavalry, military deputations from each Paris district, and a delegation of 300 from the Hôtel de Ville had assembled. Fanfares were sounded, a Te Deum was sung, and patriotic oaths were pledged, but the festival fell far short of the ideal. Tickets were required, which the poor could not afford. Aristocrats stayed away out of fear that they would be forced to show allegiance to the new order. For all the talk about ordinary citizens being actors, uniformed men—the National Guard, representatives from each district, and administrators from City Hall—sat in reserved seats. "This was not a festival for the people," the press complained. "It was a spectacle put on for them, and, as had to happen, they were very unimpressed, very uninterested."[3]

While banners were raised to yawns in Paris, another sort of celebration was taking place in Perpignan. In the words of the priest Claude Fauchet, an early supporter of the Revolution among clergy, the city's residents staged "a little lesson for aristocrats." These festivities lay somewhere between the revelry of Saint-Antoine district and the solemn oaths taken at Notre-Dame. Crowds exceeding 10,000 lined the streets, with one hundred National Guard soldiers leading the parade. People sang patriotic songs and carried placards reading "Long Live Liberty!" and "Long Live the New Constitution!" Fauchet's report is vivid in detail. Vehicles passed with banners reading "Long Live the King!," "Long Live the Law!," and "Long Live the National Assembly!" Townspeople filled their glasses with wine from a cask bearing the words "It flows only for true patriots." Another wagon carried the remains of a smashed trunk. "Storage for Special Privileges," its signs read, and "Storage for Feudal Rights."[4]

At the center of the parade walked a richly dressed man wearing a mask with two faces, leaning heavily on two enchained slaves. "He represents an aristocrat," Fauchet writes. A large contingent of similarly dressed "aristocrats" walked behind him. At the town square, a speaker proposed toasts to the health of Louis XVI, "father of the people and restorer of French liberty." A chant arose, "Long Live the National Assembly!," and the "aristocrat" cried, "No, No, No!" As a speaker read from a speech by Louis XVI pledging his attachment to the new order, the man collapsed and was pronounced dead. Toasts followed, the slaves were freed, and the parade resumed. Its mood, joyous and full of life, was far from the insolence and mockery of past carnivals. "Everything took place in the greatest tranquility," Fauchet reports, "and the people, despite the wine supplied to them in profusion, insulted no one. There was no disorder."[5] Mardi Gras in Perpignan achieved what the planners at Notre-Dame had aimed for but missed: spontaneous glee and a people in celebration of itself.

Despite the shortcomings of the Paris ceremony, the two events on this first Mardi Gras of the Revolution shared a vision of citizens as actors instead of subjects.[6] Both were calm, sober, and scripted. The power mocked in Perpignan had been defeated, which changed its laughter from subversion to solidarity between the governed and their leaders. The transformation suggests why carnival aroused such repugnance after feudalism was abolished in August 1789, an act that raised the low and humbled the proud. Revolutionaries celebrated carnival without the carnivalesque. The world had already been turned upside down.

Through the many dramatic changes of the French Revolution, concealment grew as a central preoccupation. The figure of the mask was prominent not only in polemics, politics, and festivity, but also in fundamental questions of human vice and virtue. The language of masking framed how citizens assessed others' intentions, guiding them to search for signs of loyalty or betrayal in words, acts, clothes, and bodies. The embrace of sincerity as a sign of virtue inspired tears, embraces, and earnest public avowals. Even as unmasking traitors became the national project, sentimentalism remained the dominant tone, mixing its virtuous effusions with state-sanctioned violence.[7]

The first official act to reorder carnival came not from above but from a humble neighborhood meeting in the Récollets district of Paris. In the spirit of openness and with Mardi Gras approaching, the council voted to forbid all masks. An excerpt of its deliberations, which dismissed masking for its "license and abuse," was printed on a handbill and posted throughout the precinct. The decree was sent to the city's fifty-nine other districts with the plea that they, too, ban masks. It found instant support. Four days after the Récollets council acted, the Jacobin Club of the St. Dominique neighborhood enacted a ban of its own, charging that "enemies of the Revolution . . . under the cover of a mask, could easily execute plans counter to our security and public tranquility." It forbade the sale of all masks and disguises and the public use of masks whether on foot, on horseback, or within a carriage. It also banned all masked balls, both public and private.[8] The bans were an indication of what life would be in the new order: joyful, yes, but sober and dignified, too.

Within a week, the municipal Commune reviewed and forwarded these decrees to the Paris police bureau, which ordered a citywide ban on all masks and costumes. Its language was sweeping. "It is expressly forbidden for all individuals to disguise, travesty, or mask themselves in any manner whatsoever," Article 1 states, "whether in the streets, squares, or public parks, on penalty of arrest, unmasking on the spot, and immediate transport to the nearest district office." Violators faced jail or a heavy fine, with their masks and costumes impounded. Masked balls were expressly forbidden, with imprisonment threatened for any sponsor. The decree further forbade merchants from selling, renting, or displaying any mask or "clothes intended for disguise." Notices with its text soon appeared in major Paris newspapers.[9] Within a month, carnival masks had been abolished, with the faith that degrading acts unworthy of citizens' new status would disappear as well.

For the most part they did. The heavy presence of police, supplemented by the National Guard, had much to do with this. "We are confident that you will take all necessary measures . . . to prevent every evidence of trouble and disorder, whether in the *guingettes* and other dancing establishments, in the streets within Paris, or among its suburbs," the Paris mayor Jean Bailly wrote to the police bureau a week before Ash Wednesday. Bailly's personal note to Lafayette was more blunt. "I cannot omit reminding you that tomorrow, *jeudi gras*, is when the explosion of joy among the populace is the greatest of all the days of the year. You will surely agree with me that we must take extraordinary precautions to prevent all license. . . . I needn't remind you that such precautions must also be in force on the other *jours gras*."[10]

A similar pattern held in provincial cities, where mockery gave way to wholesome instruction. The watershed of 1789 took the bite out of displays that a year earlier would have been brazen. To revile religion and the nobility was suddenly virtuous rather than daring or irreverent. Burlesque figures were paraded alongside inspirational emblems, as in the town of Morteau, where busts of Voltaire and Rousseau and allegorical representations of Motherhood, Time, and Destiny shared the streets with mitered donkeys and derisive effigies of the king and queen. Citizens posed as Marie-Antoinette in rags, "priests" shed their robes to reveal the dress of sans-culottes, and "nuns" danced the Carmagnole.[11] Here the disguises were not dishonest, since the actors' patriotism was sincere. It was a twist that Rousseau couldn't have foreseen, despite his talk of transparency: revolutionary truth shone through faux queens and faux priests, with the spirit of deceit tamed and harnessed for public good.

The distance separating this domesticated carnival from the carnivalesque is evident in a small book published in 1791 by the writer Pierre-Louis Ginguéné. *On the Authority of Rabelais in the Present Revolution* held that the mad humor of the Renaissance satirist was a necessary response to tyranny. The bawdy chronicles of Pantagruel and Gargantua were allegorical, Ginguéné writes, with their meaning covered by a "somewhat transparent veil." "Under the exterior of foolishness, Rabelais carries a profound political and philosophical message. One must simply go to the trouble of finding it."[12]

This profound message was a satire on courtly society. Gargantua's education in the mud is Louis XIII in his frivolous minority. His fearful silence before an eloquent lowly page is the empty-headed duc de Berry tongue-tied before parlement. In this reading, Rabelais's "veil" is a corollary to the two-faced aristocrat in Perpignan. Just as Rabelais the truth-teller was forced to mask his truths in a time of tyranny, hypocritical aristocrats must deceive in the age of freedom. In Ginguéné's view, Rabelais's humor was far from liberating. In this he echoes other revolutionaries' opinions of carnival. The novels *Pantagruel* and *Gargantua* are "immoderate, obscure by design, obscene without joy, trivial, insignificant, and vulgar," he writes. "I've avoided rereading it and do not approve."[13] In Rabelais's own day, this was the only way to speak the truth, he asserts. Now liberty strides triumphant with its face uncovered and head held high.[14]

The serious fun that characterized Mardi Gras in Perpignan and Ginguéné's reading of Rabelais affirmed that the hierarchies carnival mocked no longer stood: the outlandishness that had once defied them was no longer needed. As the *Révolutions de Paris* wrote in a denunciation of carnival, "We are not buffoons." Joseph-Antoine Cérutti made a similar point in his *Letter on the Advantages and Origins of French Gaiety*. Frivolity thrives under despotism, Cérutti writes, while deep contentment—*le bonheur*—flourishes in freedom. "The spirit of amusement and repartee is ill-suited to the gravitas of the Republic. . . . Ridiculous trifles count for nothing among those concerned with the public good."[15] In a world of equals united in fraternal love, sincerity replaces clever banter. Ardor resists the mask.

Yet despite the early ordinances banning masks, they never really receded from the revolutionary imagination. Masks disappeared from the streets to resurface as a central figure in speeches, in print, and in the characterizations of conspirators both real and imagined. It was against the danger of masks that revolutionaries proposed reforms in dress, both to break fashion's implied hierarchies and to bring uniformity to the populace. As the Terror approached, masks multiplied in the minds of revolutionaries. Orators warned the nation of their treacherous ubiquity. That masks remained a threat so long after their physical banishment helps explain why any lasting transparency was never, and perhaps could never have been, achieved.

MASKED MOTIVES

Many aristocrats learned firsthand the many forms of disguise during the Revolution, when they were compelled to conceal their identity. Its success could mean the difference between life and death. When the moderate Girondin Condorcet fled arrest in 1794, he took the name Pierre Simon and disguised himself as a worker wearing the "carmagnole," a dark coat in coarse material. He made it to a small inn ten miles outside of Paris, where he was recognized, arrested, and spared certain execution only by suicide. One account of how he was recognized points to a single false note: a striped silk vest beneath his rough coat.[16]

Revolutionaries equated concealment with the aristocracy for good reason. Fashion history for the high-born, with its late-century craze for peasant girl dresses and *petit-hameau* rusticity, now repeated itself not as farce but as tragedy. Many nobles donned the clothes of the people in a headlong flight to the border. Within days of the Bastille's fall, journalists sympathetic to the Revolution sounded the alarm. A correspondent described what he witnessed on a provincial highway on July 16. "We saw a disguised hussar, a milkmaid whose pail was full of gold coins, and, a little beyond them, a nobleman dressed as a coachman. Our steps were surrounded by traps; even those who volunteered their services aroused our suspicions." A week later, the newspaper reported: "They are taking to the roads under different disguises. Women have assumed the clothes of men, and men are dressing as valets, artisans, and poor farmers."[17]

The memoirs of the marquise de Rochejaquelein, who remained in France after 1789, suggest that a single disguise was often insufficient. Dressed as "women of the people," she and her mother left Paris for the Vendée in late August 1792. Arriving in Châtillon-sur-Sèvre, she writes, "I dressed myself as a peasant woman from head to toe, choosing the most tattered clothes I could find." A year later in Savenay, she adopted the custom of its local peasants, wearing a purple woolen bonnet, yellow stockings, green broken-down slippers, and a thin bedspread for a cape, held around her neck by string. She regularly rubbed soil into her hands and arms to darken her white skin. Often on the run, she and her mother tried to pass as bourgeois relatives of a supposed protector in the area. When the Terror ended, the marquise was living in Nantes as a servant named Victoire Salgues.[18] Revolution-as-carnival had transformed her identity in a manner more complete than what any legislative act could have done.

Aristocratic disguise, coupled with long-standing associations linking elites with hypocrisy, fed a climate of fear, rumor, and suspicion. From learning of clandestine emigration to imagining counterrevolution by concealed aristocrats was a small step. The fear of conspiracy, often cast in the language of disguise, suffused the popular imagination: corrupt ministers were tampering with grain prices to engineer famines; predatory priests were feasting on young girls; a network of false beggars with artificial sores roamed the countryside. A letter from a shopkeeper in Lyon complained that aristocrats still held free rein in that city, "but the more there is resistance, the more my courage rises, and the more I persist in unmasking these vile creatures who think they are superior to those they are oppressing."[19]

The writer Antoine de Baecque calculates that in the first two years of the Revolution some forty newspapers appeared with the announced goal of exposing disguised aristocrats. Their very names convey vigilance: *The Observer, The French Observer, The Spectator, The Club of Observers, The Listener-at-Doors*. The journal *Rougyff, or The Forthright Sentinel* boasted of "a thousand eyes, a thousand telescopes with a single view trained on Paris, a million electrical wires that surround me, all capable of giving me the signal to leap to our rifles, our sabers, our canons." The *National Denouncer* vowed to "speak the truth and unveil every face."[20]

The discovery of disguised aristocrats aroused legitimate suspicion. The language of masking did its part to intensify distrust. The aristocratic plot, which was prominent in Jacobin thought in particular, may well have been in part what François Furet described as "the figment of a frenzied preoccupation with power." If so, it was understandable, given more than a century of sermons, plays, novels, and commentary linking courtly dissembling to elites. Vigilant observers denounced masks of patriotism, masks of solidarity, and masks of piety or generosity. "Behind the mask of popularity, beneath the clothes of the Nation, under the toga of the senator and the vestments of religion, they are sharpening the knives of vengeance," one wrote. Writers and actors were particularly distrusted, masters that they were of manipulating words and sentiments. "The language of liberty masks their inclinations."[21]

The language of masking and disguise did more to feed the cycle of denunciation and arrest during the French Revolution than any other figure of speech. Acts of public denunciation, typically associated with the Terror, came as early as 1789, and they owed much to contemporary discussions of concealment. Brought anew to popular consciousness by the exodus of nobles, the mask came to designate all enemies, real and imagined, as dissemblers, deceivers, and therefore "aristocrats." The extent and number of plots had no limit. Printed currency bore the words "The Nation Rewards Informants."

The journal *L'Ami du Peuple* contains numerous instances of what its editor Marat called "the art of unmasking skilled dissemblers." Any public administrator "who is corrupt or suspected of being corrupt must be unmasked. The door must be open to denunciation."[22] Defended by writers representing most every political position—men as varied in their views as Honoré Mirabeau, Camille Desmoulins, Louis-Sébastien Mercier, and Marat—denunciation was eventually enshrined by law as the duty of all who witnessed any offense against public safety or the life, liberty, or security of individuals.

Denunciation was the necessary complement to transparency, the imperative to tell all and hide nothing. Rousseau's vision for openness, shared among intimates in his fiction and sketched for society in *The Social Contract*, was an inspiration for revolutionaries intent on reforming human nature.[23] A citizen named Simond spelled out this vision of transparency at the Jacobin Club: "We need no more talking, no more correspondence, we need silent meetings where each divines in others' eyes what he has to do."[24] Sentimentalism fed the conviction. To display the recesses of one's heart in public was both natural and worthy. Because this demanded the very thing conspiracy exploited, willing vulnerability, transparency also bred suspicion. Perpetual publicity justified scrutiny, probing, and calling to account, particularly since this revolution required internal cleansing.

Schooled by novels, plays, and operas intended to arouse intense emotions, revolutionaries equated sincerity with virtue and readily made powerful emotions public. Revolutionary sentimentalism initially embraced all ranks through the notion that those who felt deeply were kindred souls, whatever their convictions. As the Bastille fell, witnesses described faces "wet with tears" and spirits "intoxicated with sentiment." The painter David captured the same heightened passion among representatives in the *Tennis Court Oath*.[25]

The course of events made sentimentalism explicitly ideological. Camille Desmoulins described the scene at the Jacobin Club when news came that the king and his family had been arrested trying to flee France. Robespierre declared his readiness to die for the cause of liberty, and "more than eight hundred rose as one . . . [offering] an admirable *tableau* by the fire of their words, the action of their hands, of the hats, of all their faces, and by the unexpectedness of this sudden inspiration." Another witness declared that "the holy enthusiasm of virtue" had suddenly gripped the assembly. The "kiss of Lamourette," when a bitterly divided assembly suddenly fell into fraternal embraces, was not exceptional.[26]

Revolutionary sentimentalism was seldom far from distrust. The individual's path from openness to paranoia had already been charted by Rousseau. It was now revisited by the nation, as the language of suspicion shaded into conspiracy. Speaking at the Jacobin Club, Robespierre lauded the deep feeling for justice and humanity evident among the populace but warned that its natural goodness made it prey to "political charlatans." A virtuous population is easily "baffled by specious pretexts" and "seduced by illusory acts of patriotism," he declared.[27] The historian David Andress looks to the popular stage for comparisons, writing that in the eyes of revolutionaries the people's virtue—"like the *ingénue* victim of a melodramatic villain"—harbored dangerous innocence.

Sentimentalism was also paired with blood. In a speech demanding a purge of political impostors in early 1792, Robespierre spoke of maternal love, protection, and benevolence. He then urged all "ardent and sensitive" souls to imagine themselves triumphant among the bloody corpses of counterrevolutionaries. A version of this imaginary scene played out a year later in the town of Clamecy, where Joseph Fouché was dispatched to enforce local Jacobin rule. In June, he reported on the lighthearted songs, happy dances, and sweet tears of its citizens just after a brutal campaign had killed hundreds of priests and former nobles.[28]

The coupling of transparency with suspicion was fully present in the Revolution's first Mardi Gras, when a journalist voiced his plea for openness with a single vivid phrase. "Our faces shouldn't be any more masked than our hearts." He then invoked the danger. "The enemies of our Revolution have for now dispersed, but with the mask's help they may soon return to this assembly of citizens, who are at ease and unsuspecting."[29] Another writer echoed the menace.

> Listen: we are in the midst of carnival, and we will have masks, yes, masks. It's useless that they tried to prohibit them, we will have them. The entire aristocratic cabal has decided to adopt the popular mask. Now princes, ministers, intendants, governors, counts, dukes, marquises, financiers, bishops, abbots, magistrates, bailiffs, and attorneys . . . will speak of humanity, and of equal rights, of morals and perhaps even virtue! . . . Citizens! spy, search out, expose these perverse beings. . . . These are your greatest enemies![30]

A writer for the *Journal des clubs*, a Jacobin newspaper, recounts having overheard a child ask her mother on Ash Wednesday why there were no more costumes. The writer responds: "You ask, 'Where are the masks?' when in fact they surround you. . . . Here are former tyrants and former slaves disguised as legislators fanning the flames of discord instead of making laws, and there, humiliated aristocrats, who have donned a popular costume, affecting a popular language, acting in a popular fashion."[31]

Like the fear of conspiracy and persistence of "aristocrats," unseen masks haunted revolutionary democracy. The best hope was to instruct citizens in how to spot enemies. Marat proposed posting guards at the city gates to inspect the hands of all entering and leaving: "The softness of the skin will suffice to announce a disguised traitor."[32] Nicolas de Bonneville, whose journal *Bouche de fer* described denunciation as the essence of democracy, gave a sketch of the perfect patriot. "His penetrating vision pierces masks and sees into hearts."[33] Such vigilance had its costs. Extending the reach of the mask so widely damaged, perhaps fatally, the prospects of unworried transparency. Whom can you trust when masking wears a mask?

GHOSTS OF MARDI GRAS

As the Revolution's second carnival season approached, a most unexpected pamphlet appeared bearing the title *Carnival, 1791: Public Notice*. No author is listed, nor is the place or date of publication given, but its language is unmistakably radical. This extraordinary notice is detailed in its application of Jacobin principles, and, in the spirit of serious fun, is unremittingly earnest. Jacobins have voted to celebrate carnival this year, it announces. Since celebration comes naturally to the French, a well-ordered masked ball is in order. In fact, two balls are announced, on the Monday and Tuesday before Lent at the Jacobin Club, where doors will open to the public when the National Assembly adjourns each evening.

How to avoid the ban on masks? The pamphlet offers a solution. "The club hastens to make public the list of members who will mask themselves." In this way, it will be "a ball for friends, a national ball, a truly patriotic ball."[34] The list of attendees bears thirty-four names, including the club's most prominent members. Their costumes will feature fishwives, a linen seller, Turkish muftis, song sellers, a boot scraper, a cart driver, and an apothecary. Others reward attention. Jean-Baptiste Target, the attorney who defended Cardinal de Rohan in the Diamond Necklace Affair, will come as a fat merchant woman summoned to the court. Charles Lameth, the Jacobin leader and former noble officer who fought in the American Revolution, will come dressed in black with a round hat and rapier inscribed "The Security of France." Armand Camus, who oversaw nationalizing Church property and helped write the Civil Constitution for clergy, will come as a defrocked monk with a satyr's head.

Other costumes reveal deeper connections. Docteur Guillotin, who had introduced the machine for executions a year earlier, will come selling herbs and wearing a death mask. The journalists Danton, Marat, and Desmoulins will dress as bulldogs. The abbé Grégoire, who renounced the First Estate to join the Third, will dress in "a well-known costume, Judas." Robespierre will appear as a ghost "in a long white robe with a veil over his head." A chilling note follows: "One is urged not to be afraid. It is the last time this mask will appear."[35] As psychological indicators, the costumes are eloquent in this formative period of Jacobin principles. Some seem to offer an intimate glimpse of motive and character. This is deliberate. The *Public Notice* is a hoax published in the spirit of carnival against the men who had banned it. No such event was ever planned or took place.

An effect of the 1790 ban on masks was the appearance of lampoons that drew on the clichés of carnival. Forcing the holiday off the streets gave it new life underground. While the tone of such pamphlets varies widely—from farce to wit to pure viciousness—all are executed with relish. The irony that a revolution more sweeping than any carnival reversal had banned the holiday was not lost on these authors. In this transformed political landscape, the mask became a teller of truth. It offered a glimpse into motive through the lens of ridicule. Hence Grégoire as Judas, Camus as a lascivious monk, and Robespierre in a white sheet—every adolescent's best effort at being scary—asking for the public's trust. Another, more pointed, message is embedded in these satires. In the charged atmosphere of denunciation, the mask was code for conspiracy. In this way, the pamphlets carried a deadly serious indictment, often against revolutionaries themselves.

In the beginning, royalist satires substantially outnumbered those from the left. These were more often a ribbing than an outright attack. The first of two spoofs in the counterrevolutionary periodical *Actes des Apôtres* is cast as a dispatch from "The Revolutionary Club." Despite the recent ban on masks, it announces, a great ball has just been held in the Pantheon. Robespierre dressed in the virginal robes of a choirboy, and the abbé Grégoire danced the fandango with Talleyrand in a dark corner. Both were dressed as Muslim mystics.[36] The piece is preposterous, but it succeeds in trivializing its subjects. When the lawyer Target mounts a tightrope and receives a huge inverted pyramid from Sieyès to balance on the tip of his finger ("an ingenious emblem for the Constitution"), everything comes crashing to the ground. Target flees, confusion spreads, the room catches on fire, and revelers rush home in fear for their lives, "covered in filth, unrecognizable and disgusting."[37]

A second satire in the *Actes* turned the image of a hypocritical nobleman on its head. A patriotic wig maker has discovered a counterrevolutionary plot among his curling papers that details plans for "all the most terrible aristocrats" to launch their coup from the Opera ball. Each traitor will wear a recognizable disguise. An honest prelate will mask himself as Talleyrand. The most humane aristocrat will come disguised as Barnave, the most virtuous as Mirabeau, the wisest as Montmorency, and the least cutting as Guillotin. The most charming woman will come as Mme de Staël, and the man with the greatest dignity will disguise himself as Robespierre.[38]

The royalist press soon grew more savage in its spoofs. *The Jacobite Carnival* describes a ball at the Jacobin Club, where the walls are painted red—"the color of Foulon's blood" (a reference to the royal administrator beheaded in the street)—and the interior is lit principally by mirrors, "because mirrors, as you know, figure not a little in the new constitution."

Maskers sit at a great table as waiters serve them the heads of those recently guillotined. Jacobins plunge in greedily with knives and forks. All amusement ends when the maskers begin to throw up. "You have no idea, my friend, of the abominations that these wretches vomited up, especially Marat, Desmoulins, and Prudhomme."[39] It's worth noting that the Terror, with its steady diet of decapitations, was still three years in the future when this pamphlet was published.

Carnival literature from the left was typically more didactic. A carnival story in *Père Duchesne*, Jacques Hébert's radical journal, carries the message that masks mean counterrevolution. The narrator of "Shit-Abed" crashes a noble ball held in defiance of the ban on masks. Disguised as a German prince, he gains information from a duchess seated next to him about plans to overturn the Revolution.

> Despite all the *fucks* and *goddamns* I let fly, nobody suspected me. When it comes to drinking and smoking and swearing, the Père Duchesne is no worse than a German prince. The duchess jutted out her goddamned pointy chin and her eyes grew as round as a cat pissing in the gutter. Then she told me all their secrets.[40]

An army of émigrés will invade France, the duchess confided, and the king will initiate mass slaughter with his own hands. Others showed him their knives, freshly sharpened for the National Assembly.

> When I'd heard all these vile plans and every one of these fucking bastards had unveiled his goddamned soul to me, I told them who I was. I'd have been lost if I'd been alone, but when I gave the word a crowd of fishwives rushed in, and we all pounded the shit out of this god-damned lantern-prey, shouting at the top of our lungs, "*Chienlits! Chienlits!*"[41]

The force of this fantasy comes in its torrent of insults. None would have taken it seriously, but the absurdity carries a dark reminder that aristocrats were duplicitous, that the mask was their habitual costume, and that, given half a chance, they would slit the throat of any honest citizen.

This was how carnival proved useful long after masks were banned. Recast as weapons, masks settled scores, questioned motives, and warned of plots. Such pamphlets were a potent way to mock power through laughter. But were they in fact carnivalesque? Not entirely. Carnival was the setting but not the vehicle of their mockery. Its revelers were hypocrites and deceivers, while their masks told the truth. In this sense, the spoofs were another means of discrediting carnival.

There was at least one true rebel among carnival polemicists, however, a genuinely anarchic voice whose short book was faithful to carnival's lawless spirit. The Reasonable Fool—the name this anonymous author gives himself on the title page—leaves no party or position unscathed. The king, queen, and six-year-old dauphin are pilloried, clerics derided, and forty-eight members of the National Assembly named, each with an absurd costume. The last word in this black hilarity is derision, the last image one vulgar, irreverent soul: the indestructible Père Duchesne, who scatters ash on an entire deluded nation. It is a rare instance of the carnivalesque in a Revolution that otherwise smothered it with sincerity. The book's central showpiece is a speech by the Ghost of Mardi Gras before the National Assembly. Exiled by France's legislators and disgusted by the falseness all around, he mounts the tribune. Liars and frauds, the ghost begins, you who have invented this constitutional masquerade, you who applaud the city's attempt to destroy me, you who think that pleasure can be forbidden: heaven will have its vengeance![42]

With this, the ghost relates his vision of carnival, a vast, fantastical ceremony parading its madness through Paris. A chariot bears the drunken Louis XVI, who sits astride a wine barrel with leaves in his hair. Marie-Antoinette follows as the queen of the bacchants, drunk with pleasure and exposing her body to the leering crowd. Sparsely clad ladies of the court dance wildly around her beating tambourines and jabbing the air with thyrsi. The six-year-old dauphin is dressed as Cupid, and princes of the blood follow in clothes of thieves, rag pickers, monkeys, and satyrs.

At the Champ de Mars, General Shit-Abed, commander of the National Guard, is dressed as a woman with beauty spots and makeup; his soldiers prance about in dresses with ribbons in their hair. Priests bless the champagne and brioche, and the nation gets drunk on Holy Communion. More maskers appear: judges, officers, and municipal officials, men as women and women as children. The crowd makes its drunken way to the Hôtel de Ville, where the entire assembly begins a frenzied dance, heaving and pitching in wild exhilaration. At six in the morning, a nearly unconscious Louis XVI mumbles that it is time to receive the smudge of Ash Wednesday. The nation greets the first light of this holy day in a stumbling, staggering parade to the Palais-Royal, where the Père Duchesne waits with his stinking pipe and sailor's cap.

The king kneels before the sooty celebrant, who, stroking his forehead with a black cinder, will intone gravely,

> "You fucking French monarch, remember that you were once King, and that your idiocy and infirmity have reduced you to nothing, but that you may one day yet be King if you can ever get it up again."

Marie Antoinette presents herself, the Père Duchesne views her askance, and then he drops this morsel:

> "Listen, you bitch of a million bitches, remember King David, who after committing adultery covered himself with sackcloth and ash. Imitate his repentance. More to the point: *memento mulier quia pulvis est, et in pulverem reverteris*."[43]

MASKS AND THE TERROR

To attain true transparency among citizens after 1789 and lift the mask of appearances once and for all would mean reforming dress. While the letter of sumptuary laws announcing social position was now largely neglected, their spirit in officialdom persisted: in the long robe for the law and short robe for finance, the magistrate's soutane and scarlet gown, the violet gowns of royal counselors, short black gowns of clerks, and so on. From the revolutionaries' point of view, silks and breeches were akin to costumes intended to fabricate esteem. The coupling of such garments with deceit was evident in revolutionaries' debate over a proposal to forbid the customary dress of religious orders. "Do the police not prohibit masks and cockades that might be a sign of a party opposed to the Revolution?" the law's author, the former Bishop Torné, asked. "If the simple clothing of a citizen is susceptible to a multitude of wise regulations, would not religious costumes, which can entail so many abuses, also be submitted to police rule?"[44]

When delegates to the Estates General in 1789 appeared in traditional garb, there was instant resistance. The nobility wore black silk trimmed in silver and gold, while the Third Estate wore black fabric; the nobility wore magnificent plumed hats and lace cravats, while the Third Estate wore unadorned tricornes and muslin cravats. "Absurd," wrote Jean-Baptiste Salaville in a letter to Mirabeau, "ridiculous . . . the height of despotism and debasement." Maintaining distinctions among orders through dress is "the original sin of our nation," he added. Pledging to wear whatever he wished to the sessions, another deputy called this clothing an "indecent masquerade."[45]

In October 1789, the National Assembly granted French citizens the right to dress as they wished. Chateaubriand describes visiting a salon where men in wigs and silk stockings rubbed shoulders with bareheaded guests wearing styles from England and America. The British traveler John Moore was astonished to see a young nobleman at the theater dressed as "a violent democrat . . . in boots, [with] his hair cropt and his whole dress slovenly."[46] As with the lifting of censorship in the press and onstage, this legislation presented a dilemma. What if citizens wished to wear emblems of the old order? The general climate of suspicion, coupled with the Revolution's powerful pressures for universal equality, made citizens into connoisseurs of fashion well before Jacobin committees were interrogating intentions. The 1790 *National and Anecdotal Dictionary* defined silver buckles as "superfluous ornaments designating an aristocrat or an egoist with a heart of bronze."[47]

In this context, clothes grew politicized to an extent never before seen. The effect was not to repudiate the equation of clothes and character that had been so objectionable at the Estates General. Rather, the correlation remained but with different points of reference. Particular details—precious buckles, for instance, or a silk vest—revealed nobility. Cloth rosettes or simple breeches confirmed revolutionary virtue.[48] Over the decade, legislators elaborated a new vision of legibility by dress, whose roots shared the dual lineage of early laws linking clothes to status and the new imperative for openness. In late 1791, J. F. Duval, a deputy to the Legislative Assembly, proposed requiring clerics to wear a badge on their left breast reading "Priest, guilty of sedition." Others called for prostitutes to wear a green and red sash. Louis de Saint-Just proposed that soldiers sew golden stars on their uniforms over their wounds. Legislators wore a brass star covered with white enamel and embossed with tables of the law.[49] What are the clothes of utopia? Pure, unmediated signifiers, with perfect legibility.

A pair of examples shows the force of these convictions. When the twenty-year-old Cécile Renault was questioned about a plot to assassinate Robespierre, her accusers charged that she was dressed too well to be the daughter of a Parisian paper maker. They led her from the courtroom, stripped her of her clothes, dressed her in rags, and recommenced the interrogation. When a M. Huguenin was arrested for wearing the allegedly noble attire of an apple-green suit with pearl buttons, he proclaimed his innocence: "I'm not the one in prison. It's my clothes!"[50] Closing the gap between essence and appearance was in part the motive for reviving the law forbidding men from dressing as women. Proposed by Bertrand Barère and passed by the Convention in August 1793, it now made cross-dressing a capital crime.[51]

Two months later, the Convention reaffirmed the law forbidding women from dressing as men, a prohibition that revolutionary patrols actively enforced. Arrests included a runaway named Sophie who lived in the quarries near Passy, a woman named Marie-Anne who said she had wished to attend the opera alone, and a twenty-year-old named Euphrasie who told the police that she dressed as a man because it made her happy. Similar laws against cross-dressing would be reissued under Napoleon and remain in force throughout the nineteenth century.[52]

The most recognizable tokens of patriotism were liberty caps and cockades, both of which provoked conflict. Wearing the rosette was originally elective. Royalists baited zealots by ripping it from their clothes or sporting black ones of their own. The cockade gained such significance that the Legislative Assembly eventually made it a crime to appear in public without one, first for men, in the summer of 1792, and a year later for women. Separate legislation specified its fabric (wool, not silk) and size. The Phrygian bonnet was the cause of fistfights and an instrument of conversion. The image of the king forced to don the cap is an icon of the Revolution. The exercise was repeated, often roughly, in public gardens and on the street. When rumors circulated that royalists planned to introduce green bonnets in order to provoke revolutionaries, the *Révolutions de Paris* offered a dire observation. "Too often a mere difference of color suffices to inspire diverse opinions, and then hatred, and at last massacre. All this over the shape of a hat or some nuance in clothes."[53]

Over time, many came to see freedom of dress as a danger to the Republic. Silver buckles, black cockades, and green bonnets carried potential menace. Clothing had become a nightmare of endlessly multiplying signs: so many heads not covered by red bonnets, so many hats not adorned with the cockade, so many breeches not loose and flapping like those of the good sans-culottes. Jacques Hébert warned of plots hatched by youths in checkered coats and tight breeches, which he called the costume of subversion.[54] The more clothes were purified, the greater suspicions grew.

The logic pointed toward uniforms. The ultimate expression of a politics of sincerity, national uniforms represent the terminal point in a path that began with banning masks. They are at the far end of a continuum whose opposite pole is disguise. Disguise is deceit. Masks offer concealment, but the concealment is visible. Freedom of dress conveys liberty but risks division. Uniforms alone eliminate ambiguity. Better than tolerating difference in perfect transparency, conformity assures equality.[55] In 1792, the painter Jacques-Louis David prepared a series of sketches for a national uniform. The style looked vaguely Spanish, with a jacket and tight trousers, a sleeveless coat and short cloak, pistols, a sword, and a round hat with feathers. Later the same year, the Girondin deputy Rabaut de Saint-Étienne offered another set of designs.[56]

Another impetus came two years later from the Société Populaire et Républicaine des Arts, which issued a public call for yet more proposals. The society envisioned clothing that would join the practical with the patriotic. "National attire will meet the goal, so essential for free men," the society reasoned, "of evoking our country everywhere and at all times. French citizens will no longer be confused with peoples from nations still crushed under shackles of servitude."[57]

David drew up new designs, now with variations that would identify civic status. These included two uniforms for civilians, two for representatives, one for judges, one for legislators, one for municipal officials, and one for the military. Preparations followed in May 1794 to distribute 6,000 sets of instructions nationwide for legislative and the military uniforms and 20,000 for civilian dress. With Robespierre's fall two months later, the project collapsed. It is far from certain that the uniforms would have had their intended effect. The *Révolutions de Paris* had noted that the red bonnet itself might be worn "as though a mask . . . to poison even the most healthy of revolutions." It later warned the public of "false sans-culottes who are slipping in amongst you, adopting your manners and putting on your clothes the better to betray you."[58] Compliance was no guarantee of assent.

The same fear that had persisted from the earliest debates over dress—that seeming conformity could harbor deceit—fueled the preoccupation with masks during the Terror. As Saint-Just remarked, "Counterrevolutionaries don't dare show themselves but have assumed instead all the forms of patriotism." Robespierre declared that traitors conceal their motives "under the form of democracy in order to dishonor it by fatal, absurd setbacks, and to smother it in its cradle." He used similar terms in his denunciation of Danton, Hébert, and Brissot in the name of the people in May 1794: "The conspiracy has disguised itself in the trappings of a perfidious moderation that, while harboring crime and assassinating virtue, would lead us down a hidden though certain path to tyranny."[59]

Far from being incidental to the Terror, unmasking was its principal means of identifying enemies. It furnished a credible script for framing accusations. Conclusions drawn from efforts to reform dress were directly relevant. Revolutionary virtue expected uniformity, whose very conformism fed a self-devouring skepticism. How else to explain the language used to denounce such figures as Jacques Roux, who addressed the Convention in summer 1793 with a group of sans-culottes at his side, or the Hébertistes, whose speech was impeccably republican? "A man cloaked in the mantle of patriotism, and whom the people believed worthy of being their interpreter, has insulted the majesty of the national Convention," Robespierre responded after Roux's appearance.[60]

Sentimentalism played its part in the dynamic, as displays of political conviction brought ever more passionate responses. The Law of Suspects in September 1793, for instance, cast under suspicion those who "have not constantly demonstrated their attachment to the Revolution." Because all knew that feelings could be feigned, the effort was increasingly hard to sustain. For the historian William Reddy, such displays generated self-doubt and an impulse to accuse others. Reddy imagines the reasoning:

> Sincere expression is the root of virtue, and virtue is necessary to the defense of the Revolution. I have sincerity and my thoughts are virtuous; therefore, those who disagree with me are insincere "monsters" and merit death. . . . Am I being sincere?

Faced with such laws, Reddy writes, many felt hypocritical. "Targeting others was a means of deflecting suspicion; and it did not matter whom one targeted, since all were guilty."[61]

At each moment that it seemed on the brink of unanimity, the populace had a disturbing tendency to produce traitors. In an extraordinary speech to the Convention in March 1794, Saint-Just came to the conclusion that the battle was no longer between revolutionaries and aristocrats. It was between the revolutionary and his dangerous lookalike. This was his rationale: if someone in the old order had run through the streets shouting, "Down with the King!" he would surely have been arrested. Dissenters therefore kept quiet. Yet we know that dissenters existed in the old order, just as they do today.[62] The absence of dissent, in other words, confirms the presence of dissent. "Let us no longer judge men by their words or their deeds," Saint-Just concluded. "In a matter of days, you will receive a dossier on persons who have conspired against the country. The criminal factions will be unmasked. We have surrounded them."[63]

With the mask now a defining figure of political discourse, individuals, parties, and positions receded in importance. The country consisted of the people and its single enemy, conspiracy, whose false face was identical to that of the people. "Among individuals, it is difficult to distinguish those who belong to one or another of the factions," Robespierre said in a speech directed variously against Fabre d'Églantine, unnamed foreign agents, and a diverse group that included Hébert and Desmoulins. "The important thing is to grasp their goal and its effects: you will see that these factions draw near one another and fuse."[64]

Desmoulins and Hébert were part of a single plot, Robespierre argued, even if their convictions differed. "A few skilled stagehands are hidden in the wings operating the machinery silently behind the scenes. At base it is the same faction as that of the Gironde, except with different actors. Or, rather, it is still the same actors but they are now wearing different masks. But it is the same stage, and always the same drama."[65]

Robespierre's language describing all opponents the same in their deceit was a final role for the mask. Since 1789, it had moved progressively deeper into the political fabric even as it disappeared from society. With each step it grew less visible and ever more ineradicable. Banished from carnival, it reappeared in pamphlets to expose the enemy's true nature. Forbidden as an incitement to degrading frivolity, it was found lurking in the words of false friends and the deceptively populist dress of plotters. As the satires of 1790 and '91 gave way to denunciations and arrests in 1794, the mask became the figure for any faction that secretly opposed the people, a permanent though still more dangerous disguise now that everyone claimed to speak for the people.

Is it any wonder, then, that when members of the Convention mounted their coup against Robespierre in July they used the language of the mask? "Robespierre is right: we should tear the mask from every face we find wearing it," Billaud-Varenne announced from the tribune on the afternoon of 8 Thermidor, "and if it is true that we can no longer enjoy freedom of opinion, then I would rather my dead body serve as this tyrant's throne than be an accomplice to his crimes through my silence." Collot d'Herbois declared that it was time to unmask Saint-Just. Philippe Rühl, swept up in the chaos in the small hours of the 9th, cried, "Let's go, let's unmask the wretches or have our own heads presented to the Convention."

Later that day J. L. Tallien, receiving word of the arrest of Saint-Just, Robespierre, and fifteen others, announced the return of sincerity. "A little while ago I demanded that the veil be torn away. I have just learned with delight that it has been done, that the conspirators have been unmasked, that they will be annihilated. Now liberty will triumph."[66]

The mask's many meanings in the five years between the fall of the Bastille and the end of the Terror owed much to particular conditions: aristocratic migration produced and multiplied disguise, a polemical war in pamphlets and the press questioned opponents' motives, and there were genuine threats to the new regime from within and abroad. Framing it all, however, was the long association of concealment with elites. This legacy framed and intensified more immediate circumstances, investing events with familiar associations and providing language to make sense of them. The figure of the mask was especially potent because of associations formed a century earlier at Versailles and diffused throughout society.

The years following Thermidor brought the gradual return of festivity and public celebration. Although carnival and its costumes reappeared in the Directory, masks remained forbidden until 1805. Remnants of revolutionary transparency endured, sometimes in telling ways. David designed new attire for Directors with blue ribbons, a Roman sword, and plumed hats. The press called the clothes absurd, but in David's view ancient styles were needed: a wide range of contemporary attire was now politically tainted.[67]

Both features of the Revolution's resistance to masks—its ideal of openness and preoccupation with deceit—would survive into the Romantic age.

The popularity of balls made the mask a common possession. In the same years, Balzac, Daumier, and Hugo made a new master of disguise, the professional criminal, the era's defining figure. The mask was both domesticated and criminalized, an explosive combination of thrill and menace that proved enormously appealing to the bourgeoisie.

A foretaste of these new associations came in an obituary that appeared shortly after Robespierre's death. It was an indication of how complex the revolutionaries' early resistance to masks had become and an acknowledgment of still deeper sources of concealment. "He was crime incarnate," the notice read. "He covered his eyes with spectacles to keep people from reading into his soul."[68] Later generations would discover on their own just how hard it is to unmask the heart.

PART THREE

The Body

Phrenological Heads, 1831 (Art Resource)

The art of concealment is so advanced in our current state of civilization that we give our trust to others almost by chance. The greater a man's deceit, the more likely he is to assume the tone and look of an honest soul incapable of fraud. In such a state of affairs, experience is imperative . . . yet it is clear that such experience comes too late.

—F.-J.-V. BROUSSAIS, *Lectures on Phrenology* (1836)

"It's true," Di Blasi said, "every society produces the particular kind of imposture that suits it best, so to speak."

—LEONARDO SCIASCIA, *The Council of Egypt* (1963)

7
Century of Shadows

THE SELF-MADE MAN

When François Vidocq arrested Pierre Coignard for usurpation of titles in early summer 1818, it was a victory of disguise over imposture. Coignard had been on the run since December, when his comfortable life as André-Pierre de Pontis, comte de Saint-Hélène, came to a sudden end through a secret door in his bedroom closet. He had been a model noble officer, with the prestige that came from having escaped the Revolution, thrived abroad, and returned triumphant with the restored monarchy. The record spoke for itself. He had commanded troops in Buenos Aires, served alongside Maréchal Soult with Napoleon's army in Spain, and, after Waterloo, joined Louis XVIII to reenter France.

For the past three years, he had been master of the king's troops in Paris as Commandant of the 74th Legion of the Seine. The testimony of twelve battle scars and a long list of titles announced his merit: Chevalier of Alcantara, aide-de-camp to the duc d'Angoulême, Chevalier of the Légion d'Honneur, and recipient of the Cross of Saint-Louis, bestowed by the king himself. With his wife at his side, Rosa Maria Marcen de Suera, comtesse de Saint-Hélène, the count graced the choicest salons of the Restoration.

In fall 1817, his luck ran out. Fresh out of prison, an ex-convict named Darius happened to pass through the Place Vendôme as Pontis was reviewing troops. Darius thought he recognized the man. He asked questions, learned where Pontis lived, and knocked on his door with a promise not to expose him if he helped with a job. Pontis claimed not to know the man and turned him out. Darius went straight to the police. The chance sighting in the Place Vendôme was to be fateful. It initiated a sequence of events that shook the French Ministries of War and Justice, embarrassed the crown,

FIGURE 7.1. *The False André-Pierre de Pontis, comte de Saint-Hélène*, anon. (Bibliothèque nationale de France)

and returned Pierre Coignard to the very place he and Darius had first met, chained to a wall in the prison of Toulon.[1]

To contemporaries, Coignard's audacity was astonishing. The *Journal des débats* called his feat singular. "A man who by all appearances basked in public esteem and possessed numerous titles was discovered to be the ringleader of thieves."[2] In fact, the ruse was not unique. Versions of Coignard's feat were multiplying both in the criminal underworld and among the high circles he briefly inhabited. He and other impostors thrived on conditions that favored a particular kind of deceit. The self-made man—made honestly or not—could now be on equal footing with the well-born son.

Officials investigating the explosive claims of Darius had to proceed with care. Pontis enjoyed influence in Louis XVIII's court and was respected among officers. Without proof, any suggestion that he was a criminal could be career-ending. The War Ministry's judicial division quietly gathered information about the commandant's personal life. He was just shy of forty-three, his wife Rosa was of "extreme virtue," and they had a three-year-old son. They lived in modest circumstances on the rue de l'Échiquier and received few visitors. His conduct was above reproach.[3]

Yet there were anomalies. Pontis's file contained letters from a mayor in the Vendée who reported that the officer had once requested a copy of his baptismal record. The original was destroyed during the Revolution, Pontis had told him. For his trouble, the mayor could expect a Cross of Saint-Louis and a place for his son in the officer corps. When the official found no evidence that such a family had ever lived in the region, he conveyed this curious request to the prefect, who forwarded the report to Paris. When it arrived, there had been no reason to doubt Pontis's claim that he was born in Soissons to noble parents on November 20, 1774. Members of the War Ministry now reread the report with interest.[4]

Other details attracted investigators' attention, including a recent series of letters from Pontis to France's War Minister. They followed no clear logic. He requested a promotion in the officers' ranks; he was due back pay and wanted immediate compensation; he asked to be posted in Guadeloupe. Between midsummer 1816 and November 1817, just weeks after Darius appeared at his door, there were five such requests. Referring to himself in the third person, Pontis rehearsed his twenty-seven years of service, numerous wounds, and inviolable attachment to the king. Such was "the highest evidence of his zeal," he wrote, "which numbers him among the most faithful subjects ever to fill the duties entrusted to him by your Excellency."[5] Individually the petitions were unremarkable. In light of the accusation, they suggested alarm.

On December 5, General Hyacinthe Despinois, senior officer of the War Ministry's investigative unit, summoned Pontis to his office. Baron de l'Horme de l'Ile, Chief of Military Police, was also present. Despinois greeted Pontis with a barrage of questions about his birth, family, titles, and war record. Who were his parents? When and where did they die? Could he produce letters from them? Pontis related the outlines of his life. His father was a French count, and his mother was Argentinian. His parents left France for Buenos Aires when he was three or four, where he lived until he was fifteen. He was an only child and knew little about his extended family. After his mother's death in 1790, he and his father returned to Paris, where they soon grasped the threat the Revolution posed to aristocrats like them.

He and his father therefore immigrated to Madrid and from there took a ship to Buenos Aires, where he joined the Spanish army and attained the rank of sub-lieutenant. Transferred to Spain in 1810, he was promoted to lieutenant colonel. He led troops against Napoleon's invading armies, was captured, and, possessing valuable information about Spanish plans, defected to the French. Maréchal Soult recognized his stature and protected him. In summer 1813 he entered France as a member of Soult's general staff.[6]

Despinois asked him about his titles. Could he produce his commission as lieutenant colonel? Could he produce the citation naming him Chevalier of the Order of Alcantara? Could he produce the brevet from Maréchal Soult naming him Commandant of the 100th Regiment? Did he possess a single official document naming the soldiers he had commanded or officers he had fought with in Buenos Aires? Pontis gave the same reply to each question: "My commissions and all my belongings were lost in the retreat from Saragossa." Despinois pressed him on gaps and contradictions, which Pontis blamed on a careless secretary and his own faulty memory. When asked, he emphatically denied promising a village mayor the Cross of Saint-Louis in exchange for baptismal papers.

Despinois then asked if he understood the gravity of usurping titles. "Are you aware that in such a case neither your military position nor the honorific gifts His Majesty has bestowed on you will shield you from the law?"[7] Pontis was indignant but kept his composure. He insisted that he was a French émigré born to noble parents in Soissons. Documents confirming this, he said, were at his home.

The testimony Pontis gave is confirmed on every point in an 1813 document now held in the archives of the French War Ministry. The *État des Services et Campagnes de M. André-Pierre de Pontis* certifies twenty-three years of continuous military service beginning in 1790 under the Spanish crown in Buenos Aires and continuing, from 1811, with French forces. According to this record, Lieutenant Colonel Pierre de Pontis led Spanish troops in two separate engagements against British forces in Buenos Aires and took some eighty prisoners. It notes commissions received from the marqués de Soler Mentès, the comte de Lignière, and Maréchal Soult. A separate report from 1817 recognizes twenty-four campaigns and twelve battlefield injuries. It salutes Pontis's "very honorable military service."[8]

Despinois rejected Pontis's offer to return the next day with his documents and instead demanded an immediate inventory. From his office, he arranged for an armed guard to escort him, the baron de l'Horme, Pontis, and a recording clerk directly to the officer's home. As his three guests entered the sitting room, Pontis apologized for his appearance. The interview had been long; he was uncomfortable and needed fresh clothes. "He began to undress in front of me," de l'Horme wrote five weeks later in a futile effort to have his dismissal reversed. "As he changed his undergarments, he stepped into an alcove next to his bed and pulled the door shut, which until then had stood open. I could not have imagined that at the back of that alcove, hidden behind the wallpaper, was a secret door." Seconds later, a downstairs door slammed shut. De l'Horme rushed into the room to find the alcove empty. He sent his gendarme into the street, but it was too late. The commander of the Paris division of royal troops had escaped.[9]

MASTER OF DISGUISE

François Vidocq was in his sixth year as director of the secretive *Brigade de Sûreté*, an investigative unit within the Paris police, when he was ordered to find André-Pierre de Pontis. Two weeks after his disappearance, the War Ministry notified police that it had strong reason to believe the supposed count was in fact an escaped convict. Pierre Coignard, the investigators related, had served five years in prison for forced entry and burglary. New charges included forgery of public documents and "usurpation of both titles and civil status, to the suppression of his own."[10]

Vidocq was an ex-convict who now worked for the law. Police Commissioner Jean Henry had hired him on the premise that it took a thief to catch a thief. "These individuals are of the greatest utility for policing Paris, above all after a disastrous war, which, while blessedly over, brought a great number of criminals into the capital," Henry observed.[11] Vidocq's initial brigade of six eventually grew to twenty-eight men and women, all ex-cons who kept a foot in the underworld. Vidocq's detractors said that they had never really left it.

In his own best-selling memoirs, Vidocq boasted of the many disguises he employed as head of this motley team. He was a dandy in the gambling halls of the Palais-Royal, a charcoal carrier in the city's markets, and a proper gentleman in the city's cafés and salons. At the height of his celebrity, he was received by a credulous King Louis-Philippe as an ancient duchess from the Faubourg Saint-Germain. "A day did not pass without important discoveries," Vidocq later wrote. "There were no crimes, committed or planned, whose circumstances were not revealed to me. I was everywhere, I knew everything."[12] Finding a missing count would be easy.

New crimes were added to Coignard's warrant. Just months after his escape, the home of General Pedro Marti, a Spaniard now living in Paris, was robbed. The thieves took money, silver, linen, the general's uniforms, and a Cross of the Légion d'Honneur. General Marti reported two suspicious visits weeks earlier from an elegant Spanish lady who called herself

FIGURE 7.2. *François Vidocq*, anon. (Bibliothèque nationale de France)

the comtesse de Saint-Hélène. Her coachman, he recalled, had shown an unusual interest in the building's exterior.

The following month, Coignard's younger brother Alexandre was arrested with a set of burglars' tools inside a banker's offices on the rue de la Paix. He was recognized as the comtesse de Saint-Hélène's liveried coachman. In late May, a botched robbery left a thief named Lexcellent in the hands of the police. Under questioning, he revealed that Pierre Coignard was the head of a criminal band he belonged to and that Coignard's house at the edge of Paris was their center of operations.[13] The day after Lexcellent's arrest, Vidocq stationed twelve agents in street clothes near the house.

Disguised as a fruit seller from Les Halles, he knocked on the door. When there was no answer, he forced his way in to see Rosa escape through a back garden. As he dragged her back, she screamed that he and his dirty spies had no business treating a gentlewoman so roughly. Vidocq replied that the daughter of a Spanish tinker had no business assuming airs with him. Inside the house, agents found skeleton keys, jewels, artworks, wigs, false mustaches, knives, and pistols.

Vidocq stayed with Rosa while his men fanned out to watch the streets. At nightfall, an agent donned one of Rosa's dresses, lit a lamp in her bedroom, and stood before the window. The trick worked. Coignard and an associate named Soffiet returned and were instantly surrounded by Vidocq's men. Coignard fired two shots, injuring an agent in the hand. He was thrown to the ground, and Vidocq stomped him into submission. He was carrying gold worth 3,200 francs and General Marti's Cross of the Légion d'Honneur.

Both Coignard and Vidocq had come to crime in the turmoil of the Revolution. Coignard, older by five years, was eighteen when the Bastille fell. Born in the Loire valley, where his family raised grapes, Coignard was the first of fourteen children. Records at the Toulon prison give 1770 as the year of his birth. He apprenticed as a hat maker and fought in the revolutionary army. He was arrested for theft at thirty-one and sentenced to fourteen years. He may have been married to a woman named Délaïde Lordot at the time of his arrest; she died in the prison of Saint-Lazare in the 1810s. His features were fine and plausibly aristocratic. He stood five feet, four inches and had a broad forehead, chestnut hair, thick brown sideburns, and an aquiline nose. His eyes were gray and his chin more pointed than round.[14]

In the fifth year of his sentence, he escaped prison and fled to Spain, where he met Rosa Marcen, a tailor's daughter. In Catalonia, he joined a criminal ring led by his brother Louis. Through either stealth or persuasion, he gained access to personnel records inside the Spanish War Ministry, where he found the dossier of an officer who had fought in Buenos Aires and whose age and features were close to his own. He altered the officer's name to read André-Pierre de Pontis and added his own identifying physical details, including each of his scars. He then replaced the file.[15]

Sometime after 1808, Coignard returned to the ministry, introduced himself as the French noble André-Pierre de Pontis, and claimed to have served the Spanish throne in Buenos Aires. He said that he wished to reenlist as an officer. The falsified dossier was located and declared to be in order. Soon Lieutenant Colonel de Pontis was commanding Spanish forces against the French. From the start, his performance was exemplary, earning him knighthood in the ancient Order of Alcantara and commendation for an unrealized plan to ambush the French camp. In 1811, he was arrested by Spanish authorities for theft. He escaped and, in early 1814, crossed over to the French side, where he presented himself to the general staff as an aristocratic émigré ready to serve his country. He was soon made commandant. He was likely present at the battle of Waterloo. Once Napoleon's defeat was certain, he hastened to join Louis XVIII in Ghent, where he was received with the gratitude and pomp befitting an officer who had deserted the emperor for the sake of the king.

Once in France, he set about procuring a baptismal certificate to affirm his identity. Having failed in the Vendée, he traveled to Soissons, where he hosted local notables to a lavish luncheon. Here he rehearsed the circumstances of his birth and childhood in Soissons and escorted those willing to vouch for him to the notary public. In 1814, he received the Légion d'Honneur; in 1815, he was given command of the 74th Legion of the Seine; and in 1816, he was named Chevalier of the Order of Saint-Louis. One year later, his former cellmate Darius knocked at his door to ask for a job.

François Vidocq ran away from home at thirteen after stealing 2,000 francs and his parents' silver. As a child, he tortured animals, and by age eight he bit ears and scratched eyes in fistfights. At fourteen, he wielded a deadly saber. After a short stint with a traveling circus as a Polynesian savage who ate flesh and drank blood, Vidocq joined the army. His nickname in youth, Vautrin—"wild boar," in regional dialect—was well deserved. One of his first acts as a soldier was to strike an officer. He was assigned a guard but escaped with a fellow prisoner. To cover their desertion, they stole a policeman's cloak and cap and moved through the countryside with Vidocq posing as a convict under escort. At Vitry, they found a Jewish merchant who was willing to exchange street clothes for their uniforms, which allowed Vidocq to reenlist in another military division and claim no prior service.[16]

So began Vidocq's long series of desertions, arrests, and escapes. Each new getaway offered him a fresh occasion for disguise. He boasted of having escaped from twenty country jails and every prison in the department of the Seine. In his memoirs, he repeatedly denies wrongdoing. He admits to having killed two men in fights but insists he was justified. He also admits to being found with bloody hands near his mistress, who had been stabbed five times with his knife, but said that he had cut himself trying to keep her from killing herself.

The most consequential crime of Vidocq's early life was a forgery meant to help a fellow inmate leave prison. Vidocq was found guilty and sentenced to eight years. In Vidocq's telling, he was framed by a pair of forgers who occupied the same cell. "I protest to this day with all my might," he wrote nearly fifty years later, "against any participation in this crime." Surviving documents tell another story. A man had offered Vidocq money to falsify a document, which he did using a military seal belonging to his former regiment. It was discovered beneath his mattress. He served just one year of the sentence before escaping.[17]

Vidocq has had eloquent defenders, including Hugo, Lamartine, and a series of historians and biographers who have portrayed him as the victim of a relentlessly punitive judicial system. Others describe a secretive man without scruple or principle who abused his authority and was willing to write or say whatever served his needs. The first false name he used was Rousseau, a choice in keeping with his ingenuous tone. His *Memoirs* begin:

> I was born in Arras. My perpetual disguises, the mutability of my features, and my singular talent to advance in the world have sown considerable doubt as to my age. It is therefore not irrelevant to state here that I came into the world on July 23, 1775, in the house next door to the one in which, sixteen years earlier, Robespierre was born.[18]

This elegant opening, with its supreme assurance and faint menace, acknowledges Vidocq's guile as if in confidence. His words were as deceptively transparent as his body. He was the anti-Rousseau, a master of bluff and stranger to all sentiment.

"After the century of Enlightenment, the century of shadows," writes the critic Francis Lacassin. Vidocq was at home in the new century. His single strongest credential was an uncanny ability to change his appearance. This was no mean feat, since those who knew him described his colossal physique. At five feet, six inches he was half a foot taller than the average Frenchman, with cascading blond hair, blue eyes, a strong nose, and fleshy lips.[19] Vidocq was not especially refined. He was no seducer and not even a very good liar. Instead of sweetening his words, he altered his body.

When needed, he could add several inches by stacking playing cards in his shoes. He also developed a way of walking that made him shorter. He learned from professional beggars how to induce skin ulcers and simulate scars. He could produce a fever by swallowing tobacco juice over several days. To play a beggar, he darkened his face by rubbing it with walnut husks, filled his nose with a gummy mucus he darkened with coffee, and infected himself with lice. With a new tattoo on his left arm, he impersonated a drowned sailor named August Duval, whose traits and biography he had learned from a friend of the dead man. When he located Duval's family, the mother, father, cousins, and uncle tearfully embraced him and sent him on his way with a stash of money.[20]

Vidocq craved attention but had a horror of being recognized. As an agent, he always carried wigs and false mustaches of several colors and styles. He changed clothes several times a day. If strangers called out his name in the street, he responded with anger and sometimes violence. His unending efforts to alter his appearance point to an awareness that identification relied largely on what was observed and recalled. He claimed to have committed hundreds of faces and physiques to memory.[21]

Vidocq's arrest of Coignard at the edge of Paris was an example of the kind of work that made this former thief famous. Beyond routine stops for vagrancy and petty theft, Vidocq and his band staged scenes meant to instill fear. He passed nights disguised as a drunk in squalid taverns listening for secrets. The Palais-Royal's prostitutes trusted him enough to present him to their pimps. He accepted bribes and then betrayed their providers. He once blocked the doors of a rowdy working-class dance hall, stopped the music, and went through the crowd naming each criminal he recognized. "We were giants," he wrote with typical assurance. "No henchman was more determined or dreadful. We broke arms and legs. Nothing stopped us, and we were everywhere. I was invulnerable."[22]

The things that distinguished these two deceivers were mostly temperamental. Vidocq mastered many personas, while Coignard stayed to a single role. Vidocq manipulated his face and body, while Coignard relied more on mastering his words and manners. Vidocq favored brute force, while Coignard employed a quick mind and smooth tongue. One additional difference points to the complex place of status just after the Revolution. While Vidocq was capable of disguising himself as a merchant or a professional, his preference ran to impersonating society's dregs. Coignard aimed uniquely above his own station for the prestige it conferred. This choice was what earned him the charge of usurpation.

When he appeared in court, Coignard was in full command of his persona, mixing hauteur with lordly reserve. He faced an array of possible crimes. The 1814 Charter restored what the Revolution had stripped and the Napoleonic Code only partially restored. "The ancient nobility reclaims its titles," Article 71 reads. "The new nobility [Napoleon's titled notables] retains its own." Articles 258 and 259 from the 1810 Penal Code were still in force: "Any person who intervenes in public, civic, or military functions without authorization . . . shall be punished with imprisonment of two to five years." And: "Any person who publicly wears a suit, uniform, or decoration not belonging to him, or who claims titles . . . that have not been legally conferred, shall be punished with imprisonment of six months to two years."[23] In addition to usurping the aristocratic title of count, Coignard was accused of forging official documents, attempting to bribe a public official, participating in a string of thefts, and shooting a police agent.

Before the court could take up usurpation and forgery, it first had to prove that the so-called comte de Saint-Hélène was in fact Pierre Coignard. An initial trial was held to establish his identity. Never wavering from his insistence that he was Pierre de Pontis, he revealed an agile intellect. As the chief counsel exposed holes in his story, he improvised ever more fabulous answers. "Are you not in fact Pierre Coignard?" the judge began. "I may resemble him," Pierre replied, "but I am not he." He explained that he had met a Pierre Coignard in Spain and that the man had indeed escaped from prison in Toulon. "I knew him, the poor creature—I helped him as much as I was able, then he died."[24] He attacked his accusers' credibility, calling them spies in the pay of Vidocq.

Villagers from Langeais, however, insisted that he was Coignard. "I remember saying to my father, 'What a shame that such a handsome young man has to be a thief,'" a neighbor recalled. "He debauched a poor young girl and dragged her into crime," another testified. "She died at Saint-Lazare." A friend of the family reported that he had held her baby when she was baptized. His efforts to defend himself showed resourcefulness even when they were not convincing. When a portrait of him was produced that Délaïde Lordot had possessed in prison, he swore before God and the saints that he had never been painted. One witness, a former neighbor in Paris, testified that their concierge once received a note from the defendant requesting any mail addressed to Coignard. "It was Coignet and not Coignard," Pierre replied. "He was an officer, one of my friends, who was having difficulty with the war bureau."[25]

It took only ninety minutes to reach a verdict. The judge declared him to be Pierre Coignard, ordered him to serve the remainder of his original fourteen-year sentence, and held that his remaining charges would be heard at a later date. This second trial was marked by stubborn silences and angry outbursts. Coignard demanded to be addressed as the comte de Saint-Hélène, quibbled with the wording of questions, and refused to address the substance of the charges against him. On the strength of testimony from his former accomplice Lexcellent, Coignard was convicted of theft and three counts of forgery. The latter included his falsified military record and fictitious baptismal certificate from Soissons. The sentence was life imprisonment.

It is noteworthy that Coignard's sentence does not include usurpation, a word that had appeared on his earliest arrest warrant. Perhaps the judge reasoned that by declaring the 1813 *État des Services et Campagnes* a forgery, the titles it bore—*sous-lieutenant* (1790), *lieutenant* (1794), *capitaine* (1800), *lieutenant-colonel* (1806)—were necessarily discredited. Perhaps he thought that with the penalty for Coignard's other crimes now set at hard labor for life, the prescribed six months to two years for usurpation was unnecessary.

Or perhaps the omission was more complicated. Witnesses for Coignard in his second trial reinforced an argument his attorney had made earlier. "How can you believe that a man who has just escaped from the prison of Toulon could suddenly find himself able to fulfill the functions of a superior officer?" the attorney had asked.

> Bravery may be innate, but military knowledge is acquired only through long and grueling experience. When the duc de Dalmatie [the Maréchal Soult], an expert in judging valor and military talent, stated that he knew no serviceman more worthy of the title of *chef de bataillon*, it was because M. de Pontis combined valor, military talent, and experience in command. Without this, any usurper of the name de Pontis would have betrayed himself by his own ignorance.

The premise of the argument was wrong, but its substance—that Coignard was a gifted officer who deserved his title—was demonstrably true. At the second trial, witnesses confirmed the point. Whatever his identity, the officer was "full of honor and loyalty," "superior," "faithful," a natural "man of the parade-grounds."[26]

At some point in Spain, the lies about Coignard's noble birth and sterling record were accompanied by genuine accomplishment. He was promoted and decorated for his actions. Whatever else was false about the man, he had earned a substantial portion of the honors he claimed. The Légion d'Honneur he received in 1814 as *chef de bataillon* depended on Maréchal Soult's praise. His selection as commander of the 74th Legion of the Seine and 1816 promotion to Chevalier of the Order of Saint-Louis were based on his performance. Pierre Coignard was a hardened criminal and unrepentant liar. He doctored military records, offered bribes to a public official, and hoodwinked associates into vouching for what he knew to be false. He was a convict with unserved time from his first sentence. By the standards of the day, his crimes amply deserved the sentence he received. But his titles, at least in part, were deserved.

Such considerations indicate an important shift underway in assessing identities. At the time of his birth, the noble estate Coignard falsely claimed was a legally recognized status. When its legitimacy was denied by revolutionary legislators two decades later, so, too, were the conditions for this particular falsehood. According to the law, Coignard's supposed crime of feigned nobility had no standing. To be sure, his title as comte de Saint-Hélène was a fiction. It mocked the clause in the 1814 Charter permitting hereditary nobles to reclaim their titles. Yet Article 1 of this same document undermines the authority of titles: "The French are equal before the law, regardless of what might have once been their title or rank."[27] The grounds for usurpation were now crumbling. If all citizens were truly equal, wouldn't former usurpation be mere prevarication? If so, was it a crime?

There were still plenty of other props for swindlers to exploit: bogus degrees or certificates, invented personal connections, posh accents, hollow displays of charity or compassion. The particular allure of claiming noble birth as a commoner, however, had begun to fade. The sense of violation that Coignard's contemporaries registered would soon recede as well. His unmasking belongs to a moment when the terms of identity, and what it meant to falsify it, were undergoing fundamental change. Accused of usurpation, he was punished only as a counterfeiter and thief.

Coignard's imposture therefore differed from than that of Pierre Mêge, whose deceit more than a century earlier turned not on the fluidity of status but on the difficulty of confirming the identity of persons determined to hide it. Coignard was disturbing to his contemporaries because he was good at what he did: leading troops, holding forth in salons, and impressing the king. He lived his imposture for five years in the public eye—something Mêge did only briefly in interrogations and the courtroom—and in the process partially earned his position. The peril of the new meritocracy was not so much that it opened the door to liars, but that it risked leaving society without a justifiable objection when the liars were meritorious.

On September 22, 1819, in front of the Palais de Justice on the Île-de-la-Cité, Pierre Coignard was publicly exposed in the pillory before being branded with the letters T. P. (*travaux forcés à perpétuité*). He then attacked his guardians with such savagery that it took five men to restrain him. Three weeks later, chains were hammered around his neck and ankles, and he, along with 454 other shackled prisoners, left Paris for Toulon. A journalist who spoke with him years later wrote that he still insisted he was the comte de Saint-Hélène. Jules Michelet, who visited him in 1831, noted that he read the newspaper with gold-rimmed eyeglasses. Chained to another inmate night and day, he carried himself with assurance and distinction. He died in the prison hospital at age sixty-four, having served fifteen years of hard labor.[28]

CONFIDENCE AND DISTRUST

The outlines of Coignard's life were repeated throughout the first two decades of the century. A tailor's son from Pau named Latapie forged baptismal and military records to say that he, too, was a French émigré with battlefield experience in Spain. Like Coignard, he was made a member of the Order of Saint-Louis, thanks to forged royal letters.[29] After his arrest, which came just two weeks after Coignard's capture, a chagrined Secretary of War, Laurent de Gouvion-Saint-Cyr, demanded that the police "make an example of the man and put an end to this disorder." He did not get his wish. Latapie suffered a mental collapse and was transferred to the Asylum of Bicêtre.[30]

Another tailor's son attracted a fawning circle of aristocrats at the beginning of the century with the claim that he was Louis XVII. A runaway who had a talent for convincing French nobles he was one of them, Jean-Marie Hervagault used his eloquence and good looks to transform a string of arrests for vagrancy into a narrative just gothic enough to persuade others. After Marie-Antoinette's beheading, he said, he was smuggled out of the Temple and replaced by a child lookalike named Jean-Marie Hervagault. He had spent the intervening years incognito.

He said that he had roughhoused with George III in England ("I once allowed myself to slap him, which seemed quite appropriate for the king of France with regard to the king of England"), was secretly consecrated as king by Pope Pius VI in the presence of twenty cardinals at the Vatican ("He applied two stigmata to my body with a red-hot iron: one on my right leg bearing the French royal insignia and, on my left arm, letters forming the words *Vive le Roi*"), and was assured at court in Portugal of military support by the representatives of nine sovereign princes ("The agreement is in the royal archives"). At the height of his fame, shortly before an 1802 court found him guilty of falsehood with fraudulent intent, hopeful royalists showered him with gifts, dinners, concerts, and formal balls. According to one account, the police minister Joseph Fouché urged Napoleon to recognize the impostor as Louis XVI's son and then induce him to renounce the throne publicly.[31]

One of the most enthralling impostors in these years was Anthelme Collet, whose *Memoirs of a Condemned Man* narrate one assumed identity after another. Posing as a priest in Gap, Collet gathered donations for church renovations that were never made. As a theater director in Italy, he commissioned an array of costumes on credit that he then used for disguise. As a wealthy landowner in the Dordogne, he hired a former military officer as groundskeeper and took all his savings on the promise of fail-safe investments. As an officer of the 60th Regiment in Aix, he inspected troops, granted a rich recruit temporary leave, and, as a deposit to ensure his return, took his gold watch and a large sum of money.[32] In every case, Collet followed the same basic pattern. He appeared in each new town in the clothes of his character, attended church, and gained the trust of local notables. He then stole from his victims and disappeared.

Collet recounts visiting a French countess on her estate in clerical robes. He had been a general under Napoleon, he told her, who thanked him by making him a bishop. “What flattered me most about my position,” Collet later wrote in his memoirs, “was having the freedom to appear onstage in the theater of society in whatever costume pleased me. From this moment, I played whatever role best suited my taste. I had the choice.” When he died in prison at age fifty-five, Collet had spent nearly half his life behind bars, having been convicted on five separate occasions in the previous thirty-four years. His crimes included forged passports, falsified papers of credit, and numerous counts of theft. His pedophilia also emerged in his victims’ depositions, but the 1810 Penal Code punished sex with minors only if accompanied by violence.[33]

At his final trial, the prosecution denounced Collet as “a monstrous chameleon who takes on every shape, every color, every mask, every name.”[34]

FIGURE 7.3. *Anthelme Collet*, anon. (courtesy of Widener Library, Harvard University [Anthèlme Collet, *Mémoires d’un condamné*; HV6278.C57 A35])

With the publication of his memoirs, he became a celebrity. A fellow inmate at the Rochefort prison, where Collet spent his last twenty years, described the elation of visitors who flocked to the prison. "The ladies in particular were most eager to see him. 'What a man he must have been to don the sacred miter without compunction,' they exclaimed. Gentlemen said: 'What grace he must have displayed when he wore the officer's cap!'" His memoirs stayed in print for nearly thirty years.[35]

Coignard, Latapie, Hervagault, and Collet were the well-known impostors. The press reported still others. From the *Journal des débats*, August 15, 1821:

> One Dubois, alias Capon, a notorious robber, branded twenty years ago after ten or twelve trials, managed to . . . escape from the prison of Troyes. He came to Paris, where the police arrested him two days later, dressed in the uniform of a superior officer, wearing several decorations.

And from the same paper, November 3, 1832, reporting on a man arrested by police near the Palais-Royal gambling hall wearing the Légion d'Honneur, the July Cross, and the Order of Saint-Louis. He claimed to be an ex-colonel of a line regiment.

> Transferred to the prefecture, he was recognized as an ex-convict. In his residence . . . several stolen articles were retrieved, as well as papers proving him to be the head of a band of thieves currently at work in several different neighborhoods of Paris.[36]

Such stories, both famous and forgotten, affirm postrevolutionary France as fertile ground for reinvention. Aristocrats who had staked their lives on denying their true identity returned to claim their former place, while former revolutionaries found it in their interest to disguise their own past. Napoleon's conquests spread disruption across Europe. It was an age of dispersed and destroyed archives, fragmented families, secretive reunions, and miraculous homecomings. Balzac's Colonel Chabert—the veteran who makes his slow way back to France to find his wife now remarried—stood for a generation of soldiers who wandered home from every corner of the continent to claim their due. Many like him found that in this new regime of bureaucracy one's identity depended on having the papers to prove it.

"Moments of great political upheaval have always been marked by the appearance of adventurers and usurpers," writes the author of an 1837 book unmasking Hervagault and two others who claimed to be Louis XVI's son. "In such periods, there is a certain type of person whose acts are believed because they are incredible. Our love for the miraculous, when exploited by those who replace skill with insolence, opens a path to all manner of fraud and falsehood."[37]

There was another reason the age bred deceit. In opening careers to talent, French revolutionaries broke the straitjacket of estates. The soldier from Corsica who made himself emperor was the paradigm for a favorite Romantic script: a provincial youth comes to Paris and acquires the skills to conquer the *beau monde*. Tempered with the right caveats, the example might inspire a bright artisan or industrious shopkeeper as well to toil, enrich himself, and advance. The path was open to climbers of every status, young men on the make as well as fathers of families with an eye on their savings. It was also open to those clever enough to fake it. A society thrown open to merit after centuries of privilege blurred the line between deserving accomplishment and the artful con. This was no doubt part of Anthelme Collet's fascination. His gains, however temporary and ill gotten, were the fruit of ingenuity. The appeal was of course double-edged. Criminals more fortunate than Collet might still be at large.

The fear of such deceit was as telling as the phenomenon. Dread of the criminal impostor and its accompanying thrill fed a new appetite for crime stories. Memoirs, novels, and chronicles detailing the criminal underworld made up a growing portion of popular reading. Such was the climate that helped make François Vidocq a best-selling author. His *Memoirs* appeared in 1828. Its success prompted him to produce two more novels—*The True Mysteries of Paris* and *Metal-Workers of the North*—which were largely the work of Alfred Lucas and Auguste Vitu.[38]

In 1836, Vidocq produced the book *Thieves*, which painted an intimate portrait of the disguised criminal. Its singular message was chilling: trust no one. A promise in his memoirs had outlined the book's intent, which is to penetrate concealment. "I will unmask the thieves' methods and reveal the signs by which they recognize one another. I will describe their habits and reveal their language and dress. . . . I will place before the eyes of honest men every sort of trap into which they might fall."[39] Its elaborate subtitle advertises the book's aim: *Physiology of Their Habits and Language. A Work that Unmasks Every Crook's Tricks, Intended to Serve as a Pocket Guide for All Honest People.*

Thieves likely did more to frighten than to reassure. Violent slang fills its pages. An *abreuveur à mouches*—"flies' trough"—is a bloody wound. A *bastringue*—"doodad"—is a tube used to hide documents or small saws in the anus. A *charrieur à la méchanique*—"mechanical coachman"—is someone who strangles a pedestrian from behind as an accomplice robs him. A *défrimousseur*—"kisser-fixer"—is a hit man who ruins a face. *Tantes*—aunts—are men with the desires of a woman, the "women" of an all-male prison.[40]

For all its gruesome details, *Thieves* is pedagogical and at points even paternal. Not every criminal face bears sinister features, Vidocq notes. One must study the details of speech, dress, gesture, and comportment. Among the thieves he describes is the *chevalier d'industrie*. For Vidocq's generation, the term described a particular kind of corrupt businessman, who was both entrepreneur and confidence man. The chevalier of industry lives in an exclusive neighborhood. His clothes are made according to the latest cut. His horses are English, and his servants numerous. For all of this, "he has not spent a sou." These are the crooked bankers who receive the Légion d'Honneur for their public service while siphoning off investors' money. Their manners are smart, their names—actual or assumed—are illustrious, and their titles, "which they either truly possess or give to believe so," open all doors.[41] By Vidocq's description, most are impostors.

Others made the connection explicit. In his memoirs, the Paris chief of police Louis Canler opens his list of criminals with the chevalier of industry. The chevalier has contempt for common thieves who resort to violence. He is distinguished and agreeable. He lives well, dines at the Café Anglais, and sits in the first boxes at the theater. Canler's example is an honest farmer's son named Daniel, whom he describes as cunning, eloquent, and audacious. Daniel moved from the countryside to Paris, married a rich man's daughter, lost large sums at the Bourse, and committed a series of crimes. He escaped the law by changing his identity. Not long after, he was appointed as head of an industrial firm, where he was known as a man of perfect honor. His skills were especially effective among the "most civilized, intelligent, confident members of the population, i.e., those most easily fooled."[42]

These were the skills at which Anthelme Collet excelled. In his profile of Collet as a prisoner at Rochefort, the journalist Maurice Alhoy described him as a celebrity and said that his cell was the first stop many visitors made to the prison. He was, Alhoy writes, the "finest, most remarkable chevalier of industry" to appear in the annals of justice.[43]

STEPPING-STONES FOR THE PARVENU

There was another response to the upsurge of criminal impostors in these decades: laughter. The breakthrough came by an improbable vehicle, a sentimental melodrama from 1823 meant to bring tears. A wealthy man is robbed, an orphan finds his long-lost mother, and the bandit gets his comeuppance. Its creators had intended the scoundrel's undoing as a lesson in morality, but the brilliant acting of an unknown actor named Frédérick Lemaître sabotaged its moral. In the process, Lemaître transformed the swindler into one of the most recognized public figures in Paris. Robert Macaire lampooned *chevaliers d'industrie* of every field and profession. In the process, he became an emblem for the age.

There was little in *The Inn of Adrets* that promised success. Its setting is a small hostel on the edge of the Adrets forest, where two travelers have arrived amid plans for a wedding. Bertrand, lacking the swagger of his companion Macaire, frets that gendarmes are on their trail since their prison escape two days earlier. "What do we have to worry about?—this bandanna makes me unrecognizable," scoffs Macaire as he pulls the disguise across his face. The innkeeper meantime decides that he should tell the bride's father that his own son, the groom, is adopted. His birth mother is rumored to have spent time in prison. Clémentine's father Germeuil learns the news but has no qualms: Charles is a good lad, he says.

A beggar woman named Marie arrives at the inn, Germeuil mentions that the dowry is with him in Room 13, and, when all are asleep, Macaire and Bertrand take the money and beat him senseless. The theft is discovered, gendarmes appear, and Macaire suddenly sees that Marie is the wife he deserted years ago. When she gives her name to the police, the innkeeper points to Charles and cries out to her, "This is your son!" Macaire's bandanna falls, and Marie nearly faints: "My God, it's him!" She pleads with Macaire to avow his paternity and admit to the robbery, but instead he pins it on Bertrand and tries to flee. Bertrand shoots him dead.[44]

Without Frédérick Lemaître's inspired performance, Macaire would have stayed dead. *The Inn of Adrets* was the young actor's premiere. As he writes in his memoirs, he was dismayed to find the script "worse than your average melodrama—tired, outmoded, and with one foot already in the grave."[45] Everything pointed to a failure, and Lemaître feared being defined by the role. He therefore decided to play Macaire as a brilliant, cynical rogue. The trick was to keep the plan secret. During rehearsals, he and his Bertrand, the actor Saint-Firmin, declaimed their lines with leaden earnestness.

At the premiere, Lemaître and Firmin went to the front of the stage to display their ridiculous costumes. Macaire wore patched-over red trousers, a ramshackle top hat, and ladies' slippers. Bertrand wore a baggy, tent-like overcoat and carried an umbrella. While the rest of the cast played their parts straight, Lemaître and Firmin preened, mixing physical comedy with callousness. Lemaître's affected gallantry was supremely arrogant, and

FIGURE 7.4. *Frédérick Lemaître as Robert Macaire* (Bibliothèque nationale de France)

Saint-Firmin endured his kicks and curses. They were mocking and derisive and uttered sentimental lines with contempt, which made the public laugh at the other actors' sincerity.

Those present called the play a revolution. Lemaître was "as elegant as a salon dandy, as brutal as a market worker, as shy as a child . . . [and] as corrupt as a knave," according to one critic. Théophile Gautier called him a Proteus, able to turn from irony to tenderness to fury in a flash.[46] To write properly about Lemaître, the poet Théodore de Banville declared, one would need a blood-dipped quill and craggy perch on Patmos, where John wrote the Book of Revelation. The play ridiculed all things holy, he continued: virtue, honor, loyalty, friendship, the family. Vice became comic and attractive. Its mockery was devastating. There were "no more kings in Europe, nor royalty, nor aristocracy, nor classic poetry."[47] Months later, the Interior Ministry shut the play down as an offense to morality.

When it reappeared nine years later at the Porte Saint-Martin Theater, *The Inn of Adrets* drew a rapturous response. Spectators in gloves and polished boots mingled with the theater's more typical crowds in their workers' caps and shirts. Lemaître returned as Macaire, and an actor known as Serres played Bertrand. The pair added new desecrations. Macaire smothers a laugh when his wife Marie recognizes him, scoffs when she leaps on their son's neck, and steals the boy's watch when they embrace. In a revised ending, Macaire and Bertrand lead pursuers on a mad chase off the stage, into the audience, and up to the second boxes, where shots are fired and two bloodstained dummies dressed as gendarmes tumble into the house. A parting shot mocking melodrama follows:

> Shooting informers and killing the police
> Doesn't mean you lack sentiment.[48]

Popular acclaim increased the critics' rage. Guibert de Pixérécourt, a pillar of tradition, damned the play for offending modesty and harming the social order. Jules Janin went a good deal further to charge that Macaire had begotten Lacenaire, a murderer whose trial and beheading were a sensation in the '30s.[49] The scandal increased Macaire's celebrity. A spinoff called *Robert Macaire* premiered in 1834 at the Folies-Dramatiques. The play transformed the character into a chevalier of industry. Macaire's cynicism remains, but he now has refinement. A decisive turn comes when Bertrand produces a valise of carnival costumes he has stolen. The next scene opens with Macaire dressed as a businessman and presiding over a shareholders' meeting. As the head of a bogus insurance company, he calls himself the chevalier de Saint-Rémond. He assures investors that he has influence with the government and the police. They applaud him vigorously and buy more shares.

The play drew great crowds to the Boulevard du Temple, and its run of 155 consecutive performances was broken only by an earlier booking that took Lemaître to London. Years later, Lemaître said that the success had a simple, single explanation. *Robert Macaire* was "the personification of our epoch . . . at a time when everyone attempted to get rich without actually working." Lemaître cited as evidence the indignation the work aroused: people who had laughed through *The Inn of Adrets* cried foul at *Robert Macaire* "after having suddenly recognized themselves."[50]

By taking Macaire out of a convict's clothes, dressing him in a suit and top hat, and sending him to the stock exchange, the play's authors sharpened their satire. Macaire was still a fraud and was unmistakably bourgeois. The trust of investors affirmed his rectitude. "Isn't this really just what we see in society every day?" asked one reviewer. "Isn't disinterest in fact a charade, isn't honor an illusion, and probity a hoax? Aren't all the big words that so attract the multitude's attention—philanthropy, public good, liberty, and so on—really just stepping-stones for the parvenu?"[51]

In *The Inn of Adrets*, Macaire had been a solitary bandit, deriding the family and flouting the law. Now he was an insider who resembled many others who shared his smooth speech and fine manners. In the third tableau of *Robert Macaire*, Lemaître wore the bandit's trademark bandanna not over his face but tied as a cravat. While the gesture signaled Macaire's move from the world of outlaws to that of elites, it did not remove his mask. His deceit would henceforth not be disguise but imposture, which any aspiring manufacturer, broker, or politician might also master. The way was clear for Macaires of every profession and calling. He was suited to become an Everyman.

Robert Macaire and His Friend Bertrand, a first-person novel that appeared in 1839, made full use of this potential. As a dentist, Macaire extracts a tooth with one hand while picking a patient's pocket with the other. As a physician, he charges nothing but writes expensive prescriptions that only the pharmacist Bertrand can fill. As a philanthropist, he spends donors' money on fine meals and opulent carriages. As a voter, he says his highest calling is to follow his conscience and proceeds to cast fifteen votes for himself. In every vocation he adopts—which also includes wine seller, baker, antiquarian, philosopher, soldier, police agent, elected deputy, and government minister—Macaire wins public confidence through deceit. He tells Bertrand that he hopes his legacy will be a multitude of young adepts "who honor me as their master and treat me as their guide."[52]

The wish was granted in Honoré Daumier's series *One Hundred and One Robert Macaires*, which appeared in the satirical press beginning in 1836. The images were soon available as individual prints and collected in a two-volume set. Here Macaire stands in the guise of every conceivable calling to depict an entire society of swindlers and frauds. In all depictions, he holds listeners spellbound with his supreme confidence. As a newspaper tycoon, he vows to crush all competitors with lies. As a restaurateur, he promises to serve consommé from carriages and shower the city with roasted skylarks. As an attorney, he pleads without pause for five hours before losing the case. As a physician, he stands at the bedside of a corpse to declare the surgery a success: "Without this operation, he would have been yet more dead."

Daumier's caricatures showed that Macaire could be fashioned to undermine any role. A caricature in the popular press pictured Vidocq in his investigative firm as Macaire. In it, a woman has come seeking his services.

> —Sir, I have been robbed of a 1,000-franc note, she says.
> —Very well, Madam, I have this affair in hand. The thief is one of my friends.
> —May I reclaim my note and know who took it from me?
> —Nothing could be easier. Pay me 1,500 francs for my work, and tomorrow the thief will bring your note to you and leave his calling card.[53]

Macaire's anarchic spirit tarred a widening circle, tainting trades and professions with his gleeful hypocrisy and debunking callings, creeds, and principles. "*Marcairiansme* floats through the air as invisible molecules," announced *The Physiology of Robert Macaire*, "and each individual, whether

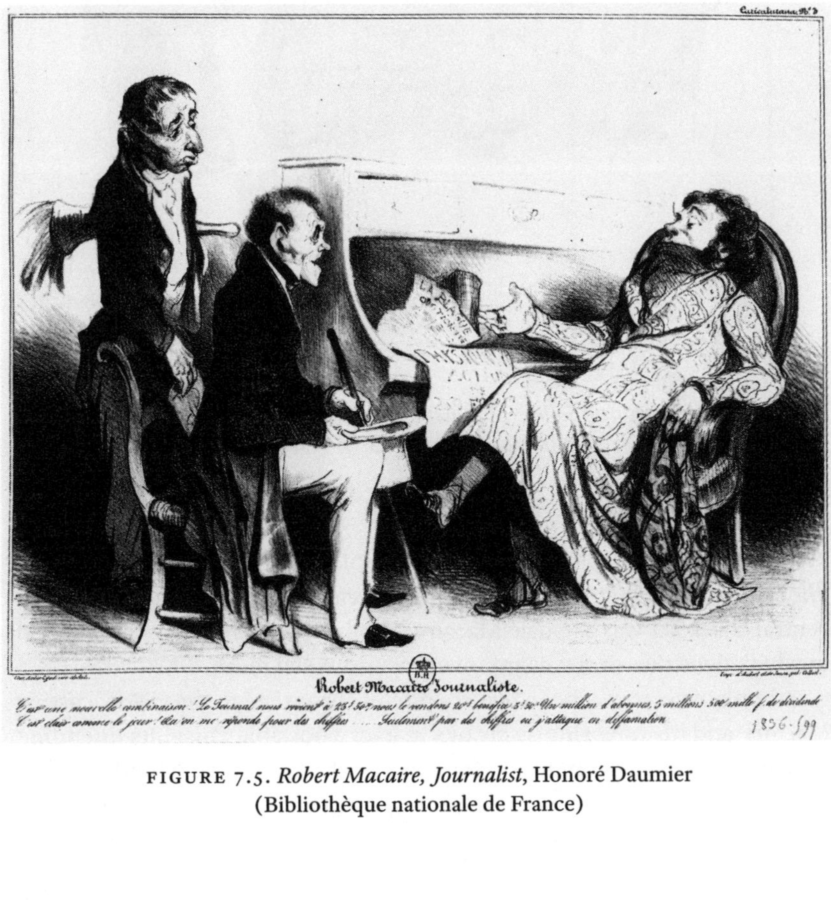

FIGURE 7.5. *Robert Macaire, Journalist*, Honoré Daumier (Bibliothèque nationale de France)

FIGURE 7.6. *Robert Macaire, Restaurateur*, Honoré Daumier (Bibliothèque nationale de France)

king or pauper, is prepared to absorb a few of its atoms." An 1836 play called *The Liberated Woman, or Five Years of Surveillance* was banned because its central character was a female Macaire.[54] The effect was a topsy-turvy world in which deceit lay at the center of every professed ideal.

A book of verse reaches a bedlam pitch appropriate to the vision, casting Macaire and his offspring as crooks in every possible guise. Its unending lists lead to a single conclusion: all the world's a Macaire. "Gentle reader, lend an ear to the tale of a crook who has no peer," one verse begins.

CROOK as a dandy,
CROOK as a poor man,
CROOK as a gentleman,
CROOK as a yokel,
CROOK as a Renaissance man,
CROOK as an Englishman,
CROOK as a Frenchman,
CROOK as a Piedmontese,
CROOK as a Spaniard,
CROOK as a German,
CROOK as Italian,
CROOK as Tyrolean,
CROOK as European,
CROOK as African,
CROOK with a telescope,
CROOK as American.[55]

FIGURE 7.7. *Robert Macaire, Attorney-at-Law*, Honoré Daumier (Bibliothèque nationale de France)

FIGURE 7.8. *Robert Macaire, Physician,* Honoré Daumier (Bibliothèque nationale de France)

Macaire was carnivalesque with no need for carnival, a figure who overturned all pieties and held nothing sacred. Together with Pierre Coignard, Latapie, Anthelm Collet, and Jean-Marie Hergavault, Macaire crystallized what was now possible: the means of forging a new identity, with forgery the salient trait. Bourgeois society's vaunted freedoms opened a path to impostures of every kind. And yet when Daumier cast Macaire as present in all trades and professions, there were still unrevealed aspects of his character. Macaire's defiant worldview also carried political menace. In the turmoil to come, he stood for revolution.

8
Reading the Body

THE HEART'S RECESSES

In his history of identity, Vincent Denis points to the years between 1792 and Waterloo as decisive in refining the protocols of documentation. Various types of official identification were already in place, including passports, identity cards, and work livrets. These served to distinguish soldiers from civilians, certify health status, authorize employment, and permit travel through designated lands. They typically carried a name, place of residence, and occupation. Until the late eighteenth century, such documents bore only the most basic identifying details, with age, height, and sometimes hair or eye color included. More particular traits were sometimes included for criminals, beggars, and vagabonds.[1] In practice, authorities relied on the word of acquaintances, relatives, and local notables for conclusive identification. The lawyer Blinière, who won the Mêge imposture case in 1712 on appeal, was typical in favoring the testimony of attorneys, priests, and students over the illiterate.

In 1792, a law made it mandatory for males age fifteen and older to carry a passport (*carte de sûreté*). According to Denis, this was the moment when new methods began to spread. Features of the face appeared in official documents, with descriptions of the nose, mouth, chin, and forehead. *A Compendium of Descriptions and the Means to Make Use of Them* offered ten different words to describe eyebrows, six words for beards, six for faces, and nineteen for eyes, including lively, bulging, drooping, viscous, and common. Assigned the job of making police records more uniform, a gendarme named Millot listed 499 specific traits from which officials could draw their descriptions.[2]

While the age's disruptions had produced an anxious need to identify strangers, the project of perfecting descriptions touched on a larger question: how to appraise others in a world whose reference points had been scrambled. Accustomed markers tying dress, speech, and manners to social position, substantially eroded by the time of the Revolution, were now gone altogether. Family reputation meant little, and lineage was discredited or deemed irrelevant. With careers open to talent, a position was no guarantee of competency. Doing business with strangers therefore turned everyday encounters into an evaluation of character. A news sheet that appeared in 1803 called *Diogenes' Lantern* used its first issue's lead article to describe the challenge.

> Is it a matter of electing a public official; of judging whether a particular defendant is guilty of the crimes imputed to him; of shaping children's hearts in the social virtues and sending them on the best paths? Do you wish to choose a wife, a husband, a doctor? To calculate the success of an enterprise? . . . In a word, are we content to live with others? If so, it behooves us to read into their soul at every moment, to raise the veil that covers it always and without cease.[3]

To raise the veil and read into the soul was the new century's project. Instructional books appeared, experts drew large audiences, and museums offered exhibits. To succeed would require grasping the inner life by external traits.

The undertaking brought a remarkable attentiveness to the features of strangers. The *Mercure de France*, for instance, carried an essay that cataloged faces its author had seen in the street. He likened them to a display of caricatures. He sees faces that are chubby, ruddy, skeletal, yellowish, rounded, flat, puffy, and long. He notes subtle differences among a drinker's florid complexion, an aging woman's rouge, and a child's creamy cheeks. He records noses that are flat, turned-up, and aquiline. His intention to judge the character of strangers is explicit, but he is at a loss over how to do so.

> For this study to be of profit, it must lead us to knowing something of the interior, which is rather like surmising the distribution of rooms in a palace from the outside. It is still possible to err, but with enough practice, one might come near the truth.[4]

This was the context that brought new attention to the ancient science of physiognomy. The previous wave of interest had been during the reign of Louis XIV, when the royal physician Marin Cureau de La Chambre wrote of its insights for those intent on penetrating deceit. After the Revolution, the need remained but its relevance was considerably wider, addressing not just a small circle of elites but society at large. Given the crimes now conceivable, mere dissembling seemed minor.

The Swiss writer Johann Caspar Lavater gave physiognomy a fresh foundation for the nineteenth century. A Lutheran minister by training, Lavater grounded his science in theology. In *Prospects of Eternity*, he writes that Jesus Christ is the perfect image of an invisible God, "an image where everything is expression, everything has unfathomable and infinite meaning." The divine body, he believed, possessed perfect transparency and was therefore wholly legible, an immaculate identity between essence and appearance. Our lost Edenic bodies were of this nature, as is our future form in the life to come. In both settings, past and future, the body's expression is "instantaneous, truthful, comprehensive, unfathomable, impossible to attain in words, and inimitable."[5]

For Lavater, this is what it meant to be created in the image of God, whose divine presence was meant to shine through all mortal features. Bodies without sin are an expression of divinity in a language unmediated by words. This explains how humans might come naturally to love God and one another and, according to Lavater, why the morally corrupt are more difficult to love. Sinful thoughts and acts leave their traces on the body. "The morally better, the more beautiful; the morally worse, the uglier." The aim of physiognomy was to grasp this divine alphabet inscribed "on the face of man and in every part of his exterior."[6]

The popular view of Lavater's theories generally neglected its religious roots. His much-publicized readings emphasized physiognomy's secular relevance. He warned a young count that his fiancée's face revealed deep character flaws; after their marriage she became a prostitute. He voiced misgivings about a priest, who was later arrested for murder. His pronouncement on the death mask of the revolutionary Mirabeau revealed a man "of horrifying power, an implacable will, inexhaustible wealth, and a haughty determination."[7]

Lavater commanded a substantial readership in France. The standard version of his major work, *Physiognomische Fragmente*, was published in ten volumes by J.-J. Moreau de la Sarthe of the École de Médecine. Its French title, *The Art of Knowing Men by Their Physiognomy*, combined refinement and practicality. Lavish plates by Rembrandt, Rubens, Poussin, Le Brun, and Hogarth helped make it a commercial success. The work went through four editions between 1804 and 1835. Editions of another translation were published in 1827, 1841, and 1845. A pocket Lavater appeared in seven additional editions between 1806 and 1826. Descriptions accompany its portraits, which include those prone to anger, joviality, egotism, pride, and other defining traits. The book's "most odious character" is the thief,

FIGURE 8.1. *Johann Caspar Lavater*, François Delpech (Art Resource)

whose face is said to show deceit, greed, and cruelty. "It would be useless for him to try to hide his spirit under the veil of hypocrisy," his description reads. "One can always spot a villain."[8]

Lavater's ideas were well known when another scientist intent on reading character from external signs arrived in France to publicize his discoveries in what he called organology. Francis Gall was born in Baden and studied medicine in Vienna, where he grew convinced that an individual's inborn traits leave traces on the brain's surface. As a young skull forms, he believed, it takes on these distinctive contours, resulting in bumps above overdeveloped regions. Skilled readers could discern their significance and discern their possessors' character. Captivated by its promise, the English physician Thomas M. Forster renamed the new science phrenology.[9]

When the Hapsburg emperor Francis I declared his claims a danger to religion, Gall left Vienna and, with the anatomist Johann Spurzheim, toured European cities giving lectures and demonstrations. They settled in France, where their theories attracted an eager following over the next three and a half decades. Gall's early lectures at the Athenée de Paris in 1807 drew 150; thirty years later, a lecture on phrenology by a member of the Académie de Médecine drew over 3,000. The Paris Phrenological Society, founded in

FIGURE 8.2. *Thief*, from *The Portable Lavater*, Johann Caspar Lavater (Art Resource)

1831, attracted 145 charter members, including eighty-two physicians and an assortment of lawyers, public officials, artists, and writers. By the end of the decade, five separate phrenological courses were open to the public in Paris, with others offered in Lyon, Toulon, Metz, and Épinal.

In Paris, the new science commanded wide attention. On one of the city's popular boulevards, a storefront business offered phrenological and physiognomical consultations. Its sign read "The external man is the projection of the internal man."[10] A considerably more sophisticated undertaking was the Museum of the Phrenological Society of Paris, directed by Pierre Dumoutier, one of the society's founders. Trained as an anatomist, Dumoutier was convinced of phrenology's applications after hearing Spurzheim speak. He became one of the city's best-known advocates, giving ten-week courses to the general public in the theory and practice of phrenology in addition to demonstrations of brain and skull physiology.[11]

A series of rooms in Dumoutier's dwelling near the Seine housed the collection. It contained 300 skulls, 200 brain casts, 600 busts, and numerous death and life masks. Its displays were divided into three large categories: the famous, the criminal, and those with severe mental illnesses. In a speech inaugurating the museum in January 1836, Dumoutier praised phrenology and its uses, which he claimed were both practical and ethical. Phrenology reveals "the complete science of man and permits him to peer into the most secret recesses of his heart," he declared.[12]

Among the masks on display were those of Rousseau, Robespierre, the marquis de Sade, Kant, and Goethe. Brains and skulls of criminals included thieves, rapists, and hired assassins. Those grouped as mentally ill included suicides, men and women with crippling obsessions, homosexuals, and a nymphomaniac. A smaller collection featured those who excelled in their pursuits and professions, including an admiral, a linguist, a watchmaker, and a child prodigy in mathematics.[13]

The museum's organization adhered closely to the writings of Gall and Spurzheim. Gall had mapped twenty-seven distinct organs of the brain. Spurzheim identified eight more.[14] The first nine comprised instincts and penchants (e.g., sexual desire, belligerence, cruelty); the next twelve, the sentiments (e.g., respect, prudence, conscientiousness); and the last fourteen, intellectual faculties (e.g., a sense of color or a memory for words). Others used research of their own. Isidore Bourdon, a French physician and member of the Académie de Médecine, was prominent in publicizing phrenology. His book *Physiognomy and Phrenology* includes the precise position of the various cerebral organs, summaries of what their bumps reveal, and examples of their influence on thought and action.

PLATE 1. *In the Street*, Constantin Guys (Art Resource)

PLATE 2. *Masked Ball at the Opera*, Édouard Manet (Art Resource)

PLATE 3. *Death at the Masked Ball*, Félicien Rops (Musée Félicien Rops)

PLATE 4. *Self-Portrait with Masks*, James Ensor (Art Resource)

According to Bourdon, the bump for Hope, or *Illusion,* is high on the forehead. This is to wait patiently without tedium or discouragement and describes Napoleon. The bump for Eventuality, or *The Gift of Conjecture,* is in the middle of the forehead. This is a memory for facts and describes physiologists, historians, and politicians. The bump for Order, or *Arrangement,* is on the ridge above the orbital cavity. This is the ability to put things in their right place and describes collectors, women, and bachelors.[15]

While the relevant evidence for phrenologists and physiognomists differed, many considered their conclusions compatible. Bourdon explained that innate dispositions seen on the skull grew evident over time in other parts of their body. The best soldiers or diplomats were predisposed to courage or circumspection, for instance, and years of acting on these inclinations left their mark on the body. For Bourdon, these "affections of the soul" were usually apparent by age thirty in one's face, gait, and posture. The lines and wrinkles of a face and the movement of its small muscles create a tableau of passions, desires, and affections. "This is an indiscreet mirror in which all things are reflected, including our most mysterious intuitions."[16]

Those convicted of crimes drew special attention from researchers in the 1830s and '40s. François Broussais was a physician who investigated the brains of thieves, murderers, and assassins. His *Course on Phrenology* opens with a warning: the art of deceit is now so advanced that any amount of trust is a risk. "I pity heads of governments, administrators, and other officials who lack the means to see through the misleading masks of those seeking to become an instrument of their power and vehicle of their plans."[17] Broussais and Félix Voisin, whose medical specialty was mental illness, used phrenology to press for reform in the educational and judicial systems. They were among a number of politically progressive phrenologists who aimed to grasp inborn tendencies in order to prepare those "poorly born" for suitable vocations. For these thinkers, biology was not destiny. Humans are malleable, Voisin wrote. Most criminals were formed not at birth but from having lived in conditions that feed humans' worst impulses. The right education, he argued, could address and correct these drives.

Voisin was scathing in answering those whose response to crime was more prisons and harsher sentences. "Sequester them, enchain them, kill them if you find it appropriate, but in the name of humanity and the respect it deserves, at least abstain from your derision. Do not demand an accounting for things that these criminals have received from neither God nor men."[18] By this, he meant the circumstances of poverty, need, and distress. The point went to the core of some basic questions. Did innate qualities lead

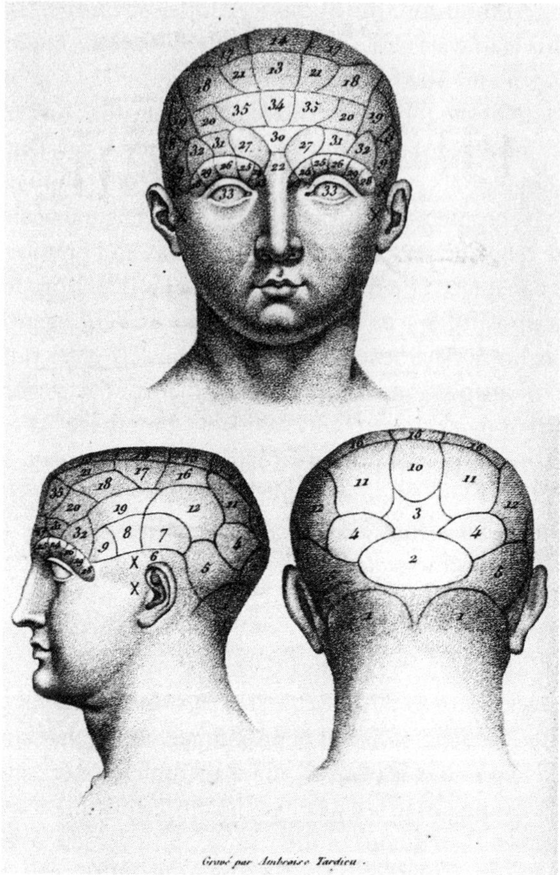

FIGURE 8.3. Phrenological chart from François Broussais, *Course on Phrenology* (courtesy of Widener Library, Harvard University [François Broussais, *Cours de phrénologie*; Phil5921.1])

some to accomplishment and others to failure? If defining tendencies were present at birth, to what degree could a person change?

The dominant view held human understanding to be the sole product of sense impressions. This blank-slate model was illustrated in a thought experiment proposed by the philosopher Condillac, who imagined endowing a statue with consciousness one sense at a time. In his telling, this was sufficient to produce language, memory, judgment, and imagination. "The self," he wrote, "is nothing but the collection of the sensations that [the statue or person] experiences and of those that memory recalls to it," he wrote in his *Treatise on Sensation*.[19] While phrenologists' accounts of inborn influences were compatible with this largely passive conception, many, including Broussais and Voisin, resisted these conclusions. The soft determinism of less subtle thinkers nevertheless often persisted. A guide written by Spurzheim's son-in-law offered advice on potential nannies and domestic servants based on the shape of the cranium, which, the book claimed, could reveal kindness and the love of children or greed and stealth. It also offered help for business owners looking to hire trustworthy employees.[20]

Despite his work for reform, Voisin had a hand in stirring anxieties about criminals. On a visit he made to the prison of Toulon, he asserted that phrenology could identify the most brutal tendencies in humans. The director then issued a challenge. Of Toulon's 372 inmates, he said, twenty-two were serving time for rape. He lined its population in rows, and Voisin, accompanied by another physician, two administrators, and a pair of military surgeons, palpated the head of each prisoner, asking those with significant swelling at the back of their neck to step out of the line. Of the twenty-two Voisin selected, thirteen were convicted rapists. Staff reported that the other nine he selected were under perpetual watch for the danger they posed to other inmates. News of the experiment made Voisin famous.[21]

THEATER OF SOCIETY

In *Laboring Classes and Dangerous Classes in Paris,* Louis Chevalier describes the dread that haunted the city in the first half of the nineteenth century. The greatest concern of Parisians, Chevalier writes, was crime. The fear was a consequence of what he calls the pathological nature of urban living. The city's population had now begun to grow from rural immigration, which largely brought single males, and the urban economy was unable to accommodate the influx. "Crime ceased to be something picturesque and exceptional," he writes. "It became commonplace, anonymous, impersonal, obscure." The threat was both vague and all-pervading, with capital punishment itself "nothing more than one settlement of scores among others."[22] Alongside the fear was a strange appeal. The "horrid gloom" and "somber glory" of great crimes held a particular fascination, at once thrilling and forbidden. Chevalier turns to Balzac, Sue, and Hugo to illustrate the preoccupation, but he considers their historical relevance as chiefly descriptive. Their fiction "sets it out," he writes of the problem of crime, "rather than breaks it down." Their work "experiences it rather than expounds it."[23]

This judgment is questionable. The teeming underworld these novelists portrayed is indeed vivid, but their works go far beyond simple description. In dramatizing the questions that troubled contemporaries, they, too, explored crime's sources and effects. Science offered advice for reading strangers and reformers offered redress, but fiction alone possessed the means to peel back layers of intent that were otherwise impenetrable. By introducing master criminals into ordinary life, novelists clarified what was at stake in the question asked by Parisians of all classes: whom to trust in a city of strangers.

Honoré de Balzac was explicit about the challenge of writing at a time when reading others had grown more difficult. The Revolution had eliminated more obvious markers of caste, and in the intervening decades still subtler signs were blurred. In his 1845 preface to *The Splendor and Misery of Courtesans*, Balzac wrote: "The flattening, the effacement of manners is on the rise. Ten years ago, the author of this book wrote that there was nothing left but nuances. Today even the nuances are disappearing."[24] The novel, set in the 1820s, conveys the power of such nuances to promote oneself and thwart others. In creating a world filled with falsehood, Balzac offered a warning to his own society. At the center of this dark work is a master of disguise. On its surface is this criminal's creation and victim, a young man who rises to the heights of society through a kind of imposture, only to be crushed.

Balzac's 1840 play *Vautrin* was a prototype for the novel. In a letter to George Sand about the work, he evoked the false André-Pierre de Pontis. "Coignard would today be a peer of France if he had not tried to be a colonel and master of a gang of thieves at the same time."[25] The lesson is not lost on the play's main character. Vautrin is an escaped convict and head of a vast criminal network. He disguises members of his band as servants and places them in important households to plot the rise of a young foreigner named Raoul de Frescas. Vautrin himself moves easily through these salons disguised as a foreign diplomat, a wealthy businessman, an aged veteran of the Revolution, a Mexican general, and a stockbroker.

Vautrin gathers his spies to explain his motives. Raoul will be his vengeance on society. He will marry into wealth, enter the corridors of power, and, under threat of blackmail or violence, follow Vautrin's orders. "I will breathe through his mouth, I will live his life; his passions will be mine. . . . In exchange for the stigmata society has burned into my flesh, I will return to it a man of honor. I enter into battle with destiny."[26] In the terms Balzac wrote to Sand, Vautrin would remain master of a gang of thieves while Raoul became a peer.

In Balzac's fictional universe, these same motives drive the killer Jacques Collin, whose nickname is Vautrin. *The Splendor and Misery of Courtesans* opens in the midst of a masked ball. Vautrin is shadowing every step of Lucien de Rubempré. His mask is black, "an assassin's mask," Balzac writes, playing on the stage associations of the domino.[27] Another of Collin's nicknames is *Trompe-la-Mort*, Cheat-Death, a fitting image for this figure of undying malevolence at the heart of the *Human Comedy*. When the novel begins, Vautrin has already plotted Lucien's rise and initiated his corruption. Since his arrest at Mme Vauquer's boardinghouse at the close of *Père Goriot*, Collin has escaped from prison and effected a crude sort of surgery to change his appearance. He has splashed acid on his face and lacerated his back to obscure the branded initials that identified convicts. He has mastered a new walk. He carries the papers and wears the robes of the Spanish priest Carlos Herrera, whom he killed in Spain.

Collin and Lucien know one another well. Before the start of the novel, the false Herrera encountered the young poet on a road near Angoulême. He was on the verge of drowning himself, distraught over his failures in Paris and the humiliations he has caused his family. He pours out his sorrows to the priest, whose talk dissuades him from the act. The convict's words are mesmerizing:

> I've fished you out of the water, brought you back to life, and you belong to me as a creature belongs to its creator. . . . You'll never lack for money. You will shine and show off while I, bending low in the mud of the foundations, shall be propping up the brilliant edifice of your fortune. . . . In short, I shall live in you![28]

Herrera's "mud of the foundations"—the money that will fund Lucien's rise—is to come from a prostitute Collin will enslave. Collin consummates his own sway over Lucien with sex.

Elements of Coignard, Vidocq, and Collet, whose stories Balzac knew well, appear in Collin's words and actions, including his return from Spain with a new identity, his colossal physique, the initials burned on his back, his disguise as a priest, and his rape of Lucien. *Collin* is close to *Collet*, and his nickname Vautrin was once used by Vidocq, whom Balzac had hosted for dinner at his home in Passy.[29] These precursors give depth and a kind of authority to the character, but their significance to the novel extends beyond shared traits. Balzac grasped that these criminals were harbingers of an age in which the successes of the respectable might rest on similar kinds of deceit. The novel's multiplying masks are fitting for a society in which a druggist's son like Lucien has a chance to enter the elite. Jacques Collin's false identities are dizzying even to readers who know his game. Also known as *Trompe-la-Mort* and the abbé Carlos Herrera, Collin appears in the book as a low-level civic bureaucrat, the English banker William Barker, the French noble M. de Saint-Estève, and a French soldier.

Other characters in the novel assume multiple identities. Collin's corrupt aunt Jaqueline disguises herself as Mme Nourisson, Mme de Saint-Estève, the marquise de San Estaban, a servant named Asie, and an unnamed baroness. The police agent Contenson disguises himself as a porter from Les Halles, the baron Bryond des Tours-Minières, a merchant, a customs guard, and a mulatto. Beyond these disguises are unseen masks: those of the prostitute Esther, for instance, who comes to the ball newly in love and imagining herself a virgin, and that of her lover Lucien, whose new clothes and rehearsed gestures will, he hopes, become second nature.

Lucien Chardon's first inkling of what reinvention might look like came just after arriving in Paris. Strolling in the Tuileries gardens, he studied others for what he lacked in his own provincial dress. The young men around him wore fitted jackets and golden cufflinks, and they carried riding whips and pocket watches. Balzac was not alone in pointing to the importance of such details. Even as the black suit of the bourgeoisie replaced earlier insignia of status, nuances not only remained but multiplied, providing ever finer points of distinction for those schooled to recognize them. Books like the baron de l'Empesé's *The Art of Tying One's Cravat* were intended to instruct and guide: "Amidst the general leveling that threatens society, amidst the fusion of ranks and conditions, amidst the universal flood of petty, inferior pretensions directed at superior grand pretensions, we have thought to render a signal service to the upper classes, to hold out so to speak, a veritable life buoy by proffering an *Art of Wearing One's Cravat*."[30] Staking a claim in this hierarchy involved minute gradations of taste.

Balzac called the general leveling "a fatal law of our own epoch." For those with Lucien's ambition, it was a boon. Managed at each step by Vautrin and supplied with money from the prostitute Esther, Lucien adopts the aristocratic name de Rubempré. He dresses in the finest clothes and is seen in high circles. Not everyone is convinced. The comte du Châtelet listens to Lucien's description of his new Rubempré escutcheon with disdain. "*Maintenant je porte de gueules, au taureau furieux d'argent, dans le pré de sinople*," Lucien says of its design: "I now bear the heraldic red, with a raging silver bull on an emerald meadow." The count responds with a haughty pun: "*Furieux d'argent*"—"Mad over money."[31]

Lucien's performance brings him to the threshold of marriage to Clotilde de Grandlieu, the scion of an ancient noble line, and the prospect of an ambassadorial appointment to Germany. His rise shows that while identity may have been movable and unstable, it was not necessarily arbitrary. Its codes were clear, its barriers policed, and its violations punished. Lucien learns this truth as Jacques Collin's elaborate scheme begins to unravel. An anonymous note has been sent to Clotilde's father stating that Lucien's fortune, the chief quality recommending entry into the Grandlieu clan, comes from a prostitute. When he arrives at the *hôtel de Grandlieu* to call on Clotilde, a footman stops him in the outer court: the Grandlieus, he declares, are not receiving guests. Lucien suddenly sees his fall.

> There is nothing more fatal than etiquette for those who regard it as the most formidable law of society. Lucien easily interpreted the meaning of this scene, so disastrous to him. The duke and duchess would not admit him. He felt the spinal marrow freezing in the core of his vertebral columns, and a sickly cold sweat appeared on his brow in droplets. The conversation had taken place in the presence of his own valet, who held the door of the coupé, doubting whether to shut it.[32]

In his distress Lucien rashly seeks comfort from Esther, whom he finds at the Opera. They are noticed by the duc de Rhétoré and Lucien's chief patroness Mme de Sérizy. "'Why do you allow Lucien to be seen in Mademoiselle Esther's box?' said the young duke, pointing to the box and to Lucien; 'you, who take an interest in him, should really tell him such things are not allowed. He may sup at her house, he may even . . . but, in fact, I am no longer surprised at the Grandlieus' coolness toward the young man. I have just seen their door shut in his face—on the front steps.'"[33]

The fragility of Lucien's mask is now painfully clear. He is discovered to be in league with an escaped convict. In a climactic police raid, Collin fires on an agent. Lucien is arrested as an accessory to murder, and his carefully maintained exterior crumbles. He is once again what he was when he first came to Paris, a frightened boy from the provinces. He recognizes each of his poses—aspiring poet, journalist, dashing wit, polished man of power and influence—as a failure. "For four hours he wept . . . enduring the subversion of all his hopes, the crushing of all his social vanity, and the utter overthrow of his pride. . . . Everything within him was broken by his Icarian fall."[34] Alone in his cell, Lucien hangs himself.

PHYSIOGNOMY AND ITS LIMITS

The close detail of Balzac's descriptions owes much to his interest in physiognomy and phrenology. He paid lavish tribute to Lavater and Gall in the general introduction to the *Human Comedy*. They were the modern equivalent of Christopher Columbus in discovering the physical emanations of thought, he wrote.[35] Lavater's work inspired Balzac to write several "scientific" tracts of his own. The novelist's *Treatise on the Elegant Life* speaks of clothes as human hieroglyphs that disclose the occupations, pursuits, habits, and even neighborhoods of their possessors. His *Theory of the Gait* is a detailed guide to reading character through bearing. In *The Physiognomy of Marriage*, he compares the combined evidence of gesture, voice, expression, and manner to the tiny glowworm, "who unwittingly exudes light from every pore." Balzac is steadfastly serious in these works. "This is not about watching and poking fun. This is about analyzing, abstracting, classifying."[36]

This same scrutiny animates his fiction. A handful of observers at the Opera ball are studying Lucien's gait at the start of *The Splendor and Misery of Courtesans*. A nervous haste undercuts his detachment, they note, which betrays bourgeois roots: he must be in a hurry to meet a lover. The truth of the body is a persistent theme in Balzac's work, sometimes in subtle ways. Balzac writes that Esther has a "love bump" on her skull and suggests that some ingrained nature acts against her futile efforts to pull herself out of prostitution. At other times, the body plays an explicit role in the plot. This is the case with the false priest Herrera, whose body—a massive torso topped by square shoulders and a frightful skull—perpetually threatens to reveal him as Collin.

An effort by police to penetrate Herrera's disguise, which is a quest to decipher his body, constitutes the novel's climax. The first thing interrogators do is strip him to the waist. If he is Collin, they reason, they will see the branded letters *T. F.*, which denoted the sentence of forced labor. Instead they find whelps, scars, and bullet marks. Herrera tells them he was brutalized by anti-royalist gangs in Spain, but the police are unconvinced. To them, his colossal chest betrays criminality. A former cellmate inspects his waist, eyes, and forehead and recognizes a scar on his arm. A questioner asks to remove Herrera's wig, which sends a wave of fear through Collin.[37] A magistrate who has watched the examination is ready to conclude that his features are "truly the physiognomy of the criminal," yet Herrera's performance continues to confound them. He begins to weep and speaks of his priestly love for Lucien, a soul so young, he sobs, so fresh and of such magnificence, beauty, and innocence. "And Jacques Collin was never more like Don Carlos Herrera," Balzac writes.[38]

At this crucial moment, the science of Lavater and Gall falters. Every witness is persuaded that this is Collin, but his powerful acting keeps them in doubt. In Lavater's terms, Collin is an Antichrist. He has destroyed his natural features and falsified the divine image. That he survives the novel's devastation when every other major character is destroyed affirms Balzac's own dismal view of human society. In the end, his power, while not strong enough to assure Lucien's triumph, has crushed all innocence, love, and hope. Balzac leaves it to readers to judge whether this flows from a malicious intent to destroy all goodness or an indifference to any notion of good and evil.

Balzac preserves this doubt to the end. Collin not only survives but flourishes as an employee of the state. In *Vautrin's Last Incarnation*, Collin signs his services over to the police. This would seem yet another move to preserve himself and increase his power. When he learns of Lucien's suicide, however, he drops his priest's disguise and declares his lifelong career of deceit to be over. "Monsieur, monsieur," he cries to the magistrate M. de Grandville, "at this very moment they are burying my life, my beauty, my virtue, my conscience, all of my strength."[39]

In language filled with religious imagery, Collin tells the magistrate that police work will be his repentance. His speech and gestures are exaggerated, but Balzac gives every indication that he is serious. Lucien's demise gives him no reason to live, he says. His limp returns, a vestige of working on the chain gang. "I want nothing more than to be an element of order and stability rather than the force of corruption itself," he avows.[40] A certain logic suggests that the conversion is genuine. Collin now faces the failure for the first time. He grasps his role in Lucien's suicide and sees the wider damage he has caused. His grief is real, and the submission to his new masters seems complete. Yet in every key passage, Balzac resists appraising Collin's sincerity, leaving the judgment to readers. Describing his pivotal conversation with the magistrate Grandville, Balzac employs the subjunctive. The former criminal's words were of a goodness, naivety, and simplicity, he writes, that "would have made one believe in a transformation."[41]

One last scene leaves unresolved the age's central question about how pliant or ingrained identities truly are. The police have given Collin instructions to visit Mme de Sérizy, Lucien's former lover and protector in the *beau monde*. She is in despair over Lucien's death, convinced that her repudiation of him at the Opera provoked his suicide. Those close to Sérizy worry that she may die. Collin dons his robes, adopts the pious mien of the priest Herrera, and tells her with saintly assurance that Lucien died loving her. She accepts his lie and is saved. "Ah, and they believe in me!" he says to himself. "I shall yet rule the world, which for twenty-five years obeyed me." His final words to Mme de Sérizy could be meant for himself as well. "Now you have no rival!"[42]

Balzac sometimes referred to himself as a "doctor in the social sciences." His announced aim in the *Human Comedy* was to present the "scientific philosophy" of his day. In this, he hoped to display the laws that shaped the tone and behavior of his contemporaries. Balzac imagined for society what Lavater and Gall had proposed for individuals: a guide for recognizing hidden influences on values and beliefs. Just as he thought that the passions and inclinations of individuals might be read in the details of the body, so, too, was he convinced that social patterns and pressures left traces on the collective.

Balzac sketched this vision in an essay called "The Pathology of Social Life, or Mathematical, Physical, Chemical, and Transcendent Meditations on the Manifestations of Thought, Considered Under All Aspects Given It by the Social State." The work echoes Rousseau in faulting society for generating false needs and unnatural vices. Balzac similarly believed that civilization had brought corruption rather than progress. His *Human Comedy*, meant as a modern retelling of the infernal first volume of Dante's *Divine Comedy*, gives ample justification for such a claim in its endless catalog of selfishness and vanity. His depiction is a devastating combination of cruelty, betrayal, and exploitation.

Balzac's focus on human vanity was not new, but he believed that its effects had been dramatically widened by the economic and legal changes brought by the Revolution. Ambition was rampant, hypocrisy reigned, and everything reeked of money. The lust for riches produced thieves who could now rely on the Civil Code to protect them: provisioners who gouged the military, middlemen who willfully overcharged, suppliers who destroyed food to inflate prices. The democratic principle of advancement provided all with equally corrupt chances to sell themselves. What better figure for this corruption than the professional thief, who thrived in the new order by repeating its pieties? What better image for climbers and arrivistes, Lucien included, than the courtesan? The novel's title is at once too narrow and too extravagant if limited to Esther and women like her.

Jacques Collin's survival at the end of *The Splendor and Misery of Courtesans* is a stark affirmation of what endures in a morally bankrupt society. This is why the critic Maurice Bardèche calls the work "a novel of the 'enfranchised,'" by whom he means prostitutes and criminals. "Their place in the natural history of society, their inner connection with other social types, and their *function* in the economy of social life, as it were, are perfectly and correctly drawn."[43] For lesser novelists, these figures were outlaws and adventurers. For Balzac they are a pathology. Balzac is unsparing about the destruction brought by Collin, yet he also gives him a kind of integrity in his defiance of society. When Vautrin is arrested at the boardinghouse near the end of *Père Goriot*, he drops his disguise, utters his real name, and states his principles: "A convict of Jacques Collin's sort is a man less cowardly than his fellows, a man who protests against the injustices of the Social Contract. . . . In a word, I stand alone against the Government with its mass of courts, police and budgets, and I can beat the lot of them."[44]

For Balzac, the bourgeoisie must now reap what it had sown. With every advance, civilization produced yet more criminals and provided them with still greater means to deceive. In an essay called "The Penal Code of Honest Men," he linked the wealth and flourishing of modern nations to an ever greater gift for imposture.

> The day someone first produced beautiful carpets—or rich porcelains, or rare marbles, or fine cashmeres—thieves, the most intelligent class in society, sensed the need to stand at the top of things.... [Thieves] are the gifted actors, the clever mimes. They seize on the tone and manner of diverse social classes, can imitate the bureaucrat, the banker, the general.

No matter how harsh the laws or severe the penalties, Balzac believed, the number of criminals would never decline. "The wound is incurable."[45]

Knowing Balzac's views on the permanence of crime and ubiquity of "prostitution" deepens *The Splendor and Misery of Courtesans*, but it does not settle the novel's equivocal ending. Collin's reformation, and the redemption from evil it might signify, would stand as a powerful statement of rebirth in a character who has until now seemed irredeemable. His transformation would also be, at least for one man, a reversal of the social pathology Balzac viewed as inseparable from civilization. Not least, it would be a human affirmation of his attachment to Lucien, however tainted it also was by greed and manipulation.

Balzac gives us none of this. Instead, Collin remains a stranger, concealed to the end. Near the close of the novel, he reflects on the significance of his last incarnation as an agent of the police. "What we do in the world concerns only appearances. *Réalité, c'est l'idée!*"[46] Is this Collin's way of consoling himself for his submission? Is it, on the contrary, another defiant challenge from a man incapable of remorse? Whatever the answer, readers are left with his ultimate illegibility. In this, Collin is our contemporary. Vautrin's last incarnation leaves us with the slightly sullied, vaguely disenchanted, all-too-familiar feeling that the line between performance and authenticity is often blurred.

HUMANITY IS IDENTITY

Balzac believed that an unceasing struggle among three powerful forces—the law, monied interests, and crime—defined society. Its outcome was uncertain, a conclusion that reflected his dim view of civilization's supposed benefits. While more progressive novelists viewed the future differently, their view of criminality was no less encompassing. Eugène Sue and Victor Hugo both called themselves socialists, and their novels offer a more hopeful vision for human wholeness and social reform. Theirs is nevertheless a world of heroes and villains. Deceit permeates every class and status, and the law is weak and often misguided. For both writers, the only sure hope for justice is through exceptional individuals acting on their own. While these writers' depictions of the criminal menace to society are yet more appalling than Balzac's, his central questions about reading strangers, whether depravity can be reformed, and why corruption exerts such a powerful appeal remain. As with Balzac, the evidence of phrenology and physiognomy is central in their work.

Eugène Sue's *The Mysteries of Paris* is a declaration of war on ignorance, poverty, and social neglect. It debuted as a *feuilleton* in summer 1842, and installments continued in the *Journal des débats* for the next eighteen months. What today reads as a wearying series of shocks—including abductions, abortions, beatings, teen prostitution, lunacy, a blinding, a rape, and deaths by drowning, strangulation, starvation, and the guillotine—kept contemporaries transfixed. Readers wrote personal letters to Sue to ask mercy for his characters, offer scenes to include from their own lives, and in one case request an introduction to the book's hero for a chance to work alongside him. One priest condemned Sue from the pulpit for glorifying crime; another wrote to say that the novel had inspired him to open an orphanage.[47] Moved by the novel's subject and success, Hugo started writing *Les Misérables* in 1845.

Disguise both criminal and benevolent dominates the action of *The Mysteries of Paris*. It opens in the medieval warren of streets near Notre-Dame. A convict whose face has been slashed by a prostitute is about to strike back in fury when a stranger appears from nowhere and beats him into submission. The stranger's features are a curious mix of hardness and distinction. He wears a worker's blouse and hobnailed boots, but his hands are soft and unblemished. He speaks street slang to the convict and the woman he has rescued but resists addressing them by the familiar *tu*. He tells them he is a craftsman named Rodolphe Durand and adds that his parents were rag sellers at Les Halles before they died of cholera.

In reality he is Prince Gustave-Rodolpe, Grand-Duke of the German duchy of Gerolstein, in Paris to expiate an unnamed sin of his youth by aiding strangers with anonymous acts of kindness. As he watches the young prostitute dull her senses with liquor, he detects "depths of goodness, grace, and wisdom." The next day he buys her freedom and spirits her to the country to live with a kindly woman, who educates her in virtue.[48] She is in fact his daughter, a fact he discovers approximately 1,000 pages later. Conceived out of wedlock, she was sent by her mother to be raised by a wicked nurse, who sold her to an abuser and claimed she had died. The girl ran away and did what she could to survive.

Disguise is also a tool of evil in the novel. At one end of the social scale is the Schoolmaster, who was serving a life term for counterfeit, theft, and murder when he escaped from prison, snipped the cartilage in his nose, and rubbed his face with acid. The result is a "frightful mask": blue-black scars crease his features, ghastly holes open where his nostrils once were, and his lips are monstrously large. At the other end is Jacques Ferrand, a notary by profession and adviser to the titled and monied. He is the very model of piety and probity. He is also a rapist, extortionist, and ringleader of a network of thieves and killers. The novel's crisscrossing paths of kidnapping, murder, and suspicious suicides all lead back to this evil genius. Ferrand's seeming ordinariness makes him less colorful than the Schoolmaster, but to contemporaries it likely made his ruse many times more frightening.

In Sue's view, such human debasement was the product of injustice and abuse. Ignorance and systemic poverty had produced this criminal class with its distortions of body and spirit. Wickedness was the predictable outcome. "Sweep clean these sewers, and in their place propagate education, a love of labor, equal pay, and fair salaries. At once you will see these afflicted faces and weakened bodies reborn to the good, which is the health and life of the soul."[49]

Disguise is equally pervasive in Victor Hugo's *Les Misérables*, whose central character Jean Valjean is himself a kind of impostor. First jailed in his youth for stealing bread, Valjean serves his term, commits and is arrested for more crimes, and serves fourteen years of a life sentence before escaping prison. Determined to live an upright life, he fashions a series of false names to evade recapture, but the torment of his equivocal identity runs deep. Hugo asks whether a good man defeated by a vicious system is redeemable.

> Can a human created good by God be rendered evil by man? . . . Is there not in the soul of every human, was there not in the soul of Jean Valjean in particular, a first spark, a divine element, incorruptible in this world and immortal in the other, which good may develop, fan, ignite, inflame, and irradiate with splendor, and which evil can never entirely extinguish?

Hugo answers for his contemporaries: "Every physiologist would have probably responded *no*."[50]

The science of reading bodies was less certain for the guardians of Cosette, the orphan whom Valjean later adopts. The respectable exterior of her foster parents M. and Mme Thénardier hides depths of cruelty. The husband in particular—"unsettling for a physiognomist"—is thickset and stooped, with coarse hair on his hands and arms, thin lips, and black teeth. His face is flat, "like a death's mask," and his small eyes are invisible behind his green glasses. Thénardier is a grifter who in Napoleonic times rummaged for valuables among the dead and dying on the battlefield. He now specializes in extortion. His aliases—Jondrette, Fabantou, Genflot, don Álvarez, Balizard—match the identities he assumes in fraudulent correspondence as a poor artisan, actor, playwright, Spanish grandee, and matron.

Late in the novel, Thénardier attempts blackmail by posing as a diplomat. When his target sees through the ruse, he replies, "Well, then, let's make ourselves comfortable" and proceeds to take off his face "as one might lift one's hat," peeling putty from his nose, pulling off the green glasses, and sweeping back the hair from his forehead. Hugo explains the disguise. Near the Arsenal on the rue Beautreillis, an ingenious Jewish merchant has the ability to transform a crook into an honest man. For a small fee he rents costumes, and from each nail in his shop hangs a complete identity and social condition. "This creature was the costumier of the immense drama performed by the swindlers of Paris."[51] Criminals enter his storeroom, pay thirty *sous*, and emerge as judges, priests, bankers, bureaucrats, officers, and intellectuals. The nickname Hugo gives the man, *Le Changeur*, intensifies the antisemitic stereotype to still more damning intent. A moneychanger's trade may be shady, Hugo implies, but criminal disguise is sinister. This single evil genius underpins a network that threatens an entire city.

The question of whether identities are mutable or fixed is vividly present in Valjean's own anguish. He is unable to think of himself as wholly reformed from the criminal he once was. As M. Madeleine, the rich mayor of the small northern town of Montreuil, Valjean's crimes continue to haunt him. As Ultime Fauchelevant, a humble gardener in the Paris convent of Picpus, his surroundings are a constant reminder of his sins: here, nuns pray for the guilty. At all times, he turns over the agonizing question of who he truly is. To show outward virtue without acknowledging his crimes is deceitful. To confess his escape and declare himself a criminal is to betray his resolve and sully the good he has done. He knows, too, that if his heart is truly corrupt, any effort for lasting reform is pointless. He comes close to turning himself in, an act that would be at once the greatest sacrifice and the most painful victory for truth. Perhaps the physiognomist was right, he reasons: perhaps he is destined to be a criminal and Fauchelevant is a false self. After years in this maze of troubled thought, Valjean has an epiphany: these very questions constitute his truest self and, with them, his redemption.

The revelation comes in the novel's climactic scene, when Valjean carries a youth injured in street protests into the Paris sewers to save him. In this tomb, the site of humans' foulest corruption and fertile source of life, rebirth is possible. Hugo describes it as a place where all secrets are known and nothing is concealed. It is the "last veil" of false identities, where deceit is no longer possible. "The sincerity of this sewage pleases us; it calms the soul," Hugo writes. His bitter catalog of human pretense is far-reaching:

> When one has spent time on earth enduring the airs assumed in the grand spectacle of state power—in solemn oaths, political wisdom, worldly justice, professional probity, circumstantial prudence, and incorruptible robes—it is consoling to enter into a sewer and see the filth that belongs there.[52]

Valjean comes close to suffocating in the quicksand of muck, which soon reaches to his neck. He somehow manages to keep the wounded man's head aloft. He frees himself, gasping and exhausted, and feels a strange clarity. He will reveal his true name, Jean Valjean, to those who know him, and in so doing transcend his identity as a criminal.

Hugo identifies this "third identity" as conscience. To follow this inner voice entails a rectitude that the criminal Valjean never considered and a candor that Fauchelevant never dared. Before this moment, to act fully in either identity was impossible: helping others was tainted, and deceiving them was untrue to himself. An affirmation of his real name is a way out by breaking the link to deceit. To act on conscience is what the ingrained criminal cannot do, motivated as it is from volition instead of fear. Hugo describes the tempest within Valjean, who reels between conviction and guilty defiance. The past floods back to him, he sobs and then writhes.

> We are never done, then, with conscience! Make up your mind, Brutus; make your choice, Cato. It is fathomless, for it is God. Into this pit you throw the work of your entire life: your fortune, your wealth, your success, your liberty, your country. Into it you throw your contentment and your joy. More, more, still more! Drain the vase! Empty the urn! You must end by throwing in your heart.[53]

Valjean's resolve to be true to his name is the claim of authenticity. Silence is no longer endurable: "I would taste—and taste again every day—my fraud, my indignity, my cowardice, my treason, and my crime."[54] He tells his truth to the newly married Cosette and Marius, the man he has saved, and dies not long after.

For both Hugo and Sue, the human face was divine, and to hide or obscure it was a kind of blasphemy. An analogy in *Les Misérables* describes these distortions. Hugo imagines human endeavor as mines that reach far beneath the earth's surface. The lowest, darkest pit houses ignorance, wretchedness, and crime. It is society's id, where brutish appetites control its inhabitants. This black abyss is the dwelling place of Thénardier and his band of criminals. Here Hugo describes larvae instead of faces.[55] "Humanity is identity," Hugo declares near the end of this infernal descent. To recognize oneself in the face of the other is the foundation of all human truth. Disguise—the mask, the larva—describes the face of the criminal. It is not just the social order that this "hideous swarming" destroys. This devastation undermines science, philosophy, law, and progress itself. Every endeavor in the upper regions depends on trust and recognition. The redemption of society is therefore a common cause that involves universal education, a humane political order, and just economic arrangements. "Destroy the cave Ignorance and you will destroy the vermin Crime," he writes. "Philosophy and progress strive for this with every means, by amelioration of the real and contemplation of the absolute."[56]

Masks fill the final scene of *The Mysteries of Paris*. It is a slice of Hell worthy of Hieronymus Bosch. Revelers stagger out of workers' taverns at sunrise to watch a pair of executions. Some of the men are in muddy dresses; drunken women clutch one another as they dance an obscene cancan. Faces are "blasted by debauchery" and "marbled by drink." Familiar costumes are present, but there is no sport. A freak known as the Skeleton—a killer for hire with parchment-thin skin, long teeth, and fingers as strong as iron—is dressed as Robert Macaire. He and his companion, another murderer, have just escaped from prison. The latter is the son and brother of the two women about to be guillotined. His taunts are as vicious as any in the mob.

Sue shows the degradation of every creature. A woman wearing a police bonnet dances before the Skeleton, her face swollen and red. A crippled child scampers through the crowd wearing a devil's costume and a hideous green mask, provoking raucous laughter with each obscenity he shouts. The throng contains all that is "lowest, most shameful, and most monstrous in this lazy, insolent, greed-driven, bloody, and godless mob." Sue includes a warning: "May this final, horrible scene stand for the peril that threatens society at every instant." This is the monstrous fulfillment of carnival's worst threat, anarchy. There is no amiable intermingling of different orders. Carnival has instead stirred up the "muddy, fetid scum of the Parisian population."[57]

"Death to all good people!" the Skeleton calls out as he dances. "Long live killers and thieves!" A stylish carriage comes into the street, and before the driver can turn back, the mob encircles it. The Skeleton leans inside. "Everyone gets a turn," he tells its aristocratic passengers, a father and daughter. "Yesterday you crushed the rabble. Today the rabble crushes you." Ripping open the door, he demands their money. The father lunges for his neck. A knife flashes, and the Skeleton lifts his arm to strike. An honest worker seizes him from behind, and the Skeleton, still in the clothes of Macaire, wheels around to plunge the knife into his chest.[58]

In *Les Misérables*, the wedding day of Cosette and Marius falls on Mardi Gras. Hugo paints the scene in chiaroscuro: sacred love in the midst of an orgy. Earnest Marius endures insults and sarcasm, and the angelic Cosette comes face-to-face with prostitutes. Women without shame don masks and bare their torsos. Profane jeers from *The Fishwife's Catechism* ring out from elegant coaches. That this abuse should bring such delight, Hugo writes, and that such shameful acts and words should bring applause, are an offense to humanity. "The laughter of all is complicit in this universal disgrace."[59]

For Balzac, Hugo, and Sue, the concealment of carnival masks stood for a greater negation. For them, carnival encouraged the worst in humans, which festered and spread among the most corrupt. In the criminal, humanity itself was concealed. Yet as beastly as they might seem, these delinquents were the products of society's own corruption. For Balzac, true reform remained uncertain, and even for the reformers Hugo and Sue the darkness was profound.

In these novels, and in the larger questions they raised about human nature and its capacity to change over a lifetime, the body carried signs that might address questions of identity. The questions themselves, however, went well beyond physical attributes to the soul itself. A protector of status in the seventeenth century and a figure for social hypocrisy in the eighteenth, masks in the nineteenth century began to take on modern associations that still hold today: as an instrument for embodying another identity and possible first step toward becoming a different person. The prospect was indeed destabilizing, not only for individuals but for the social and political order.

PART FOUR

Politics

Our Women Are Cuckoo (Bibliothèque nationale de France)

The mask was given to man to reveal his thoughts.

—TAXILE DELORD, *Another World* (1844)

The mask is chaos become flesh.

—GEORGES BATAILLE, "The Mask" (1934)

9
The Mask's Anonymity

CARNIVAL CALM

Such as it was, the tranquil Opera ball that opens *The Splendor and Misery of Courtesans*—the last masked ball of 1824—represented the carnival's peak during the sober years of the Restoration. A semblance of the festive spirit that had reigned before the Revolution returned with the new century but with nothing near its former energy or interest. Restrictive laws, a heavy police presence, and little apparent taste for public merrymaking under Napoleon or the two kings to follow dampened the former mood. The popular violence that had marked prerevolutionary carnival was also gone. Scripted public events and sedate masquerades for the well-to-do were the most prominent features of the season in the century's first three decades. With the 1830 Revolution, the mood would change dramatically, as a new political landscape and fresh commercial interests helped fuel uproarious displays. Sue and Hugo were not wrong to tie carnival in these years to social and political provocation.

The earliest Napoleonic decrees permitted costumes but forbade masks. The glitter of elite entertainments returned, as did some celebration among the populace. With them came a modicum of normalcy. "The return of our former pleasures is a sign of the new government's stability," the *Journal des débats* announced on Mardi Gras 1800.[1] A series of orders from the police detailed additional restrictions for carnival. No costume could threaten or disturb public order. No one wearing a costume could utter words or jokes deemed insulting, indecent, or inappropriate. None could carry a weapon or enter shops or homes uninvited.[2] An 1803 regulation prohibited costumes that alluded to the Revolution or mocked religion, and it threatened arrest for any reveler whose dress ridiculed the government. Two years later, a ban explicitly forbade revelers from dressing in clerical garb.[3]

Despite the ban, masks gradually appeared again in public, which the police generally tolerated. When Opera balls resumed in 1806, newspapers were soon reporting carriages filled with maskers on the rue St. Honoré. A decree from the following year acknowledged their presence in its prohibition on anyone wearing a mask from carrying knives, swords, or lead-tipped canes. It also forbade masks in public after nightfall and prohibited mask wearing in shops at any time. An 1815 "Ordinance Concerning Masks" added a clause meant to protect civility: "It is forbidden for any individual to provoke or insult persons masked, disguised, or costumed."[4]

After becoming emperor, Napoleon refurbished a popular tradition to turn carnival into a display of grandeur. The ceremony of the *Boeuf Gras*, a traditional procession that led bulls through the city to their death, was an especially dramatic enactment of the flesh that carnival feted and feasted on. Some writers pointed to ancient sources for its origin, citing Egyptian sacrificial rituals for spring or Roman agricultural festivals. In France, its earliest organizers were butchers' guilds, whose members guided immense bulls adorned with black ribbons and laurel branches along Paris streets. Fiddlers and fife players accompanied the parade, and a child with a sword or small scepter rode on the animal's back. It always ended at the slaughterhouse. The first verifiable account is from 1739, when the animal and its entourage passed before the homes of prominent magistrates and halted outside the Paris parlement. The processions, which likely predated the eighteenth century, were not regular. They were nevertheless frequent enough to be banned by revolutionaries as a barbaric custom.[5]

Under Napoleon, the procession gained a military escort and large supporting cast. Rather than a single animal led to the slaughter, there were now three, each with its own ceremony on Mardi Gras and the two days before. Handlers wrapped the bull's horns in gold leaf, twined its forelock with flowers, and rubbed its coat to a high sheen. The escort included a dozen apprentice butchers carrying knives and whips. These men dressed as hussars, the soldiers associated most recently with Napoleon's light cavalry. They wore powdered wigs and a purple chapeau, striped vests and breeches, white cravats, scarlet capes, and knee boots with golden spurs.

Two Mamelukes drawn from a contingent of horsemen Napoleon had brought from Egypt flanked the bull. Ten other Mamelukes in jewels and velour accompanied the procession, along with six Africans, six costumed Roman warriors, four costumed Greeks in ancient armor, six Polish horsemen, and six Spanish horsemen. Six French officers rode horses with plumes and braided manes. An advance cavalry unit led the procession, which was followed by infantrymen marching in close order. On the bull rode a child dressed as Cupid.[6]

FIGURE 9.1. *Ceremony of the* Boeuf Gras, 1824, V. Adam (Bibliothèque nationale de France)

Formal procedures were eventually introduced to select bulls from across the country. The city of Paris added a budget line to reward farmers whose animals were chosen. Butchers who marched were paid with state funds. Aging Mamelukes eventually gave way to gods and goddesses. It was customary to stop the procession at the Tuileries Palace, where officials often appeared on the balcony to receive the cheers of the throng below.[7] After Waterloo, elaborate floats replaced the military escort. Cupid received a float of his own in the '20s after a boy fell from his mount and broke his nose. The central features remained constant: to salute and slaughter the beast.

Hopes by the government to keep order among revelers were more or less met. Police reports for carnival early in the century consistently describe calm. "Frank, boisterous joy, without trouble or disorder" (February 1801). "We heard not a single degrading word. People everywhere spoke of enjoying the perfect calm" (February 1803). "Everywhere order reigned" (January 1804). The 1806 *Journal de Paris* echoed official assessments: "The boulevards were filled with curious onlookers of every age, along which—and with great orderliness—strolled masqueraders of every kind, on foot, on horseback, on carts, and in carriages, in theater costumes, in foreigners' costumes, in character masks and many more in plain dominos, but not a single indecency, nor a single violation of the law."[8]

Masked balls returned after the Revolution. Even at the season's peak, they were peaceful affairs with little social mixing. The police noted a private ball composed uniquely of former nobles and returned émigrés in a residence on the rue du Bac during the 1803 carnival. Organizers of an imperial ball at the Tuileries several years later had an extra 500 costumes on hand and encouraged guests to change their dress freely. Options included Swiss maidens, vestal virgins, and pagan priests. The ball "had the appearance of renewing itself three or four times during the evening." Balls at the Opera remained a pastime for the privileged. Of all the exclusive gatherings in Paris, noted a society newspaper, this was the most illustrious. "In short, nothing lacks for all to be smothered there . . . *decently*."[9]

In these years, most masks were simple dominos—usually black, white, or pink—and were either handheld or tied on with a ribbon. Women usually attended balls masked, while men were typically barefaced. There were a few character costumes; most instead wore black suits or elegant dresses. The attire adhered to a Napoleonic order recommending a domino and formal dress at balls. The few costumes present were among women. "The taste for disguise is entirely passé," wrote a visitor to the ball in 1825. "In the first boxes they yawn; in the second and third they sleep." Another described its "platonic promenades," adding that "one did not dance."[10]

In these decades, most carnival pastimes were segregated by wealth. For those not drawn to the Opera, the wine mills and dance halls at the city's periphery offered an alternative. After watching the *Boeuf Gras* pass, the playwright Victor de Jouy elbowed his way into a guinguette on the boulevard du Temple and was soon sitting alongside two Amazon women, Chinese sisters, a pair of old hags, and an Apollo. Warmed by the wine and happy with his plate of rabbit and cheese, he struck up a conversation. The Amazons were fringe makers, the sisters were laundresses, and the old hags young embroiderers. Apollo was an attorney's clerk.[11]

In the streets on the Sunday, Monday, and Tuesday before Lent, celebrations were animated and often merry. Crowds still gathered in the faubourg Saint-Antoine, as well as the boulevards Saint-Denis and Saint-Martin. Some costumes were traditional: the *Journal de Paris* deemed fishwives, apothecaries, Arlequins, and Pierrots "too easy," "tiring," and "unamusing." Others were more imaginative, including musketeers, a family of apes, Louis XV's wedding party, nomads from the Tartar steppes, and a band of "wild men" who went screaming through the streets with enough racket "to make elephants abort."[12]

FIGURE 9.2. *Carnival in Paris*, 1826, anon. (Musée Carnavalet)

Revelers threw candy from every possible conveyance, including handcarts and donkeys. The standard mode of travel was in packed carriages. A blue and gold platform pulled by a dozen horses was sponsored by a wealthy manufacturer and bore some sixty "grotesque persons," all of them employees. Maskers on horses acted as their escort. In another popular quarter, "Mardi-Gras's Burial" took place as it had for decades. A reveler covered with a sheet lay motionless on a ladder in a torch-lit convoy amid shouts and songs.[13] This being carnival, there was also mischief. Policemen in 1801 recognized an army deserter among a group of maskers but were held off long enough by his comrades for him to escape. The next year, police arrested several costumed pickpockets among maskers crowding the quays and bridges. Together they had stolen eleven watches and four snuffboxes.[14]

Police took note of the political sentiments they heard. Among them were toasts to Bonaparte's health from costumed revelers in a workers' cabaret and a group in costumes on the rue Saint-Denis.[15] Of course the revelers might have known they were being watched, and it would have been in keeping with carnival to offer lusty praise in perfect insincerity. It nevertheless seems true that under Napoleon and the Restoration monarchs the protection of a mask gave rise to remarkably few taunts or protests. This would soon change.

CRIMES OF CHARACTER

In 1834, the year the impostor Pierre Coignard died, the Théâtre de la Porte Saint-Martin staged a spectacle that combined the day's most popular stage character with the new mania for masked balls. At 2 a.m. on Mardi Gras, all dancing in the theater stopped, the stage was cleared, and the theater's resident troupe of actors performed the first act of *The Inn of Adrets*, whose star was the convict Robert Macaire. The hour, the raucous crowd, and the drama's irreverence assured a riotous performance. This version carried an additional twist: the participation of spectators. Notices in the press had given them their cue, urging revelers to flood the stage when the villagers danced with the Macaire and Bertrand. Maskers did just that, joining the actors in a romp that lasted until dawn. One of the most popular costumes among its gaudy revelers was Macaire himself.[16]

With the 1830 Revolution came an explosion of masked balls. Until now, the Opera had held the exclusive right to stage balls, which were reliably sedate through the 1810s and '20s. After 1830, it maintained the rights only on Saturday, which allowed other theaters to hire orchestras and clear their floors of seats for dancing on Friday and Sunday. From early January until Mardi Gras, notices appeared in the papers announcing each week's offerings. Some theaters offered up to a dozen balls a year. Establishment newspapers, whose writers were dismayed by what they saw, were quick to label the balls immoral. The Variétés ball was a place of "debauchery," the Saint-Martin the scene of "saturnalias," and the Odéon "bacchanalian." In the early 1830s, by contrast, the Opera ball remained resolutely conservative, "without dancing, without masquerades, without the confusion of costumes."[17] The atmosphere here, too, would soon change.

Robert Macaire was in fact a fixture in the city's commercial balls, which were now the central feature of carnival in Paris. Maskers improvised variations on his signature dress. The classic costume was a tattered green cutaway with tails, dented silver buttons, dirty red trousers, and a waistcoat but no shirt. Macaire's mask remained, a black bandanna pulled down to cover one eye. Any comic effect was lost on those who considered the play and its carnival spinoffs an outrage. "Their hideous rags and atrocious language have become as essential in masked balls as the music and candles," a critic wrote of the Macaires and Bertrands he saw at the balls. "The truth is, their laughter is without joy. Their merciless sarcasm gives off the nauseating stench of the prison cell."[18]

The poet Heinrich Heine lamented the "Robert-Macairianisme" he witnessed at balls. He wrote that its sneering spirit profaned all it touched, undermined sexual and social relations, and subverted loyalty, heroism, and faith.[19] Yet it wouldn't be right to say that all elites in attendance felt victimized. In many cases—and despite the claims of scandal the press repeated—they, too, donned a mask and joined in the jeers. For many, criminal disguise was in character during carnival.

The carnival costume most emblematic of the age was Chicard, a shambling figure who radiated irreverence. He was a walking scrapheap of France's fallen regimes: a "swift kick," as one writer put it, to "every taste, every epoch, every glory." His knee breeches were eighteenth century, but his knees were bare; the fraying epaulets recalled the Revolution's National Guard, but his boots were Napoleonic. A feathered centurion's helmet was made of painted cardboard or an upturned pail. "Every rag is derision. . . . His castoffs contain the whole of today's morality: bow before the lord of all, before the god of parody!"[20] Chicard's defiance exerted universal appeal. Those who wore his clothes were students, dandies, cobblers, clerks, notaries, and druggists. "Here, all hierarchy disappears," reads a small volume devoted to Chicard. "There are no more categories, no more conditions; all are leveled, everything melts together in the great whirlwind of the costumes and dances."[21]

Along with Macaire and Balochard—the latter the parody of a swilling worker—Chicard treated everything with cheerful contempt, "especially those above him." A pamphlet from 1841 coauthored by "Chicard and Balochard" called Chicard "above all, Republican," since he lives and dies by liberty: "the liberty of the dance." Whatever political content the pamphlet carried was softened by its silliness, but the derision is clear. Balochard deems Chicard a dictator of dance, which he says has put him on a level with Adolphe Thiers, the once and future prime minister who cast a long shadow over much of the nineteenth century.[22]

The female counterpart to Chicard was the Débardeur, a term first used to describe men who loaded wood for riverboats. The costume was a symbol of muscular freedom, and the women who wore it, classed as *lorettes* or *grisettes*, embraced its associations. The dress was simple: an untucked, flowing white shirt, form-hugging black trousers, and a worker's cap. When worn by a woman, the costume carried a charge. While it was still illegal for women to wear pants, an adjustment in 1800 had granted exceptions for

FIGURE 9.3. *Chicard,* Gavarni (Bibliothèque nationale de France)

FIGURE 9.4. *Balochard*, Gavarni (Bibliothèque nationale de France)

reasons of health, which required written police permission, as well as for carnival.[23] Débardeurs took full advantage, adding touches of their own: a red sash, a counterfeit mustache, a pipe or cigarette. By all accounts, they spoke like dockworkers.

The Débardeur was her own woman, at ease, another masker reported, "in the costume of the opposite sex." Débardeurs were unashamed to use words "that make you blush right down to the cotton in your ears." Many

FIGURE 9.5. *Débardeur*, anon. (Musée Carnavalet)

were equally bold in asking men to dinner after the ball or in refusing invitations that displeased them. "The Salic Law has been revoked," announced the author of a book called *Le Débardeur*. "Women rule."[24] The loose-limbed independence of the Débardeur that the popular illustrator Gavarni depicted was a joyous repudiation of the constraints of dress and behavior that defined women at midcentury. In the topsy-turvy world of carnival, the erotically charged freedom of the Débardeur was tolerated and even embraced.[25]

The same cannot be said of men who came to balls as women. To the *Coulisses*, a theater journal of the 1840s, the sight of men at balls wearing off-the-shoulder dresses was "ignoble," "scandalous," "hideous." For some this was no doubt what made flirting with Chicards such fun. When Jacques Renaudin was arrested in the summer of 1846—outside the carnival season—for wearing a dress in public and apparently not for the first time, police could not press charges. The 1800 law that forbade women from dressing as men did not prohibit the reverse: "an extremely rare state of affairs," an internal report commented, "that may give rise to polemics in the press."[26]

The signature dance of Macaires, Chicards, Balochards, and Débardeurs was the cancan. It went by other names as well, including the *chahut*, the *cahucha*, and the *Robert Macaire*. Revelers danced it only when the ball had reached a boiling point, which typically came during a quadrille. Its social mockery was clear: the quadrille, a group dance whose origins were in French ballet, was highly favored under Napoleon. When the orchestra

FIGURE 9.6. *"Yes, I do like lobster, but I do not care for Pierrot,"* Gavarni (Bibliothèque nationale de France)

FIGURE 9.7. *"A particular way of dancing,"* Émile Bayare (Bibliothèque nationale de France)

reached the moment for danced solos, the Chicard improvised outlandish moves, circling his Débardeur with high kicks, knee bends, and erratic twists. Women often responded in kind. By the standards of the day, it was shockingly sexual. Reporting on an especially riotous ball, an observer came to the cancan and then paused: "Here the pen refuses." "Its very name is trash," a fashionable news sheet reported.[27] That the cancan went on to become a gaudy symbol of *La Vie Parisienne* late in the century attests to its enduring appeal.

Contemporaries understood the dance to be a travesty of all serious sentiment. "It's not really even a dance, it's a parody—a parody of love, of grace, of French delicacy," wrote an enthusiast. It must be accompanied by "strident howls, convulsive yelps, guttural moans, and unimaginable positions."[28] Edmond de Lingères, a dandy who earned his carnivalesque bona fides by espousing absolute monarchy, a constitutional king, and republicanism with equal fervor, boasted of having been one of the first to dance the cancan, which he described as sensuous, taunting, lustful, mocking, contemptuous, brutish, and clownish. He added that it should be made the national dance of France. "Throwing her head back, with her mouth half-open," Lingères wrote in a spirited evocation of the dance, "Margot faints before the gaze of her partner. Then she kicks her foot to his nose, which he grasps and blesses." Other versions were less allegorical. At a masked ball at the Variétés theater, a woman came enveloped in cashmere and at the height of the quadrille slowly emerged from her wrap to dance the cancan in the nude.[29]

A Paris police manual for the municipal guard was a sign of the times. It detailed the procedures for booking revelers who danced indecently during masked balls: issue a warning, it advised, and if it remains unheeded escort the subject to the nearest station for charges under Article 330 of the Penal Code, Outrage Against Public Morals.[30] A dozen male students costumed as marquises and their maids and calling themselves *Les Badouillards*—"Rounders"—were arrested for dancing obscenely at the Théâtre de l'Odéon's carnival ball. They were hauled to the prefecture still wearing their dresses. A month later, the same group struck again, this time at the Théâtre du Panthéon's carnival ball, where they overwhelmed four policemen on duty. When reinforcements arrived, they responded with violence. When the mayhem ended, twenty students faced charges of indecency or resisting arrest, and eight were sentenced to jail.[31]

Officers charged with keeping order over these chaotic crowds were at constant risk. They suffered insults, shepherded drunks, learned to tell play-fighting from real danger, and endured the din of noisy orchestras in packed halls. Henri Gisquet, Prefect of Police in the early 1830s, regularly appealed to the Interior Ministry to limit the number and frequency of carnival balls and urged him to permit only women to mask themselves. On rare occasions, municipal guards joined in the antics to please the crowd, sometimes to their professional discredit. More commonly, their patience ran thin. Maskers at balls "go about hopping and leaping as they taunt the police," a journalist reported, "who end up looking petty and small."[32]

A dossier filed by the Inspector General of the Variétés lists instances of police brutality during balls. A youth in a first-level box, costumed as a simpleton and playing the part, used his feet to lift the hat of a sergeant standing below him. He was seized, beaten, and thrown into the street "with the greatest viciousness." Another night, agents surrounded a man in a sailor's costume whom they heard complaining about "dirty spies" in the hall. The sailor offered to leave on his own accord, but instead they removed him from the hall, drove him down the stairs kicking his back and kidneys, and dragged him along the sidewalk by his cravat.[33] "Voilà carnival!" proclaimed an anonymous pamphlet by a self-described masked scoundrel: "the despair of husbands, secret desire of women, triumph of shop-girls, hope of thieves, and damnation of gendarmes!"[34] Given the battles with police, it was fitting that when Sue's *Mysteries of Paris* began its run, maskers came to balls as characters from its underworld of thieves, kidnappers, and killers.[35]

To a season growing more coarse, the cholera outbreak of 1832 added the macabre. At one ball that year, an Arlequin ripped off his mask in a spasm to reveal a bluish, terror-stricken face. He and others who suddenly fell ill were loaded into a coach and taken to the Hôtel-Dieu, where most died. By one lurid account, some corpses were hurried into their graves still wearing their costumes to prevent contagion, at rest forever "as gaily as they lived."[36] Other stories convey an atmosphere of delirium. Two shop assistants from the countryside were arrested for obscenity at the first Opera ball they ever attended. One described his chagrin. "My mistake was that I cannot dance." He had watched others and tried to do the same. "I had hardly even touched the parquet when, in half a minute, I was in jail, where I looked miserable in my fishwife's costume." Some were proud and indignant. "I danced as I've always danced, which is by watching others and taking care of my own education myself."[37]

One reveler could not live with her shame. An agent later explained his arrest of the woman, who had come to the Opera ball as an eighteenth-century marquise, by saying that her dancing was revolting. Witnesses had tried to defend her as officers led her out of the hall. She had had too much champagne, they said, pulling off their masks; she was stirred up by the frenzy and would calm down if they would only let her go. Without naming them, the agent said that her defenders were socially prominent. For that reason, he had granted her wish to change clothes at home before going to the police station. The *Gazette des Tribunaux* carried his account:

> The young woman, who had shown intense distress on the way but whose tears stopped the instant we arrived at her domicile, apologized for having to ask the agents to wait in an unheated room, and, passing into her bedroom, told them she needed only five minutes to dress. She had scarcely uttered these words when the agents heard a window being opened in the next room. Then a loud scream rose from the street, and a falling body sounded on the cobblestones. We rushed into her bedroom. The young

> women was no longer there, and, looking through the open window, we saw her lying motionless on the sidewalk in the midst of a group of neighbors who had run down at the sound of her fall.[38]

Alongside the high spirits was a headlong and at times desperate mood, fueled by the concussive music, overheated spaces, and heaving mass of bodies. Writers used infernal analogies. The balls were like a witches' Sabbath, they said, or Milton's congress of demons, with their extravagant laughter, curses rising above the roar, and the deafening thunder of dancing. Today the terms seem cartoonish, and some of the hyperbole may well have been knowing. But descriptions also convey the crowd's frightening force and menace. "Chicard, finally, is Satanic, with his blazing eyes and depraved acts, his animal leer and florid complexion, his gait, his allure.... He comes to intoxicate us, to deaden us, and to teach us the words of his master: 'In Hell there is only dancing.'"[39]

Entrepreneurs devised ways to maintain the exhilaration beyond the usual battery of brass, drums, and cymbals. The signature finale of one conductor was to bring dancers to a fever pitch and, when they were careening at a suitably breakneck pace, fire a pistol loaded with blanks into the air. In later years, he discharged a howitzer packed with gunpowder in the direction of the dancers. "At the sound of the cannon, the crowd, intoxicated by the smell of the powder, goes mad, shrieking, howling, stamping their feet, and kicking their legs into the air." The cannon was a signal for the so-called infernal galop, which came at the ball's climax. Participants described the moment as an "electric wave" and a "terrible melee." At the packed balls of Mardi Gras, such moments brought genuine danger. Couples might fall and be trampled, and panic could provoke a stampede. G.-M. Mathieu-Dairnvaell, who published *The Carnival of Paris* under the pseudonym "Satan," likened its ecstatic terror to the last judgment.[40]

METROPOLIS IN MICROCOSM

As the popularity of masked balls grew in the 1830s and '40s, carnival largely disappeared from the streets. Daily police reports mark a sharp decline in public displays. Mardi Gras in 1840 brought "very few masks," a typical entry reads; in 1841, there were "few masks"; in 1843, "almost no masks in the streets but immense crowds in the masked balls"; and in 1844, street maskers were "very few." This continued for the rest of the century. By the 1880s, apart from grand processions of the *Boeuf Gras*, public carnival celebrations were scarce. Those that did occur seldom featured masks.[41] Income and attendance

FIGURE 9.8. *The Infernal Galop*, anon. (Musée Carnavalet)

figures at indoor masked balls, by contrast, register dramatic growth. In the mid-1820s, door receipts at the Opera averaged only 4,732 francs per ball. Ten years later, each averaged more than 8,600. Between 1839 and 1848, they grew still higher, nearing 14,000 francs a night. Whereas the season had had between six and eight balls in the 1820s, in the 1840s the Opera offered twelve.[42]

After 1830, even the smallest establishments offered masked balls. Their sudden growth and sheer number are startling. In 1836, the Paris police counted 182 public balls and another 874 private balls on Mardi Gras. The following year brought "infinitely more" requests to hold balls in the city. A year later, according to police records, there were "exactly three times more requests than last year." The anonymous author of a book called *Carnival* offered a rough calculation based on these figures. Assuming each private

FIGURE 9.9. *Galop Fantastique*, anon. (Bibliothèque nationale de France)

ball drew 100 people and each public ball drew 300, nearly half the city's population was behind a mask on Mardi Gras. A question on *Carnival*'s title page captures the mood. "One must ask oneself: Am I among those who dress in rags to make a drunken spectacle, shouting and carousing, for whom there is no longer sex, nor modesty, nor morals, nor respect for oneself or others?"[43]

A startling glimpse of the resources ball organizers drew upon came in a circular the police prefect Gabriel Delessert sent to commissioners in Paris and the suburbs. It was in response to complaints about outdoor orchestras that "overexcite the dancers, push them into disorder, and at the same time disturb neighbors' sleep." Delessert directed officers to inform all such establishments that musicians were forbidden from using bass drums, snare drums, kettledrums, cymbals, bells, hunting horns, smoke bombs, firearms, or artillery pieces.[44]

The Opera's monopoly on Saturday night balls still stood. Other theaters—including the Opéra-Comique, Variétés, Porte Saint-Martin, Odéon, Ambigu-Comique, Folies-Dramatiques, and Cirque Olympique—opened their doors on Sundays and on the three days leading to Lent.[45] Initially there was a rough correlation between admission prices and the expected clientele, but social inversions soon scrambled any map of status. Prices for a single ticket at major theaters ranged from ten francs at the Opera and Opéra-Comique to three francs at the Odéon. Admission at smaller theaters, cabarets, and cafés was less. Forged tickets could be had in cafés and restaurants near the Opera for five or six francs, which drew a complaint from the Interior Ministry that "our premiere ball" was being undermined, but the Opera itself offered season subscriptions that came to three francs per ball. At the Opéra-Comique, a ten-franc ticket permitted a "cavalier and two ladies" to enter. The very words evoked intrigue. Single-entry tickets were six francs.[46]

By the mid-1830s, character costumes were common at balls in theaters both large and small. The Opera employed a costumier inside the hall for last-minute rentals or purchases. Its exclusive provider was *Babin et Sanctus*, which published a catalog each season of its costumes. Other providers—such as the tailor M. Thumann on the rue Neuve-des-Petits-Champs and the dressmaker Mme Déserteur on the boulevard Montmartre—sewed costumes on demand. The booming market meant a rich and varied selection. This 1848 account is typical: an Arlequin seizes the waist of a Débardeur, a monk sweeps up a willing Columbine, a Pierrot approaches a lady in black domino, and a seigneur from the time of Louis XV clutches a Swiss milkmaid.[47]

There was a full social mix in these masked balls. A newspaper described the Opera ball as "a happy mingling of aristocratic elegance and popular merriment." At the rapturous height of quadrilles, the fusion was complete. One ball-goer claimed to recognize a banker, an aristocrat, a notary, and a broker at the Bourse caught up in the general frenzy. Another identified a diplomat in the costume of an Iroquois with scalps on his belt. For the wry chronicler of society Louis Huart, the Opera ball of the 1840s was like an imagined golden age, "for all ranks and stations there were confounded."[48]

Masked balls were by and large a gathering of strangers. The pool of willing revelers from the city's population was immense, the choice of venues large, and the likelihood that any one of them would be packed great. These balls were the metropolis in microcosm, a swirling city of strangers whose covered faces provided no clues to their identity. By most accounts, the mask's anonymity was genuine. The writer Charles de Boigne made the point with a brutal comparison. Society women flock to masked balls, he wrote, for the same reason they watch the beheading of criminals: to feel the rush of alien emotions.[49] The mask's anonymity gave hypocrites a chance to be authentic. "Under the domino one says everything, and one blushes at nothing."[50] Women might lust, and "loyal" husbands forgot their vows. The mask's anonymity lowered inhibitions and the barriers that policed polite society. The writer Paul de Kock described the thrill of speaking to strangers with the intimate *tu*. It carried a frisson—"pleasure, playfulness, lusciousness"—that both parties surely felt.[51]

A letter from one Julie Schott, who was instantly smitten by a masker she had met at the Opéra-Comique ball, expresses the dreams that masked balls could inspire. Published in the press on a Saturday before Mardi Gras, the letter was effusive. "My God! What a noble air and elevated tone! What expressive dark eyes! What grandeur and poetry in his features!" Julie writes. "If he really is a former notary from a town in the Midi, if his family is really rich and well regarded, and if everything else he told me is true, then may he return to the ball this Sunday. I'll be there in the same costume, standing in the same place."[52]

In the popular imagination, masked balls were a fertile ground for romance or marriage. They fostered physical contact and free-wheeling conversation at a time when arranged unions were in decline and the ideal of romantic love had begun to spread among the middle classes. The mask was at once guardian and goad, a shield for modesty and a prompt to share confidences. The pleasures of the balls, according to one fervent account, were in "seeing without being seen, confirming what you have always feared, . . . following and being followed, holding a hand and then losing it."[53] Some might call it an education in deceit—a way of producing intimacy while protecting oneself—but the mask was also a useful medium for a new dynamic between the sexes: two strangers might meet, fall in love, and marry. Where else, and how else, could such conversations occur? A journalist reported overhearing a young woman in a mask respond to a man who had told her he was a broker. "Our stock exchange is a masked ball," she said.[54]

The mask abetted romance by giving the imagination free rein. At 6 a.m., spent maskers at the Opera ball gathered in a foyer adjoining the dance floor for *souper*, a spread of lobster, meats, cheese, and champagne. Most ladies went with a man. Some accepted the invitation on the condition that they remain masked. By common understanding there was no further obligation. One author likened the occasion to conversation between travelers in a coach from Paris to Bayonne: after the *souper*, the two might pass in the street and say nothing. Some surely wanted this, and the mask was accommodating, but the *souper* might also be a first step toward affection. For women, it was an occasion to speak to a man on terms impossible elsewhere. Today a woman will take the arm of a man at a ball, a book devoted to the *Débardeur* observed, and ask for dinner as naturally as people once asked for a bit of snuff. For every woman who insists on keeping her mask on to eat, it continued, there are 930 who toss it aside.[55]

The frequency of stories involving unknowing husbands who attempt to seduce their own wives at balls testifies to the growing centrality of bourgeois marriage. The specter of infidelity was always present. Other misjudged seductions, some laughable but others ugly or unsettling, suggest that sexual currents weren't far from the surface. In "The Countess's Domino," a spiteful marriage prompts a husband to don a mask and wear one of his wife's favorite gowns to the Opera ball, where he intends to humiliate her by making a spectacle of himself. Instead, he draws a loud display of affection from her drunken lover, who grasps his hands and pleads for understanding. All farce is absent in this sober account.[56]

"An Adventure at the Opera" is a still darker tale in which the mask's secrets carry a warning. The story is set during the Napoleonic Wars, when a young officer just back from five years' service goes to the ball and meets a pretty masker. She addresses him as if they are intimates. Her white teeth and gentle voice inflame him, and they stroll together at length. She refuses his invitation to *souper* but says he may drive her home. She steps into his carriage, her foot slips, and she utters a cry. From nowhere a liveried servant appears, takes her to her own coach, and drives away.

The next morning, the young officer calls on his mother, but a servant tells him that she is unable to receive visitors: she has injured her ankle and is in great pain; the doctor is with her now. The story's last sentences leave much to the imagination. "In 1812, at the time of the Russian campaign, it was necessary to find a replacement for Captain Arthur de C***. Since his Paris leave, we have had no news from him, and no one knows what might have happened."[57]

The mask's gift of freedom opened a clear route for more direct propositions. A single man might be approached by a shapely masker who would take his arm, banter for a time, and then tell him that a gentleman of such obvious distinction would please her still more if he dressed in pants made by Blain, or a shirt by Charver, or boots by Clerx. A journalist looked into these stories to learn that there were six such women working the Opera balls for twenty francs per evening, hired by a publicist for Paris shops.[58]

Despite the cover the mask provided in the 1830s and '40s, some still came unmasked. To do so in an elegant gown or a black coat and tails, as most had done in the 1810s and '20s, was an assertion of status. To do so in the full regalia of a Chicard or Débardeur had an entirely different effect, which announced its gleeful vulgarity barefaced. For many, the season was sufficient to authorize inversions. Jules Janin, in *A Winter in Paris,* was taken aback when he recognized a magistrate dressed as Arlequin at the Opera ball. The man was in a circle of dancers with a former convict, who was dressed in a judge's gown. "What shame such men would feel if they knew . . . whose sullied hands touched their own!"[59] But who was to say that the two didn't also know who their partners were?

This moment marked an important turn in the history of masking. Breaking into a dance that the authorities called indecent, wreaking havoc in defiance of the police, playing the part of someone higher or lower in the social order: these were sights seldom seen before in Paris masquerades. Many today have the misconception that masking has always produced this behavior. In fact, it grew widespread for the first time in these years, when social and political conditions were now favorable. In the name of carnival, costumes and masks turned public gatherings into occasions to audition new roles. Many maskers found anonymity a necessary starting point. Some dispensed with the mask and made the role a second self.

Masked balls were a theatrical version of what Parisians increasingly experienced year-round. They were an exaggerated script of the rapid rise and fall of fortunes more common in the market economy. This meant that given roles were more fluid than ever before. Revelers in the 1830s could plausibly imagine themselves without a mask in a different social position. For a worker to don the clothes of the rich during Carnival, or a seamstress to propose dinner to a banker, or the rich to dress in rags, might not have been a fantasy to be dreamed and then forgotten. Whether society could deliver on its promise of greater gender equality or social mobility to those who embraced it during Carnival was another matter.

These things were surely in the minds of those who worried about the social mix of balls. It wasn't just that a magistrate who dressed as a clown, or a diplomat as an Iroquois, might tarnish the luster of elites. It was that when judges and counts joined hands with brigands and seamstresses, the whole social order, which rested on the authority of position, might lose some of its glue. The true risk, or promise, of carnival's leveling was that it offered a glimpse of a world in which identities were not fixed. Masked balls' fantastic popularity in the 1830s and '40s was evidence of a population ready to act on that possibility.

DEFIANCE AND DISORDER

The anonymity that prompted maskers to imagine themselves in different social roles produced an additional effect in these years: a feeling of impunity. As social and political tensions grew, so did the potential for conflict. Three major confrontations with police within five years revealed just how explosive these balls could be. The first two came in the Latin Quarter, with its concentration of students. Its population had been active in the revolution that brought Louis-Philippe to power, and its carnival celebrations continued to carry political overtones. Officers noted that maskers sometimes belted out "bloody refrains" of Jacobin songs at masked balls and harassed royalists.[60] For a regime trying to hold the center steady in the midst of attacks from leftists and the ultra-royalist right, these details were unsettling.

Initially authorities viewed the balls as a chance to blow off steam. The tolerance proved costly. When police tried to contain the chaos that erupted at a ball at the Théâtre du Panthéon, maskers fought back. Police stopped the event, made seventeen arrests, and evacuated the hall. An investigation reported "uncontrolled disorder, scandalous scenes . . . and violence against armed officers." Still there was hesitation to close the balls. Citing the business they brought, neighborhood merchants circulated petitions for the king to keep them open. The Minister of Commerce initialed his agreement, and Louis-Philippe let them continue.[61]

Two years later, maskers at the nearby Théâtre de l'Odéon went on a rampage that brought considerably greater damage. The Odéon dated from before the French Revolution and enjoyed a status second only to the Comédie-Française. This season included tragedies by Corneille, comedies by Molière, and contemporary plays by Eugène Scribe. Maskers were well aware that the boxes they ravaged hosted elites on other nights of the week.

Their destruction was not merely symbolic. It was aggressive, with clear social and political targets. Revelers tore chairs apart and walked across benches in their muddy boots. They wrenched gas candelabra from the walls and cracked the chandeliers' crystal globes. Punch pooled in the central foyer. Paintings were defaced, and statues of Molière and Corneille were mutilated. The bust of Louis-Philippe was smeared with charcoal. Someone hacked chips from the marble staircase. Theater boxes were used as latrines, with feces smeared on the floor and trails of urine on the walls. Police had been present but were unable to control the crowd, even when reinforcements arrived.

"To complete this tableau," a theater administrator who surveyed the damage wrote, "would require describing scenes and relating the language from this brutal orgy, but the pen refuses." The police prefect Louis Gisquet was less reticent in his presentation to the interior minister. "Agents under my authority could not pacify this debauchery. In addition to the obscene dancing, there were quarrels, fistfights, nudity, and the most shameless scenes."[62]

This vandalism was a prelude to a yet more destructive riot in 1837. Until now, the Opera had resisted the forces that affected masked balls elsewhere. Its high ticket prices had kept its balls mostly upper-class affairs, and fashion rather than concealment dictated dress. There had been fewer character costumes, and masks remained optional. When present, they were worn chiefly by women. While the guardians of tradition defended these sedate occasions, the Opera's management judged them to be a failure.

Louis Véron's appointment as Opera director in 1831 was meant to revive the institution's sagging fortunes. He was an inventor, businessman, and entrepreneur, and his monumental productions of Grand Opera quickly drew larger audiences. Véron also looked for ways to make masked balls more lucrative. In 1833, he dropped ticket prices from ten to five francs, which brought dire predictions that the "crapulous class" would invade this sanctum of art.[63] He sold raffle tickets for prizes finely tuned to bourgeois tastes, including fashion lithographs, a Japanese silver tea service, and an original oil painting of Jean-Jacques Rousseau eating cherries. He brought the famed horses of Franconi's "Equestrian Circus" onto the dance floor for synchronized stunts. Crowds still stayed away.[64]

As a response, an administrator named Duponchel leased rights for masked balls to the entrepreneur Antoine Mira, who proposed a surefire solution: Philippe Musard, one of Europe's best-known conductors and famous for his raucous balls at the Variétés theater. Having traveled to England in his early twenties, where he had led dance orchestras at the Vauxhall, Musard returned to Paris to perfect the pastiche. Working closely with promoters to rent halls and recruit audiences unaccustomed to classical concerts, he programmed single movements from Beethoven or Mozart and a potpourri of operatic excerpts set to dance rhythms. This was the conductor who fired blanks to excite maskers. In 1835, a French newspaper christened him Napoleon Musard. Around the same time, Hector Berlioz publicly burned Musard's quadrille based on tunes from *Don Giovanni*.[65]

Mira's instructions to Musard were to bring to the Opera what he had created at the Variétés, a genuine masquerade ball where men and women came in costumes and hid their identities behind masks. It was a move fully keeping with the populist spirit of Véron. On the Sunday before Lent 1837, posters two and a half feet tall appeared throughout Paris with "GRAND BAL MUSARD" emblazoned in black. This was code for the kinds of abandon the Opera had yet to see, with "Costumed" and "Masked" emphasized to denote a sharp break with tradition. The ball would be on Mardi Gras. The Variétés' formula, which was cranked-up music and a crowd of Macaires, Chicards, and Débardeurs, was about to enter the sanctum.

The response was excitement and sudden fear. When Duponchel saw the posters, he went straight to Interior Minister Adrien Gasparin to demand a cancelation. The Variétés crowd would cheapen the refined atmosphere, he said. The populace would bring their coarse words and crude dances. Given experiences elsewhere, violence could not be ruled out. Gasparin agreed, and workers immediately started pulling down the posters. The Opera was ordered to stop selling tickets. On Monday, Mira met with Gasparin with ominous news: discontent over the cancelation was brewing, and anger would erupt if the Opera's Mardi Gras ball did not take place. By the afternoon, large crowds had formed outside the Opera and were demanding that the ball go on. By nightfall, the government received regular reports on their size and mounting restlessness. Sometime after midnight Gasparin reversed himself and authorized the ball. Their one stipulation was to remove the name *Musard* from the poster.[66]

This made little difference. On Mardi Gras, handmade signs went up at the Variétés that read "Musard Ball at the Opera." In early evening, maskers drove through the city with their own signs on carriages.[67] Police Commissioner Bruzelin prepared for the crush by ordering thirty armed officers and gave them careful instructions on how to handle indecent dances and obscene language: take care to issue a warning before any arrest so that maskers would not be provoked.[68] The scruple showed that he had no idea what was coming. The interior of the Opera was bathed in dim red light when maskers streamed in near midnight.[69] Estimates put their number at five to six thousand. The tide rushed in, and Commissioner Bruzelin quickly saw that he had underestimated the task. In no time, maskers paralyzed officers

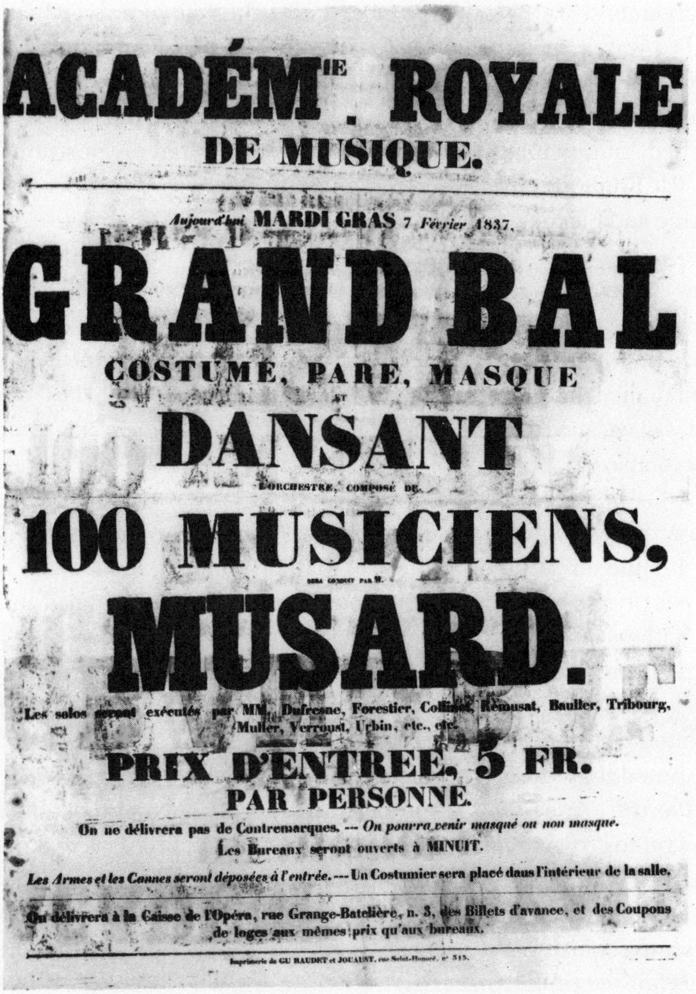

FIGURE 9.10. *Poster for Musard Ball* (Centre historique des Archives nationales)

at the hall's perimeter and pinned others in boxes above the fray. Bruzelin managed to send word that thirty more officers were needed and instructed his agents to make no arrests, sensing that the crowd might turn hostile.

Costumes of every kind filled the floor, where the spectral light transformed elated maskers, as one of them related, into a strange spectacle resembling phantoms. They moved together in couples or bands of four or eight as the whole assembly slowly pinwheeled the hall. Throngs continued to stream onto the floor, and the mass grew chaotic. Bruzelin sent out a small party to block the doors so that no more maskers could enter.

Reinforcements were slow in coming, and as he waited he watched—was forced to watch, as he later wrote—the scene unfolding before him. He reported that women abandoned themselves to things no carnival had seen and which even the loosest morality would condemn. "For six hours I watched, an unwilling and silent witness: I deplored my position!" The journalist Émile de Girardin, clearly enraptured, wrote that people were "pressing and pushing and knocking into one another."

> They turned and twirled and passed by again and again, never stopping, and there were bells ringing and drums pounding and the merciless orchestra never slowing and now even accelerating, and when there was no moment even to think the gunfire began, perfectly imitated. One could hear cries, and wailing, and laughter. It was a civil war, it was a massacre. The illusion was complete.[70]

Musard moved into his trademark infernal galop and was firing blanks from a pistol in the direction of the crowd. Maskers jimmied the lock on Louis-Philippe's private box and spread out on his couches to drink punch and raise toasts. Others broke into his son the duc d'Orléans's box, where they lit the candles on his branched chandelier. Revelers smoking cigars burned the carpets of a nearby box belonging to the Spanish banker Alexandre Aguado.

Around 6 a.m., someone in the crowd came across a discarded crown and shouted that Musard must be made king. A cry of *Vive Musard!* went up as Pierrots, Arlequins, and Robert Macaires dragged him out of the orchestra pit to crown him, lift him onto their shoulders, and carry him twice around the hall.[71] Commissioner Bruzelin, at last having gotten the reinforcements he had called for hours before, gave orders to begin making arrests and requisitioned a stage-level theater box to use as a holding cell. Officers hoisted troublemakers in from the front, who forced the door at the back and scampered out to rejoin the fray under the cover of their masks.[72] Damage was in the thousands of francs, with broken light fixtures, damaged tiles, and smashed chairs.[73] Many said it could have been much worse. Commissioner Bruzelin's prudence in not provoking the crowd with early arrests, a high-stakes gamble since they were clearly beyond controlling, likely averted greater violence and even bloodshed. Eventually the drunken and exhausted crowd, kept on their feet all night by Musard's baton, stumbled out into the morning air.

"What an exquisite example of the delicate pleasures of society! All honor to the most gallant nation in Europe! Highest thankfulness for the emancipation of July!" The sarcasm was to be expected from the royalist *Quotidienne*, whose readers considered the Opera a victim of the vulgar populace. "What we have dreaded for six years has now come to pass: the Opera has opened its doors to the scum." The centrist press was hardly less scathing. "Before long, we will be seeing 'No Smoking' signs on the walls of the world's premiere stage," commented the *Corsaire*. "Soon they will be selling cider and chestnuts in the corridors."[74]

The government realized the seriousness of the rampage. In an internal memo written largely to protect his own position after having approved the ball, Interior Minister Gasparin wrote of the need for "severity" in punishing Opera management. A special commission was convened and on Gasparin's recommendation faulted Henri Duponchel for having lacked proper authority to cede the balls' entrepreneurial rights. It was a technicality. Duponchel had been the first to urge the ball's cancelation, and the government had acted against his wishes in permitting it to go on. He received the maximum fine of 10,000 francs and was ordered to pay for all damages to the hall.[75]

Given the acrimony, the story's postscript is both telling and unforeseen. After the next two lackluster seasons of Restoration-style carnival balls at the Opera, Musard was invited back as their principal conductor. His triumphant return was greeted with the eager consent of the government and the theater's regulatory bodies. With him came his signature smashed chairs, pistols, and howitzers, as well as the cancan, infernal galops, and a familiar assortment of Robert Macaires, Chicards, and Débardeurs. His status as the premier maestro of Parisian masked balls would last for another ten years, from 1839 until 1849, with attendance and revenues that eclipsed all other establishments.

A condition imposed after the 1837 fiasco—that ticket prices be doubled, presumably to keep the "scum" away—narrowed the clientele but did little to diminish the crowds' exuberance. It was at the Opera where Heinrich Heine had watched masked dancers kick their legs high into the air with the dawning conviction that the French held nothing sacred and where the poor "marquise" had been arrested before plunging to the pavement from her bedroom window.

Outside the Opera's doors and along the nearby boulevards, projects were underway to bring restaurants, hotels, luxury goods stores, and banks. The crown jewel would be the monumental Palais Garnier, the Opera's future home. In the coming decades, the area would draw the Jockey Club on rue Scribe and the spectacular dining room of the Grand Hôtel. The burgeoning opulence that maskers of modest means saw as they made their way to the ball during carnival no doubt sharpened the gibes of those disposed to mock. It likely stirred resentment as well. It surely had other effects, too, quickening the dreams of those who longed to live above their station.[76]

10
World Upside Down

"SILENCE, CENSORS"

In the nineteenth century, it was standard practice to publish the sermons of notable priests. This was sometimes done for special occasions—a royal visit, military victory, or baptism of a convert—or on the dedication of a new mission. A priest's final message to his congregation before retirement might also be published. Small printing runs for a parish or diocese could include personal news and notices. When the last sermon preached by Father Barnabas, a curé in the village of Vesses, was published in the form of a prayer book, local information appeared on the reverse of the title page. It was a mix of social notes, diplomatic appointments, and marriage announcements. "On the twenty-fifth of this month, the comte de Turde-Nosh was admonished for having failed to take up his weapon against the marquis de Millefleurs. . . . The marriage of Herr Lingua-Keister and Miss Innit-Sniffit was announced several days ago. . . . The Ambassador Flatus-Mortis will receive the vicomte de Chomp-All in his *hôtel* on the rue de la Morellerie."[1]

Father Barnabas's final sermon, delivered on Mardi Gras 1830, summarized his calling, which had been to watch over the spiritual and physical health of his parishioners. Its primary message was on the abiding inner spirit that "produces within each one of us such surprising and advantageous effects." Its title: *A Description of Six Types of Farts*. The fart is majestic and mysterious, Father Barnabas began. Its range surpasses the mightiest pipe organ yet miraculously issues forth from a single tiny opening. Its marvelous effects are made without the help of a keyboard.

How could a single hole produce the tones of a hundred pipes? Simple analogies aid the understanding, Father Barnabas explained. Just as the report of a musket comes from a well-seated wad, so too might a stomach packed with sausage acquire an explosive state. Its tubes grow clogged and swollen, just like the narrow streets of a country village. The spirits want liberty, they begin to clamor and brawl, until at last a spark breaks through all obstacles. "Oh wonderful winds that leap forth from a small shift of the buttocks, to resound now as a trumpet, now a bugle, and now a flute . . . that should arise within the mortal frame to reawaken the sleeping senses, bring laughter to the cheerless, make straight the twisted bowels, and chasten the nose of all whose sniff has gone astray."[2]

A Description of Six Types of Farts was an especially ripe expression of anticlericalism, which surged in response to the Restoration's militant Catholicism.[3] It was an early instance of the carnivalesque pamphlets, books, songs, and poems that soon appeared in abundance. They reveal in gloriously disgusting detail the upturned world of carnival: a world of unchecked license and appetite, where taboos were banished and indecency was embraced. They were subversive in ways that most pranks of masked balls were not. The cancan could only pantomime moves that these verses recounted with relish. Their virtuoso insults—dazzling, inventive, often foul, and sometimes violent—were altogether more elaborate than what most maskers could produce on the spot.

Unless of course they happened to have a copy to declaim or memorize. That was apparently the purpose of *The Fishwife's Catechism*, which carries the subtitle "An Indispensable Collection for Spending Carnival Pleasantly." Maskers made good use of it. In 1830, the Paris police added a new clause to its 1815 "Ordinance Concerning Masks" that forbade any masked, disguised, or costumed person from insulting others with coarse words or "reading or reciting from offensive books, most notably *The Fishwife's Catechism*."[4] The book was a collection of dialogues and speeches set during carnival. Its vitriol reeked of the sewer. A preface written in pidgin and signed by Badoulard introduces the book's author, "the slovenly Mme Gutter-Mouth" whose description sets the tone. Her hair is as soft as an old broom, her nose as fine as the heel of a boot, her cheeks as rosy as a shriveled beet, and her lips as sweet as a chamber pot.[5] The book's scenes include an oath-laden argument between two market woman that ends in a long series of slurs.

> COCO: Get away, you bandage pus, bottom-face, shriveled fowl, toad's whore, ruined cadaver, crusty rump, lover's remedy, seducer of little boys, broken clock, reptile's squeeze-box.
>
> MARGOT: Shut yours, you toilet-pipe, oozing wound, mercury-box, trollop's bidet, poultice-face, canker-tooth, lamb-shank, tombstone, crocodile, animal.[6]

The Fishwife's Catechism circulated alongside a number of other carnival collections, including *The Prodigal Tongue, or the New Vadé*, *The Robert Macaire: A Salacious Songbook*, *Carnivaliana*, and *The New Fishwife's Catechism*.[7] Readers sometimes saw the same material in different books, as snatches of dialogue and especially impressive curses were spliced into new scenes. Their crude tenor was consistent. The opening harangue in *The Fishwife's Catechism*, for instance, "An Indignant Rotter to the Parson's Wife," also appears in *The Prodigal Tongue* as the words of a worker. Stretching over five pages, its ferocity is unremitting. "Your breath is as fresh as herring in vinegar, and your nose has the look of a burnt piece of tripe," runs one of the more muted lines.

More typical are insults about the rant's main subject, venereal disease: "Plenty of men who had the pox have shared their pepper sauce with you. . . . Go hide yourself, you old mercury-sponge." Toward the end, a cascade of abuse cranks up the tempo:

> Go ahead, cry in rage,
> Just like an old Camembert;
> It gives me the pleasure
> Of seeing your fair features:
> You sausage-grinding,
> Chestnut-gobbling,
> Baguette-yanking,
> Gherkin-licking
> Poison-box.
> Soiled doormat,
> Used pouch of charcoal,
> Unplumbed well,
> Bottomless drum.
> Go scratch yourself in the rump.
> Just get away from me, she-ape.[8]

Like *The Fishwife's Catechism*, *The Prodigal Tongue* announced itself as a handbook for carnival. It was "appropriate for merriment in diverse encounters among maskers whether at balls or in the streets."[9] In addition to more extended sequences, it offered short insults for specific costumes: to a baker (you color your bread with a harlot's piss), a woman in men's clothing (a beard isn't the only thing you lack), an apothecary (medicine and love, you give both from behind), a Turk (you can lock all the doors in Constantinople, but the little slit still makes you a cuckold), a lawyer (your mouth is so big as to catch turds on the fly), and Punch (hump-backed, shark-chinned, comma-nosed vampire). On and on they went, in endless variety fashioned for most every masker: valets, shepherdesses, coachmen, charlatans, street sweepers, peasants, wet nurses, Arlequins, Pierrots, savages, cooks, milkmaids, and shoemakers.[10] The sheer quantity is numbing, the wit runs thin, and the rough humor is often odious, but the energy it exudes commands a kind of awe.

While the pamphlets consider everyone and everything potential prey, three broad targets are especially vulnerable: love, the Church, and social elites. *The Prodigal Tongue* contains a declaration of sentiment from Gadouilleux, master vintner, to a laundress. Its enraptured tone mimics the ecstasies of romantic verse, and its filth is without limit. It begins:

The sweeper of sewers who drowns in the lees,
And the vintner who dies from the dross that he eats,
Feel torments less bitter than those that arise
In my turbulent heart when I gaze in your eyes.
Between you and a turd, my God! what resemblance!
The very same odor announces your entrance.

The poem continues in this spirit as the swain relates seeing an image of his beloved during his morning *toilette* ("Oh surprise! Oh delight! Your face seemed to swim / In the midst of the turds just beneath the rim"). It concludes with a promise to worship her likeness always.[11]

"The Liquefied Bride," from *The Robert Macaire*, brims with the same essential substance, although it lacks the exalted style. The ballad describes an unlucky bride who has diarrhea on her wedding day. Its eight stanzas narrate the progress of poor Marguerite from her home to the village square ("It colored her blouse and got on her feet / When she tried to clench her bum in the street"), from the square to the church, where she and the groom kneel at the altar ("Both received the benediction / In the midst of defecation"), and from the church to the marriage bed ("The clasp gave way, at last he had her, / Then he was sprayed with fecal matter"). The pair sink into a steaming brown sea until only their noses show. The lyrics smear both matrimony and religion. A moral-of-the-story ending parodies ladies' advice books:

Daughters, sisters, heed this lesson
Should you ever have the runs,
Take this warning and its wisdom,
Tuck a cork between your buns.

Deri dera, la, la,
Deri dera, la, la.[12]

The song's exaggerations, the obsessive iterations of its subject, and its ornate rhyming make "The Liquefied Bride" an especially elaborate farce. Its broad humor also carries a sting. The message of defecating in the marriage bed or at the high altar is not particularly metaphorical. The oceans of waste that sweep across these verses perhaps distract from the desecration, but two holy sacraments are polluted. Its response? Deri dera, la, la. The language alone would have been enough for police to prohibit the ballad, but readers would have also discerned a venomous undercurrent that was not just sport.

By comparison with the libertine literature of the eighteenth century, accounts of sex in these songs are relatively tame. By nineteenth-century standards, however, they were plenty risqué, offering a wide array of uncensored appetites and acts. "Silence, censors, if you're appalled— / All is done in carnival," runs the refrain of a song called "Carnival" that glories in desire. While its scenes are riotous, most depict lawless urges rather than deviance or force: the teacher Rigodon lectures blandly in the schoolhouse while his wife gives private lessons to a student; Martin thought he had found an honest bride, so imagine his surprise to learn that he was a father before the wedding; Blaise is all heart and a pure soul, so he shouldn't mind sharing his wine and his wife. The last verse of "Carnival," however, is of an entirely different order, using the season's liberties to embrace the forbidden:

My dear mum, from morn 'til night,
Sought for me a tender wife.
In the name of bringing help
She at last procured herself.
Silence, censors, if you're appalled—
All is done in carnival.[13]

The sexual themes sometimes included a social dimension, as in the title song of *The Robert Macaire*. Its refrain is a call for revelers to taunt the municipal guard by dancing the cancan, here called the *Robert Macaire*. The emphasis is on class:

Workers, proles, *Parisiens*,
Laundresses whose rags are clean,
It's time to dance *Robert Macaire*
To show the sentry what we mean.[14]

Its stanzas survey different strata, each irresistibly drawn to dance. By comparison with the workers' defiant sensuality—repeated in this refrain after each verse—upper-class pleasures are spoofed. Wealthy families attempt the cancan at exclusive addresses, dukes and duchesses go to seedy cabarets to learn it, the king dances it in *petits appartements* with his "little mignons." The song is joyous and lacks the foulness of other carnival lyrics. In the end, the dance bridges social differences. "Thanks to the cancan, the court and Courtille join hands," the song concludes, naming the working-class neighborhood just outside of Paris.

Other carnival verses targeted elites in harsh terms. These, too, invoked feces, rotting food, pustules, and pestilence, but their scenes are without the silliness of incontinent brides or cuckolded schoolmasters. Stripped of levity, the singsong verses carry menace. "Doesn't he simply make you swoon? / This golden boy with a silver spoon—" a fishwife sneers in the direction of a dandy. The poem appears in *The Prodigal Tongue, or the New Vadé.*

> He has a title, his words are sweet,
> Let's light a fire beneath his seat. . . .
> Look at how he pecks at turds:
> His legs are as skinny as a bird's.
> If the butcher should grant him grace,
> It's surely not to spare his race.
> It's only that for fatty filling
> Someone has to spend a shilling;
> In other words, you're not worth killing,
> Not worth the straw that we would waste
> To light a path to your resting-place.
> You'd waste the water we would pipe
> To rinse your stinking guts for tripe. . . .
> If someone served your guts in slices,
> He'd waste his time and waste his spices.
> If he drained your blood for *boudin*,
> It would poison the whole human clan.[15]

The carnival songs and lyrics that gloried in abuse were part of a long history of carnivalesque mockery. The Mazarinades from the seventeenth-century Fronde had a similar mix of insult and hilarity, and eighteenth-century tracts like *Diarrhearama* reveled in excrement. The violence of this poem, made all the more chilling by its cold banter, also had precedents. These included Scarron's little book on the detesticulation of Cardinal Mazarin and the acrostic a century later vowing to drink Chancellor Maupeou's blood. Carnival's expected license often blurred the line between what was and was not permitted. In periods when political tensions were high and social agitation overt, the carnivalesque carried genuine threat.

Carnival in the 1830s and '40s was nevertheless more explosive than during the Fronde or in the years before 1789. Police in the nineteenth century were well aware of the mood of maskers at carnival balls, by turns withdrawing when the chaos spiraled out of control and intervening with redoubled force. In masked balls, the mayhem was often without a target. In these packed, crowded spaces, its frenzy was contagious. Malice toward the Church and social elites was a common feature, present in much of the destruction in balls and on the streets. At the Odéon, maskers covered prime theater boxes with urine and feces, vandalized the private box of the duc d'Orléans, and defaced the bust of the king. At the Opera, they snuffed out cigars on the carpet and propped muddy boots on the balconies of bankers' boxes.

The anonymity masks conferred accounts for a portion of the havoc. More fundamental differences of temperament and setting, however, separate these carnival crowds from their earlier counterparts. Since 1789, and especially with the 1830 Revolution, legal equality changed the grounds and altered the terms of defying privilege. To the populace, the official denial of inborn qualities that had once been enshrined by law gave their taunts a greater purchase. All now shared the same rights, enjoyed the same civic status, and belonged to the same community of citizens. To elites who acted as if nothing had changed, revelers responded with scorn.

The genuine social mixing of masked balls also had a hand in making defiance easier. The eagerness of elites to mix with the working classes made them fair game. This dynamic was explicit in the warnings some sounded. The Chicard's costume may have attracted students, cobblers, and clerks, wrote the anonymous author of *Physiology of the Chicard*, but his real essence was the "distinguished gentleman who debases himself to act at being baseborn for several days." The *Journal de Paris* lamented the new fashion of the privileged to "wallow in the mud" at masked balls. Another newspaper noted with grim sarcasm that recent shifts in taste at the Opera ball now reflected "this century's allure."[16]

Revelers now brought a level of social and political defiance to the streets seldom before seen in carnival. Maskers performed impieties in ecclesiastical garb. Police spotted and strongly admonished maskers carrying guns. A man dressed in a tattered suit and sporting a tricolor cockade wore a mask made to look like Louis-Philippe. He went through the crowd shaking hands with "all the rubes and cads" he could find, to the mocking cheers of onlookers. "The police kept an eye on the masker without daring to arrest him for fear of a riot," a witness reported. Two nights later, the mockery was stripped of merriment when several hanged effigies of the king were discovered bearing tags that read "Louis-Philippe's Judgement." Revelers continued to mock the king and his ministers in the carnival season in the years to come.[17]

As the social and political menace grew more pronounced, Parisians found new relevance for the *Boeuf Gras* parade, which continued to lead bulls through the city to their death at the slaughterhouse. They still passed by the Tuileries, where Louis-Philippe sometimes saluted the procession as it passed. The satirical weekly newspaper *La Caricature* published a poem during carnival that described the encounter between "the two fat and powerful monarchs." A blithe tone belies its ominous doubling.

> His bulk was fat and formless,
> With a weight that was enormous,
> His face was large and thick
> On a wide and heavy neck,
> And he bellowed loud complaints
> From his tiny, feeble brain.
> . . .
> It's the end of the parade,
> And soon this momentary king
> Will shed his ribbons and flowers.
> His withered crown
> Will roll in the dust
> Along with all our glory.
> . . .
> Revel in this single day
> That destiny has given you.
> For king, O my king, for a day,
> Tomorrow will pass without return.[18]

Five years before the revolution that overthrew Louis-Philippe, an anonymous pamphlet drew the parallel more closely. "What a joy to be the Fatted Calf, with his sad, big eyes and beautiful horns! . . . But his reign is ephemeral, like all monarchies. He knows, the poor monarch, that his crown and its splendor are only passing. . . . Better to die from a heart attack or the stroke of an axe than to waste away in work and pain."[19]

The next year, one of the butchers took the parody too far. When the procession passed in front of the Tuileries, the king motioned from the balcony for it to stop so that he and the queen could greet the child Cupid. They descended to the street, kissed the boy, and mingled with the entourage. Suddenly the young butcher appeared on the royal balcony, grandly saluting the crowds assembled in the courtyard. They responded with cheers and cries of "*Vivat! Vivat!*" Royal aides rushed onto the balcony, where they punched and kicked the butcher as they pushed him out of view.[20] The season had always inspired disrespect, but rarely had it pointed so directly at the head of state.

NOSTALGIE DE LA BOUE

Of the many familiar rites in the heyday of carnival—the broken chairs, brazen cancans, and infernal galops, mustached women in brigands' clothes, cupids and slaughtered bulls—none embodied its headlong irreverence with greater gusto than the Courtille Descent. The post-festum Descent was as much hangover as final fling. Assembling on the outskirts of Paris as the sun rose on Ash Wednesday, maskers joined a parade that obliterated all differences in mud, blood, and alcohol.

Those otherwise indulgent about carnival's excesses had nothing good to say about it. To the disapproving, it was the sorry product of the ball season's two-month binge. They called it both indecent and inhuman. That it appealed to the wealthy in particular was of special concern. In this, it captured the essence of Parisian carnival in the 1830s and '40s, which was broadly popular and widely censored. For many, the season was incomplete without the Courtille Descent. In the early nineteenth century, the village of La Courtille lay at the eastern edge of the city. Beyond it was the countryside. Not far from the Saint-Antoine district, it was home to farmers, vintners, shopkeepers, and urban workers. Situated beyond the city limits, it had a reputation for lawlessness, a view unfair to those residents who more or less played by the rules.

The reputation was also not entirely wrong, especially on weekends. Wine was cheaper in the guinguettes clustered on the Courtille side of the Barrière de Belleville, which was close enough to attract workers from Les Halles and Saint-Antoine. Streetlights were few, fights were frequent and sometimes fatal, and the police, despite a post at the barrier and frequent patrols into the village, avoided some areas at night. A broadsheet from midcentury described the horrible sounds that penetrated the darkness from curses, quarrels, and combat with fists or knives. The light of day often revealed human debris, "the largest number having collapsed in drunkenness, but others, with gaping wounds, no longer breathing."[21]

The Courtille's celebrated wine shops included the *Red Bull*, *Brazen Cock*, *Wooden Sword*, and *Savage*. The largest and best known, which also served food, was *Papa Desnoyers*, the "Élysée of miscreants" and a frequent stop for police. Regulars called its atmosphere Homeric. Sides of beef and skinned sheep ready for cooking hung from the walls. Tables piled with charcuterie, fruit, and bread stood nearby. "If master Rabelais had known La Courtille," a visitor wrote, "he would have certainly made it Gargantua's home."[22] *Desnoyers* was dark, smoky, and loud. Nonstop music from noon until midnight mingled with merchants' cries and criminal slang. Its denizens had "a horror of normal walking," a visitor reported. "They either danced or staggered."[23] This was where the ex-convict François Vidocq came at the start of his career as the new chief of the Security Brigade to stage an attention-grabbing dragnet. Positioning his agents on the streets outside, he ordered the customers to leave one by one. With a piece of white chalk, he marked a large X on the clothes of each man he recognized as a deserter, thief, or escapee.[24]

Desnoyers was the destination of choice when Mardi Gras balls in Paris finally wound down. Revelers began arriving on Wednesday around 6 a.m. Crowds that had been growing since Saturday prevented more than a token cleanup, and much of the rubbish of those four days stayed where it had fallen. Visitors described cloth napkins with every sort of stain used and reused. Gnawed bones, broken cups, and shards of bottles littered the floor, which was slick with drink and discarded food. It was a "hideous atmosphere, stinking of wine, liquor, cooked meat, and nauseating excretions." A brass band played raucous tunes on the first floor, which was large enough for twenty couples to dance. A journalist likened the cancans he saw to the same scenes that now defiled the Opera.[25]

After breakfast, maskers tumbled into the streets to begin a motley parade into Paris. They headed down the sloping boulevard de Belleville, their "clothes in disorder, muck up to their knees, their faces pale and some covered in dust." Witnesses did not hide their disgust. "Women screamed like veritable bacchantes, which incited their husbands to become still more drunk."[26] The procession of revelers down the muddy slope singing, shouting, and fighting was "like an overflowing sewer" in its waves of "crude, brutish, besotted maskers." Some were on foot, with others in open coaches or perched atop carriages, "as though on pedestals from which to insult those they passed."[27]

Spectators watched as the "dirty ocean" passed before them. One of them described seeing Pierrots, milkmaids, marquises, Débardeurs, shepherdesses, rag pickers, and Chicards. From the windows overhead, residents rained down bits of chicken, old fish, and stew. "This delirious mass, a river of humanity, snaked its way down the street singing, shouting, dancing the cancan, squealing, shrieking, stopping for more liquor and responding with yet more swinish delight than before, abusing onlookers and treating them to gestures impossible to describe."[28]

Benjamin Gastineau, whose 1855 volume on the history of carnival ends with an account of the Descent, recounts seeing women dressed in men's clothing and swearing at the top of their lungs. Women and men alike were guilty of blasphemies, he writes, as they spewed out infamy on God, their elders, and their spouses, "interrupting themselves only to vomit." The aftermath was ghastly. By noon, Gastineau continues, most of the "peasants, pompadours, financiers, Débardeurs, savages, shepherds, dominos, Robert Macaires, and brigands" had left La Courtille. Street sweepers moved in to face the aftermath, sickened by the "human filth," kicking those who had passed out, giving others a hand but not knowing where to take hold, and fending off the insults of those who continued to curse and shout.

"Who are these drunken, dirty crowds, who spent the night in sordid debauchery and at daybreak delight in wallowing in mud and insulting others?" The question came from a writer in the *Journal de Paris*.[29] He provided various answers, beginning with the Courtille's own residents, who made the most of the annual attention. They, too, drank and ate at the cabarets' wooden tables, he wrote, danced to the small bands assembled there, and took their place in the Ash Wednesday procession down the long hill.

To another observer, the moment was a release and a happy reversal, an "admirable compensation" for twelve months of poverty and want. "Let them have the indescribable fun for an hour or two of insulting everyone to their face and calling them '*tu*.'" Some in fact claimed the revelers were all working class, a description that combined censure, condescension, and relief that kept such filth at a safe distance from respectable people. "When you stop and think that these people have to go back to being laborers after Mardi Gras," as one writer put it, "one can only pity them, since they will surely repeat these shameful pleasures."[30]

There were also the same rumors as those spread before the Revolution that the government paid the poor during carnival to keep them pacified. The police prefect Henri Gisquet had a reply for such notions. "Any government would have to be an enemy to its own dignity and authority to encourage such depravity." He had a point. Carnival in these years was open season on the government and police, spirited to be sure but seldom happy or submissive. "Haven't you seen these people in disguise," Gisquet asked, "ready with their outrageous gibes and taunts against our magistrates, our ministers, and even the head of State?"[31]

A far greater number reported that most of the Courtille revelers were reputable and well off. "Good Parisians whisper the names of society figures whom they know will participate in the Courtille Descent. They are even willing to brave the February wind to see them more drunk than normal."[32] A British aristocrat and founder of the Jockey Club in Paris, Lord Henry Seymour, was a fixture at *Desnoyers*, where he distributed exploding cigars and called himself Milord Arsouille, "Sir Souse Pot." For the Descent, Arsouille rode in a carriage drawn by six English horses and amused himself by holding coins under a flame until they were scalding to throw to children. One year a dozen musicians rode with him playing the William Tell Overture. Milord Arsouille may have been the most flamboyant regular at the Descent, but he was not the only society figure there. Every class came to the Courtille, a contemporary wrote, "mingling and confounding ranks until there was no longer any distance."[33]

For the authorities charged with keeping order, the Descent's makeup was substantially more unsettling than if the troublemakers had been strictly working class. This was why Prefect Gisquet, who reported that elites gleefully imitated the "abject classes" during carnival, denounced the privileged for embracing such squalor.[34] Others, too, condemned the conduct, which was not so much topsy-turvy as the rich slumming it. The effect was a kind of equality, with a strong pull toward the lower end. It was as if elites had forgotten their place, one observer commented, and were now hurling themselves into degradation "with such fervency and fire" that it looked second nature.[35] It was a troubling thought for those who still believed that order depended on hierarchy.

This social mix accounts for much of the anxiety the Descent provoked. The privileged classes took on what they pictured as the gross pleasures of the working classes. They dressed in their clothes, ate in their neighborhoods, and were drunk before noon. Tastes among those who came in costumes reflected this. One account drew attention to the decline of historical and exotic costumes and the rise in "ignoble" and "hideous" outfits, and another called the display "trashy."[36] By comparison with carnival during the Empire and Restoration, these years saw a coarsening of the public mood. The humor was more cruel, the taunts more personal, the pranks more rough. One merrymaker's insolence brought calamity. A coachman amid the throngs of Mardi Gras knocked the hat off an elderly man with his whip. As the man stooped to pick it up, the horse jostled him. He fell, struck his head on the paving stone, and died in the street. The coachman did not stop.[37]

THE FOOL'S TRUTH

When does carnival point to revolution? In the days before Lent, its predictable antics blur the line between the permitted and forbidden, but the defiance is usually understood to be temporary. Its topsy-turvy truth mocks the rich, scoffs at marriage oaths, and lampoons the Church, but whatever insolence or blasphemy it voices is usually couched in merriment. The Courtille's bacchanalia, however much it resembled Eugène Sue's vision of Hell, was over in a day. Exhilaration, even when genuinely anarchic, does not mean revolution. Yet carnival's upside-down world can sometimes shift thought and prompt more radical action. One remarkable book that appeared partway through Louis-Philippe's reign used carnival's distortions to frame a searing social critique. Now forgotten, it was among the most revolutionary works of its day.

The Testament of Robert Macaire: Thoughts and Maxims of This Storied Character is an improbable vehicle for this generation's most famous swindler. It is substantial and sober, without dramatic action or apparent humor. It is, in fact, a thoroughgoing rejection of worldliness. Its author, Benoist de Matougues, was a scholar of ecclesiastical history whose work was devoted to religious subjects. He edited the writings of St. Jerome, wrote a biography of Pope Pius IX, and assembled a multivolume geographical dictionary of the Bible.

Matougues turns Macaire's cynicism into a wholesale denunciation of the reigning order. An opening letter in the voice of Macaire to his accomplice Bertrand serves as the preface. Here Macaire states that the present day needs its own Molière, who unmasked hypocrisy at a time of blind faith. Who will do the same for commercial chicanery? Society is "one continuous, unending trumpery, with each class specializing in its own variety." Cheating is universal, permanent, and absolute. There can be only one conclusion: fashion for yourself a better mask and take full advantage. "You may do whatever you wish so long as you preserve appearances and seem not to violate the social code. This is the issue in its entirety. . . . Therefore, Bertrand, cunning alone will save you. Society merits your most profound contempt. It is a collection of imbeciles, hypocrites, and perverts."[38]

So begins this 335-page treatise on wealth and poverty, morality and the claims of conscience, and what remedies might exist for this corrupt world. The content is classic Macaire, but the mood is dark, animated not by cheerful expedience but fierce accusation. The urgency of its central theme—the malign power of money—is unswerving. Money does not just influence views of a person's worth. Money creates it, regardless of merit.

The *Testament* describes with two funerals, beginning with a common worker. A naked cart clatters to the cemetery, perfunctory verses are read by a priest, and two salaried men dump the body into a hole. In the second, a train of stylish mourners follows a rich man's coffin. There are respectful salutes along the route, solemn hymns and eulogies, and a waiting monument. Notice the response of strangers in particular, Matougues remarks. Why do the two processions receive such different reactions? "The world pardons everyone except the proletariat."[39] In the eyes of society, he observes, every impulse and action of a poor man reveals innate depravity. When a worker speaks, he is a liar; when he eats, he is a glutton; when he drinks, he is a drunkard; and when he rests, he is lazy. When a worker flares up in anger, he is a savage, and when he is silent, he is a cretin. When he is cool to others, he is proud, and when he is polished, he is a fraud.

The rich man's actions and desires, by contrast, are a testament to his judgment. Is he a drunk? He only likes to have fun. Does he gorge himself with food? He knows how to live well. Does he break the law to make money? He knows how the game is played. Macaire describes the underlying psychology in his preface:

> Everyone says [the worker] is free. This is a lie. . . . No one has lived as he lives, with his terrible burden. . . . You heap up mud in order to cast him into it, you spit in his face and then announce that you have rendered fair judgment.[40]

The book provides examples of this hypocrisy. If a rich man kills someone in a duel over insulting words or acts, he is honorable. If a poor man kills someone to feed his starving family, he is a murderer. Vengeance underlies both judgments. In the first instance, it is the due justice of the offended; in the second, it is an obligation to society. Matougues responds bitterly: "And this is what you call morality! This is what makes up good and evil!"[41]

The power of money to define values leads him to a radical conclusion: the supposed laws of morality are fictions devised by the powerful to subjugate the weak. What the world calls ethics has no sanction from God or any grounding in earthly or divine justice. It therefore has no legitimacy over conscience. The same features that render these laws arbitrary—greed when they succeed and revenge when thwarted—make them inviolate to the privileged. "Woe to those who infringe the code! . . . Prison, exposure, forced labor, death: these things await those who violate the social code."[42] In the name of this fiction, society judges, condemns, and executes.

This is half of Matougues's equation in explaining the social genesis of morality. It remains to explain why anyone would accept such an arrangement, most especially the powerless, at whose expense these corrupt codes were erected. The answer lies in human nature, which for Matougues is fundamentally selfish. He first sounds the theme in the preface. It is not true indignation, Robert Macaire asserts, but rather envy that feeds criticism of his crimes. If his detractors were honest, they would stop invoking words they don't believe and try harder to be like him. "What actually bothers them?" he asks. "Our success. What do they really want? Our money. At base, every one of them is as guilty as we are—if there's any guilt in the matter. We at least have the courage of our morality. Our critics don't even have the courage of their hypocrisy."[43]

Matougues draws the conclusions that follow. Driven by greed, the rich and poor alike use the language of morality to elevate their victories and console themselves in failure. Moral censure is the expression of those whose own selfish desires have been thwarted: to call the successful immoral is gratifying. Yet Macaire's words urge an additional response. Those who grasp the corruption of society's values should use them for their own ends. Matougues offers a set of maxims that counsel distrust, dissembling, and concealment.

> Mediocrity and cunning usually succeed: mediocrity draws no umbrage, while cunning disguises and deceives.
>
> In questioning the judgment of children, one forms them early for hypocrisy. This education is logical and necessary for a habit they should employ for the rest of their lives to avoid starvation or social rejection.
>
> One is free to speak at length, but prudence recommends saying nothing.
>
> Do not attempt to enlighten others, which would be foolish on your part. People do not change their minds. Leave them in the company of their own pride, and laugh at their stupidity.
>
> The human heart is a toxic dump that one must take care not to dredge. Its fumes are fatal.
>
> Whoever expresses gratitude is a liar.[44]

A series of assertions resembles claims that Karl Marx made in works from this same decade. Commercial society's thoroughgoing dishonesty authorizes rejection of its so-called morality, Matougues writes: "Ideas are nothing more than the realization of the mores of their epoch, and if these ideas are money-obsessed it is because mores are built on money." Political authority itself is inseparable from the interests of property: "Financial interests will not forgive my words against men of money, for these are the powers of the age. To attack them is to attack property and to attack the state."[45] Because law is a product and defense of this society, it has no legitimacy. Humans may therefore violate it, curse it, and seek to abolish it: "Everything in this world turns on force."[46] Matougues's conclusion therefore justifies meeting force with force.

> How can you expect us not to kick the dust of our sandals into the face of this society, which oppresses the proletariat and leaves it to starve? . . . Do you think we can leave society untouched, cursed and dissolute as it is? Impossible. We will haunt it, torment it, attack what is called society's rights, laws, and principles, and call all its enemies to its ruin.

The logic foretells conflict: "I do not understand how a rich man and a proletarian can look at one another without destroying one another."[47]

In a series of statements to follow, Matougues announces revolution. Society is at war, he writes, between the haves and the have-nots. The right to property is not sacred and can survive neither examination nor criticism. The final phase of industrialism will push workers to bring its own fateful consequences. "Nothing is more powerful in overturning human works than revolutions: the strongest and most ancient institutions will not survive. . . . Revolutions are prepared by theory but put into place by interests."[48]

Matougues addresses the wealthy and powerful directly. The poor were hungry and you offered no food. The poor were homeless and you provided no shelter. "Now it is your turn to suffer! Be cursed, cursed forever!" You have profaned our wives, corrupted our daughters, and debauched orphan boys and girls. "Suffer, you accursed ones! Vengeance is at last come!" Interspersed with passages that clothe the struggle in biblical language, the warning is apocalyptic. "Rise from the grave, ye dead, awaken, throw yourselves against the society, whose corruption is ranged against you!"[49]

After this climactic vision, Matougues suddenly seems reluctant to follow where his own words have led. His call to arms remains in suspended animation. "Don't believe that I intend to work for the betterment of humanity: this least of all! Such a wish has always struck me as foolish and useless. Trying to make people better is assuredly a sign of madness." The statements are puzzling and unexpected. The book's final sentences remain defiant, but the tone is defeated. What is left for workers who cannot feed themselves? They must either steal or die. And if they steal, how does society respond? "Send the wretches to prison! To prison!"[50]

The Testament of Robert Macaire is an eccentric mix of advocacy, critique, and exhortation, consistent in its outrage but filled with incongruities. It curses society in religious terms but seeks no comfort in faith or divine justice. Its denunciation of injustice is uncompromising yet ends in discouragement. Animating all of it is the spirit of Macaire, the master of bluff. Is this his biggest caper yet? One is tempted to consider it. "What is behind the magnificent, indignant language [of moralists], these tears and lamentations?" Macaire asks in the preface. "Nothing but envy of Robert Macaire." Is Macaire also laughing at Matougues? Probably not. The opening letter has a hard edge that the charismatic Macaire never showed. "The consequences of violating [society's] morality are horrifying: imprisonment, forced labor, and the executioner, the great ruler of this world."[51] Here Macaire's knowing wink looks more like contempt.

If Macaire's bitterness in the *Testament* was unprecedented, it was not entirely out of character. Matougues took the premise of a farce based on the power of appearances, drained it of all humor, and followed its logic. Macaire had taught that one must manipulate others to avoid becoming their victim. When money is the sole source of morality, and when that morality is used to victimize the poor, the proletariat's destruction of the ruling class is both just and certain.

Such claims serve to connect Macaire's mocking laughter to the religious themes of Matougues's other works. Macaire-as-misanthrope—a crook whose upside-down worldview is the one accurate vision in a contemptibly perverted society—is not so far from the belief that the human heart is corrupt and all is vanity. Matougues's Macaire ends his prefatory letter by invoking Pascal. The philosopher renounced earthly morality, he reminds readers, showed contempt for the hypocrisy of courtiers, and died in obscurity. A century later, Voltaire declared Pascal a madman, mocked religion, and basked in his international celebrity. "Conclusion: respect for divine morality is foolishness, while respect for human morality is brilliant."[52] The fool speaks the truth.

TO BE RENEWED

The best-known writer on the experience and effects of carnival is the Russian critic Mikhail Bakhtin. Since 1968, when his 1940 doctoral dissertation appeared in English, scholars have regularly turned to his work to make sense of the subject. Bakhtin's *Rabelais and His World* now holds such commanding authority that his account of the carnivalesque has gone beyond describing the popular celebrations before Lent to encompass transgression against structures of power more broadly, including in politics, status, class, gender, and culture. Among historians, the temptation has been to read this interpretation as the definitive word on carnival in all times and places. In fact, carnival's customs, significance, and meaning have varied so widely across places and periods that no single interpretation, even one as appealing as Bakhtin's, can encompass its many expressions.

For Bakhtin, Rabelais's novels *Pantagruel* and *Gargantua* embodied the spirit of carnival's topsy-turvy world. In Rabelais's joyously distorted universe, carnival is an inversion of all official hierarchies and affirmation of humans' essential equality. Carnival celebrates "temporary liberation from the prevailing truth of the established order." The individual becomes "an indissoluble part of the collectivity, a member of the people's mass body." Carnival is rebirth through costume, mask, and common physicality. "In this whole, the individual body ceases to a certain extent to be itself; it is possible, so to say, to exchange bodies, to be renewed."[53]

In this account, carnivalesque hilarity celebrates things more elemental than ideas, culture, or religion. Its essence instead is renewal. What Bakhtin calls the lower bodily stratum—Bernard of Clairvaux's acknowledgment of being born "between feces and urine"—occupies a heroic place in the carnivalesque. Here the stuff of standard Rabelaisian insult becomes a wondrous affirmation of fertility. "Excrement was conceived as an essential element in the life of the body and of the earth in the struggle against death. It was part of man's vivid awareness of his materiality, of his bodily nature, closely related to the life of the earth."[54]

According to Bakhtin, this was why the body's urges, functions, fluids, odors, and orifices are so prominent in *Gargantua* and *Pantagruel.* It is also why they are essential to the carnivalesque. Rabelais's "grotesque debasement," Bakhtin comments, was not with mud but with excrement.[55] This is the register of *Diarrhearama* from the eighteenth century and "The Liquefied Bride" from the nineteenth. For Bakhtin, laughter gives voice to the powerless. As a spontaneous eruption of a universal life force, laughter resists dogma, intolerance, and intimidation. The carnivalesque, guided by the drives and desires all humans feel, follows its own law of freedom: "everyone participates because its very idea embraces all people." During carnival, there is no distinction between spectator and actor. All who participate are both playwright and performer. A more direct way of putting it is that carnival laughter—"gay, triumphant, mocking, and deriding"—spares no one, including oneself.[56] The season's insults, curses, and abuses are all a rejection of hierarchy. "People were, so to speak, reborn for new, purely human relations." This for Bakhtin is genuine liberation: the triumphant freeing of human consciousness by a "new immortal people."[57]

Carnival at the Courtille, in masked balls, and as expressed in its exuberantly foul songs and poems lends support to this vision. Here the humble set the terms: laundresses in their cheerful rags, Father Barnabas and his pious farts, the slovenly Mme Gutter-Mouth, and, in Benoist de Matougues's reading of Macaire, the revolutionary proletariat. In the 1830s, supposedly respectable revelers joined in as well. For the poor to insult the rich implied social tension. For the rich to imitate the poor insulting the rich meant a temporary dissolution of all such roles. These moments were a plausible version of what Bakhtin called true equality. Yet other elements of carnival in the 1830s and '40s do not fit his descriptions. Unlike the laughter of Rabelais, the nineteenth century's japes were vicious and targeted. It's one thing to go from the Opera ball to Desnoyers to hoist a greasy joint and slosh beer with prostitutes and thieves. It's another to have them tell you you're not worth the water to rinse your guts.

In Bakhtin's account, carnival liberates in the moment of hilarity. If it is seditious, the rebellion lasts only as long as the laughter endures. Its offenses are authorized, predictable, and therefore contained. These are among the reasons that numerous scholars have concluded that carnival brings no true political or social change. Some go further to argue that it is in fact conservative. The critic Umberto Eco, for instance, took issue with Bakhtin's claim that carnival is transgressive. The season's supposed utopia, Eco writes, is not only fleeting but has the effect of strengthening the status quo. Comedy and carnival "remind us of the existence of the rule."[58] Their antics, however outrageous, do not threaten the social order, Eco concludes. On the contrary, they reinforce the law.

This is in line with those who view carnival's seeming anarchy as a safety valve. The anthropologist Victor Turner makes the point by casting carnival's traditions in terms of ritual. Its seasonal regularity is part of a larger, stable order, he writes. Its ridiculous transformations highlight the reasonableness of the everyday. Such rituals of status reversal, Turner concludes, strengthen the status quo in two respects: they acknowledge the accustomed order and, in returning to it, affirm the legitimacy of those who hold authority.[59] Whatever changes such moments of radical inversion might bring are therefore incremental.

Incrementalism can nevertheless alter an established order. This is the frame within which Natalie Zemon Davis finds "unruly women" of the early modern period—those who dressed as men, cursed grain hoarders and shameless officials, or claimed authority as writers—to have weakened encrusted hierarchies. These carnivalesque inversions, Davis writes, did not strengthen the accustomed order but weakened its hold in small but significant ways. They expanded the reach and authority of women beyond the limiting expectations for wives and daughters. By doing so, they "made the unruly option a more conceivable one."[60]

The study of carnival across history defies generalization. In fact, carnival has been scripted and spontaneous, ceremonial and anarchic, a celebration of state power and its insolent rejection, a stately parade and a scene of drunkenness, blood, and filth. Despite claims of its supposed conservatism, it is not hard to find disruptions of the social and political order that go beyond mere play to have lasting effects. Its upheavals were not always part of a fixed ritual, nor its consequences an affirmation of the everyday order.

In *The Politics and Poetics of Transgression*, a masterful analysis of the carnivalesque in literature, history, and criticism, Peter Stallybrass and Allon White cite social historians who have chronicled both conservative and revolutionary effects of carnival. Their conclusion is reasonable: it is unproductive to ask whether carnival is intrinsically radical or conservative, they write. Carnival may be a stable ritual for long periods with no transformative effects and then bring bedlam. In the presence of "sharpened political antagonism," it may act "as *catalyst* and *site of actual and symbolic struggle*." The observation is a reminder of the value of understanding ritual in both its unchanging structures and lived experience. "The politics of carnival," Stallybrass and White conclude, "cannot be resolved outside of a close historical examination of particular conjunctures."[61]

France in the 1830s and '40s confirms these conclusions. Its carnival forms were much the same as in earlier eras, but their effects were entirely different. Carnival in the eighteenth century had mostly preserved the status quo. While its individual confrontations could be explosive, the overall atmosphere defused any serious challenge to the order. There were taunts and mockery at masked balls, but the readiness of social superiors to unmask themselves in indignation held more serious defiance in check. The violence and greater insolence during carnival in the two decades before 1789 were evidence of profound social and economic pressures. Carnival indeed provided means of defiance and occasions to display it, but it did not bring bedlam or inspire visions of a new order.

Only in the decades after the Revolution did carnival's disruptions threaten political upheaval. The king's vulnerabilities, an increasing mismatch between the regime's promises and policies, and overall popular discontent played their part, but relevant, too, was a population of men and women now able to dream plausibly of changing their fate by their own volition. Equality before the law was the formal articulation of a society now open to genuine social and economic mobility. The mask's anonymity, coupled with their sheer numbers in balls and on the streets, offered a protection that earlier celebrations lacked. These antagonisms and opportunities were what turned a long period of mostly peaceful rituals into confrontations that were potentially revolutionary.

11
The King's Execution

HEROIC-COMIC UPROAR

Less than a year after the revolution that brought Louis-Philippe to the throne, carnival helped spark a protest that soon spread to other parts of the city. The politically driven devastation, which would recur in the coming years, showed the explosive potential of carnival in these early years of the new regime. It began on Mardi Gras, 1831. As the sun rose, revelers from the city's masked balls joined a crowd that had already begun to grow near the Louvre. Their taunts mixed carnival mockery with hostility against royalists and the Church, and before long crowds of rioters that were at once jubilant and savage roamed through Paris.

The spark was a memorial mass held the day before for Charles d'Artois, duc de Berry, whose 1820 assassination now took on fresh significance. D'Artois was the son of Louis XVI's younger brother, who, as Charles X, had been forced to abdicate when revolutionaries took to the streets in 1830. This mass was the first formal occasion for old-blood aristocrats to gather publicly since the moderate Louis-Phillipe had assumed power. The service was held across from the Louvre at the traditional parish church of kings, Saint-Germain-l'Auxerrois. It was eleven years to the day after Berry died, having been stabbed as he left the Opera by a veteran loyal to Napoleon. He had just been to a ballet called *The Carnival of Venice*.

The mass had also drawn bitter opponents of the Bourbon line, who were primed to cry foul at the first hint of resurgent royalism. What they described was an outrage. At the end of the service, an image of the duc de Berry's young son was lifted up. Known as the comte de Chambord, he was, apart from his dethroned grandfather, the only living heir to the Bourbon line. The image was crowned with flowers, and a flag with the monarchy's *fleur-de-lis* was unfurled. As mourners began to leave, protesters poured into the church to have the last word. They broke windows, overturned candle stands, trampled priests' vestments, and destroyed the central platform where memorial wreaths had been placed. National Guard troops could do little to control the spreading chaos. François Arago, a charismatic public figure who had seen the service with the novelist Dumas, gave an impromptu speech denouncing the mass as a sacrilege against the memory of revolutionaries killed on the barricades. Chants rose against the Jesuits, and groups outside hurled rocks against the church.[1]

Someone called attention to a *fleur-de-lis* carved on the cross atop the church's facade. Chants of "Down with the *fleur-de-lis*!" rose up, and some climbed onto the roof to bring it down. After two hours of hacking, the cross crashed to the ground to cheers and renewed cries of "Down with the Jesuits!" A new chant arose: "To the Archbishop's!" A large group set out for the palace, which was on the Seine near Notre-Dame. When they arrived, they forced their way inside and began a rampage that would stretch over two days, destroying tables and chairs, breaking mirrors, overturning bookshelves, upending cabinets of precious manuscripts, and destroying paintings. Others went to the church of Saint-Roch, where they vandalized the interior and burned all items bearing the *fleur-de-lis*. The socialist Louis Blanc described what he saw. "No one dreamed of such pillage. A thirst for destruction, like a fatal intoxication, gripped everyone. . . . It was all done amidst a frightful storm of cheers, laughter, burlesque shouts, and wild cries."[2]

Such was the mood when Mardi Gras dawned. The police commissioner Canler was at Saint-Germain-l'Auxerrois at 6 a.m. and took note of those arriving from the city's theaters still in their carnival costumes. He estimated their numbers to be two to three hundred. There were well-dressed men in black suits and gloves, as well as a group of "convicts, con-men, pimps, low-class idlers, [and] . . . professional rioters." The groups had nothing in common, Canler wrote—"neither their language, nor look, nor dress"—and yet they stood shoulder-to-shoulder, shouting and assaulting the doors of the church.[3] When the doors gave way, rioters streamed in to finish the previous day's devastation. They sacked ancient relics, overturned confessionals, ripped paintings from the walls, pulled down chandeliers, and upended seats and benches to victorious cheers.

One of the costumed revelers mounted the pulpit and sang *La Parisienne*, a revolutionary song from 1830. Another found his way to the sacristy and emerged in a priest's full regalia. "He climbed onto a heap of debris and began beating time to an infernal dance," Dumas recalled in his *Memoirs*. "He resembled Satan, mockingly clothed in sacred garments and presiding over a witch's Sabbath." A witness described screams that transformed the sanctuary into a "theater of mad bravado." "The savages struck wildly in every direction, ripping apart, pulling down, blaspheming against God, religion, and the clergy as they danced on the debris of sacred objects and works of art." Physical violence against those who tried to protect the church sent a cross bearer to the hospital, where he later died.[4]

Rioters then set out for the archbishop's residence to resume Monday's rampage. They broke windows, pulled up carpets, gutted desks and cabinets, and tossed papers, books, chairs, and tables into the Seine. A journalist described seeing furniture, silk curtains, footstools, books, missals, and precious manuscripts dumped into the river. The water was soon white with feathers from a mattress. Crowds gathered on the bridges, and fishermen retrieved what they could to sell. At the residence, now an empty shell, rioters began tearing through portions of the roof to cheers from the crowd below. When the National Guard arrived around noon, half of the roof was gone. The rioters were sufficiently satisfied to disperse. Some returned to Saint-Roch, and others gathered at the church of Notre-Dame-de-Bonne-Nouvelle, which they entered and vandalized. Still others went to the seminary of Saint-Sulpice, where they threw rocks and broke windows. At the church of Saint-Paul, rioters fueled a bonfire with objects bearing the *fleur-de-lis*.[5]

A German tourist named M. L. Börne was in Paris that day, thrilled to observe such historic events. On one side of the Seine, the *Boeuf Gras* procession was underway with its entourage of butchers. On the other, another parade marched with their spoils on proud display, including a portrait of the archbishop and church censers, with which they raucously blessed passersby. To convey the grandeur, Börne invoked great works of art and literature. "It was a Beethoven symphony that laughed while crying, it was Shakespearean drama," he wrote. "Yet neither Shakespeare, nor Swift, nor Jean-Paul risked such bold juxtapositions." For Louis Blanc, the madness was of a piece with the season. "We were in the midst of carnival," Blanc began.

> Every extravagance of Mardi Gras mingled with the emotions of the rioters. The streets of opulent neighborhoods resounded with the wheels of coaches. Maskers ran through the city in a frenzy. In the evening, Paris was illuminated. Where the Archbishop's mansion rose the day before there was nothing but ruins.

A newspaper reported the same stunning contrasts. "Shouts of laughter and carnival buffoonery punctuated cries of hatred against the cross and the congregation. The pranks of Arlequin and Punch were mixed with serious speeches."[6]

National Guard troops struggled to control events. Crowds mistook a solitary young man for a priest and threw him from a bridge into the Seine. He was retrieved unconscious by fishermen and taken to the hospital, where he was identified as an American. He did not live. A priest was attacked in the Latin Quarter. He was Belgian, also visiting the capital. Word spread that a member of the National Guard, a merchant named Valérius, was among mourners who had saluted the duc de Berry's image the day before. A group invaded his shop as other members of the Guard rushed in to protect the property. At the Place des Victoires, crowds damaged the equestrian statue of Louis XIV and its surrounding grille.[7]

Until midday, the rioters' targets had been the Church and presumed royalists, with the centrist monarchy of Louis-Philippe left largely unchallenged. In the afternoon, more pointed political protests began. A large group marched along the quay toward the Chamber of Deputies waving two flags, one of which was topped by a liberty bonnet. They chanted, "Down with the Chamber!," "*Vive la patrie!*," and "Down with the Milieu!"—the latter being a reference to Louis-Philippe's promised third way between royalists and republicans. An armed detachment confronted them, and in the midst of the clash protesters wrested away an officer's sword, which they shattered. They dispersed, shouting "To arms!"[8] Another crowd gathered at the Palais-Royal, where protesters encountered mounted troops.[9] National Guard reserves moved to surround the Hôtel de Ville. The Louvre and Tuileries were closed and remained under heavy guard. That night, troops prevented rioters from setting fire to the offices of the royalist paper *La Quotidienne*.[10]

The government's response was to declare the service for the duc de Berry a provocation and cast the riots as a defense of Louis-Philippe. Camille de Montalivet, who was in the king's inner circle, condemned the "factious ceremony" at Saint-Germain-l'Auxerrois as a hostile act against "our Citizen-King and the July Revolution." He added that the Parisian populace was rightly offended. The police prefect Jean-Jacques Baude went further, calling the royalists' service a failed attempt at civil war. He urged Parisians to demonstrate France's strength by uniting against their common enemy to defend the king. Baude then announced the names of eleven men arrested for having participated in the memorial mass, including the officiating priest and the Guardsman Valérius.[11]

Newspapers favorable to Louis-Philippe repeated the government's line. The *Constitutionnel*, which called Mardi Gras a "day of magic," declared the events an expression of people's natural gaiety. The paper claimed that Parisians of every stripe—revelers in masks, elegant ladies, young people, men and women in grotesque costumes—had paraded alongside National Guard troops in a display of unity, gratitude, and just indignation, "a heroic-comic uproar."[12]

To say the protests were a show of solidarity with the regime was both a pander and a dodge. There were benefits to be gained from framing the rioters' violence as justified outrage and not mob violence, but the script omitted the protests' anti-governmental tone. It also failed to acknowledge carnival's anarchic energy, which fed the passion and shaped much of its expression. The rancor against what protesters took to be a royalist display was real and their distrust of Jesuits' political influence well founded. For authorities to believe that the upheavals came solely from these sentiments, however, was to misread events. When Louis-Philippe and his cabinet were the butt of a widely publicized carnival farce a year later, the government would have a different view of the people's natural gaiety.

FIREBRAND SUNDAY

In these years, the carnivalesque was combustible. Just beneath the hilarity simmered belligerence. Violence came in fierce momentary eruptions: in shoving matches with police, in student rampages that trashed elite theaters, in the destruction of holy places by carnival mobs. These explosions expressed grievances about political affairs, social inequities, and Church power in the anarchic terms of the season. Unlike in earlier years, these acts were collective rather than individual. Carnival in the 1830s and '40s did not strengthen the status quo.

The hostility was not the unique product of revelers running amok. In the nineteenth century's single worst instance of carnival violence, it was the forces of order who struck first. In 1832, a politically provocative masquerade in the southwestern city of Grenoble set off a chain of events that ended with the army plunging into a peaceful crowd of civilians with bayonets. The masquerade was not innocent. It dressed the king in a clown's suit and cast military officers in degrading roles. The brutality it provoked was by any measure wildly disproportionate. Louis-Philippe's regime not only defended the assault but blamed the victims for their injuries and called the maskers traitors. The response showed just how dangerous the government considered carnival and its masks to be.

In the posturing and rancor that followed, most ignored the fact that the assault had come a full day after the maskers had put away their costumes. Most also disregarded the more immediate circumstances that caused troops to converge on the crowd, which had more to do with an inept response than any threat of insurrection. What both sides agreed on was that mockery of the king had nearly brought about insurrection. Given the right conditions, carnival could imperil the government.

Firebrand Sunday—*le Dimanche des Brandons*—was a rural festival of fertility traditionally celebrated in Grenoble on the weekend after Mardi Gras. Practices varied across France, but most involved a torch-lit parade of young men who had married in the past year. It culminated with a bonfire and dancing in the town square.[13] By the early nineteenth century, parades with flaming torches that gave the holiday its name had evolved into an extra weekend of carnival mischief. When two carriages moved through the streets bearing absurdly costumed maskers on the first Sunday of Lent, the local population took it in stride.

Two locals who were dressed as Englishmen led the procession on horseback.[14] Behind them was a pair of French officers on foot, one carrying a giant ecclesiastical candlestick and the other brandishing a comically enlarged rectal syringe. One of the Englishmen held the end of a ribbon that looped around the neck of a dignitary, who drove a carriage. Inside sat a red-robed judge and a priest with ass's ears. The second carriage, driven by another faux priest, bore a bloated creature with flaming cheeks who wore the label *Budget*. Two figures in gunny sacks labeled *Supplementary Credit* sat on either side of him.

Two horsemen followed, one dressed as a National Guardsman in a worker's smock and the other as a Polish soldier with a black armband. Overseeing the whole shambling procession—at the rear of the first carriage, where lackeys ordinarily stood—was a fat clown whose hat was fashioned to resemble a gigantic pear. The crew periodically improvised scenes of self-importance. "Gentlemen, let us deliberate!" a dignitary would command: "Rise!" In response, the procession stopped and all stood solemnly until the next order came: "Now be seated!" In every instance, the fat clown called out, "You shall all have medals!" The farce drew laughter along its route.[15]

The masquerade made its way outside the town gates and along an esplanade lined with Sunday picnickers and strollers. When the maskers approached the gates on a drawbridge to reenter the town, soldiers from the army's 35th Regiment blocked their path. The troops had been newly assigned to Grenoble and were garrisoned just outside the city limits. Some bystanders jeered, and the maskers played up their roles. The officer with the syringe struck a fencer's pose. The dignitary in the driver's seat rose and declared this to be "another opportunity to save France." He then commanded the soldiers to retreat.

The police arrived and moved toward the maskers, but the crowd's catcalls convinced them to withdraw. When some threw rocks, the carnival fun suddenly lurched toward a confrontation. On an officer's orders, soldiers snapped their bayonets into place and advanced two steps. The maskers kept to their roles and continued to ham it up. More rocks flew. Then, just as suddenly as tempers had flared, an officer ordered the troops to withdraw.

Local authorities had known of the planned masquerade and intended to prevent it. The day before, an anonymous letter describing preparations was received by the town commissioner, who forwarded it to the mayor and prefect. The latter, Maurice Duval, had been in his post just a month and had done nothing to alter his reputation as a hard-nosed functionary. Duval had served Napoleon in Italy, was close to Interior Minister Thiers, and typically favored force over dialogue. The mayor instructed the police to monitor the maskers. Duval, whose authority exceeded the mayor's, instructed the police to arrest them.

Passions cooled on the drawbridge, and the masqueraders filed back into town. Duval then issued a new order. No masks could be worn at the Firebrand Ball later that day. By local tradition, the ball was the climax of carnival. Duval would later testify that he possessed information about plans to mock the king, his ministers, and the military with "allegorical" masks.[16] Fearing further outrage, the mayor pleaded with him to reverse his decision, but Duval was adamant. Organizers responded by canceling the ball altogether: a carnival ball without masks would be worse than no ball at all.

Discontent grew through the evening and into Monday, especially among the town's younger population, who singled out Prefect Duval as responsible for both provocations. Plans were drawn up for a protest—the word its organizers used was *charivari*—at Duval's residence early Monday evening.[17] When he got wind of it, he sent a note to baron de Saint-Clair, lieutenant general of the 35th Regiment, to prepare his troops. Demonstrators began gathering in the courtyard outside the prefecture just before nightfall, and a sizable crowd quickly formed. Menacing chants began to ring out. *Down with the prefect! To the lamppost with him! Down with Louis-Philippe! Long live the Republic!*

Soldiers cleared the square and ordered the crowd into the rue du Quai, a narrow adjoining street. Duval sent two policemen to summon the troops. Just after they left, the 35th Regiment's two commanding officers left the soldiers for Duval's residence on their own initiative. When the policemen arrived at the barracks, there were no officers to consult. The crowd was in high spirits and buoyed by the growing numbers. They continued their mocking chants, mingling threats with laughter. Suddenly the demonstrators saw that two units, one a company of light-infantry troops and the other of grenadiers, had blocked either end of the rue du Quai and were advancing at a trot with their bayonets lowered. Panic swept the protesters as they realized there was no escape.

At the front of each group, soldiers began driving their bayonets into flesh. Screams echoed through the small street. Some soldiers thrust their bayonets into the walls to make it harder to escape. Many fell and were trampled, others crouched to the ground, and some flattened themselves against the walls on either side. It was a "scene of horror," testified an attorney who witnessed the scene from a nearby shop. "Soldiers were striking left and right, high and low." Someone passed a bleeding child to the attorney through a window and then boosted the boy's sister through as well.

Witnesses reported having heard no warning. Those at the periphery reported hearing the words "Fix your bayonets, forward, march." Other shouts rose above the struggle. "Surround them! Strike them!" Some in the crowd loosened cobblestones to throw in self-defense while others pleaded, "No rocks! No rocks!" A law student was knocked to the ground by the flat of a sword and held immobile at bayonet point. He broke free, but the blade tore through his thigh. "Don't let him flee!" a soldier shouted.

A cabinetmaker came face-to-face with a group of soldiers, and as he begged for mercy one of them stepped forward and drove a bayonet into his groin. A shopkeeper's assistant was already on the ground when a soldier struck him twice in the head with the butt of his gun. "Bourgeois thief," the soldier said, "I'm going to kill you." When a recruit on leave stooped to save a mother and small daughter from being trampled, he was stabbed three times. Witnesses described troops striking in every direction, "blindly, furiously." One man, staggering from three wounds in his side, had his head opened by a rifle butt.[18] People forced doors open and broke through the windows of shops and cafés. Those who could pushed their way inside; others lay where they fell. Soldiers continued to advance from either end. Some watched silently. Others boasted. "Did you see how I skewered him?" one called out to a comrade.[19]

The violence eventually ebbed, leaving the population aghast. Miraculously there were no deaths, but casualties were heavy. The summary report, issued by doctors who treated the injured on the scene and at the hospital, detailed forty-two bayonet wounds on twenty-six civilians. A third of the blows came from behind. One woman and two children, ages ten and twelve, were struck. Four victims were stabbed in the face or head. Only one of the attacking soldiers went to the hospital, for a wound in the same spot that had been treated two weeks earlier with a dose of mercury. This time he was kicked in the testicles. No other troops were injured.[20]

For the townspeople, the harm to neighbors meant more than the raw numbers. The furniture merchant Tivan, who was walking with his wife, was struck three times. Claude Pellat, an apprentice carpenter, had four wounds. Giraud the glover had three. The wig maker Reymond, the baker

Guillot, and the bank teller Giraud all had bayonet wounds. Mme Ch***'s chambermaid—the press chose discretion in abbreviating the name—was bayoneted in the knee. A law student named Huchet watched as a bayonet passed through his upper arm. One of the city's newspapers launched a subscription drive to raise money for the injured, which swelled quickly with a broad cross section of donors. Among the fund's first contributors were professionals—a banker, doctor, and attorney—but the list also included merchants, shopkeepers, a silk dealer, a printer, and municipal administrators.[21]

What had begun as a masquerade was starting to look like insurrection. After the confrontation, residents erected barricades throughout the town. Troops dismantled them as soon as they went up, but efforts resumed through the night. Early Tuesday morning, Prefect Duval ordered the local National Guard to reinforce army positions. Its members, viewing the maneuvers as an occupation, did nothing. At mid-morning, residents armed with pitchforks and hunting rifles, some of them wearing red liberty bonnets of the Revolution, began moving toward the Hôtel de Ville. "We're on our way to hear what that bunch of aristocrats has to say," one of them called out to a university professor who had stopped to watch. "Come with us," another told him, "we're going to hear Huchet talk about Robespierre."[22]

Alexandre Huchet, the law student whose arm had been pierced, was in a state of fury. Moving through the crowd, he shouted to anyone who would listen that the monarchy was about to end, that the spirit of Marat and Robespierre lived on, and that a Republic was coming. At the prefecture, the crowd swelled to 1,500. With his arm in a sling and flanked by youths carrying rocks and pistols, Huchet made his way to the front to deliver a fiery speech. In it, he demanded that the army withdraw from the town, called for a Republic, and announced the immediate establishment of a provisional government in Grenoble, by which he meant himself and the small band around him.[23]

Inside the prefecture, Duval huddled with Lieutenant General Saint-Clair and members of the National Guard, who had come to press their case for a full military withdrawal. Saint-Clair agreed to replace his troops now stationed throughout the city with National Guardsmen. As he moved to the courtyard to announce the agreement, he was seized by Huchet and three others, who declared them hostages. Officers in the building rushed to barricade Duval inside one of the rooms before the armed group could seize him, too. In midafternoon, he escaped and took shelter in the military barracks outside the town. After four hours of negotiations, officers of the local National Guard convinced the youths to free Saint-Clair. In return, he issued orders for National Guardsmen to replace his troops in town and promised to move the army out from Grenoble.[24] With that, the revolution ended.

Residents were gratified when the 35th Regiment was replaced with the 6th, but news from Paris erased any good feeling. Louis-Philippe dissolved the Grenoble National Guard, punished its members for insubordination, and congratulated Prefect Duval for his actions. Maréchal Soult, the Minister of War, thanked the 35th in the name of France and its king. Within ten days, an additional 12,000 troops from the army's 7th and 19th Divisions had massed in Grenoble and the 35th was ordered by the king to return to the city, where they pulled cannons into the public gardens and made a show of keeping a torch alight to fire them.[25] The occupation stretched on for two months. Public calm returned, but private rage smoldered. Despite pleas from the authorities, fistfights, duels, and on occasion all-out brawls broke out between townspeople and soldiers. Journalists and the local population kept up their appeals for redress. For its part, the national government never ceased to praise the soldiers' work.

The 1832 carnival in Grenoble was a tripwire, not a safety valve. There were factors beyond the masquerade that contributed to the assault and military occupation. Discontent with Louis-Philippe's government was widespread, and self-described republicans like Huchet were growing more bold in their defiance. While some other spark might as easily have set off an explosion, it was carnival maskers making fun of the king that touched off these events. In the minds of those who both condemned and defended the maskers, their Sunday farce was what had provoked the violence. This is an indication of how potent their affront had been.

A MASK THAT UNMASKS

On the day Grenoble's local newspaper *Le Dauphinois* reported the bloody charivari outside the prefect's residence, another story ran bearing news of a related crime. Charles Philipon, editor of the satirical newspaper *Le Caricature*, had just been convicted by a court in Paris for having published seditious drawings. In one, a worker strained under the weight of enormous bundles labeled *Taxes, Fees, Indirect Contributions on Wine and Tobacco*, and *Salt Tax*. Among the spectators applauding his efforts were Louis-Philippe's ministers. The king, pictured from the rear as a stout, well-dressed man, held a bag open to receive the load. Another caricature depicted a coat of arms labeled *Grand Poulot*. Its insignia included a peacock with a paper cap, panpipes, castles made of cards, and toy horses. *Poulot*—Chickie—was the family nickname for Louis-Philippe's twenty-two-year-old son

Ferdinand. The caption read: "Blessed are the poor in spirit, for theirs is the kingdom."[26]

It was fitting that news of Philipon's conviction shared space with the first reports of the masquerade. The Grenoble maskers had taken their characters from the pages of *Le Caricature*, and Prefect Duval understood Sunday's events within the larger context of the paper's political satire. In bringing charges against Philipon, government officials claimed that his images were a provocation. For them, events in Grenoble confirmed this fact. The verdict was a vindication.

La Caricature was among a new crop of Paris newspapers to appear in the 1830s. In the beginning, there had been no more fervent defender of the king than Philipon. The son of a hatmaker from Lyon, he had fought on the barricades and held great hopes for the regime, which promised to restore the freedoms of 1789. Initially the paper stayed out of politics, and Philipon recruited artists and writers to provide wry commentary on Parisian life.[27] Balzac wrote most of the copy for the first issue, which appeared in November 1830, and much of the content in its succeeding six weekly numbers. Honoré Daumier, another of the paper's young recruits, said that his career would have never taken off without Philipon. Within two years, the public taste for this new style of journalism, which offered serious social commentary alongside irreverence, was strong enough for Philipon to start a second newspaper featuring caricature and opinion. It was a daily, which he called *Le Charivari*.

It didn't take long for Philipon to lose faith in the king. By early 1831, Louis-Philippe had begun to shed liberal advisers in favor of conservatives. When ministers of the deposed Charles X were put on trial for having repressed revolutionaries in July, Louis-Philippe prompted riots by urging leniency. He publicly undermined General Lafayette, who had built republican support for him. A series of resignations and dismissals among cabinet ministers shifted the balance of his inner circle steadily rightward. Former admirers began to say that his liberal rhetoric had been a ruse to secure power.

Philipon described his experience as having left "the land of liberal illusions" to enter "the saddest kingdom of reality."[28] His first caricature of Louis-Philippe ran in January. A month later, the government brought charges against him and his publishing house. This was to be the first of sixteen suits against him in the next year and a half. Of the six that reached the courts, Philipon was convicted three times and forced to pay 10,000 francs in fines. In September 1835, pilloried by a series of government officials as criminally seditious, Philipon published the final issue of *La*

Caricature. With such publications squarely in its sights, the government pushed through a bill later that month requiring advance authorization for any image published in the press.[29]

Even as he suffered these legal setbacks, however, Philipon was winning the wider public. In his trial, which had begun four months before the Grenoble masquerade, he and his lawyer crafted a defense that produced an enduring image of royal idiocy. Offenses against "the person of the king," forbidden by an 1830 law on the press, had been premised on the monarch's inviolability. They were punishable by up to five years in prison and a fine of six thousand francs.[30] To counter the government's claims, Philipon argued that the sketch of a squat, round figure with full face and bushy sideburns was not the king. "It is the king's resemblance, and not his person, that we have employed," his lawyer Étienne Blanc explained. "We haven't touched his person, only his resemblance, which as far as I know does not belong to him."

As Blanc addressed the jury, Philipon roughed out four additional images from his seat in the courtroom. The first was Louis-Philippe and the last was a pear, with the two others bearing traits of each. Philipon displayed the sheets in his summation. Where will you stop, he began, if you convict artists for mere resemblances? "You must condemn the pear, because it resembles the previous, and the previous resembles the king! You will have sentenced a man to prison for two years for drawing a pear!"[31]

The maneuver did not convince the jury, but it was a triumph in the court of opinion. *Le Caricature* published the sketches in January, and soon pears were sprouting up all over France. A newspaper estimated that four to five hundred thousand pears were on the walls of Paris alone. A shopkeeper was arrested and charged with disturbing the peace for exhibiting cardboard pears atop moneybags in his windows. Hats in the form of pears made their way into vaudeville and farce. In Auxerre, the mayor forbade two things: the dumping of trash and the drawing of pears. As he served his sentence, Philipon watched fellow prisoners draw pears on the walls of cells and corridors. Today *pear* in French, *la poire*, is also a term of abuse, meaning meathead. Scholars trace its sense to these years.[32]

Once the pear was identified with the king, artists for *Le Caricature* used it with cruel abandon. A month before the Grenoble masquerade, the paper published "M. Mahieux, Pearicide" by Traviès, depicting a hunchback dwarf about to sever the top of a pear with his dinner knife. A week before the masquerade, it printed the image of two clowns hauling a huge pear across a muck-filled landscape. Its caption was "The Juste Milieu Soils Itself."

FIGURE 11.1. *"You must condemn the pear,"* Charles Philipon (Beinecke Rare Book & Manuscript Library, Yale University)

FIGURE 11.2. *The Juste Milieu Soils Itself*, anon. (Beinecke Rare Book & Manuscript Library, Yale University)

Other caricatures equal the violence of "M. Mahieux, Pearicide," including Daumier's "Enormous Pear Hanged by Men of the People." Here, faceless laborers hang the bloated fruit from the rafters of an empty barn by night. Philipon's "Monument Expiapoire" is a fanciful structure on the spot of Louis XVI's beheading. The violence was coupled with humiliation. One image scores a triple visual pun by superimposing the king's features onto a pear that is itself the back end of a cow. Its caption, "The *Boeuf Gras* of 1834," links the king to the annual carnival slaughter. Another shows Philipon at a masked ball teasing a dumpy figure in a clown suit while a reveler whose sash reads *Charivari* draws a pear on the man's back. Its title: "I Recognize That Clown."

Within the year, a courtroom stunt intended to show the absurdity of linking the humble pear to disrespect for the king had succeeded in doing just that. In the pear, caricature found common cause with carnival. In 1833, *Le Charivari* announced the coming of "political carnival" and predicted that "the streets [would] open out like the pages of a newspaper: lined with sarcasm, on foot, on horseback, and by carriage." When carnival revelers that same year wore pear masks, revelers' traditional riposte—"*Je te connais, beau masque*"—produced fresh hilarity. Heinrich Heine wrote that Louis-Philippe's halo was gone and in its place was a pear.[33]

The popularity of Philipon's works inspired Charles Baudelaire to call the July Monarchy the Belle Époque of caricature.[34] Its polemical edge turned laughter into a weapon. Charles Blanc, the author of a political dictionary in 1842, deemed caricature the people's means of exposing bad government. An attorney defending youths charged with heckling a provincial official echoed the point. Caricature and charivari, he said, were "tools of political condemnation."[35] Caricature's inversions were extravagant, and, like *The Fishwife's Catechism* or *Six Types of Farts*, their fun was not always innocent.

Derived from the Italian verb *caricare*—to charge, load, or fill—the word *caricature* suggests portraiture by exaggeration, an overstuffed version of a person's essential features. For Baudelaire, its impulse was demonic. To distort nature using nature's own traces—depicting a man with a Cro-Magnon forehead or woodpecker's nose—was a kind of blasphemy in its willful distortion of the divine image. It also contained a doubling akin to carnival masks. Behind the semblance, Baudelaire wrote, was "the scathing, veiled idea."[36] Philipon's own words about caricature shared these features. "God

FIGURE 11.3. *The* Boeuf Gras *of 1834*, anon. (Library of Congress)

FIGURE 11.4. *M. Dudessert,* Honoré Daumier (Beinecke Rare Book & Manuscript Library, Yale University)

FIGURE 11.5. *M. Prune*, Honoré Daumier (Beinecke Rare Book & Manuscript Library, Yale University)

FIGURE 11.6. *M. Fulchir*, Honoré Daumier (Beinecke Rare Book & Manuscript Library, Yale University)

FIGURE 11.7. *The Leading Actor of a Tragicomic Imbroglio*, anon. (Library of Congress)

knows, there are plenty of *grave individuals* who say that I'm not serious! But there have always been the venturesome few who, like myself, find the sound of a jester's bells amusing and who can recognize serious thought under the mask of play."[37]

The description was fitting for the time: caricature's jolly front often hides belligerence. The critic Champfleury, who claimed that caricature represents the mob, made the connection explicit. "Caricature predominates only in times of revolt and insurrection. Does one imagine in these moments that the crowd is tranquil, reasonable, just, equitable, moderate, gentle, and indifferent?"[38] Masks permeate the caricatures of Philipon and other artists he published. In one of them, the king sits on a money chest holding a smiling mask to his face. His words are beguiling: "My comrades, my dear comrades! I am a Republican just like you. . . . I love liberty and equality. . . . I desire only your profit. . . . The profits of all. . . . The profits of the whole world!" In another, the king's amiable mask and bourgeois trappings are sloughed off to reveal a despot. His face is vicious, the umbrella has become a scepter, and beneath the hat is a crown.[39]

Daumier's "Masks of 1831," which appeared in the last week of carnival, renders the faces of the cabinet and the ever-present pear as masks.[40] A sardonic commentary describes having seen the ministers carousing in the streets. "No sooner had this group of jokers donned their disguises than the masses began to thank them—in the form of boos and scathing shouts." The caricatures sharpened the barb: these ministers were two-faced in their very essence. A variation appeared, with a fox examining the same masks stacked in duplicate in a storeroom. In the center of the image, directly beneath a clown's suit and topped by a dunce's hat, is a likeness of the king. "Pretty faces," the caption runs, "but they have no brains"—a quote from a fox in a fable by Lafontaine as he regards statues of heroes.[41]

In his farewell column of *La Caricature*'s final issue, Philipon wrote proudly of having "unmasked actors of the last fifteen years," who had preached liberty but practiced despotism. Even if they silence our pens, he wrote, no censor can erase the "stigmata of shame with which we have stamped them over the past five years."[42] Stigmata—scars burned on the body—leave traces that can't be easily obscured. Once you see the king's head as a pear, it's hard not to imagine it every time you think of him. Caricature reveals truths that resist all attempts to conceal. At the very time when physiognomy commanded its greatest authority, caricature offered its own evidence that the body reveals character.[43]

Baudelaire made a similar point in writing about Daumier. "Every poverty of spirit, every absurdity, every neurosis, every vice of the heart is seen and read clearly on these animalized faces. . . . [Daumier] possessed the subtlety of an artist and the precision of Lavater."[44] "Masks of 1831" made explicit what was implied from Philipon's first disillusionment with the king. Under the guise of amusement, caricature used the body to expose the deceit of its words. Caricature: a mask that unmasks.

LOUIS-PHILIPPE'S JUDGMENT

The Grenoble masquerade was certainly meant to unmask, and most of its characters came from caricature. The clown wearing a pear hat was of course the king, and a priest in jackass ears was unambiguous. The officer's

FIGURE 11.8. *"Pretty faces but they have no brains,"* anon. (Bibliothèque nationale de France)

two-handed enema had long been a slapstick gag, but since General Lobau of the Paris National Guard had dispersed protesters with a fire hose the previous year, *La Caricature* regularly pictured military men with the same syringe. The officer's companion in the Grenoble masquerade, who wore a uniform and carried a large candlestick, followed the newspaper's spoofs

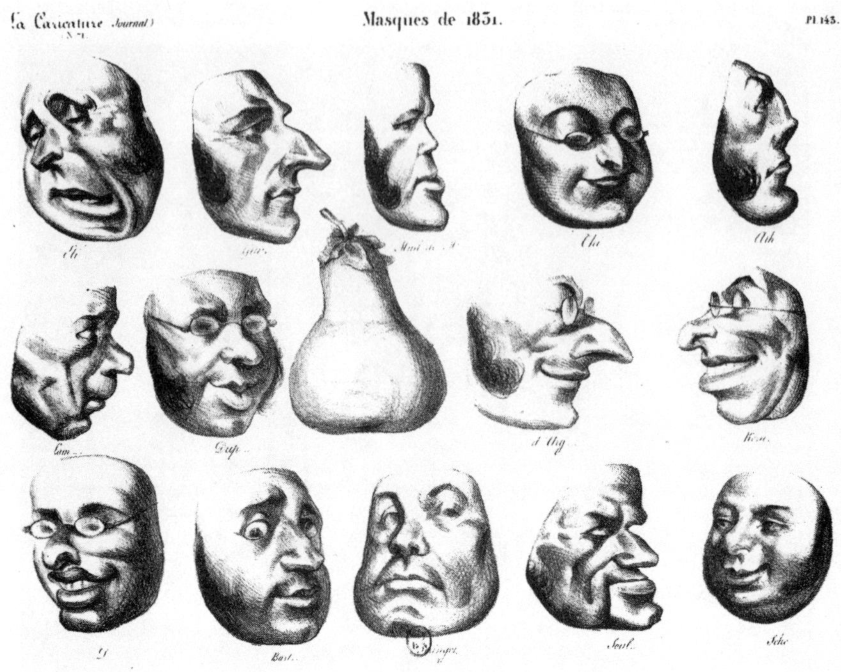

FIGURE 11.9. *Masks of 1831*, anon. (Bibliothèque nationale de France)

of Maréchal Soult, whose plunder of church treasures while commanding Napoleon's troops in Spain was well known.

As the assault on unarmed civilians began to draw national attention, its fault lines recalled Philipon's trial. On one side, local journalists and some city officials claimed the parade had been in good fun and denied that the clown in a pear hat was meant to be the king. On the other side were members of Louis-Philippe's cabinet and legislative supporters, who used images from *La Caricature* to link the maskers to the newspaper's crime of attacking the king. Prefect Duval announced that the "allegorical masks" had mocked the king and insulted French ministers, officers, and legislators. It had been his duty, he said, to stop this threat to public order.[45] Lieutenant General Baron Delort, who commanded reinforcements sent to Grenoble, denounced the "despicable masquerade, whose obvious intent was criminal." Duval added that French troops were its real victims. He then blamed protesters for having "thrown themselves on the soldiers' weapons" in an effort to seize them. Maréchal Soult called the civilians in the rue du Quai anarchists who were drawn from the "lowest, filthiest part of the population."[46]

One week after the assault, two members from Grenoble rose in the Chamber of Deputies to demand how officials could make such claims without first launching an inquiry. The chamber exploded with jeers, and the chamber's president André Dupin called them rebel sympathizers and disloyal to the nation. Anyone who criticized the army was pushing the country toward civil war, he declared, and those who claimed that soldiers had attacked women and children were liars: it was anarchists who had attacked the soldiers. "And these troubles, Gentlemen, came from the most atrocious offense conceivable. This was not an innocent masquerade, it was an abominable crime. It was the mock execution of the King. They were not intending to entertain. They wanted a revolution."[47]

To call the masquerade the symbolic murder of the king may well have been calculated to rally supporters. Given the context, it was also logical. The press law forbidding attacks against the king's person had been used to jail Charles Philipon for caricatures. Images of the hunchback Mahieux beheading a small pear and two workers hoisting the fruit through the mud had appeared just weeks before. Only days before Dupin's speech, in a final defiant carnival gesture, revelers had hanged effigies of the king throughout Paris with the label "Louis-Philippe's Judgment."[48]

A single deputy, the republican Odilon Barrot, rose to rebut Dupin. Barrot defended the maskers in the name of carnival. Even the despots of antiquity had permitted a season of license, he argued. "Never before has disguise of any sort become an affair of state!" Few were inclined to agree. The prime minister and Grenoble native Casimir Périer brought the debate to an end with a blistering attack on Barrot for failing to condemn the "criminal allegory against the king's authority." The national press largely shared Périer's view. Mocking the king played into the hands of royalists, wrote the *Constitutionnel.* Now that people could vote freely and publish what they wished, it asserted, masquerades were unnecessary.[49]

That so few establishment figures were willing to defend Grenoble's maskers at the very time so many citizens were drawn to the mask highlights its danger and the appeal. The political upheaval of these years did not of course depend on masks. Dissent and demonstrations were evidence of the political divide that Louis-Philippe's centrist policies failed to bridge. Conflict persisted among royalists and republicans, the monied and workers, and old wealth and the *nouveaux riches*. Yet the mask in its several forms—physical, allegorical, and in caricature's travesties—did on occasion encourage and abet political violence. Its nineteenth-century uses encompassed disguise and imposture, social ascent and dressing down, and unrelieved mockery. Each could be used for political ends. The anonymity that masks brought to the streets and riotous balls was a decisive variable. The government, which had been eager to claim carnival's riotous spirit in 1831, learned a year later in Grenoble that masks owed no allegiance.

IDENTITIES IN THE NINETEENTH CENTURY

According to those who followed drama in the first half of the nineteenth century, the age's greatest actor was a man who never uttered a word onstage. Jean-Gaspard Deburau was a mime who enthralled Paris audiences for the better part of three decades. Adopting the costume and persona of the commedia character Pierrot, Deburau performed at the popular Funambules Theater, where elites joined the larger working-class crowd whenever he was on the bill. In each role he played—as humble worker, soldier, musician, poet, rag seller, or merchant—the perfect legibility of his body declared his identity. Victor Hugo and George Sand hailed him. The historian François Guizot brought him up in conversation. Louis-Philippe invited him to the Tuileries for a private performance. One extravagant review pronounced him the Amerigo Vespucci of a new world of drama.[50] The rapturous praise says as much about the age as it does about the actor. Deburau was an Everyman.

In the century's opening decades, the means to take an active role in shaping one's own identity were available to a wider share of the population than ever before. Public education, equality of opportunity, and an expanding economy opened new opportunities for charting the future according to one's own lights. Inequity of course endured, and the limiting conditions many faced were unyielding. By law, however, birth no longer dictated one's place in the world. The scope for defining one's own identity was wide. For his audiences, Deburau embodied this freedom for self-fashioning. He showed onstage what was possible in society.

Deburau's power was in his seeming transparency. Unlike earlier Pierrots in the commedia tradition, he shunned the mask and covered his face instead with bakers' flour, just as Fat William had once done. He colored his lips lightly with rouge and darkened his eyebrows. Where earlier Pierrots had worn a fitted costume, his was loose and flowing. He wore wide white trousers, a white blouse with large buttons down the front, and a simple black skullcap. Spectators felt an instant kinship with Deburau, singling out his sangfroid and self-possession. George Sand called his relation to audiences "homogeneous." "In this narrow room, the stage is scarcely separate

FIGURE 11.10. *Jean-Gaspard Deburau*, Nadar (Art Resource)

from the audience," she wrote. "All are fascinated and energized by the calm presence and majestic lead of Pierrot."[51]

The novelist Jules Janin described the same quality. Become drunk, he wrote, hug your child, fall into debt, pay your debts, marry off your daughter, make fun of your physician, and mock your confessor. Show respect to the police commissioner, weep when you feel like it—and weep fully—and then be a jokester, a charmer, a smooth talker, a dashing young man, a lucky man. Janin drew his conclusion. "Gilles is not such and such a man with a proper name or determinate social position," Janin wrote, using the name Pierrot also went by. "Gilles is the people."[52]

In his influential book *Sources of the Self*, the philosopher Charles Taylor describes modern identities as consisting of three related qualities: a view of ourselves as beings with inner depths, an affirmation of ordinary life, and a sense of connection between an inward moral source and a universal or providential order. He refines the terms further for the nineteenth century. Personal ideals and inclinations, he writes, now figured in one's selfhood. Meaning came to depend on one's "powers of expression." Discovering a framework for that meaning, Taylor observes, was "interwoven with inventing."[53]

Taylor's descriptions are a fair summary of individuals' accounts from the middle third of the century. For some in this generation, writing about oneself in explicitly personal terms seemed new and remarkable. In an 1836 autobiography, the novelist Stendhal—the pen name for Henri Beyle—spoke of his own individuality as an intrusion. "I have always been put off by the awful problem of the *I's* and *me's*," he writes early in the work. "Who on earth will be brave enough to read this excessive heap of *I's* and *me's*?" He calls their presence in his writing an impertinence and describes the distracting misery of ruminating on the *I's* and *me's* in the book. "Yet if I do not probe more deeply into the character of Henri, which is so hard for me to know, I am not conducting myself as an honest author trying to tell all he can about the subject."[54]

The shadow of Rousseau, whom Stendhal invokes with admiration and some fear, is a constant presence. Any comparison of his own efforts with this great writer, he says, is ludicrous. Perhaps so, but his intense self-scrutiny was thoroughly Rousseauean. Like Rousseau, Stendhal documents the precise nature and sequence of his thoughts. He transcribes them "*exactly as they were*," with the announced aim of depicting events not as they occurred but solely in their effects on him. "Where to find the reader who, after four or five volumes of *I* and *me*, won't want to throw a bottle of ink rather than a glass of dirty water at me?" He also gives himself some warrant: ordinary people in the nineteenth century are speaking and writing in much the same way, he writes.[55]

Despite its powerful legacy, Rousseau's imperative for sincerity was giving way for Stendhal and his contemporaries to a more austere authenticity. This inner call among them was not so much to bear effusive witness to one's feelings as to hold true to one's own uniqueness, an identity at once discovered and self-defined.[56] Rousseau's sincerity, a torrent of sentiments that proclaimed unfailing fidelity to his own heart, did not rule out inconsistency, contradiction, or distortion. Authenticity, by contrast, claimed a deeper congruence between one's words, actions, and individual essence. In explaining his motives for writing another autobiography, *Memoirs of an Egotist*, Stendhal begins: "Let us see if, in making my examination of conscience, pen in hand, I will arrive at something *real* and that remains *consistently true* for me." Stendhal's difference with Rousseau is evident in both tone and address. The open displays of feeling common in the late eighteenth century had a correlate in Rousseau's emotional exhibitionism. Stendhal was more tentative in describing the task of sounding his own character, which was "so hard for me to know."[57]

The restraint, a deepening sense of selfhood, and sharp focus on singularity in Stendhal's autobiography were consistent with responses more generally. Tocqueville noticed and commented on this as well, linking the rise of modesty and self-mastery to democracies. He observed that great passions and heroic acts were far more fitting in the aristocratic past. Tocqueville's efforts to correlate manners and morals with governing structures were similar to what Montesquieu had done a century earlier, now updated for an age of growing equality.

Similar shifts were evident in the arts. Listeners described being moved by music in the new terms of depth and intimacy, but few now swooned or wept openly in theaters. The practice of reading aloud before others in salons, workshops, and town squares now gave way to silent reading. Museumgoers still sometimes gathered in groups to talk freely about what they saw, but the meditative, reverent, and largely private experience of museum-going familiar to us today was now starting to spread. In each domain, an interior, individual, and less communal experience replaced more public displays. To speak of a deepening sense of selfhood is a figure of speech, but the spatial analogy captures the experience of many such listeners, readers, and art lovers.[58]

Those who thought explicitly about such things developed new accounts of cognition that connected identity to self-invention. Some tied their work to the current state of France. The philosopher Victor Cousin, for instance, who articulated a prevailing view of selfhood, wrote that he wished to help heal a fractured nation. Well known for his early work *Lectures on the True, the Beautiful, and the Good*, Cousin was sometimes called France's "pope" of philosophy. He was a professor at the Sorbonne, director of the École Normale Supérieure, a member of the Institut de France and Académie Française, and, for seven months during the July Monarchy, Louis-Philippe's Minister of Public Instruction.[59] In his teaching and writing, he offered a sure means of recovery from the collective traumas of war and revolution: individual initiative. His program, detailed in a series of published lectures, was read widely. Its goal was to train each pupil, most all of them young men, to study, shape, and master his own self.

As the historian Jan Goldstein writes, Cousin's account of selfhood was a "highly articulated subjectivity."[60] Rejecting blank-slate models of cognition from the Enlightenment, Cousin urged an assertiveness appropriate for a social order based not on birth but on accomplishment. The mind was not simply the inert sum of sense impressions, but a site of active reflection, introspection, and self-creation. The description was apt for men determined to make their mark in the world. The result was an individual at once enterprising and highly conformist. The heroic and unfettered self claimed by Cousin's followers was a defender of the status quo.[61]

According to Cousin, this *moi* possessed a vital force apart from all reflection. Its essence was spiritual, an immaterial foundation that underlay all human thought, feeling, and experience. While Cousin described the *moi* as possessing varying levels of depth, he believed that it was fully accessible through self-scrutiny. There was no unconscious.[62] For those well trained, methodical contemplation brought order to the flood of impressions. Cousin recommended "voluntarily inserting oneself into this entirely interior world" and wrote of "giving oneself to oneself as spectacle." This self was independent of others and gloried in its freedom. "The will alone is the person, or the *moi*," Cousin wrote. "Our personality is the will and nothing more."[63] Cousin's official connections ensured that his program was taught in universities and secondary schools throughout the country. Its main audience therefore comprised members of the respectable bourgeoisie who had a stake in meritocracy. According to its tenets, those unexposed to the curriculum were more subject to the force of circumstances and less likely to distinguish themselves. Put another way, those who succeeded had earned their superior status.[64]

Social and economic conditions created fertile ground for Cousin's ideas. They also encouraged individual initiative quite apart from the program of any philosopher. The Napoleonic Code and 1814 Charter affirmed the principle of equality before the law, opening careers to talent and removing legal obstacles to ascent. Napoleon's new "notability"—created chiefly to displace the former aristocracy by birth—carried prestige but brought no significant social or political privileges. The qualities it honored were instead individual. "True nobility resides in morality," he declared. "All men are equal before God: wisdom, talents, and virtue constitute the sole difference among them." Of the 3,200 individuals who possessed noble titles at the end of the Empire, only one in five had been an aristocrat in 1789.[65]

What later generations called social leveling was more accurately the law's promise of equal access. Hierarchy remained, but it was based more on achievement than birth and measured chiefly by wealth. The mayors, administrators, and functionaries who staffed the regimes of the Restoration monarchs Louis XVIII and Charles X were by and large former bankers, notaries, lawyers, and solicitors.[66]

These were the defining elements of the self-made man. The values that fueled his rise—institutional recognition, specialized knowledge, industriousness, and some degree of luck—were widely celebrated. "I have permitted each to arrive anywhere, from everywhere," Napoleon said of his new notability. "My act is popular because it consecrates equality from the very start: talent, courage, and wealth decide the rest."[67] This particular process, which necessarily produced inequality, became the creed of political liberals, who declared that those with talent and determination could remake themselves. "Anyone of the inferior classes who has the intelligence and property will, along with his family, enter the ranks of the bourgeoisie," the *Journal des débats* stated in 1830.[68]

Most who rose quickly also knew they were not immune to reversals. A recurrent image in Balzac is the wheel of fortune, which could just as likely bring failure as success. In the late 1840s, the *Journal des débats* repeated the warning. "The bourgeoisie is not a class, but a position. You acquire it, you lose it."[69] Before 1789, to squander a fortune might sully a reputation, but an aristocrat would still be an aristocrat. For this new elite, bankruptcy or scandal might be irredeemable.

These were the dreams and risks that helped make masked balls of the 1830s and '40s unlike before. The taunting of social superiors seen in the eighteenth century was now replaced by a different kind of boundary testing, one as likely fed by possibility as impertinence. A book called *Carnival's Masquerades and Indiscretions* evoked the startling confusion of status and class: counts danced with laundresses, magistrates supped with seamstresses, girls without their mothers played house with their lovers. In carnival, the book went on to say, one shouldn't be judgmental. "In a world where everyone is an actor, we must all wipe the slate clean from time to time."[70] The mask's anonymity was not the only factor in the role reversals on display. The prospect of remaking oneself inspired maskers to sample new roles.

It was in these decades that the notion first appeared that carnival masks give license to express our true self. This belief—that masks reveal a more authentic self—rests on particular conditions: personal autonomy to shape one's identity, adequate economic means, and the presence of ideas and institutions that make such self-definition possible. The palpable sense of individuality that emerged in the middle third of the century was not absent in earlier centuries, but the barriers to its free public expression were considerable. For these reasons, masks in the 1830s and '40s assumed a new power and significance. They still served to conceal, but they also revealed the truth of a dream or new possibility. Among women, they brought a degree of parity with men and may well have prompted greater freedoms than their accustomed roles permitted.[71] Both men and women used masks to escape the constraints that decent manners supposedly dictated. Masks also helped those who longed for bourgeois stability to imagine themselves more secure. That criminals were said to have dressed in judges' gowns was in its own way an emphatic assertion of another life, however irreverent.

The promise masks offered was related to the extraordinary appeal of the mime Deburau. Night after night, before audiences of ordinary families struggling to survive, Deburau invented and embodied a new self in each of his roles. His success was measured in the assurance, recounted in numerous sources, that he truly was the person he portrayed. The claim of merit was also the currency that numberless Macaires in print and in person used to hoodwink others. Beyond the many young professionals inspired by Cousin's words for honest striving and self-creation, meritocracy also motivated impostors like Coignard and Collet. Success may have indeed rewarded the meritorious, which doesn't mean that all who succeeded were deserving. It shouldn't be forgotten that Deburau was an extremely good actor.

PART FIVE
The Psyche

Self-Portrait, Eugène Carrière (Musée d'art moderne et contemporaine de Strasbourg)

The symbolic efficiency permitted by masking deploys resources often repressed by individuals before they have become who they are. It transfigures them beyond shared laws and ancient prohibitions. . . . The mask forcefully introduces the relativity of current identity. It brutally announces the precarious, accidental nature of the current moment, when so many faces are possible.

—DAVID LE BRETON, *Faces* (2003)

Each one fixes his mask up as he can, the exterior mask. . . . Because inside there is another one, often contradicting the one outside. Nothing is true! True is: the sea, the mountain, a rock, a blade of grass. But man: always wearing a mask, unwillingly, without knowing it, without wanting it, always masked with that thing which he, in good faith, believes to be handsome, good, gracious, generous, unhappy, and so on.

—LUIGI PIRANDELLO, *On Humor* (1908)

12
Modern Masks

THE POET OF MODERN LIFE

In his account of the 1859 Salon, Charles Baudelaire included a description of two sculptures that were not part of the exhibit. Their creator Ernest Christophe had shown Baudelaire the unfinished works in his studio, and the impression was profound. Baudelaire praised them in the review and dedicated a poem to each in his collection *Les Fleurs du mal.* Christophe's names for the works—*Comédie humaine* and *Danse macabre*—evoked themes that recur in Baudelaire's prose and poetry. These included a fascination with disease and death, the seductions and delusions of the flesh, and the modern experience of urban life, which was at once ecstatic and forlorn.

Christophe's *Human Comedy* is a commanding nude who draws a cloth across her thigh and holds a piece of fabric to encircle her face. In his review, Baudelaire calls the statue an allegory, a word he also includes in the poem's title, "The Mask: Allegorical Statue in the Style of the Renaissance." The poem opens in wonderment. The woman's grace evokes the city of Florence in its power and sophistication. Her form is strong and slim, a miraculous body "Made to reign on sumptuous beds / And charm the ease of a pope or prince." Every trait of her face is triumphant. Its expression is at once languid, sly, mocking, and self-satisfied. "Sensuality calls and Love enthrones," it seems to say.

> What a thrilling spell her kindness confers
> To this creature endowed with majesty!
> We come near to walk around such loveliness.

But circling the statue brings a sudden shock. "Oh blasphemy of art! Oh fatal surprise!" A side view reveals this kind face to have been a mask. The

FIGURE 12.1. *Comédie humaine*, Ernest Christophe (Art Resource)

woman recoils behind the false front and her shoulders twist back in agony. What was inviting and adorable is now seen to have been an illusion.

> Yet why does she cry, this perfect beauty,
> Who can bring vanquished humanity to her feet?
> What strange sickness gnaws within?

. . .

She weeps, you fool, because she lives! What she laments above all,
What causes her to shudder to her very soul,
Is that tomorrow, alas, she must still live!
Tomorrow, and the next day, and always!—as we, too, must do![1]

The tone in these final lines shifts from outrage to compassion to despair. Her lies are intoxicating, but behind her mask tears flow. Her unending tomorrows are also ours. What is the allegory? Baudelaire is explicit. Hers is "the universal mask, your mask, my mask," which we wear "to veil our suffering and remorse from the eyes of the world."[2]

Dance of Death, the second sculpture Baudelaire saw in Christophe's studio, could be from a nightmare. A decaying corpse emerges from a rumpled, billowing gown. An exposed rib cage lies against the glistening fabric. A swarm of bees plays at its collarbone, and near the pedestal a coiled asp has begun to mount. The woman's eye sockets are dark and vacant, and her skull, adorned with flowers, rests on fragile vertebrae. She is about to go out for the night. The poet seeks to protect this ghastly beauty from the crowd's mockery and disgust.

Obsessed with flesh, they do not understand
The unspeakable elegance of the human frame.

The corpse holds a mask just below her torso. "Has anyone ever seen a slimmer waist at the ball?"

Baudelaire was not alone in coupling masked balls with death. Remembering the frenzy that had consumed revelers earlier, Victor Hugo conjured the dance of death. How strange it was, he thought, that revelers had embraced the mood with such exuberance. "People willingly danced the *danse macabre*, and, still more bizarre, they did so without realizing it. . . . Musard's baton could have been a tibia."[3] In Baudelaire's poem, death laughs with contempt at the living.

Who has not held a skeleton in his arms?
Who has not fed upon things of the tomb?
What matters the perfume, dress, or costume?
Whoever shows disgust thinks that he, too, is handsome.

Lost in their own pleasures, most fail to see the abyss or to hear the Angel's trumpet already sounding. The poem's closing words are spoken by this unmasked skeleton.

"In each clime, under every sun, in all your contortions,
Death admires you, ridiculous Humanity,
And often, scenting itself with myrrh,
It brings irony to your insanity!"[4]

In these two poems, the mask carries few of its earlier associations. In the first, its distortions are forced and inescapable. Worn unhappily, it is a source of anguish, and the sickness it hides is existence itself. In the second, the mask hides the truth of all mortal things, which is death. Here it is welcomed by most all who wear it, whether in denial, distraction, or consent. In Baudelaire's vision, both masks go beyond outward deceit to conceal a more intimate suffering. Beneath each lies an inner world of unspoken cruelty, shame, and fear.

Baudelaire was one of the first late-century writers, artists, and cultural critics to use the mask to probe the interior landscape of the psyche. As masks disappeared from the streets and balls, they assumed associations closely tied to the new science of psychology. For his and later generations, the mask signified the facelessness of life among strangers in the city. It also signaled a foreignness to oneself. In these decades, masks pointed to human motives that were neither rational nor fully knowable. They signified an unmoored self and the elusive pursuit to understand one's own nature. For some, the response was to unmask: to tear off the false front of custom and propriety, give voice to more authentic impulses, and expose the true desires of oneself and others. In this view, the mask stood for civilization's unnatural demands and the damage they did to mental and physical health. This unmasking revealed things that society might wish to deny, including violence, sexual deviance, and madness.

Vast transformations in urban life contributed to these changes in private experience. In 1830, more than half the Paris population had been born outside the city. By 1850, the population had surpassed one million, swelled by migrants from the countryside. "There is no Parisian society, there are no Parisians," a contemporary lamented. "Paris is nothing more than an encampment of nomads." In 1865, 1.7 million people lived in the city.[5] The urban landscape changed to accommodate the new population. Early in his administration, President Louis-Napoleon Bonaparte vowed to cut new roads and open crowded neighborhoods so that sunlight would penetrate the city "as the light of truth illuminates our hearts." Just months before declaring himself emperor two years later, Bonaparte announced a massive new undertaking to modernize roads, harbors, railway lines, and canal and river transportation. To manage the undertaking, he named

FIGURE 12.2. *Charles Baudelaire,* Étienne Carjat (Art Resource)

Georges-Eugène Haussmann as prefect of the Department of the Seine. Haussmann vowed to remake the population as well by either reforming or relocating the "floating and agitated ocean" of the urban poor.[6]

Building on its role as the national hub of culture and commerce, Haussmann streamlined movement within Paris itself, connecting rail lines to the city center, improving access to the marketplace Les Halles, and clearing space for monumental buildings of finance, commerce, and the law. Over ninety miles of new boulevards were laid and more than 100,000 buildings demolished, eliminating entire neighborhoods, opening wide vistas where narrow tenements had once stood, and forcing the working class to the city's perimeter. Critics denounced Haussmann for moving the poor to the suburbs, where conditions were harsh. "We have built two cities, quite different and hostile: the city of luxury, surrounded, besieged by the city of misery," the prefect's most vocal opponent Louis Lazare wrote. As with all Haussmann's projects, this, too, was by design. To ensure that there would be no more revolutions, he wrote in his memoirs, he "disemboweled" neighborhoods most likely to rebel by building wide central avenues through their center. By his own estimate, Haussmann's projects displaced between a quarter- and a half-million people.[7]

New construction brought blocks of residential space, hotels, department stores, and public parks. David Van Zanten, a historian of urbanism, contrasts what had once been a city of hidden spaces—of private gardens, narrow tenements, walled hotels, and shops squeezed against the street—with palm courts, spacious lobbies, soaring staircases, and grand restaurants, "all tinkling and tantalizing."[8] Haussmann's master plan with its cream facades and straight-arrow avenues spread uniformity across what were once distinct neighborhoods. Two decades earlier, Balzac had recorded the physiognomies of Paris streets and districts, citing noble streets, merchant streets, dowager streets, and worker streets. The stronger impression now was an overall sameness.

With the 1860 incorporation of Belleville into Paris, the squalid spectacle of the Courtille Descent receded and a new kind of public display emerged: that of spectacle and commodification. This was deliberate. Haussmann and the emperor preferred Parisians to be dazzled by opulence, abundance, and imperial power. Consumption increased, but the greater point was its conspicuousness. Public life became spectacular, a performance fueled by the new consumer society, mass press, and the crowd's shared voyeurism. A book devoted to the city's boulevard culture dwelled on its "feast for the eyes." "The real Parisian spectacle," its author wrote, "is where we have found it: in the street, on terraces, in restaurants."[9]

With these changes came a shift in experience. Edmond and Jules Goncourt took note of the new conditions.

> I see women, children, households, families in this café. The interior is going to die. Life threatens to become public. . . . I am as much a stranger to what is coming, to what is, as I am to these new boulevards without turnings, without chance perspectives, implacable in their straight lines, which no longer smack of the world of Balzac and make one think instead of some American Babylon of the future.

The scale, wealth, and abundance were at once inhuman and intimidating: "Faces are eclipsed by clothes, feelings by landscapes."[10]

The architectural historian David Harvey puts his own gloss on this change. "The mask now became more significant than the reality as daily life came to mimic the facades displayed at the masked ball or during carnival." T. J. Clark makes a similar point in *The Painting of Modern Life*, describing a new emphasis on ostentation rather than luxury, fluff rather than fashion, and consumption rather than trade. "And here above all was *uncertainty*—a pantomime of false rich and false poor, in which anyone could pretend to be anything if he or she had money for clothes."[11] One set of figures points to a particular space in which strangers might want to turn their face into a mask. Between 1855 and 1860, the annual number of omnibus passengers in Paris grew from 36 million to 110 million. Anonymity, whether cultivated or unwilled, was unavoidable.[12]

These changes gave birth to terms that now describe the modern condition: estrangement, alienation, aloneness in the crowd. "The deepest problems of modern life," begins the 1903 essay "The Metropolis and Mental Life" by the German sociologist Georg Simmel, "derive from the claim of the individual to preserve the autonomy and individuality of his existence in the face of overwhelming social forces."[13] Baudelaire's language, swinging from elation to despair, was more poetical. In the city, he wrote, the self dissolves in a sea of strangers. This was a rare privilege for artists, he believed, an opportunity to merge with an unknown being. To give one's poetry and charity wholly to these strangers was "holy prostitution," "mysterious intoxication," an "ineffable orgy." How to explain this urge for intimacy with the unknown? It is as if "a fairy has infused the taste of disguise and the mask in the cradle," he wrote.

For the poet Baudelaire, the urban spectacle populated an inner world that came to define, and at times defy, the world around him. Paradise exists within oneself alone, he wrote. He watches a poor, wrinkled woman through a window, narrates to himself what he thinks her sad story to be, and weeps. Her imagined suffering brings him satisfaction. "What does the reality outside of myself matter, if it has helped me to live, to feel that I am and what I am?"[14] Never far from such comfort was a terrifying solitude, which came to him in the dead of night. "Dreadful life! Dreadful city!" His plea, conveyed in an entry called "One O'Clock in the Morning," is for redemption from his own self-loathing. "Lord, my God! Grant me the grace to produce a few beautiful verses to prove to myself that I am not the lowest of men, and that I am not inferior to those I despise!"[15]

Baudelaire knew, too, of the fears, passions, and perversions that lived behind strangers' masks. *Paris Spleen* includes intimate portraits of the city's loners, workers, dreamers, and beggars, who exist mostly unseen among the privileged. It also depicts the vain, cruel, and depraved. A gloved gentleman in a new suit grandly salutes a poor donkey being whipped by its master. A family in tatters stops in wonderment before a brilliant café, and a woman inside, announcing her disgust, demands that they be made to leave. Two children, one rich and one poor, torment a rat imprisoned in a small box. A woman he calls "Miss Scalpel" has a sexual craving for surgeons with their sharpened tools and bloody gowns. The spectacle of modern life produced ever more sophisticated masks.

Baudelaire found a kindred taste for the mask in the artist he believed best embodied modern life. Constantin Guys was a prince who "sees society, is at the center of society, and remains hidden from society."[16] A Dutch painter who spent most of his career as an illustrator for the popular press, Guys settled in Paris in the 1850s. His works predated Impressionism but shared its embrace of the transitory. His chance scenes are of carriages and cafés, from the theater or at races, and in doorways and bordellos. Baudelaire deemed Guys the painter of modern life as much for his temperament as for his work, which he seldom signed. He preferred to be invisible and unacknowledged. Learning that Baudelaire planned to write about him, Guys forbade him the use of his name. In the essay he remains M. G.

"The Painter of Modern Life" appeared in *Le Figaro* in three installments. In it, M. G. is a "great lover of the crowd and anonymity." His passion is "*to marry the crowd.*" Unseen among its multitudes, he conveyed the feel of their own facelessness. He was a *flâneur*, the obsessive observer who became a public fixture in these decades. He strolled endlessly, watching, assessing, evaluating, and recording. Before a regiment had passed, Baudelaire writes, Guys had absorbed its high sheen and fixed expressions. He was a self insatiable for the non-self, Baudelaire writes, an immense mirror floating in a reservoir of electricity, "which he rendered into images more alive than life itself, forever fugitive and unstable."[17]

When Baudelaire's essay appeared in 1863, the word *modernity* was still rare. The poet Gautier had used it several years earlier in defense of stylistic innovations. Baudelaire's associations were closer to the evanescent sensations Guys sought to depict, as well as his own experience of the city. "Modernity," he wrote, "is the transitory, the fugitive, the contingent."[18] The view was strongly shaped by Paris and its transformations, both physical and psychological, which marked the course of their lives. Guys's cultivated anonymity, as well as Baudelaire's interior communion with strangers, were versions of a mask the metropolis induced many to assume (see plate 1).

THE DECLINE OF BALLS

Édouard Manet's 1873 painting *Masked Ball at the Opera* is a crowded, claustrophobic scene whose content belies the title. The setting is not in the Opera's main hall but in a corridor just outside the boxes. A lady's leg dangles from an overhead walkway, which crowds the space below. Top hats bunch together in close quarters. The women in front by turns implore, defy, and resist the men who far outnumber them. The mask of a rosy-cheeked woman in a cap, white blouse, trousers, and laced boots lies on the floor like a discarded piece of clothing. Despite the Débardeur's costume, there is nothing masculine about her. She peers up with a cool gaze and curls her long fingers on a man's chest. He looks down as if appraising her and gently tests an arm. Just above them—to the left of a red-booted foot—are the knees and gold-trimmed culottes of another Débardeur (see plate 2).

Two women are pressed nearby in a dark jumble, one with an orange, a fan, and a bouquet of flowers. The other grasps her bunched gloves as a bearded man looks down with delectation. To their right, a woman touches a man's cheek. Another bends in close to a seated man with her chin in her hand, an elbow resting on the man's left leg and a finger between her lips. At the far left, a Polichinelle draws back in dismay. A woman in a hat whose trim matches his costume—his likely companion—stands with folded arms as a man leans in to cup her breast. Another man watches intently. The faces beneath these black hats show monied satisfaction. A contemporary who saw the painting described the men's eyes as "alight with truffles and Corton" and their pockets "full of *louis d'or*."[19] In this masked ball, only five people are masked.

The painting, rejected for the 1873 Salon, has none of the disruptive glee that described Opera balls of the 1830s and '40s. The art historian Linda Nochlin, whose essay on the work calls it a vivid example of Manet's "slice of life" vision, writes that it "refused—and still refuses—to comply with its subject." It has no "merry-making," "gay abandon," or "lighthearted revelry."[20] Writing a generation after Manet's death, a critic called it the "multicolored life of the flesh market." He continues:

> The scarcely-concealed lust of the gestures of the soliciting men, the women offering themselves (while parrying certain offers), the calculating glances, groping hands, brutal winks, all the typical gestures of the proceedings, metropolitan in every nuance, are employed to create a style.[21]

For this critic, the modern city and its mores had stifled all play.

Thirty years earlier, Baudelaire described the black suit as the "outer husk of the modern hero . . . the necessary dress of our suffering age, which wears the symbol of its endless mourning on its thin black shoulders." With the coming of democracy, he wrote, all had an equal share in the loneliness of existence. "We are each of us celebrating some funeral." Manet read and corresponded with Baudelaire, and he may have remembered the passage. If so, its commentary adds a grim layer to his painting.[22]

Manet's cheerless atmosphere is a fair characterization of masked balls in the last third of the century. With the prime years of masking now past, these gatherings had a dull, routine-like quality, both at the Opera and in dance halls that still offered balls. Most women came wearing masks, and many dressed in costumes. Few men wore either masks or costumes. Most dressed instead in the formal black suit and top hat. The frenzied galops and infernal dances of Musard were gone, and dancing of any kind was secondary. Whatever was gained in orderliness came at the expense of excitement. There remained a social mix, but even at the Opera public interest was a fraction of what it had been earlier. The taste for disguise was in decline. Soon the masked ball itself would disappear.

Balls at the Opera and the roughly twenty other theaters that staged them after 1850 differed from gatherings two decades earlier in many ways, beginning with their poor attendance. Revenue from Opera balls was a fraction of what it had once been. In an effort to draw a larger public, the price of admission for men was reduced first from ten francs to seven, and then from seven francs to five. This was half of what admission had been for both men and women in the 1830s. In the 1871 season—three years before Manet painted *Masked Ball*—admission for women was lowered to two francs.[23]

The tone had changed, too. Suave luxury replaced license, and festivity shifted to signal wealth and sophistication. Ostentation replaced concealment. At the Opera, champagne, great buffets of food, and fifty tables for formal dining welcomed ball-goers. Couples and small groups spoke backstage or in the corridors outside the hall. Inside, the orchestra was an accompaniment to a slow circulation of women and men, most of whom talked while a relative handful danced. The boxes above were their own spectacle, which was the main reason many attended. Here sat France's social and political elites, who relished the attention they received. A prominent newspaper listed the names of thirty-two notables its reporter recognized among the first-tier boxes in 1875. These included the Rothschilds, Louis-Philippe's grandson the comte de Paris, the Russian ambassador, and members of the Aguado family, which possessed one of France's largest banking fortunes.

First-tier boxes were also held by members of the city's private clubs, including the Jockey Club, the Sporting Club, the Union, the Champs-Élysées, and the Cercle de la rue Royale. "We have not cited all the distinguished and celebrated personalities who were in attendance," a reporter noted. "May it suffice to know that in this great assembly we saw everyone who is pleased to be seen at Parisian events." Perhaps this was why beggars had also begun appearing outside the Opera on ball nights to open its doors for revelers and then ask for money.[24]

For those who wore them, costumes were more elaborate than the century's earlier, simpler attire. Shops near the Opera rented used costumes that had first been worn in performances. Their prices ranged from two to ten francs, with a largely middle-class clientele. The most popular women's costumes were Bohemians, Alsatian maids, wet nurses, schoolgirls, and shepherdesses. Men could come as musketeers, grenadiers, noble lords from François I's or Louis XIII's day, or astrologers. Clown costumes, Arlequins, and Pierrots were also available.[25]

The few men who came in costume were usually mocked. There was some amusement when several showed up as the same Neapolitan fisherman: the Opera had just sold its stock of chorus costumes from an Italian production. Police arrested a Polichinelle who had his own reasons for disguise. A search found him carrying two stolen wallets, two bracelets, three brooches, four scarves, a pair of opera glasses, and six pairs of pince-nez. At the Opera, authorities asked a man whose costume was judged too political to leave his hat in the coat-check room. He had come as Jacobin, and on the hat—a black bicorne popular during the Revolution—was a large tricolor cockade. The rental shops also did brisk business in another kind of disguise. Men in cloth coats and workers' smocks often came to rent black suits and top hats for the balls.[26]

Authorities also watched for men who came to the Opera ball in women's clothes. A contemporary whose studies in "social pathology" included both female and male prostitution asserted that this ball in particular was a rendezvous of those looking for sex with other men. He described the hall's private boxes, guarded by well-compensated attendants, as especially active. Police took testimony from some who met, danced with, and went home with seductive maskers to learn that they were not women. The author of a book called *Paris Corruption* relates recognizing one such beauty at the Opera from police photos of him without makeup and wearing men's clothes. Officers also patrolled the Opera and other ball settings for what they described as gangs of pederasts.[27]

In the balls of these decades, those with means put their wealth on display. One man came in the expected black suit and white tie but wore a lace shirt studded with diamonds, rings set with sapphires, and boots with golden heels. "Our masquerades of society aim more for brilliance, luxury, and amazement than merriment," an observer wrote of the gatherings. "Costume balls are now little more than a glittering procession." This witness found it telling that ball administrators hired professional dancers in matching costumes to populate the floor.[28]

There was much speculation about why many women but so few men came masked. Most male observers rendered moral judgment. A journalist estimated the portion of honest women at balls to be an "infinitesimal minority" and added that even these soon forgot their virtue. Another surmised that "delicate ladies" in particular were attracted by the balls' disreputable elements.[29] Others were less quick to assume that masks signaled vice. One evoked the legacy of Débardeurs. With balls now more formal, he wrote, a simple mask conferred this same independence, freeing women from the modesty expected in other settings. "With a mask, they feel strong. While demure in their own homes, at the Opera they can hear things without blushing—things they would never dare to read." This writer also voiced concern. In a mask conversation breeds intimacy, and when the mask comes down strangers speak freely. "They may even share their most secretive thoughts."[30]

One writer's first memory of a ball conveyed a more disturbing dynamic. Posters had promised splendid costumes and a sparkling atmosphere. Instead he found "sad men" in coats and top hats slowly circling the floor. It put him in mind of caged animals. A company of young and not-so-young women in their "costume of the sidewalk" teased and flirted. Aristocrats of birth and finance sat in rented theater boxes above, watching and being watched. Some men lingered backstage. Others stood on the dance floor, where five or six maskers danced. In the corridors outside the hall, a "hunt for women" went on all night. When the "prey" was exhausted, he reported—when she was "at the end of her defenses and all her tears"—there was "a sickening feeding-frenzy" in the corners, an orgy of pinching, pulling, and scratching. The spectacle was like "an undertaker's wedding," he wrote, which he called the "cruel and morbid nuptials of *Tout-Paris* in a black suit."[31]

The change these scenes convey from the raucous popular balls of forty years earlier started just after the 1848 Revolution. Two weeks before that year's Mardi Gras, troops loyal to Louis-Philippe had opened fire on protesters objecting to a ban on political banquets, killing twenty. Rioters poured into the streets, the king fled into exile, and on February 25 the Second French Republic was declared. Among the executive decrees was one from the new interior minister ordering theaters to reopen. The stated reason was to reestablish public order, but just as important was an effort to project normalcy after this third revolution since 1789. Musard's masked balls at the Opera resumed on the Sunday before Lent. Attendance was one-third of what it had been the year before.

The poor showing was a sign of things to come. Masked balls entered a decline that was never reversed. Revenues at the Musard ball in 1848 and the following year were the lowest since the conductor's arrival ten years before. A shortened schedule in later years did little to boost attendance. Most no longer came to dance but to watch others dance, which a dwindling number now did. "The actor became a spectator," a contemporary reported. Tickets were sent to young clerks in department stores offering free access to balls on the condition that they come in costume and dance. Complimentary passes were widely available for women.[32]

Some looked to the political climate for an explanation. One writer attributed the change to the spirit of freedom and equality, which had shifted how citizens of this new Republic viewed themselves. True liberty has produced "a new regard for oneself," he wrote, and "the end of a taste for disguise." A more jaundiced view from an 1855 book on carnival linked the decline of balls to the reign of money, distinction, and display:

> Today we no longer have classes, or faces, or characters, or moral constraints. . . . Now that money is the sole mark of nobility or distinction, now that the mask of money disfigures every face and all are free to disguise themselves to play their little comedy, what good is carnival? . . . Carnival is dead. A masked, disguised, made-up, papered-over civilization has buried it.[33]

The historian François Gasnault singles out an additional factor that tarnished the city's pleasures. In the months after February 1848, the promise of fraternity met the reality of a steadily worsening economy, desperation among the urban poor, and much of the countryside resistant to the new order. Tocqueville described a society split in two: those who had nothing joined in common need and those who had something joined in common fear. When laborers and the unemployed erected barricades in late June to protest the closure of national workshops, the army's six-day assault produced casualties in the thousands and sent thousands more into forced exile. "To dance after April," Gasnault writes in reference to elections in which monarchists and other conservatives dominated, "would seem suspiciously frivolous. To do so in July, given the hatred, pain, and fear that was fixed in hearts of Parisians, was indecent or dangerous."[34]

A determined effort followed to elevate the tone of the balls. By government order, the Opera raised ticket prices to ten francs at the start of the 1850 season. It issued new requirements for men and women to wear evening attire or come "in domino," a designation for formal dress that excluded the motley gear of Chicards, Balochards, and Macaires. A theater box on the lowest level was permanently reserved for police surveillance.[35] Additional guidelines limiting maskers' freedom appeared after Louis-Napoleon's 1851 coup against the Republic. These forbade wearing masks in public before 10 a.m. or after 6 p.m., including on Mardi Gras. No disguise that harmed public decency would be tolerated. Ecclesiastical dress could not be worn as a costume, and all religious symbols were forbidden. Provocative words or gestures were explicitly banned. All masks and disguises after noon on Ash Wednesday were illegal.[36]

Two years into the Second Empire, Napoleon III's new regime assumed direct control over the Opera's balls. Decrees strengthened dress codes and formalized distinctions between women and men. Women were required to attend masked and in a costume or formal gown. Men were to come in a black suit or costume, with no requirement to mask. Any man dressing as a woman, it added, or any woman as a man was intolerable.[37] In keeping with the new mood, Phillipe Musard's contract was terminated and a suitably tranquilizing replacement was found. The conductor, Isaac Strauss, was known best for his soothing performances in the spa town of Vichy.[38] Napoleon III's own example also played a part in shifting the mood. He and Empress Eugénie appeared at the Opera on Mardi Gras two months after declaring himself emperor, along with his cabinet, members of the diplomatic corps, and officers of the court. He moved to the front of his box, saluted the crowd, basked in its applause, and then left with his entourage to visit other theaters.[39]

In their early years, Opera balls of the Second Empire drew a wide social range. Wealthy bankers spoke to journalists, society women and shop girls shared the floor, and workers mixed with artists and professionals. Whatever mingling went on, however, there was little taste or occasion for suspending social roles. At most other venues with balls in the last week of carnival, the profile was more popular. These included the Salle Sainte-Cécile on Friday, the Salles Valentino and Barthélemy on Saturday, the Vauxhall on Monday, and the Prado on Mardi Gras. Apart from their scattered masks and costumes, the balls here differed little from the dances held at other times of the year.[40]

Such were the influences that changed masked balls from the carnivalesque 1830s and '40s to the staid '60s and '70s. Political upheaval, the prominence of wealth and ostentation, and the ubiquitous poor just outside the theaters' doors contributed to an experience whose festivity was increasingly staged. A hardening class structure meant that society was less in flux than before. Balls now featured little that was topsy-turvy. With the Empire's collapse, the sheen of privilege and sophistication that had reigned at balls also disappeared. Sumptuous buffets of shrimp, truffles, and champagne were replaced with sauerkraut and beer.[41]

As with the tumultuous events of 1848, some looked to the French defeat of 1870 to draw fresh conclusions about the shared effects of national trauma. After the war, a journalist observed, French gaiety did not return. A new generation "grown old before its time and indifferent to all things" had replaced the carefree, youthful spirit of earlier years. Former pleasures now seemed like "old, obsolete games."[42] News spread in 1903 that Opera administrators had decided to make this the final season. The theater's last masked ball, held on Saturday instead of Mardi Gras, was a far cry from the spontaneous displays of the Musard years. At 1 a.m., an hour after doors opened, a parade of women who had entered the gown competition processed through the hall. At 2 a.m., prizes for the most beautiful dresses were awarded. At 3 a.m., revelers assembled for a "monster cake-walk," the new dance craze inspired by American jazz.[43]

After a run of two hundred years, this marked the end of the Opera's masked balls. Much had changed since its boisterous days. The move away from true concealment had shifted the tone from spontaneity to arranged spectacle. Willing reversals in status had given way to self-display. True festivity was replaced by something closer to commemoration. A telling instance of their decadence came in the only masked ball *Le Figaro* listed for the 1905 carnival season, a "Grand Masked Ball for Children" at the *Casino de Paris*. It started in the afternoon. There were children's dances, the distribution of toys, and, for those who came in costume, a token entitling them to have their photograph taken.[44]

CARNIVAL IS DEAD

Carnival's street celebrations also declined in the second half of the nineteenth century. After the bloody June uprising of 1848 and the abrupt turn from Republic to Empire, costumes grew rare in public and masks all but disappeared. The gleaming metropolis was worlds away from the muddy streets that saw such violence in the late eighteenth century, when coaches packed with maskers on Mardi Gras clogged working-class neighborhoods. Now some wore costumes with advertisements for shops and stores, and carnival carriages bore commercial signs and banners. "Onion Tablets for Your Pot-au-Feu, invented by M. Rozière de Romainville." "A Cure for Corns, by M. Galopin, *Artiste Pédicure*." "Insecticide by M. Vicat." Publicity now travels in disguise, a writer quipped.[45] Some street revelers still dressed in costumes, but most found them eccentric. Just as there are cemetery fanatics, an observer commented, so, too, are there carnival fanatics: a carriage passes with three or four freezing Pierrettes and a Musketeer inside; you wait another fifteen minutes before another passes.

The grand insults and scatological songs were also a thing of the past. Carnival today, a witness claimed, is merely an excuse for drunkenness. "As for wit or a salty gibe or some sly intrigue, forget about it. You yawn at the Opera and then go shout in the streets until you're hoarse. Such are the accumulated pleasures of carnival in Paris."[46] The season's pranks were nevertheless harsh. A common amusement in the early '50s had been for a man and woman to dress as a homeless couple with battered hats, shredded clothes, and soot smeared on their faces. Their exaggerated pleas for food or small change drew insults and laughter. "Such mockery of the poor brings the greatest success in Paris," an onlooker noted, describing the sport of "reviling and abusing" the would-be beggars.[47]

Years later, when masks and costumes no longer appeared on the streets, the heartless amusement lived on without the buffer of make-believe. The poverty was no longer a disguise. "Masks and masquerades are no longer with us," a journalist wrote during the 1870 carnival season. "What do you see today along the boulevards? A few poor devils covered in rags chased by children shouting insults."[48] The opulent city made inequities more glaring. Carnival, known for making the unsaid sayable and the forbidden permissible, now gave the privileged an opportunity to flaunt their place in the order.

This same year, a poem called "Elegy" appeared in *Le Figaro* that cast carnival as a wheezing angel on the verge of death. Its author remembered the Chicards and Balochards of his youth.

> You surely recall the cavalcades,
> Today there is none of that!
> Now nothing remains but barricades,
> At least the *boeuf* is fat.

In place of disguise, the poem continued, is vanity: boulevards have become a fashion show. In some neighborhoods, men and women in elegant clothes threw confetti at one another. "Gaiety today is nothing more than commerce." "Elegy" ends in bitterness. Farewell Scapin, farewell Polichinelle, it reads, the politicians have usurped you. "It's only in the Chamber that you see false faces."[49]

An enveloping sobriety in the national mood made common festivity more difficult. An essay on traditions of masking in France recalled earlier customs: gentlemen of the Renaissance who rode through the streets masked; ladies at the time of Louis XIV who went to church, concerts, and salons masked; masked throngs of the Saint-Antoine district on donkeys and in carriages during carnival; and the riot of disguises in the 1830s that made it hard for mask makers to meet the demand. "No one will amuse his contemporaries voluntarily," the essay concludes. "Carnival is dying. Masks are disappearing." The current age is "serious and literal."[50]

The elegiac mood was widespread, and it persisted into the twentieth century. "In the streets, carnival is in agony, awaiting its final breath, God willing!" reads an account from 1879. Twenty years later, a journalist reported that the young had no taste for disguise. In 1904, *Le Figaro* published

FIGURE 12.3. *Mardi Gras on Paris Boulevard*, anon. (Bibliothèque nationale de France)

"The Ballad of Cheerless Mardi Gras," whose snatches of conversation register little notice of the day.

> —What do you think of England?
> —Will Japan be defeated?
> —This warfare on the seas worries me.
> —So far, Wilhelm has stayed silent.
> —But what if his policy suddenly turns brutal?
>
> "Tell me, handsome masker, what do you say?"
> "This Mardi Gras is awfully thin."[51]

For the novelist Jean-Richard Bloch, the disappearance of shared festivity marked a turning point. Bloch published a collection of essays at the end of World War I that he called *Carnival Is Dead*. It is an especially heartfelt expression of national loss. The book's desolate introduction, framed as a prayer for countrymen killed in the war, describes a dying civilization. There is now no moral connection among people, Bloch writes, no faith by which any common cause might be made. Secularism has destroyed all spiritual ideals but provides nothing to nourish the soul in their place. For Bloch, the death of carnival stands for a culture stripped of all higher meaning. Without the vital conviction of wrongdoing, repentance, and redemption, he writes, carnival's exultant release is hollow. "Freedom has no festivals."[52]

What the French have instead is perpetual, empty excitement. How can costumes and confetti compete with photography, the telegraph, or the rotary press? What are Christmas lights in a city filled with automobiles? Carnival's former passions are now sated by entertainment and politics, with one important difference. Unlike the holiday's cyclical release and renewal, the effect of these modern stimulants is perpetual agitation and anxiety. Modernity's excitements offer no renewal.

Bloch points to mass democracy in particular, which he claims unleashes waves of emotion while limiting authority to a small number. If Christian pessimism in its cycle of sin and repentance fueled popular joy during carnival, he writes, democratic optimism has brought emptiness to the people. Bloch found the same dynamic in spectator sports, which unleashed ecstatic passion that vanished just as quickly. For this writer, the death of carnival signified a sterile public spirit. Modern festivals are joyless because they cannot address the needs of individuals. "These are by definition movements for the masses, whose events are bureaucratic and centralized, where man only watches or listens and is allowed to act only with a rare gesture, both false and emphatic."[53]

Despite this powerful postmortem, one carnival tradition lived on. The procession of the *Boeuf Gras* still flourished. The parade that ended at the slaughterhouse had in fact grown yet more grand than before. Since its elevation as a formal feature of carnival by Napoleon in 1805, the tradition had survived with minimal interruption through the Restoration and July Monarchy, Second Republic and Second Empire, and now well into the Third Republic. With the 1848 Revolution, processions had been suspended on humanitarian grounds. They returned under Napoleon III with unprecedented pomp. Four bulls received an escort that included Roman warriors, medieval foot soldiers, Renaissance chevaliers, royal musketeers, and modern French guards. Monkeys carried banners along the route, which included stops at major hotels, department stores, the Jockey Club, the Banque de France, and the home of the Rothschild family. The contingent of deities reached fifteen, and the number of bulls killed rose from four to six. After the slaughter, meat was distributed to dignitaries.[54]

The *Boeuf Gras* was again suspended in 1871, a consequence of international and domestic crises. The humiliating armistice ending the Franco-Prussian War, signed on the Germans' terms at Versailles, came in late

January. Deep social and political divisions soon burst into civil war, and the population had little interest in festivity. A "scarcely provisioned Paris was in need of meat," an account from these months explained. "It was in no mood to cart living bulls or other carnival floats through its empty streets."[55] When the ceremony returned twenty-five years later, its connection to carnival was largely historical. Tens of thousands lined the sidewalks in street clothes to see its fourteen floats and hundreds of participants. On the first day, the parade stopped at the Élysée Palace, where President Félix Faure and his family raised a toast to the bull. It continued for two more days, winding its way to the Hôtel de Ville and the Bastille, to the Madeleine, the Opera, and the grand boulevards, to Place Clichy and Montmartre, and to Notre-Dame and the Luxembourg gardens.

The refurbished spectacle was an explicit display of nationalism. A bull was still at its center—a Normande on Sunday, a Limousine on Monday, and a Nivernais on Tuesday—with an entourage far larger than it had ever been. Armed executioners were mounted and rode before and on either side of the bull, who stood on a float pulled by six horses. Other floats followed with products from the soil and trophies of foreign conquest. The Agriculture Float bore ten farmers, twenty village musicians, and an assortment of turkeys and geese. The Pastoral Float had ten sheep, two shepherds, and two shepherdesses. The Charcuterie Float featured four pigs in a giant bathtub, and the Wine Float had a pair of champagne bottles that were each two meters tall. Near the end came floats for Beer and Benevolence.[56]

The press described a "human sea" on the boulevards near the Porte Saint-Martin. Ten thousand gathered in front of the Opera; twenty-five thousand were packed along the rue Lafayette; and thirty thousand gathered at the Place de la Concorde. Two floats drew tremendous cheers. The first to do so was the centerpiece, the *Boeuf Gras*. Among the broadsheets and fliers sold by hawkers on the streets were verses prepared for these three days of celebration, whose fatal culmination came on the afternoon on Ash Wednesday. Each carcass would then be auctioned, slaughtered, and sold to Paris restaurants.

The other display to draw great cheers was the Float of the Colonies, which featured "colonists, natives, soldiers, and cavalrymen."[57] An illustration from the *Petit Parisian* conveys its intended message in both words and images. Along its sides are emblems that read *Algeria*, *Tonkin*, *Tunisia*, *Cochin*, and *Sudan*. On its platform are eight colonial subjects, including an African couple, five men with characteristic headgear, and an Asian woman who stares fixedly ahead. Just before them is a colossal soldier in a greatcoat, who is armed with a pistol, saber, and rifle bayonet. On a pedestal above stand a sailor and two explorers, one of whom holds an axe. The tricolor waves on high.

In 1896, the year the *Boeuf Gras* returned, France's growing colonial empire drew wide support from across the political spectrum. The colonial enterprise, which stretched from the Caribbean to Africa and the Orient, bridged political differences by laying claim to Napoleon's vaunted "civilizing mission." Contemporaries now understood the phrase in explicitly racial terms. The popular prime minister Jules Ferry spoke of the rights "superior races" possessed by virtue of fulfilling their duty "to civilize the inferior races."[58] There were clear economic reasons for possessing colonies overseas, which could address the damaging effects of domestic overproduction and the need for resources. "Once the French genius is put to colonization," read a front-page editorial from the country's best-selling daily newspaper the *Petit Journal*, "we will find an outlet for the overflow of our factories, and at the same time we will be able to secure . . . the primary materials needed in our factories."[59]

Such convictions helped feed the popularity of France's Universal Expositions, which drew tens of millions of visitors to Paris in the 1880s and '90s. The 1889 Exposition displayed four hundred subjects from sub-Saharan Africa, Tahiti, and New Caledonia. These "human zoos" included indigenous peoples in cages, as well as in reconstructed "natural" settings. "We see colored people in canvas encampments, under reeds, surrounded by straw and cow dung," a guidebook reported. "Young and old clamor to see the savages."[60]

The Universal Exposition of 1900, attended by more than fifty million people, devoted twenty-eight buildings to French colonies and protectorates. Visitors to a pavilion sponsored by the Alliance Française could watch instructors instruct Senegalese and Dahomean men, women, and children in the French language using the new Berlitz Method. In 1900, the total population of France's colonies was more than sixty million.[61] Colonial culture was spread through children's books, novels, travel literature, geographical societies, and religious organizations. Promising to transcend party politics, it claimed national unity through universal ideals. It did so in the full awareness that such aims entailed coercion and bloodshed.

The juxtaposition was sometimes striking. In 1897, General Joseph Gallieni, who had served in the French colonies of Senegal, the Sudan, Martinique, and Tonkin, received a medal from the French Anti-Slavery Society for his "humanitarian act" of ending slavery in Madagascar. His victory, which abolished a centuries-old monarchy that had used the forced labor of men captured in Africa, secured the island nation as a French colony. Two months later, Gallieni imposed an annual requirement of fifty-nine

FIGURE 12.4. *Float of the Colonies*, anon. (*Petit Parisien*, February 23, 1896)

days' uncompensated work for French colonial administration from every male Malagasy. Historians estimate that within six years this requirement had caused the death of 20 percent of the male population.[62]

What was in the minds of spectators of the *Boeuf Gras* as they cheered float after float celebrating the fruits of French soil, French benevolence, and the French empire? In 1890, Sir James Frazer published *The Golden Bough*, a founding work in the new field of anthropology that connected carnival to ancient fertility rites. At the center of these rites was a scapegoat, whose sacrifice brought a turning from winter's darkness to the rebirth of spring. Drawing from myth, religious belief, and an array of practices across the ancient world, Frazer found a common thread of death and resurrection that was at once communal and individual. "In name and detail the rites varied from place to place," he writes of such rituals in the ancient world. "In substance, they were the same."[63]

Remnants and echoes of carnival violence persisted in modern and early modern Europe. "Wild man" hunts were a carnival rite throughout the Pyrenees, Switzerland, Austria, and the eastern Czech lands, where young men dressed in animal skins, blackened their faces with soot, and were then chased, caught, and ritually "killed" to be borne motionless through the streets. In Italy's Piedmont region, an honored carnival turkey was brought to the main square, impaled by the neck on a post, and clubbed by youths on horseback until the head broke loose, spattering the victor's clothes with blood. In eighteenth-century Venice, patricians regularly sponsored "bull hunts" during carnival in which packs of trained dogs attacked bulls before raucous crowds. For Frazer, such rites strengthened and renewed community. It bound its members in common guilt and in the elation of the moment brought a shared feeling of rebirth.[64]

The language of sacrifice pervaded popular and official descriptions of France's *Boeuf Gras*. Verses celebrated "the terrible fate of an innocent beast," and printed accounts devoted attention to each year's "*sacrificateurs*," a term once used to describe priests involved in the ritual killing of animals in ancient Israel, Greece, or Rome. In the 1870 procession, four sacrificers flanked the bull, along with soldiers dressed in uniforms from the armies of Louis XIII and Louis XV. In 1896, a mounted sacrificer preceded each bull, which was accompanied by fifteen Roman horsemen and twelve lictors. Four more sacrificers surrounded the bull on each float. In 1897, when over 1,400 people had a role in the procession, twenty-seven sacrificers on horseback preceded each float bearing a bull.[65]

Whatever thrill came in seeing the bulls and their sacrificers together with the eight colonized subjects who were surrounded by soldiers, it was probably not experienced as an offering to an offended deity or a rite to cleanse wrongdoing. Walter Burkert, a classicist who has studied the origins of myth, describes how rituals of symbolic or actual violence may become "sacred" and self-perpetuating without carrying explicitly religious content. "The fact of understanding is more important than what is understood. Above all, then, ritual creates and affirms social interaction."[66] The tens of thousands who cheered these displays were above all cheering an imagined ideal, however justified or illusory, of their own solidarity.

At the end of the century, carnival was no longer the occasion for social hostility that it had once been. It did not generate riotous or obscene insults in the name of fun. It no longer served to audition new identities, desecrate church property, or foment political revolution. The terrain was the same, but the atmosphere of Paris, especially in the last half century, had changed fundamentally. The sheer mass of its population, the ascendency of conspicuous wealth and spectacle of commodities, and a drab seriousness momentarily relieved by empty excitement all worked against the festivity that carnival and masked balls had once embodied.

13
The World Within

A NEW WORLD APPEARS

"The unknown: this is the lion's share." So begins a chilling story in the collection *Cruel Tales* by Villiers de l'Isle Adam. The epigraph first appeared decades earlier. Written by a physicist, it had been used by scientists, explorers, and military men to describe conquests and discoveries. In "The Guest of Final Feasts," Villiers points to another alien terrain: the human unconscious, which researchers in science and medicine had now begun to probe. In the *fin de siècle*, revelations from the new field of psychology became central preoccupations for physicians as well as writers, artists, and the general public. To many, the world within was an unknown landscape.

"The Guest of Final Feasts" begins as the narrator and a friend are leaving the Opera's masked ball. They recognize a trio of women who have just removed their masks, and the five agree to dine together. A dignified stranger appears, whom the narrator recalls having seen somewhere before. To make the group an even six, they convince him to join them. The stranger, who withholds his name but asks to be called Baron Saturn, says that he is theirs until sunup. They make their way through the frigid night to the Maison Dorée, where waiters bring rich dishes to their private dining room. Maskers' cries echo through the streets. Two of the women lie entwined on a sofa, as the third plays the love duet from *Tristan and Isolde* on the piano. The stranger is quiet and slightly aloof, his pale hand dangling a glass of champagne above the carpet. Unease gathers in the narrator's mind. "How to align my familiar memories with such intense, indistinct ideas of murder, of profound silence, of fog, of terror-stricken faces, of torches and blood?"[1]

The lurid atmosphere of *Cruel Tales* is characteristic of the *fin de siècle*'s decadent writers. For this generation, themes of death, disease, and decline exerted a powerful appeal. Alongside the sparkling Belle

Époque—represented by the Eiffel Tower, early motion pictures, and beaming men on velocipedes—was a dark vision of cultural decay. Some glimpsed the end of civilization in society's rampant materialism and the soulless reign of science. The German author Max Nordau captured the mood in a widely read book called *Degeneration*. The *fin de siècle*, he wrote, was at once a confession and a complaint. "The prevalent feeling is that of imminent perdition and extinction . . . [like] the impotent despair of a sick man, who feels himself dying by inches in the midst of an eternally living nature blooming insolently forever."[2]

Hours pass in the restaurant's private room. The horizon reddens, and Baron Saturn rises to leave. Someone remembers that there is to be an execution at sunup, and the narrator now recalls where he has met the man: at a beheading in Lyon. The irrational thought strikes him that the stranger is to be this morning's executioner. "Messieurs," Baron Saturn says as a farewell at the door, "I assure you that I am as blind and deaf as God permits!"[3] A voice calls the others back inside. It is a physician who recognized the man and has studied his obsession, a case also known by doctors in Munich and Berlin. Baron Saturn has traveled in the East to witness executions and watch sessions of torture. His fantasy, the physician explains, is to be the world's torturer-in-chief. He now travels throughout Europe paying executioners great sums to let him do their work. If he cannot participate, he stands close to the guillotine or hanging tree to watch the victim's face. One of the women speaks up, calling him a creature from hell. "An actual hangman would leave me untouched. This horrifying creature fills me with indescribable fear." The women don their masks as the morning bells of Paris sound six o'clock.[4]

In the *fin de siècle*, masks evoked the psyche. In works of art and literature, their proximity to madness and moral decay was widespread. This was a new turn in a long series of associations. As the physical object receded from public spaces, the mask took on new meaning. No longer common in theaters and the street, it loomed large in depictions of the deepest human drives. For the decadent novelist Jean Lorrain, the mask was at once enthralling and repulsive. It was "the turbid, troubling face of the unknown," he wrote in his collection *Stories of Masks*, which appeared in 1900. In his depictions, masks are the portal into a dreamworld of violence, dread, and sexual perversion. If masks were for some a sign of the crowd's facelessness, they were for Lorrain a figure for truths often kept concealed.

The collection's opening story begins with an extended series of assertions. The mask is "the smile of the lie," "lust laced with fear," "the delicious, tormenting risk embraced on a dare from one's curious senses." The sight of ball-goers stirs illicit desire.

FIGURE 13.1. *Jean Lorrain*, Wilhem Benque (Art Resource)

> What instincts, what appetites, what hopes, what cravings, what sickness of the soul lie behind this cardboard? . . . Into what hashish- or morphine-induced stupors, into what escape from the self, into what dubious or dangerous adventures will this lamentable, grotesque parade plunge itself on days of masked balls?

Lorrain recounts following solitary maskers returning home in the dark and imagines their fate. "Is she ugly? Is he attractive? Is he young? Is she old?" The evening may end in shame or with blood, he writes, in a hotel, a police station, or the cemetery.[5]

In the story "With One Like Her," the narrator comes upon a desolate masker staring into the Seine on a cold February night. The Opera ball has just ended. Shivering—with bare legs, slippers, and a thin gray coat—the masker appears to be on the verge of suicide. The man approaches and offers his arm in solace, which the figure seizes, brushing bare legs against his own as they speak softly. They are soon arm in arm. The narrator suggests a hotel, and the masker names an address on the rue Git-le-Coeur.

> It was in an alley that was so foul-smelling and dark, with a lamp sputtering at the base of its stairs, that I stopped dead, as if on the doorstep of an assassin. "No," I said to this creature, "I will never enter there." Then she said, with a voice caressing and unerring, "Go on, enter! There is no danger. I am the hotel-boy here."

A maid shows them to a room. As Lorrain writes in the story's last sentence, the two men said nothing more that night.[6]

As with Baudelaire, whom he names in "The Man with a Bracelet," Lorrain considers the effects of the city on its occupants' thoughts. In this story, they are uniquely sexual. The setting is a working-class neighborhood on the outskirts of Paris, where Haussmann's new buildings are out of place alongside the dirty hovels. On paydays, men cluster outside wine shops. Women's painted faces line the windows above, "lit like masks in the streetlights' colorless halo." Their appeal is strongest on modern men, Lorrain writes, especially those living in cities, "where imaginations are exhausted and made sick." Here the vertigo of the abyss is intensified by the prostitutes' smiles, which Lorrain describes as menacing and welcoming. He compares them to the new buildings' facades, "dismal and bricked up, like a mask."[7]

For the title character in Lorrain's 1901 novel *Monsieur de Phocas*, the sight of masks everywhere he looks provokes terror. He cannot shake visions of decapitation. He sees severed heads mocking and soliciting him. The conviction grows that every face is disembodied. A journal entry begins "April '98: Masks! I see them everywhere."

> The horrible vision last night of a deserted city filled with all its masked cadavers at doorways, a morphine-ether nightmare that has implanted itself within me. I see masks in the streets, I see them onstage at the theater, I find them again in the box seats. . . . The ushers who hand me my overcoat wear masks . . . and the coachman who drives me home has this same cardboard grimace affixed to his face![8]

The menace Lorrain describes also lives in Phocas's own thoughts. Walking through Paris, he feels hatred for everyone he sees, which brings still more self-loathing. He curses shopkeepers' petty greed, the bourgeoisie's trivial preoccupations, and the ravenous smiles of women. He remembers the hateful words about him from servants he overheard as a child and now hears them taken up by the crowd. "Death to the Army!" "Death to the Jews!"[9] Phocas is every bit as violent, murderous, and lust-driven as this filthy crowd, he tells himself, pouring curses on the strangers around him.

For Jean Lorrain, the mask is a permanent feature of a species that can never fully conceal its depravity. His stories expose the pervading presence of malice and carnality. Of the many artists and intellectuals who evoked masks in the *fin de siècle*, Lorrain was most explicit in linking them to humanity's darkest urges. His maskers are closer to specters than to the living. Their joy is barren. Why else would they "cease to be what they are—in a word, evade themselves?"[10] The answer is both confession and accusation. "As terrifying as the mask is, the human face is yet more frightening."[11] Nervous and subject to terrors, addicted to ether, and an expert on prostitutes who specialized in unusual acts, Jean Lorrain likely lived his own fictions.[12]

For those in the *fin de siècle* who shared Lorrain's obsessions, a placid face was no security. Perhaps this was a factor in the return of Pierrot as a sociopath. The essence of an innocent naïf in commedia and an earnest Everyman at the Funambules, Pierrot was now portrayed as mad. In Henri Rivière's novel *Pierrot*, a young artist is inspired to become a mime when he sees Deburau play a barber. As his professional reputation rises, his mental state begins to unravel. He watches actors known for playing cruel or evil characters and spends hours studying Lavater's sketches of criminals. "I no longer wanted to be the Pierrot who trembles before a naive devil with a red tail and horns. I wanted that devil to tremble before me." In Paris, he is asked to step in for the ailing Deburau. The sketch is the very one he saw at the theater years ago, with a rival performer now sitting in the barber's chair. To the spectators' great hilarity, the mime makes a show of tying his customer's arms to the chair just as Deburau had done, unsheathes a large gleaming razor, and beheads him.[13]

The same demon possessed other late-century Pierrots. Paul Margueritte was the sole actor in his avant-garde play *Pierrot, Assassin of His Wife*. It begins with Pierrot's announcement that he has just killed Colombine. He tied her to the bed and tickled her to death, an atrocious end, he explains, that came amid her own shrieking laughter. Margueritte then played both roles, screaming with the laughter of each and ending with Pierrot's own howling death. The playwright Fernand Bessier was present at the premiere. The instant Pierrot fell dead, he reports, the relief was palpable, "as if awakening after an atrocious nightmare."[14]

Such brutality was widespread. In J. K. Huysmans's *Pierrot the Sceptic*, the character beats and stabs his visitors before setting his rooms on fire. Edmond de Goncourt's novel *The Brothers Zemgano* describes a terrifying pantomime in which a drunken Pierrot beheads members of Colombine's family and lashes out violently at his hallucinations of an undertaker. The bloody dreamscape of Arnold Schoenberg's song cycle *Pierrot lunaire*, set to poems by Albert Girard, is another instance of this Everyman's haunting afterlife. "Pierrot! My laughter is / All forgotten!" sings the soprano in "Prayer to Pierrot":

> Black blows the flag
> That flies at my mast.
> Pierrot! My laughter is
> All forgotten!
>
> O give me back—
> Pierrot—my laughter![15]

For the artist Félicien Rops, the mask was tied to morbid eroticism. Born in Belgium, Rops spent many years in Paris, where he declared himself an enemy of the bourgeoisie. He spent time with artists and intellectuals, including Hugo, Degas, Rodin, Baudelaire, and Verlaine. His embrace of decadence, which he described as a renunciation of all ideals, led him to claim that the prostitute—corrupting, deadly, and irresistible—was now society's chief source of community. In a letter to a friend, Rops wrote that his sole artistic task was to render what his nerves and eyes registered. A painter must depict his own time, he claimed. For him, this comprised moral sentiments, passions, and psychological impressions.[16] In his depictions, women are insatiable, diseased, and often demonic. His version of the temptation of St. Anthony, for instance, puts a naked woman in the place of Christ on a crucifix, which bears the word EROS rather than INRI. Satan wears a red cassock, and skeletons hover above. Rops's works, including a considerable amount of pornography, contain depictions of the deranged and possessed. In some images, he adapts the contorted postures and expressions in photographs of women diagnosed as hysterical.[17]

Masks signal the physical or mental threat Rops believed women represented. In *Hypocrisy*, the misogynist trope is unambiguous. In *Human Parody*, a man trails a skeletal streetwalker who lures him with a pleasing mask. In contrast to Ernest Christophe's sufferer in *Human Comedy*, about whom Baudelaire had written with compassion, this mask hides malice. Rops may well have had Christophe's *Dance of Death* in mind in his ghoulish *Death at the Masked Ball* (see plate 3). Flanked by two men in top hats and clad in a shroud and elegant slippers, a woman throws her skull back in ecstasy. In a letter, Rops characterized modern life as "the end of a perpetual masked ball." The assessment was desolate. His rendering of *The Absinthe Drinker* is set just outside the entrance to a ball, where a hollow-eyed woman stares out blankly.[18]

Rops designed the frontispiece to a collection of literary portraits called *Modern Masks* by the late-century writer Félicien Champsaur. It features a naked woman with a Phrygian bonnet and jester's doll. Masks (or are they

FIGURE 13.2. *Hypocrisy*, Félicien Rops (Musée Félicien Rops)

FIGURE 13.3. *Human Parody*, Félicien Rops (Art Resource)

FIGURE 13.4. *The Absinthe Drinker*, Félicien Rops (Art Resource)

heads?) line the wall and table. Just below the shelf, closest to the woman's belly, is a leering Gustave Flaubert. Near the curve of her back is Émile Zola. Above him to the left is Alphonse Daudet and, above Daudet, Dumas fils. In the hand of the woman is the crenellated, steaming head of Champsaur himself. The associations are multiple, combining Judith, Circe, and Salome. The Paris seal appears with the phrase Baron Haussmann adopted as the city's motto: *Fluctuat Nec Mergitur*, "Wave-tossed but not sunk." In this setting, the feeling is more seasickness than resolve.[19]

Soon after *Modern Masks* appeared, the critic René de Gourmont published his own two-volume *Book of Masks* with vignettes of the lives and work of fifty-three contemporary authors. He rejected the term *criticism* to focus on what he described as a new form of inquiry. “A writer creates his own aesthetic in creating his work,” he observed. “We must therefore appeal more to sensation than to judgment.” The claim implies a subject in flux, better captured by impressions than fixed truth. Gourmont called the approach “psychological analysis.” Unsure of capturing the true face of his subjects—which included Lorrain, Rimbaud, and Villiers de l’Isle Adam—Gourmont instead rendered their masks.[20]

Of all late-century depictions of masks, those of the artist James Ensor are the most frightful. For Ensor, public life was a perpetual carnival of the haunted, mad, and depraved. His canvases depict maskers whose fixed

FIGURE 13.5. *Modern Masks,* Félicien Rops (Art Resource)

smiles do nothing to conceal their torment. The clarity of his depictions, with many set in city streets under blue skies, intensifies the effect. *Intrigue* features a bulging, masked crowd on a sidewalk at midday. A spectral figure in a towering black hat seizes a masked woman in *Skeleton Arresting Maskers*. People stand transfixed before a narrow plank in *Maskers Watching a Tortoise*. Masks recur in Ensor's work with grimaces or sneers, sharpened teeth, gaping mouths, and porcine or absurdly pointed noses.

As a boy, Ensor lived surrounded by the masks on display in his parents' souvenir shop. He later remembered them as "hard shells that gave shelter to soft beasts." The image stayed with him. In a speech in Paris at the opening of an exhibit, he spoke of his era as marked by "suffering, scandalized, insolent, cruel, malicious masks."[21] His *Self-Portrait with Masks*—in which fifty human, animal, and unearthly masks crowd around him—offers a glimpse into his own inner landscape (see plate 4). "Oh! You see them, masks, under our immense opal skies," Ensor wrote to a friend. He described the vision: they were by turns insolent and timid; their gestures and expressions were like wild animals; their voices were now like a flute and now like an unhinged trumpet. "Then I saw all and my heart trembled and my bones shook and I grasped the enormity of such distortions and I glimpsed the modern spirit: a new world has appeared."[22]

REVEALING THE UNCONSCIOUS

This late-century interest in the psyche grew in part from the work of scientists. As researchers mapped a psychological terrain beyond their subjects' control, intellectuals and public figures weighed its implications for free will. At the Salpêtrière Hospital in Paris, diagnoses of a new illness termed *hysteria* deepened the conviction that French culture was in crisis. Patients afflicted by this condition experienced visions and trancelike states, sudden tears or laughter, and seizures. Cases grew into the hundreds and then thousands, and hysteria was soon an alarming presence in the popular imagination.

Jean-Martin Charcot first worked as a young intern at the Salpêtrière. In 1862, he was made chief physician in one of its largest sections. Over the next three decades, his research came to define the hospital's work, which drew national and international attention. The Salpêtrière, founded by Louis XIV, had long been a place of care and incarceration for beggars, criminals, and those judged insane. A women's prison was added in the 1680s. Its inmates included prostitutes, the pregnant and unmarried, and women awaiting execution or deportation to the colonies. Over the next two centuries, the compound steadily grew, eventually coming to resemble a bustling, self-sufficient city. In Charcot's day, its capacity was over 10,000. The grounds contained more than 100 buildings, with Protestant and Catholic churches, recreational gardens, walkways and benches, orchards, a reservoir, post office, and cemetery. While a range of ailments brought both male and female patients to the hospital, it was known chiefly for the women in its care, many of whom also served as nurses' assistants, cooked, sewed, and staffed its markets and kitchens.

In the nineteenth century, the former prison basement was made into a common space that housed a library, gymnasium, and large hall for plays, concerts, and dances. It also hosted masked balls. Each year to mark carnival, the hospital held a "*bal des folles*," the so-called Madwomen's Ball.[23] In the words of a journalist who covered the 1881 ball, these masquerades were meant to bring a ray of light into patients' monotonous existence. Physicians working with Charcot were often on hand. As with other events Charcot supervised, the masquerade was designed to be therapeutic. Three hundred women gathered for the ball. Most had been patients at the hospital for months or years. A woman with long blond braids came in traditional Alsatian dress. Another came as a fortune-teller, distributing small strips of paper that each bore a prophecy. A popular illustration depicts clowns,

FIGURE 13.6. *Ball at the Salpêtrière Hospital*, anon. (Alamy)

a short-skirted wizard, a sultana, one or two masks, and a small, somber jester. A musician plays in the upper left, and two ward nurses watch. Parisians in evening wear coolly inspect the patients.

Observers claimed that the costumes offered some relief. "They acquitted their roles perfectly," the journalist wrote of these patients. His account ends in surprise and some wonder. "The dancers' attitude and manner were so calm and reasonable in appearance that it took the presence of doctors . . . to remind us that we were in the presence of hysterics and epileptics and that these women were, in a word, the famous *subjects* of Dr. Charcot."[24]

Because Charcot believed that hysteria's origins were physiological, he resisted describing his patients as insane. He had studied other neurological conditions, including lateral sclerosis, multiple sclerosis, and degenerative brain disorders. In his initial research on hysteria, he devoted considerable effort to finding brain lesions or other malformations. Hysteria was most severe among women who had suffered sexual trauma, he noted, and among men who had experienced sudden physical injury. An early published paper discussed the case of a physician deemed hysterical who had been seriously hurt in a railway accident.[25]

While he treated both men and women, Charcot's more numerous female patients drew the greater public attention. Accounts in the press and from the hospital's many prominent visitors described women of all ages and conditions gripped by an uncontrollable force. They suffered crippling convulsions. Some heard voices and claimed to see Satan or Christ and the saints. They described lovers who came secretly to their beds. Some engaged in self-mutilation or tried to starve themselves. At night they sleepwalked, some for hours at a time, washing and dressing themselves, strolling wide-eyed in apparent self-command, touring the grounds, and responding cogently to questions.[26] Under hypnotic suggestion, they replicated the contorted gestures and positions common during hysterical attacks, turning suddenly rigid, holding unnatural postures for minutes or hours, baying like dogs, and permitting researchers to cut or pierce their flesh without registering pain.

Augustine Gleizes, who entered the Salpêtrière at age fourteen after suffering repeated seizures, became the public face of hysteria through a sequence of photographs documenting the condition. Her "passionate poses"—so named by one of Charcot's associates—occurred during sleep, when the attacks took her through a series of scenes by turns rapturous and harrowing. In these images, published annually and disseminated in the *Photographic Iconography of the Salpêtrière*, the patient is pleading, prayerful, mocking, terrified, and ecstatic. One photograph shows Gleizes, dressed in a ward nurse's uniform, in a state of perfect rigidity. Her only support is the back of two chairs, one beneath her neck and the other at her ankles. Prepared by the hospital's in-house photography studio and published annually from 1876, the *Photographic Iconography* did much to publicize the affliction.

Equally famous was Blanche Wittmann, who came to the Salpêtrière in 1877. Born to abusive parents and sent to live at age twelve with a predatory guardian, Wittmann had suffered convulsions before coming to the hospital. Her admittance coincided with Charcot's early experiments with hypnosis. While many rejected Franz Mesmer's earlier practice of "magnetism" as unscientific, brain researchers in France, England, and America continued to study techniques that could induce trancelike states. Charcot's lectures and papers, many based on his work with Wittmann, were decisive in convincing the larger scientific community of hypnotism's legitimacy. Charcot claimed that only those with hysteria could be hypnotized. He also believed that hypnosis offered unfiltered access to the hysteric's psyche. The implications of these findings, detailed in an 1882 paper entitled "The Diverse Nervous States of Hysterics as Determined by Hypnosis," were unsettling. Its conclusion was that the mind harbors thoughts that act independently of an individual's own will.[27]

Thanks to an iconic painting, Blanche Wittmann did much to anchor hypnosis in the public imagination. She is the unconscious, partially unclad center of attention in André Brouillet's *A Clinical Lesson at the Salpêtrière*. Depicted at the instant of her collapse, Wittmann falls back into the arms of an assistant. A nurse stands ready to help as Charcot turns to address his audience. Beyond its drama and immediacy, the work carries more subtle means of persuasion. Every spectator is identifiable, and together they represent the highest levels of learning. They include professors of psychiatry, anatomy, and neurology, renowned physicians, members of the Chamber of Deputies and Senate, a respected art critic, a novelist recently elected to the Académie Française, a poet, and an eminent political journalist. Their presence attests to Charcot's wide reach, and their reputation conferred esteem.[28] The immense painting was a central attraction of the 1887 Paris Salon, which drew more than half a million visitors to the Palais de l'Industrie.[29]

Charcot shared his findings about hysteria widely. On Tuesday mornings, he examined new patients in an amphitheater that could hold five hundred. These sessions were open to the public. They drew curious spectators, medical professionals, public officials, and society fixtures eager to see and be seen. Philosophers, novelists, and stage performers also attended. On Tuesday evenings, Charcot hosted receptions in his sumptuous home on

FIGURE 13.7. *A Clinical Lesson at the Salpêtrière Hospital*, André Brouillet (Art Resource)

the Boulevard Saint-Germain. On Friday mornings, he presented his research on neurology to students and physicians.

Depending on one's perspective, Charcot was otherworldly, opportunistic, or a little of each. The writer Jules Claretie called him "a Bonaparte of the scalpel," listing physical similarities in their dark eyes, wide forehead, and implacably grave presence. An obituary in *Le Figaro* praised him as "the first traditional scholar who dared to cross the threshold of mystery," surpassing the boundaries of accustomed science to reach the "occult and unknowable." Endowed with supreme pride and a commanding presence, it concluded, the physician was equal parts healer, sorcerer, and showman.[30]

After the collapse of Napoleon III's regime, the new government elevated science as a guide to social policy. Positivism, a doctrine that shaped policy in the new Third Republic, claimed that all aspects of human experience—including all social, moral, and religious questions—were subject to scientific understanding. The view fueled a state campaign of anticlericalism meant to limit the influence of the Catholic Church. Science would replace superstition, proponents held, and the doctor would supplant the priest. Moral and social influence no longer belonged to the Church, but instead to "the masters of the body: the providers of treatments and prescriptions."[31]

While Charcot was a singular embodiment of this secular priesthood, others drew comparable attention. In the eastern city of Nancy, the physician Hippolyte Bernheim treated a range of illnesses with hypnosis, which led him to modify Charcot's claims. He showed that all people, not just those with hysteria, could be hypnotized. He also found hypnosis effective in treating diseases of the nervous system and gastrointestinal disorders. Bernheim's description of the hypnotic state carried relevance for the wider culture. Under hypnosis, he wrote, the subject remains "motionless, insensible, the face inert like a mask, detached in appearance from the exterior world." For Bernheim, the force of suggestion was the most important lesson hypnotism offered, and its implications—that free will might be intermittent or even illusory—affected the everyday lives of all.[32]

Acknowledging the public role of science, some also expressed concern about its reach. Citing an alarming rise in nervous ailments, the writer Octave Mirbeau declared Charcot's influence more consequential than that of

FIGURE 13.8. *Jean-Martin Charcot* (Art Resource)

Napoleon. The judgment was not entirely positive. In discovering the root cause of mental and social ills, Mirbeau wrote, Charcot approached the secrets of human experience. Power will come to those who hold this knowledge, he continued. Imagine a population under hypnosis, who walk, act, see, and suffer on the command of scientists. Those who know the mind's secrets also have the power to enslave. "The future is for these men of learning: they will be the masters of all who are led only by their hearts, their nerves, or their imagination."[33]

Among hypnotists' discoveries, those pointing to the unconscious caused the greatest distress. Charcot showed that this was a place of ungovernable urges. Here, he wrote, coherent ideas "settle themselves in the mind in the fashion of parasites." Describing these ideas as unwilled personality fragments, he concluded that in some subjects they could coalesce to form multiple personalities. The psychologist Pierre Janet, who worked closely with Charcot at the Salpêtrière, described such fragments as a force outside of individual volition. "Like a malign virus, the obsession is implanted and develops in a place inaccessible to the subject, acting subconsciously, troubling the conscious mind, and bringing about all the disorders of madness and hysteria."[34]

Novelists were quick to grasp the haunting prospect of actions driven by such powers. In Guy de Maupassant's chilling tale *La Horla*, the narrator is possessed by an alien presence. It is "another being, like ourselves, greater than ourselves . . . the domination of a mysterious will over the enslaved human spirit." In the encroaching madness, his journal entries grow steadily more desperate. When he thinks about the Salpêtrière's experiments and the physicians overseeing them, the image of children playing dangerous games comes to him. "A calamity for us! A calamity for mankind!" Determined to destroy the beast inside of himself—to strangle it, poison it, tear it apart with his teeth—he sets fire to his house, realizing too late that servants are trapped inside.[35]

Discussion of hypnosis and its dangers was widespread in the *fin de siècle*. Writers described "crimes of the laboratory," in which unprincipled doctors urged patients under hypnosis to injure others. During one session, Blanche Wittmann was instructed to "poison" a colleague with beer said to be tainted, and, once out of her trance, she convinced the man to drink it. Gilles de la Tourette, who had participated in the experiment, pointed to another risk. The threat of rape ordered under hypnosis was real, he warned. Tourette was part of a panel that confirmed six such cases in Paris, and he was vocal in urging changes to the penal code.[36] This was the context in which hysteria became a generalized fear, affecting not only those under the care of physicians but throughout the wider population. The dread at once universalized the disease and made its symptoms vividly insidious. For many, the affliction was as much moral as physical, and its name came to describe the beleaguered, fractured, irrational experience of the masses.

In *Parisian Life*, Jean Claretie called hysteria among women and men the new *mal du siècle*. The century's sickness was everywhere, he wrote, "coursing through the streets and through the world." Claretie, a member of the Académie Française, included in its causes the "spectacle of public life." Raucous public assemblies, slanders endured in the press and salons, and the unrelenting pressure to impress others had "heated the brains" of his contemporaries. Hysteria, he wrote, was a moral illness as well as a mental disorder. Its symptoms were widespread and familiar: unnamed sadness, a broken spirit, despair for no clear reason.[37]

A 1905 book called *Parisian Hysterics* begins with a description of the city's everyday assaults on mental health. Steam and electricity, a flood of commodities, immediate gratification, too little sleep, and too much alcohol have made Paris subject to hysteria. "They circulate in the faubourgs and boulevards, in tiny interiors and millionaires' mansions, they pass and return, all of them ardent and impassioned, this crowd of hysterics."[38] Émile Zola put it more simply: "We are sickened by our industrial progress, by science; we live in a fever. . . . Everything suffers and complains in the works of our time."[39]

The crises attributed to these pressures, both personal and cultural, led many to doubt the power and reach of reason. The debilitating effects of the modern city, combined with an awareness of irrational urges from within, raised familiar questions about self-mastery in new and troubling ways. The most committed positivism, as the historian Jan Goldstein observes, had led to "a legitimation of the realm of unreason."[40] In this context, the stable, consistent, and predictable self that Victor Cousin had described at midcentury now looked to be naive. When the physician Hippolyte Bernheim described the faces of subjects in a hypnotic state as resembling a mask, it was not in the sense that Baudelaire had meant. The mask was not a protective shell donned to keep a distance from the crowd. It was the passive look of a self in whom reason was not the master.

UNMASKING THE PSYCHE

"Does one live a whole life behind a mask?" The question comes to the central character of the novel *Brother Pelagius* as she faces the man she was once meant to marry. It is the eighth century, Saracens are attacking the fortresses of southern Gaul, and Marguerite of Carcassonne has vowed lifelong virginity if God will spare her people. Carcassonne is liberated. On her wedding day, Marguerite keeps her vow and renounces marriage. She dons a monk's robe, renames herself Brother Pelagius, and enters a monastery. Marguerite lives and dresses as a man. She finds comfort in what she now understands to be her true nature. "Is it really you wearing this man's garment?" she asks herself. The answer is affirming. She grows certain that God has made her a unique vessel to preserve and protect her homeland. Hers is "a virilized soul," which has gained sovereignty over her woman's nature. On her deathbed, a divine vision tells Marguerite that her spirit will return one day in the person of Joan of Arc.[41]

The author of *Brother Pelagius* was Jane Dieulafoy, a writer, archaeologist, and war veteran who spent most of her adult life dressed as a man. Like her fictional creation Marguerite, she was a faithful Catholic and devoted nationalist. She married early, and when her husband enlisted to fight in the Franco-Prussian War, she went with him to the front. Barred from enlisting, she fought as a sharpshooter, folding her experiences into the novel *Volunteer*, the story of a woman who fights in the French revolutionary army disguised as a man. After the war, Jane and Marcel Dieulafoy led archaeological digs in Persia that brought a series of historic discoveries. Working with local excavators, the two unearthed the palaces of Xerxes, Darius, and the Achaemenid dynasty. Jane was often seen in the saddle with her rifle. They returned to France with crates of artifacts, adding substantially to the knowledge of the ancient Near East. In 1886, Jane received the *Légion d'honneur* for her work.

Jane Dieulafoy thrived and was accepted in a society whose laws still forbade cross-dressing. The particular ordinance from 1800 was consistent in spirit with prohibitions stretching back through the Revolution to the Renaissance. Its opening sentences declare that women in men's clothes generate "great unpleasantness and indeed contempt from the police." Any "disguised" woman—that is, any woman wearing pants—was subject to arrest. Its only exceptions were for reasons of health, a remnant of the law's earliest versions that had cited hermaphrodism. Such "reasons of health" had grown more broad since the Revolution. Early in the century, a female equestrian petitioned and won the right to wear pants when using a standard saddle. At midcentury, a female professional musician received permission to dress in a man's suit for public performances.[42]

During Jane Dieulafoy's life, the sight of women in men's clothing was rare and often scorned, but examples were also growing more numerous. The owner of a printing press on the Left Bank, for instance, appeared in court in 1889 on charges of having worn a beret and men's shirts and trousers. According to the press, the shop's employees and regular patrons were

FIGURE 13.9. *Jane Dieulafoy in her home*, Dornac (Paul Cardon) (Art Resource)

shocked to learn that its owner was a woman. At the hearing, the magistrate showed disdain. It was a woman, he announced with emphasis, *not a boy*, who stood before him.[43] A newspaper the following year reported that ten women in Paris held rights from the police to wear men's clothing.[44] Jane Dieulafoy was among them, as was the critic Marc (née Marie-Amélie) de Montifaud and the decadent novelist Marguerite Eymery, better known as Rachilde. Most of their contemporaries described women who dressed as men in terms that ranged from eccentric to hysterical. Some identified them as menacing instances of the late century's "New Woman," a disparaging reference to those who sought higher degrees and entry into the professions.

The literary scholar Rachel Mesch describes the commitments of Dieulafoy, Montifaud, and Rachilde as more personal than programmatic. In her book *Before Trans: Three Gender Stories from Nineteenth-Century France*, Mesch proposes using present-minded concepts unavailable in their day to understand her subjects. Their dress, she writes, was an expression of their identity. "We should stop thinking of them exclusively as women but rather as individuals pushing against that very identity," she writes.[45] In doing so, they were at once ahead of their time and shared in its presumptions and possibilities. Mesch is hesitant to provide a particular gender designation for Dieulafoy, Montifaud, and Rachilde, resisting *trans* as anachronistic.

On occasion, Montifaud and Rachilde used masculine pronouns. In the last scene of Rachilde's *Monsieur Venus*, when the central character wears both men's and women's clothes, the narrator switches to *they*. Dieulafoy, Montifaud, and Rachilde all married and were by all indications comfortable in sexual relationships with men. Of the three, only Montifaud seems to have been attracted as well to women. "Their stories reveal a complex relationship between gender and sexuality that cannot be easily delimited by modern terminologies," Mesch writes.[46]

As writers, the women framed their lives in part by the books they wrote. Jane Dieulafoy's novels, in which male-identified women fall in love with men, are one example. Rachilde's *Monsieur Venus* follows the Parisian Raoule de Vénérande, a wealthy woman who dresses as a man and initiates a working-class florist named Jacques Silvert into brutal, hashish-fueled sex acts. Groomed by Raoule, Jacques embraces a female persona, dressing in silk gowns and submitting to Raoule's demands.[47] The novel's last scene is a necrophilic consummation of marriage between the "husband" Raoule and a wax effigy of his dead "wife" Jacques. It drew Rachilde a prison sentence for pornography in Belgium, where the book was published.

Rachilde's calling card read "Man of Letters." She was championed among the French avant-garde, associating with the literary club *Les Hydropathes* and frequenting the bohemian café *Le Chat Noir*. Her lovers included Catulle Mendès and Maurice Barrès, the literary celebrity and partisan nationalist. She sometimes went to balls dressed as a man, accompanied by Jean Lorrain, dressed as a woman. Her application to the Paris police to wear pants cited her profession as a journalist. "This is to earn my daily bread," she wrote, adding that she wished subjects and readers to "address my pen and not my person." In 1899, Rachilde married the writer Alfred Villette and stopped wearing pants. "I buried my life as a boy," she later wrote.[48]

Trained as an artist, Marc de Montifaud worked as a professional journalist and critic. At age nineteen, she married the Spanish count Juan Francis Léon de Quivogne, who took her surname. Her historical and fictional works scandalized readers. One detailed the sexual pleasures of prominent women in early Church history, and another was a frank biography of Mary Magdalene. She was repeatedly sentenced to prison for obscenity, successfully petitioning in each case to serve her time instead in a mental ward. When Francis Magnard, the editor of *Le Figaro*, slighted her husband in print, she cut her hair short, donned a tuxedo, and, as he left his box at the Comédie-Française, slapped Magnard across the face. She fled to Brussels with their young son and retained her male attire and short haircut. When she returned to Paris three years later, she petitioned and received police permission to wear pants, which she did for the rest of her life.[49]

Does one live a whole life behind a mask? The question posed by Dieulafoy's Brother Pelagius resounds in the stories of these and other women in the *fin de siècle* whose masculine attire was the more fitting expression of identity. In French, *pélage* means coat, peeling, or fur, suggesting that the monk wears a false front. In the novel, it is instead Marguerite who concealed her true masculine identity to others and possibly herself as well before entering the monastery. The mask Pelagius rejects is his former female self, expressed in dress, demeanor, and self-understanding. These women and perhaps others who petitioned to wear men's clothing defy the charge that they sought to disguise themselves. Use of the term "disguise" in the law against cross-dressing assumed that attire was the natural expression of gender, but it entailed a deeper assumption as well: that no woman would have a natural desire to be a man, nor any man wish to be a woman.

Their intent was not to conceal an identity. It was instead an unmasking, done in the name of truth to oneself. Rachilde wrote something similar to explain her preference for masculine attire: "One shouldn't imagine that I wanted to cross-dress."[50] Just as her preference for men's clothes was no disguise, cross-dressing was also a misnomer: there was no "crossing over." Marc de Montifaud wrote simply, "I am myself, myself alone. Which is certainly not enough, but ultimately, I am me."[51] These responses corresponded with the reconsideration of other elements of identity once thought natural. The *fin de siècle* brought a series of firsts for women, including the first female reporter, attorney admitted to the bar, professor at the Sorbonne, pharmacist, and astronomer. Between 1885 and 1900, the number of women earning *lycée* degrees rose from 4,300 to 13,000. The legalization of divorce in 1884 granted a new degree of autonomy to those who wished to escape an unhappy marriage.[52]

It was therefore fitting that the figure to crystallize publicly questions of identity in the *fin de siècle* was a woman. Few made a more convincing case of women's unimagined powers than the actress Sarah Bernhardt, who embodied self-transformation in her person and in her performances. The questions her acting raised about women's roles in particular undermined assumptions about the fixity of gender. In Edmond Rostand's *The Eagle*, she was the duc de Reichstadt. In François Coppée's *The Passerby*, she was a man named Zanetto. She was Werther in a stage adaptation of the Goethe novel, the prince in Maeterlinck's *Pelléas et Mélisande*, and King Ahasuerus in Racine's *Esther*. Her 1899 depiction of Hamlet was legendary.[53]

Audiences described what they saw as unimaginable. Bernhardt possessed a "strange and special duplicity," at once "extraordinarily virile" and a "woman superior to all women." As Hamlet, a journalist wrote, she was "the most profoundly *woman* that a *man* can be," a confounding claim that turned on just how convincing Bernhardt's depiction truly was. Another critic described Bernhardt's convincing naturalness with the observation that the men beside her onstage seemed disguised. "She is constantly recreating herself," a critic wrote. "Every day . . . she perfects the masterpiece that is her personality."[54] The celebrity and dismay that Bernhardt provoked reflected a public uncertain and divided about inherited roles. That Bernhardt was a consummate performer was understood, but her astonishing command opened questions that extended beyond the stage. Was gender itself—women's supposedly natural dress, roles, aptitudes, and attractions—a performance?

The historian Mary Louise Roberts points to the words of Bernhardt's contemporary, the female critic Daniel Lesueur, for their wider applications. "She is constantly creating and recreating herself," Lesueur wrote. "Every day, despite inconceivable fatigue, despite the passing years, she perfects the masterpiece that is her personality." Bernhardt was "a model for how women could 'create' and 're-create' themselves throughout the course of their lives," Roberts comments. Her art was evidence that femaleness was "decidable and fluid" rather than "predestined and fixed."[55] Evidence for this ranged from the thousands of newly educated women, many of whom worked outside the home, to those who questioned the very category of woman.

IDENTITIES IN THE *FIN DE SIÈCLE*

Near the end of Maurice Barrès's novel *A Free Man*, the narrator travels to Venice. At twenty-five, Philippe is both driven and aimless, determined to forge his own path in defiance of "barbarians" who dominate society. He has no clear direction in life, and his habitual mood is disgust: at society's anarchy of values, at the impossibility of finding any creed by which to live, and at the absence of any true guide. Months intended to steel his mind in a monastic retreat have brought some clarity but yet more self-loathing. A revelation comes in Venice. Content that he has seen enough of the city in a single day of sightseeing, Philippe shuts himself in his hotel room, eating his meals in bed, smoking cigars, and conjuring mental images yet more sumptuous than what he has seen in this dream city. The most sublime experiences are within, he realizes. "My memories, soon altered by instinct, presented me with a Venice that exists nowhere. In place of all the charms of this noble city, I substituted a beauty yet more certain to please me, a beauty according to myself."[56]

A Free Man is the second of three novels Barrès wrote in his midtwenties. The name he gave to the trilogy, *The Cult of the Self*, captures his generation's determination to define oneself on one's own terms. Dismissed by establishment writers, the books attracted a passionate following among the young. In an early review, Léon Blum, the Socialist leader and future prime minister, compared Barrès to Voltaire and claimed that he had inaugurated "a new cast of mind and sensibility."[57] To his critics, Barrès was defiant. "A self that does not submit: such is the hero of our small book," he wrote of *A Free Man*. "Never submit! When besieged by a lawless society, whose throng of doctrines has destroyed all discipline, this is our salvation."[58] His introduction to the trilogy is a modern Genesis: "It is we who create the universe."[59]

Maurice Barrès was among many writers in the *fin de siècle* to take up the project of finding themselves by unmasking. Decadent artists and authors had revealed violent and irrational elements that lay just beneath the veneer of civilization. The choice of Dieulafoy, Montifaud, and Rachilde not to live their lives behind a mask acknowledged the psyche in individual terms.

FIGURE 13.10. *Maurice Barrès*, Eugène Pirou (Art Resource)

For Barrès, unmasking was both personal and civilizational. In this, he was characteristic of an age grappling with the new science of psychology. With the discovery of the psyche, the very terms of identity—of how one understands one's uniqueness and one's place in society at large—changed in fundamental ways.

For this generation, the individual faced unprecedented personal and civic stress. Specialized work, a growing gulf between the rich and poor, and the loss of shared beliefs each played its part in this malaise. In the *fin de siècle*, few leading thinkers championed the solitary, sensitive stance of Rousseau, who judged society from a distance. Nor was Victor Cousin's well-trained and proudly independent self-made man a prominent model. Larger numbers of women and men now possessed the means to shape their fate, but the very circumstances responsible for this greater autonomy—rising affluence, educational diversity, and vocational specialization—made the project more dependent on others. The anonymity Baudelaire had once relished in the metropolis, experienced now by entire populations, was deeply alienating. Rather than elevating individualism in these years, leading social and political critics instead looked to strengthen community.

For Barrès, the unconscious was essential to this higher wholeness. It was in the psyche that the soul of a people dwelled. In his youth, Barrès had been keenly interested in hypnosis. In Paris, he attended lectures on experimental psychology and wrote articles for the press on psychiatry.[60] The power of this unconscious was Philippe's Venetian revelation as he gazed at Tiepolo's vaulting church interiors. The feasts, silks, saints, horses, and cascading angels that fill these skies, he realized, were an inheritance from Tiepolo's ancestors. Tiepolo's tragic lesson was that even those civilizations replete with the many-souled past are at risk: within two decades of Tiepolo's death, the thousand-year-old Venetian Republic would fall. When Barrès wrote, Prussia's annexation of Alsace and Lorraine was a daily reminder of France's own humiliation in 1870.

Soon after his best-selling *Cult of the Self* novels appeared, Barrès announced that individualism must be transcended for a higher unity in the nation. "We are not the masters of thoughts born within us. They do not originate in our intelligence," he wrote. "The whole cortège of descendants constitutes a single being." When war broke out in 1914, Barrès welcomed the renewal it promised. "I've wanted nothing more than for Frenchmen to unite around the great ideas of our race," he declared. "Blood has not yet rained upon our nation and war has already made us feel its regenerative powers."[61]

Barrès was not the only prominent thinker to write of the psyche as a source of individual and collective identity. Gustave Le Bon, best known for his work on crowd psychology, asserted that the unconscious housed the instincts, passions, and sentiments of one's race. Like Barrès, he wrote of defining racial characteristics, and he repeated antisemitic claims of the day. Le Bon's large conclusions reached beyond those whom he termed "inferior races." The unconscious was formative in all people, not only across centuries but in every moment. "Our conscious acts stem from an unconscious substratum created above all by the influences of heredity," he wrote in his book *Crowd Psychology*. These "secret causes" are ancestral residues that constitute the soul of a race. "Most of our daily actions are but the effect of hidden motives that escape us."[62]

While many rejected Barrès's and Le Bon's proposed cure of a militant nationalism, their account of collective malaise from a lack of shared purpose found wide resonance. The sociologist Émile Durkheim observed that personal uniqueness and social relations pulled in opposite directions. "On the one hand is our individuality," he wrote. On the other is "everything that expresses something other than ourselves."[63] He was responding in part to the new term *anomie*, a state of living without norms, which the philosopher Jean-Marie Guyau had coined to describe the moment. Guyau's book *A Sketch of Morality Without Obligation or Blame* celebrates what public education had at last made possible, the ability to live one's life free from religious demands or constraints. "Consult your instincts, your sympathies, your aversions," Guyau wrote. "You are free to follow your own self-government."[64]

Durkheim found nothing liberating in this. To move from the country to the city was to leave close communities for a sundered, anonymous crowd. Dense urban centers with their ranks of workers might bring a certain degree of interdependence, but it came without true belonging. For large numbers to live in such conditions, without fellowship or guiding principles, was fundamentally new. So, too, was the particular alienation it produced. Cities excited hopes and desires far beyond the means of most to satisfy them. Affluence fed the craving in its constant display of opulence. The effects of this normlessness were "conflicts and disorders of every kind." In his classic work on suicide, Durkheim singled out anomie as a "regular and specific factor" in this uniquely contemporary plague.

Insofar as humans might find relief, it would not be in self-created individualism. In a valueless age animated by unrealistic desires, most were incapable of finding meaning on their own. Instead, Durkheim wrote, human wholeness came in recognizing one's place in the "collective consciousness," society's shared source of mores, worth, and morality. Durkheim endorsed communitarian programs designed to foster joint duties and a sense of belonging. These collectives made explicit the ways in which communities of teachers, workers, owners, and professionals were mutually dependent.[65]

The political expression of this vision went by the name Solidarism, a set of principles that government officials actively promoted. Fashioned as a moderate response to revolutionary socialism from the Left and threats to democracy from the Right, Solidarism elevated shared duties over rights and emphasized citizens' mutual obligations.[66] Alfred Fouillée, a professor who helped fashion the intellectual underpinnings of the movement, asserted that interdependence was fundamental to human nature. His argument was psychological. Consciousness itself, he wrote, was not individual but collective.

> There is nothing so singular that is not also multiple and nothing so much mine that is not also held in common. . . . I cannot feel singly, nor think singly, nor speak, wish, or exist singly. Why complain of a law that, once understood and accepted by our intelligence, becomes a law of solidarity and universal fraternity?[67]

The poet Arthur Rimbaud amplified the cross-currents affecting identities in the *fin de siècle*. Rimbaud plumbed the fractured selfhood Baudelaire had embodied. For the latter, urban experience had both loosened the hold and sharpened the solitude of individuality. In the same spirit, Rimbaud's response was a renunciation. His version of a more encompassing wholeness—akin to Durkheim's collective consciousness or Guyau's imaginative leap—was to cast off his subjectivity. The series of exertions to deny his own selfhood involved drugs and other intoxicants, as well as humiliating and sometimes violent sexual episodes, which he described as "every form of love, suffering, and madness."

His rendering of the self's incompleteness and effort to find identity with a larger whole has become iconic: "I is an other," he wrote. As a poet and human being, Rimbaud wanted to be both the author and spectator of his own alien selfhood. It is wrong to say "I think," he continued. Instead one should say, "*On me pense*," that is, *One thinks me*, or *It thinks me*, or perhaps *I am thought*. From his common starting point with Baudelaire, Rimbaud expressed a selfhood far from Durkheim's, Guyau's, or Fouillée's vision of fraternity. It was nevertheless consistent with an expansive sense of identity that aimed to find completion outside of oneself. These writers and their contemporaries expressed a shared need to transcend individualism.[68]

What were the prospects for the kinds of community such thinkers urged? In the *fin de siècle*, the obstacles were considerable. Deep social and economic divisions defined the population. Napoleon III's grand infrastructure projects had transformed society's wealthiest members into a caste, making the kinds of class mobility that had characterized the century's early decades no longer possible. An 1869 study concluded that 183 individuals engaged in banking, finance, shipping, rail, steel, and chemicals controlled twenty billion francs in stocks and bonds. Its author described the condition as "financial feudalism."[69] A depression that devastated European economies in 1873 rendered the inequity yet more entrenched. Public life remained segmented, with social movement largely foreclosed.

The stagnation lasted for more than twenty years. Prices fell by 40 percent, industrial production slowed, and the kinds of property transfers that bred new wealth after the French Revolution were now rare. Violent demonstrations made class conflict explicit, and anarchists' bombs kept the population on edge. Opportunities for substantially improving one's condition, which had plausibly inspired individual hopes two generations earlier, were now difficult for all but a relative few. The consequence was a society at once insecure, sclerotic, and highly stratified.[70]

This was the context in which the mask receded from public life to inhabit the precincts of psychology. In the first decades of the century, the promise of remaking one's identity had generated quick fortunes as well as convincing frauds, bringing both imposture and new means meant to expose it. The charged inversions of ball-goers in the 1830s and '40s were an indication that other roles were thinkable. Their disappearance later in the century was also revealing. Social mobility grew less realistic, even as psychology opened new paths for inward transformation. In this sense, the means of shaping identities were expanded, despite the dim prospects for substantial change in circumstances.

Among decadent writers and artists, the response was to render the inner world aesthetically. Their motives were to expose the hypocrisies or shameful obsessions of a self-satisfied society. They aimed as well to probe the true nature of what many were quick to declare deviant. In some cases, they savored the corruption. A potent heritage of their work was the modern imperative to strip away the false front of propriety or prejudice and live in accordance with—or at least in full awareness of—one's inmost nature.

The varied legacy of unmasking the psyche was defining in the twentieth century, and it continues to spread in our own time. Sigmund Freud, who studied with Charcot at the Salpêtrière in 1885–1886, made it the central feature of psychoanalysis. Maurice Barrès, who denounced the "masquerade" of those who refused to be true to their deepest instincts, articulated the terms and logic of a nationalist ideology that announced a triumph of the will. The unmasking Brother Pelagius embodied, and the truth by which his creator Jane Dieulafoy lived, announces an identity historically denied to the women and men who were mocked, arrested, whipped, or put to death for wearing clothes deemed criminal.

To unmask the self in its full depth is a project we recognize today. Jean-Marie Guyau's voice from more than one hundred years ago, the culmination of a long history toward greater autonomy in forming one's own identity, remains resonant. "Consult your instincts, your sympathies, your aversions. You are free to follow your own self-government." If only it were so simple. Another legacy of unmasking is to ask, and often to doubt, who we truly are.

Afterword

We know what it is to wear a mask. The twenty-first century's pandemic that killed millions and sent the global economy into free fall made masks universal. Masks were the first line of defense, and their concealment was disorienting. How to judge the stranger's intentions? How to convey warmth or sympathy? How to build trust or show skepticism? Our masks gave us a glimpse of the experience of populations centuries ago who wore them to protect not their health but their very identities.

Insofar as masks stripped us of some means of expression, they made others more explicit. Intimacy among friends required an extra effort. They also made indifference easier. We avoided people we didn't want to speak to by pretending not to see them. We discovered that we could dispense with polite smiles and found we could meet others' words with a grimace or a smirk. In masks, introverts grew still more reticent and extroverts still more demonstrative, and vice versa. Employees felt like cogs when they did routine jobs in masks. Wait staff endured more abuse from diners.

In its more ordinary times, modern life has brought the disappearance of most physical masks. They no longer evoke infernal powers as they did in ancient societies. They no longer possess the face-saving role they played for beggars and the indigent hoping to preserve their pride. They no longer assert the modesty they carried for women who wished to move independently in public parks and markets. Their prominence in carnival, once a means of defying the social order and imagining other identities, is now sustained chiefly by a tourist industry expert at recreating traditions no longer lived. Most masks that define our time are strictly utilitarian: to provide oxygen and protect against infection.

Yet the mask still reveals as much as it hides. One indelible legacy of the pandemic is the militant resistance it aroused. Heads of state refused to mask themselves for the weakness it supposedly showed. Parents kept masks from their children and boycotted classrooms with claims that they blocked airflow and damaged young brains. Many thousands belligerently refused masks as an infringement on God-given freedom, despite the lives it sacrificed for the sake of principle. They burned them, cursed those who wore them, and threatened death to authorities who required them. Store clerks, security guards, bartenders, and bystanders were beaten, stabbed, and shot for asking patrons to put on a mask.

In our time, masks are unnatural and unwelcome. For many, they are an infringement on individual choice and the wide circle of rights that autonomy implies. Some consider masks by definition an affront to human dignity. These were among the reasons given in 2011 to prohibit Muslim women in France from wearing the burka in public. The legislation, submitted by President Nicolas Sarkozy, forbade any attire "intended to hide the face" in public transportation, streets, markets, government buildings, and private businesses. Arguing in favor of the bill, Jean-François Copé, an ally of the president and member of the National Assembly, stated that the full veil "is not a garment, but a permanent mask, which constitutes a threat to our society." Michèle Alliot-Marie, Minister of Foreign and European Affairs, asserted that to wear a burka demonstrated a refusal to belong to the national community. "The Republic is lived with an uncovered face," she declared.[1]

The roots of such sentiments are in the eighteenth century, when human flourishing meant a rejection of society's falsehoods for the truer voice of conviction. Its advocates argued that mutual trust, the foundation of communities that aspire to be self-governing, relies on openness. Sincerity, the avowed congruence between feeling and expression, is registered in the face. The political expression of this view was fully present in the French Revolution, when masks were banned and transparency was demanded in all matters. Liberty stands unbowed, its exponents proclaimed, with its face uncovered and head held high. Animated by a similar spirit, Victor Hugo's resounding claim in rejecting the masks of ignorance and depravity remains powerful: "Humanity is identity."

Opponents of mask mandates and full-face veils are part of this history. In its contemporary meaning, identity implies autonomy and reciprocity. Both groups object to the submission that masks imply, whether to a faceless government official, religious authority, or husband who demands obedience. There is some logic to this response. To reject masks is to oppose hierarchy, real or merely perceived.

The long history of masking puts contemporary resistance to masks into a wider context. Yet in a health emergency, defiance in the name of freedom is also a rejection of the common good, a feature of the contemporary world foreign to earlier settings. It should be said, too, that some Muslim women have asserted that the full veil offers protection against sexual objectification. The choice to wear the veil, they insist, is wholly their own. This is a modern version of the mask women in the seventeenth century wore to protect their own privacy in public.

Strategies of masking and unmasking are seldom wholly personal. *Paris Concealed* chronicles many moments when individual choice has confronted social or political demands. Masks have served to assert, protect, efface, and alter identities. They have also preserved, defied, and subverted larger structures within which people have ordered their lives. In many corporate settings today, just as in Versailles's courtly context, one's own status depends on the judgment of those with greater power. Here, masks are prudent. Unmasking political figures' deceit by a vigilant press is no less vital to democracy today than it was to French revolutionaries. And while few now consult phrenological maps or pocket physiognomies to penetrate appearances, facial recognition technologies with their data banks of criminal and civil infractions perform a similar, if exponentially more intrusive, function.

Selfhood in our own world is still strongly shaped by forces that appeared in the nineteenth century, when masks were a vehicle for fashioning one's own identity and unmasking became a project of self-discovery. The imperative to unmask oneself remains powerful. This is a legacy of the *fin de siècle* and the emergence of psychology, but its deeper roots rest on the more enduring conviction of an essential core selfhood to which one should be true. Marivaux wrote of essential defining qualities "that are with us, that are within us, that are ourselves," a slightly looser formulation of a still earlier founding myth that aristocratic virtue was passed in the blood from father to son in "seeds of untold power."[2] Maurice Barrès identified the bedrock of identity as race, a category his contemporaries embraced as France's colonial empire grew to become the second largest in the world. For Jane Dieulafoy, Marc de Montifaud, and Rachilde, unmasking meant affirming the truth of gender.

Apart from medical uses, we live in an age that has little use for physical masks but is awash in technological masks. We have the means to shape identities online and to alter permanently our physical features through surgery. This is in dramatic contrast to the time when identity was so firmly fixed that imposture or cross-dressing was punishable by death. Where does this leave us? Lives spent online risk assuming the same unreality as the unending stream of images, in which no thought seems original, no identity unique, no presumed core essential or defining. In this space, to fashion one's own identity means to curate a series of posts and photos. The ability to construct more credible masks for ourselves than any previous population possessed has led many to the view that all aspects of identity are fluid and a matter of personal volition.

Oscar Wilde opposed the *fin de siècle*'s eager embrace of unmasking. For Wilde, imperatives to be authentic were too tediously earnest. His well-known claim that life's first duty was to be as artificial as possible—with the second, he claimed, yet to be discovered—has been taken by some to be the unserious pose of a dandy. As with most of his quips, however, there was substance behind the stance. Wilde rejected the idea of fixed identities as especially fatal to art, which he believed should not be the expression of some supposed essential self. True individuality, he claimed, was the freedom to create oneself anew against all consistency or conformity. "Man is least himself when he speaks in his own person," Wilde wrote. "Give him a mask, and he will tell you the truth."[3] In this regard, he was a prophet.

Acknowledgments

Since beginning this book many years ago, I have accrued many debts. May these acknowledgments serve as partial thanks to the institutions and people who have helped me along the way. Research for this book was done with support from the American Council of Learned Societies, the Liguria Study Center, the Carmargo Foundation, the Fulbright Scholar Program, and the John Simon Guggenheim Foundation. Boston University's Center for the Humanities provided financial support for the production of this book. I have gained much from having presented my research publicly: in Jan Goldstein's workshop on French history at the University of Chicago; Stanford University's seminar on early modern Europe led by Keith Baker; Vincent Denis's seminar at the Université de Paris 1; a seminar on French history run by Caroline Ford at the University of British Columbia; Steven Kaplan's seminar on French history at Cornell University; the National Humanities Center in North Carolina; and panels of the Society for French Historical Studies in Cambridge, Nashville, and Washington, DC. Portions of the book have appeared in *Representations* ("Versailles, Meet Les Halles: Masks, Carnival, and the French Revolution," *Representations* 73 [Winter 2001]: 89–116), *French Historical Studies* ("The Face of Imposture in Postrevolutionary France," *French Historical Studies* 35, no. 2 [2012], 291–320; © 2012 Society for French Historical Studies; all rights reserved; republished by permission of the publisher; see https://www.dukeupress.edu), and the *Journal of Urban History* ("Urban Development and the Culture of Masked Balls in Nineteenth-Century Paris," *Journal of Urban History* 40, no. 4 [Fall 2013], 646–62, doi:10.1017/S0963926813000205; © 2013 Cambridge University Press).

I've benefited immensely from conversations and correspondence with friends and colleagues, including Keith Baker, David Bell, Rick Caldicott, David Charlton, Vincent Denis, Barbara Diefendorf, William Doyle, Steven Englund, David Garrioch, Jan Goldstein, Dan Gordon, Colin Jones, Steven Kaplan, Laura Mason, Sara Maza, Robert Nye, Michael Prince, Jeffrey Ravel, Jonathan Ribner, Christopher Ricks, Jean-Paul Riquelme, Sophie Rosenfeld, Paul Scott, Pierre Serna, Daniel Smail, Roger Shattuck, Jay Smith, Jean-Yves Vialleton, James Whitman, and Diana Wylie.

My thanks to Séverine Pascal for her help identifying handwriting in archives of the Bibliothèque de l'Arsenale, as well as to Michel Ollion and Isabelle Foucher of the Archives Nationales, whose work was essential in determining the outcome of an eighteenth-century court case involving carnival violence. I am especially grateful for the help provided by Thomas Bonnell, Andrew Jainchill, and Gabriel Sabbagh in sorting out the abbé de Choisy's works and biography. I appreciate Gerald Honigsblum's hospitality in Paris on an early research trip; his later help on a particular point of research was especially valuable. My soulmate Lydia Moland has been by my side with love and support at every stage of this book.

I have been fortunate to have two colleagues whose warmth, humor, and scholarly integrity have strongly shaped my own teaching and writing. Christopher Ricks's sharp mind and generous heart, delight in what words can do, and healthy distrust of common pieties have taught me to see familiar things in fresh ways. Roger Shattuck's love of literature, ear for music, and eye for art have showed me ways to write about works of the imagination that retain their life, spark, and mystery.

Illustrations

FIGURES

PART OPENERS

COLOR PLATES (FOLLOWING P. 178)

Notes

A full bibliography is available online at https://press.uchicago.edu/sites/johnson/index.html.

PREFACE

1. Jean-Jacques Rousseau, *Émile, ou, De l'éducation*, in *Oeuvres complètes*, 4 vols. (Paris: Bibliothèque de la Pléiade, 1969), 4:515.
2. Marcel Mauss, "A Category of the Human Mind: The Notion of the Person; the Notion of the Self," trans. W. D. Halls, in *The Category of the Person: Anthropology, Philosophy, History*, ed. Michael Carrithers, Steven Collins, and Steven Lukes (Cambridge: Cambridge University Press, 1985), 18, 22.
3. Charles Taylor, *Sources of the Self: The Making of the Modern Identity* (Cambridge, MA: Harvard University Press, 1983); Jerrold Seigel, *The Idea of the Self: Thought and Experience in Western Europe since the Seventeenth Century* (Cambridge: Cambridge University Press, 2005), 5–7.

CHAPTER ONE

1. Mme de Sévigné, quoted in Alain Mazère, *La Rochefoucauld: Le duc rebelle* (Bordeaux: Le Croît vif, 2007), 321, 319. Unless otherwise noted, all translations in this book are the author's.
2. François, duc de La Rochefoucauld, *Réflexions ou Sentences et maximes de morale*, in *Oeuvres complètes* (Paris: Bibliothèque de la Pléiade, 1964), 411, 412; La Rochefoucauld, *Oeuvres de La Rochefoucauld*, 3 vols. (Paris: Hachette, 1868), 1:359.
3. Jean-Jacques Rousseau, *La Nouvelle Héloïse*, in *Oeuvres complètes*, 5 vols. (Paris: Bibliothèque de la Pléiade, 1959–95), 2:373; Brendan Donnellan, "Nietzsche and La Rochefoucauld," *The German Quarterly* 52 (1979): 303–18.
4. Morris Bishop, *The Life and Adventures of La Rochefoucauld* (Ithaca, NY: Cornell University Press, 1951), 5.

5. Mazère, *La Rochefoucauld*, 126.
6. La Rochefoucauld, *Apologie de M. le Prince de Marcillac*, in *Oeuvres complètes*, 19.
7. Quoted in Mazère, *La Rochefoucauld*, 118.
8. La Rochefoucauld, *Manuscrit du Liancourt*, in *Oeuvres complètes*, 356, 358; Jean Starobinski, "Introduction" to La Rochefoucauld, *Maximes et mémoires* (Paris: Union Générale d'Éditions, 1964), 12; Vivien Thweatt, *La Rochefoucauld and the Seventeenth-Century Concept of the Self* (Geneva: Droz, 1980).
9. La Rochefoucauld, *Réflexions ou Sentences et maximes de morale*, 438.
10. La Rochefoucauld, *Réflexions diverses*, in *Oeuvres complètes*, 507.
11. La Rochefoucauld, *Réflexions diverses*, 507–9.
12. La Rochefoucauld, *Réflexions diverses*, 507.
13. La Rochefoucauld, *Réflexions ou Sentences et maximes de morale*, 429.
14. La Rochefoucauld, *Réflexions diverses*, 520–21; La Rochefoucauld, *Réflexions ou Sentences et maximes de morale*, 414.
15. Louis de Rouvroy, duc de Saint-Simon, *Mémoires: Additions au Journal de Dangeau*, 8 vols. (Paris: Bibliothèque de la Pléiade, 1983–1988), 2:214.
16. Jean de La Bruyère, in *Oeuvres complètes* (Paris: Bibliothèque de la Pléiade, 1951), 235.
17. La Bruyère, in *Oeuvres complètes*, 256, 266, 236.
18. La Bruyère, in *Oeuvres complètes*, 267, 235; Charles-Augustin Saint-Beuve, quoted in Maurice Pellisson, *La Bruyère* (Geneva: Slatkine Reprints, 1970 [1892]), 18.
19. La Bruyère, in *Oeuvres complètes*, 265.
20. Pellisson, *La Bruyère* (Paris: Lecène, Oudin & Cie., 1892), 28.
21. La Bruyère, in *Oeuvres complètes*, 267.
22. Saint-Simon, *Mémoires*, 5:294.
23. Orest Ranum, "Courtesy, Absolutism, and the Rise of the French State, 1630–1660," *Journal of Modern History* 52 (1980): 426–51.
24. *Le Mespris de la Cour*, quoted in Robert Muchembled, *La Société policée: Politique et politesse en France du XVIe au XXe siècle* (Paris: Éditions du Seuil, 1998), 157.
25. Under Louis XIV, the "sons of France" were Louis, known as the *Grand Dauphin* or *Monseigneur*, and the king's brother, Philippe, duc d'Orléans, known as *Monsieur*; the "grandsons of France" included the three sons of the *Grand Dauphin* (Louis Dauphin, duc de Bourgogne; Philippe, duc d'Anjou; and Charles, duc de Berry) and the son of *Monsieur* (Philippe, duc de Chartres); the "princes of the blood" were Henri III Bourbon, Prince de Condé, and François Louis, Prince de Conti. See Emmanuel Le Roy Ladurie, *Saint-Simon and the Court of Louis XIV*, trans. Arthur Goldhammer (Chicago: University of Chicago Press, 2001), 24–35.
26. Gilles André de La Roque, *Traité de la noblesse, de ses differentes especes* (Paris: Estienne Michallet, 1678), 18.
27. Henri Brocher, *Le Rang et l'étiquette sous l'ancien régime* (Paris: Félix Alcan, 1934), 24–37, 67–68.
28. Saint-Simon, *Mémoires*, 3:26–32.
29. Saint-Simon, *Mémoires*, 3:19.
30. Norbert Elias, *The Court Society*, trans. Edmund Jephcott (New York: Pantheon Books, 1983), 88; concerning status and etiquette, see 87–91.
31. Saint-Simon, *Mémoires*, 1:782, 781.
32. Saint-Simon, *Mémoires*, 1:37.
33. Saint-Simon, *Mémoires*, 1:45.

34. See Germaine de Staël, *Politics, Literature, and National Character*, trans. Morroe Berger (New Brunswick, NJ: Transaction Publishers, 2000), 220–21. Born a half century after de Staël, the mathematician Antoine Cournot coined a phrase for courtiers' judgments that has endured: "cascades of disdain" (quoted in Guy Chaussinand-Nogaret, *Une Histoire des élites, 1700–1848* [Paris: École des Hautes Études en Sciences Sociales, 1975], 192).
35. Christophe Losfeld, *Politesse, moral et construction sociale: Pour une histoire des traités de comportements (1670–1788)* (Paris: Honoré Champion, 2011), 53.
36. Maurice Magendie, *La Politesse mondaine et les théories de l'honnêteté, en France au XVIIe siècle, de 1600 à 1660*, 2 vols. (Paris: Félix Alcan, 1925), 1:355; Nicolas Faret, *L'Honneste homme. Ou, l'Art de plaire à la court* (Paris: Toussaincts du Bray, 1630), 12.
37. Faret, *L'Honneste homme*, 89.
38. Faret, *L'Honneste homme*, 165.
39. Michel de Montaigne, "Of Husbanding the Will," "Of Presumption," in *The Complete Essays*, trans. Donald Frame (New York and London: Alfred E. Knopf, 2003), 941, 596.
40. Pierre Bardin, *Le Lycée*, quoted in Magendie, *La Politesse mondaine*, 1:376; see also Emmanuel Bury, *Littérature et politesse: L'Invention de l'honnête homme* (Paris: Presses Universitaires de France, 1996).
41. Eustache du Refuge, *Traicté de la Cour, ou Instructions des courtisans* (Amsterdam: Chez les Elzeviers, 1616), 86, 3, 5, 2, 158.
42. Antoine Furetière, *Dictionnaire universel*, 3 vols. (The Hague: Arnout & Reinier, 1690), 1:n.p., 3:n.p.; Refuge, *Traicté de la Cour*, 158.
43. Refuge, *Traicté de la Cour*, 115, 158–59.
44. Faret, *L'Honneste homme*, 166, 169.
45. Antoine de Courtin, *Nouveau traité de la civilité qui se pratique en France parmi les honnestes gens* (Amsterdam: Jacques le Jeune, 1679), vii, 58, 63, 21, 57, 117–18, 24.
46. Courtin, *Nouveau traité*, 107, 86–89. The historian Roger Chartier comments on Courtin's rather awkward position. "Either the individual fails to act as his rank and the circumstances demand—and for this Antoine de Courtin coined the neologism *décontenance*—or he fails to have sentiments that conform with his visible behavior. Then *civilité* becomes pretense; it changes from a legitimate representation to a hypocritical mask" (*The Cultural Uses of Print in Early Modern France*, trans. Lydia G. Cochrane [Princeton, NJ: Princeton University Press, 1987], 87).
47. Courtin, *Nouveau traité*, 88.
48. Furetière, *Dictionnaire universel*, 1:n.p.
49. Esprit Fléchier, *Oraison funebre de tres-haut et tres-puissant seigneur, Mre Charles de Ste Saure, Duc de Montausier* (Paris: Antoine Dezallier, 1690), 13; Fléchier, "Sermon pour le troisième dimanche de l'Avent [1682?]," in *Oeuvres complètes de Fléchier*, 10 vols. (Paris: Boiste fils, 1825), 2:142. See also Losfeld, *Politesse, morale et construction sociale*, 51; Peter France, *Politeness and Its Discontents* (Cambridge: Cambridge University Press, 1992), 59.
50. Quoted in Paul Bénichou, *Man and Ethics: Studies in French Classicism*, trans. Elizabeth Hughes (New York: Anchor Books, 1971), 114.
51. Faret, *L'Honneste homme*, 236–37.
52. Brillon's additional observations about the court carry the same tone. "Truth is unwelcome everywhere, but at court it is received with horror." "The art of

flattering the powerful is so common that even the petty and uneducated practice it." "The great have been so flattered that flattery itself is becoming exhausted and the flatterers are admitting defeat." Pierre Jacques Brillon, *Suite des caractères de Théophraste et des Pensées de Mr. Pascal* (Paris: Estienne Michallet, 1699), 68–69.

53. Jean-Baptiste Morvan de Bellegarde, *Réflexions sur la politesse des moeurs* (Paris: Jean et Michel Guignard, 1700), 338; Jean de La Chétardie, *Instructions pour un jeune seigneur, ou l'Idée d'un galant homme* (Paris: Chez T. Girard, 1684), 92–93.
54. La Bruyère, in *Oeuvres complètes*, 373, 122; Antoine Gombaud, chevalier de Méré, *Oeuvres posthumes de M. Le Chevalier de Méré* (Paris: Chez Jean & Michel Guignard, 1700), 10–11, 256.
55. Marin Cureau de La Chambre, *L'Art de connoistre les hommes* (Paris: Chez Rocolet, 1660), 1–2.
56. Jean-Jacques Courtine and Claudine Haroche characterize the two periods of European history when physiognomy held the greatest appeal, 1500–1670 and 1780–1850, as moments of "political and social reconfiguration." The dates correspond to "the formation of an absolutist state and gradual establishment of civil society conceived on the court model" and "the birth of a democratic state and of mass society" (*Histoire du visage: Exprimer et taire ses émotions (XVIe-début XIXe siècle)* [Paris: Éditions Rivages, 1988], 46). See also Graeme Tytler, *Physiognomy in the European Novel: Faces and Fortunes* (Princeton, NJ: Princeton University Press, 1982), 36–44.
57. La Chambre, *L'Art de connoistre les hommes*, 8, 271, 10.
58. La Chambre, *L'Art de connoistre les hommes*, 75, 214–33, 237–39, 243.
59. La Chambre, *L'Art de connoistre les hommes*, 53, 36, 49.
60. Jennifer Montagu, *The Expression of the Passions: The Origin and Influence of Charles Le Brun's "Conférence sur l'expression générale et particulière"* (New Haven, CT: Yale University Press, 1994), 17, 111.
61. Charles Le Brun, "Conférence sur l'expression générale et particulière," quoted in Montagu, *The Expression of the Passions*, 115–20.
62. Montagu, *The Expression of the Passions*, 24.
63. Saint-Simon, *Mémoires*, 4:361, 2:303–5, 1034–35.
64. Saint-Simon, *Mémoires*, 1:164.
65. Saint-Simon, *Mémoires*, 1:134–35, 158–59, 163–66, 285–86; 2:893–95, 1034–35, 1155. Saint-Simon found grim amusement in Harlay's association with one of France's best-known actors, Domenico Biancolelli, who played the masked Arlequin of commedia dell'arte. "Society, who knew all about this," he wrote, "claimed that Arlequin made better faces and was more shrewd than the magistrate, but that the magistrate was easily the superior actor" (2:1157–58).
66. Saint-Simon, *Mémoires*, 1:7.
67. Saint-Simon, *Mémoires*, 5:381.
68. Saint-Simon, *Mémoires*, 5:428–39.

CHAPTER TWO

1. "Loup," Antoine Furetière, *Dictionnaire universel*, 3 vols. (The Hague: Arnout & Reinier, 1690), 2:n.p.; Édouard Fournier, ed., *Variétés historiques et littéraires; Recueil de pièces volantes rares et curieuses en prose et en vers*, 10 vols. (Paris:

Pagnerre, 1863), 10:27n1; *Dictionnaire de l'Académie française*, 2 vols. (Paris: J. J. Smits, 1799), 1:437.

2. Sébastien Locatelli, *Voyage de France: Moeurs et coutumes françaises*, trans. Adolphe Vautier (Paris: Alphonse Picard, 1905), 325–26. Locatelli's visit was in 1664–1665.
3. "Loup," "Masque," Furetière, *Dictionnaire universel*, 2:n.p.; "Promenade du Cours, à Paris, en 1653," Fournier, ed., *Variétés historiques et littéraires*, 10:25–34; Victor Fournel, *Les Rues du vieux Paris* (Paris: Firmin-Didot, 1879), 218.
4. Henri Estienne, *Deux dialogues du nouveau langage françois, italianizé et autrement desguizé, principalement entre les courtisans de ce temps*, 2 vols. (Paris: Isidore Liseux, 1883), 1:181–83; *An Agreeable Criticism, of the City of Paris and the French* (London: Ben. Bragg, 1704), 16.
5. James H. Johnson, *Venice Incognito: Masks in the Serene Republic* (Berkeley: University of California Press, 2011), 114–17.
6. William W. Sanger, *History of Prostitution: Its Extent, Causes, and Effects Throughout the World* (New York: Harper & Brothers, 1895), 120–22.
7. Catherine Meurdrac de la Guette, *Mémoires de Madame de la Guette, Escrits par Elle-mesme* (The Hague: Adrian Moetjens, 1681), 251; Marie de Rabutin-Chantal, marquise de Sévigné, *Correspondance*, 3 vols. (Paris: Éditions Gallimard, 1972–79), 1:64 (November 27, 1664); François Nicolas Napoléon Ravaisson-Mollien, *Les Archives de la Bastille*, 19 vols. (Paris: A. Durand, 1866–1904), 1:63–68 (April 21, 1664); G. B. Depping, *Correspondance administrative sous le règne de Louis XIV*, 4 vols. (Paris: Imprimerie Nationale, 1851), 2:571 (February 24, 1683).
8. Décrirai-je ses bas en trente endroits percés,
   Ses souliers grimaçans, vingt fois rapetassés,
   Ses coiffes d'où pendoit au bout d'une ficelle
   Un vieux masque pelé presque aussi hideux qu'elle?

   From Satire X, "Les Femmes," Nicolas Boileau, in *Oeuvres complètes* (Paris: Bibliothèque de la Pléiade, 1966), 70, 928.
9. Ravaisson-Mollien, *Les Archives de la Bastille*, 6:296 (August 13, 1680).
10. Claude Noirot, *L'Origine des masques, mommerie, bernez, et revennez es iours gras* (Lengres: J. Chaveau, 1609), 87, 90–93, 103–4, 108.
11. Jean Savaron, *Traitté contre les masques* (Paris: Pierre Chevalier, 1608), 15, 7, 14, 19; Johnson, *Venice Incognito*, 66–68.
12. "Ordonnance du Roi, qui defend d'aller le visage embruché d'un Chaperon," March 11, 1399, in *Collection Delamare, Traité de la Police*, Ms. Fr. 21625, Fol. 180, B. N.; Daniel Jousse, *Traité de la justice criminelle de France*, 3 vols. (Paris: Chez Debure, 1771), 3:829–30; Sara Beam, *Laughing Matters: Farce and the Making of Absolutism in France* (Ithaca, NY: Cornell University Press, 2007), 63.
13. "Ordonnance du Roi cy-dessus a éte lûë & publiée à haute & intelligible voix à son de Trompe & Cry public," *Collection Delamare, Traité de la Police*, February 4, 1719, Ms. Fr. 21625, Fol. 195, B. N., Paris.
14. "De Par le Roy," February 2, 1718, Ms. 21625, fol. 195, B. N., and "Ordonnance de police," February 5, 1746, in Jacques Peuchet, *Collection des lois, ordonnances et réglements de police*, 8 vols. (Paris: Lottin, 1818), 5:326.
15. Jean Baptiste Thiers, *Traité des jeux et des divertissemens, qui peuvent être permis, ou qui doivent être défendus aux Chrêtiens selon les Regles de l'Eglise & le sentiment*

des Pères (Paris: Antoine Dezallier, 1686), 320–21; *Offices propres à l'Eglise paroissiale de Saint Jean en Grève*, 2 vols. (Paris: Le Bercier & Boudet, 1742), 2:137–41.

16. Thiers, *Traité des jeux*, 328–42.
17. Pierre Jean Guyot, *Répertoire universel et raisonné de jurisprudence civile, criminelle, canonique et bénéficielle*, 64 vols. (Paris: Visse, 1784), 39:356n6.
18. *Journal d'un bourgeois de Paris sous la règne de François I (1515–1536)* (Paris: Jules Renouard, 1854), 54–55; Fournel, *Les Rues de vieux Paris*, 228–29; Benjamin Gastineau, *Le Carnaval ancien et moderne* (Paris: Poulet Malassis, 1862), 17–18.
19. Jacques Bonnet, *Histoire générale de la danse* (Paris: Houry, 1724), 150–51; Louis Moréri, *Le Grand dictionnaire historique*, 6 vols. (Paris: Jacques Vincent, 1732), 5:328; J. De La Tynna, *Dictionnaire topographique, étymologique et historique des rues de Paris* (Paris: Chez De La Tynna, 1812), 360.
20. "De Par le Roy," February 11, 1683, in *Collection Delamare, Traité de la Police*, Ms. Fr. 21625, Fol. 119, B. N., Paris.
21. Edmond-Jean-François Barbier, *Chronique de la régence et du règne du Louis XV (1718–1763), ou Journal de Barbier*, 8 vols. (Paris: Charpentier, 1857), 1:252.
22. Assavoir l'un une poularde,
    Un autre, un baril de moûtarde,
    Un autre, un reste de jambon,
    L'un, du pain, l'autre, du bon-bon,
    L'un, dans deux plats, trois amelettes,
    . . .
    Qui, des salades, qui, du fruit,
    Qui des marons, qui, du biscuit,
    Qui, du sel, du ris, du fromage
    Qui, de la soupe et du potage.

    Jean Loret, "Lettre onziéme, du onziéme mars [1656]," *La Muze historique ou Recueil des lettres en vers*, 4 vols. (Paris: P. Daffis, 1857–78), 2:169.
23. *Advis très important sur les affaires présentes* (n.p.: n.p., 1651).
24. J. C. Nemeitz, *Séjour de Paris*, 2 vols. (Leiden: Jean van Abcoude, 1727), 1:184–89.
25. Philippe de Courcillon, marquis de Dangeau, *Journal du marquis de Dangeau*, 19 vols. (Paris: Firmin Didot, 1854–60), 7:250, 226, 243–45, 259–60, 262; Louis de Rouvroy, duc de Saint-Simon, *Mémoires: Additions au Journal de Dangeau*, 8 vols. (Paris: Bibliothèque de la Pléiade, 1983–1988), 1:702.
26. Anne-Marie-Louise d'Orléans, duchesse de Montpensier, *Mémoires de Mademoiselle de Montpensier* (Paris: Le Breton, 1728), 3:37–38, 4:24–26, 4:154–56; Dangeau, *Journal*, 7:244, 259.
27. Saint-Simon, *Mémoires*, 1:698; Dangeau, *Journal*, 7:244, 259–60.
28. Dangeau, *Journal*, 7:247, 7:252.
29. Charles-Philippe d'Albert, duc de Luynes, *Mémoires du duc de Luynes sur la cour de Louis XV (1735–1758)*, 17 vols. (Paris: Didot Frères, 1860–65), 5:299 (January 15, 1744); Bonnet, *Histoire génerale de la danse*, 152.
30. From Furetière, *Dictionnaire universel*: "Incognito. Term imported directly from the Italian, which is said of the highly born who enter a city and pass through its streets without pomp, ceremony, their accustomed retinue, or other signs of their magnificence. The Prince traveled through France *incognito*. Grand and

prominent persons of Italy are not pleased if they are acknowledged as they stroll *incognito*" (2:331). See also Johnson, *Venice Incognito*, 129–40.

31. Saint-Simon, *Mémoires*, 1:469; Émile Magne, ed., *Le Grand Condé et le duc d'Enghien: Lettres inédites à Marie-Louise de Gonzague, reine de Pologne, sur la cour de Louis XIV (1660–1677)* (Paris: Émile-Paul Frères, 1920), 14, 125.
32. Saint-Simon, *Mémoires*, 1:699.
33. Saint-Simon, *Mémoires*, 1:701.
34. Saint-Simon, *Mémoires*, 1:1507; Magne, *Le Grand Condé et le duc d'Enghien*, 16.
35. Antoine de Courtin, *Nouveau traité de la civilité qui se pratique en France parmi les honnestes gens* (Amsterdam: Jacques le Jeune, 1679), 157–58; Pierre Rameau, *Le maître à danser* (Paris: Jean Vilette, 1725), 58.
36. Dangeau, *Journal*, 7:248.
37. Rameau, *Le maître à danser*, 49–59; *Encyclopédie méthodique. Arts académiques, équitation, escrime, danse, et art de nager* (Paris: Chez Panckoucke, 1786), 312–16, 313–14; Saint-Simon, *Mémoires*, 2:578; Barbier, *Chronique de la régence et du règne du Louis XV*, 1:199 (March 8, 1722).
38. Rameau, *Le maître à danser*, 35.
39. "Bal," in *Encyclopédie méthodique*, 314.
40. Magne, *Le Grand Condé et le duc d'Enghien*, 142.
41. Magne, *Le Grand Condé et le duc d'Enghien*, 131.
42. Magne, *Le Grand Condé et le duc d'Enghien*, 131.
43. Colin Jones, *The Smile Revolution in the Eighteenth Century* (Oxford: Oxford University Press, 2014), 39–40.
44. Laurent Laffemas, *Ballet dancé devant le roy et la reine regente sa mere par le trio Mazarinicque pour dire adieu à la France* (Paris: n.p., 1649), 16; *Mazarin Poulonois. Pour le iour du mardy gras* (n.p.: n.p., n.d.), 3–4.
45. Bougre bougrant, bougre bougré,
Et bougre au supreme degré,
Bougre au poil, & bougre à le plume,
Bougre en grand, & petit volume,
Bougre Sodomisant l'Estat,
. . .
Bougre à chevres, bougre à garçons.
On te coupera pauvre Iule
Et l'un & l'autre Testicule,
Et lors ô Cardinal Pelé,
Cardinal detesticulé.

[Paul Scarron,] *La Mazarinade* (Brussels: n.p., 1651), 6, 13.

46. Gustave Attinger, *L'Esprit de la commedia dell'arte dans le théâtre français* (Paris: Publications de la Société d'Histoire du Théâtre, 1950), 95, 101–4; Jean Marie Bernard Clément, *Anecdotes dramatiques*, 3 vols. (Paris: La Veuve Duchesne, 1775), 1:340–1, 3:203–4, 219; Henri Sauval, *Histoire et recherches des antiquités de la ville de Paris*, 3 vols. (Paris: Charles Moette, 1724), 3:36–39; Pierre Louis Duchartre, *The Italian Comedy*, trans. Randolph T. Weaver (New York: Dover, 1966), 307–8; Virginia Scott, *The Commedia dell'Arte in Paris, 1644–1697* (Charlottesville: University of Virginia Press, 1990), 223–24.

47. Clément, *Anecdotes dramatiques*, 1:338–40.
48. Pierre de l'Estoile, *Journal de Henri III, 1574–1580*, quoted in François Parfaict and Claude Parfaict, *Histoire de l'ancien théatre italien, depuis son origine en France, Jusqu'à sa suppression en l'Année 1697* (Paris: Chez Lambert, 1753), 189; Attinger, *L'Esprit de la commedia dell'arte*, 96–99.
49. Parfaict and Parfaict, *Histoire de l'ancient théatre italien*, 14–15.
50. Beam, *Laughing Matters*, 4; Charles Mazouer, *Le Théâtre d'Arlequin: Comédies et comédiens italiens en France au XVIIe siècle* (Paris: Presses de l'Université de Paris, 2002), 33–34; Scott, *The Commedia dell'Arte*, 241–42.
51. Scott, *The Commedia dell'Arte*, 97–98; Ducharte, *The Italian Comedy*, 79.
52. Constantin Mic, *La Commedia dell'arte: ou Le Théâtre des comédiens italiens des XVIe, XVIIe & XVIIIe siècles* (Paris: J. Schiffrin, 1927), 118–19.
53. "Nécrologie, Carlin Bertinazzi," October 18, 1783, *Mercure de France*, 137.
54. Claude-François Ménéstrier, *Des Ballets anciens et modernes selon les regles du theatre* (Paris: Guignard, 1682), 67, 80, 131, 139; *Encyclopédie méthodique*, 315; Rebecca Harris-Warrick, *Dance and Drama in French Baroque Opera* (Cambridge: Cambridge University Press, 2016), 121–22; Georgia J. Cowart, *The Triumph of Pleasure: Louis XIV and the Politics of Spectacle* (Chicago: University of Chicago Press, 2008), 8–12.
55. Jean-Georges Noverre, *Lettres sur la danse et les ballets* (Stuttgart and London: Delaroche, 1760), 243–44, 256. See also Sophia Rosenfeld, *A Revolution in Language: The Problem of Signs in Late Eighteenth-Century France* (Stanford, CA: Stanford University Press, 2001).
56. Marco Baschera draws this connection in a passage on *sprezzatura*—"naturalness"—in Baldassare Castiglione's *Book of the Courtier*: "In semiological terms, the courtier *disincarnates* the signs of human expression, which permits him to *incarnate* a social persona in the human comedy. To understand the difference, the process resembles that adopted by actors of commedia dell'arte, although in the latter case the actor displays the transformation while the courtier, at the risk of being unmasked and socially disgraced, is obliged to dissemble" (*Théâtralité dans l'oeuvre de Molière* [Tübingen: G. Narr Verlag, 1998], 155).
57. Dancourt, *La Fontaine de Sapience* (1694), quoted in Yves Moraud, *Masques et jeux dans le théâtre comique* (Lille: Université de Lille, 1977), 99.
58. Pierre Corneille, "Epître, *Suite du Menteur*," in *Le Menteur* (Paris: Éditions Gallimard, 2000), 162.
59. Émile Picot, *Bibliographie Cornélienne* (Paris: Auguste Fontaine, 1876), 42–43.
60. Je disais vérité.—Quand un menteur la dit,
    En passant par sa bouche elle perd son crédit.

    François-Marie Arouet de Voltaire, "Commentaires sur Corneille," in *Oeuvres complètes de Voltaire*, 71 vols. (Basle: Tourneisen, 1784–90), 5:381.
61. Corneille, *Le Menteur*, 47, 99, 158.
62. Pierre Corneille, *Oeuvres de P. Corneille*, 12 vols. (Paris: Hachette, 1862–1868), 4:123–24.
63. Some scholars have claimed that these words are apocryphal. See Pierre and Thomas Corneille, *Oeuvres des deux Corneille*, 2 vols. (Paris: C. Louandre, 1850), 1:386–87; François Bouquet, "Examen critique d'une anecdote littéraire sur *Le Menteur* de P. Corneille," *Revue de la Normandie* 5 (1865): 210–21.

64. J. F. La Harpe, *Lycée ou Cours de littérature ancienne et modern*, 16 vols. (Paris: Depelafol, 1825), 5:252.
65. Voltaire, in *Oeuvres complètes de Voltaire*, 5:359; Molière, "Préface" to *Tartuffe, ou l'Imposteur*, in *Oeuvres complètes*, 2 vols. (Paris: Bibliothèque de la Pléiade, 2010), 2:93.
66. Scott, *The Commedia dell'Arte in Paris*, 168; Ducharte, *The Italian Comedy*, 23; Attinger, *L'Esprit de la commedia dell'arte*, 139.
67. Molière, *Le Bourgeois gentilhomme*, in *Oeuvres complètes*, 2:293; Molière, *Le Misanthrope*, in *Oeuvres complètes*, 1:651, 695.
68. Donneau de Visé, *Lettre écrite sur la comédie du Misanthrope* (1666), quoted in Molière, in *Oeuvres complètes*, 1:636.
69. Molière, *Oeuvres complètes*, 1:643.
70. *Mercure historique et politique*, quoted in Pierre Mélèse, "A propos de l'expulsion des comédiens italiens en 1697," *Revue d'Histoire littéraire de la France* 44 (1937): 534; William Brooks, "Louis XIV's Dismissal of the Italian Actors: The Episode of *La Fausse Prude*," *Modern Language Review* 91 (1996): 840–47.
71. Ducharte, *The Italian Comedy*, 38–39; Scott, *The Commedia dell'Arte in Paris*, 183.
72. Scott, *The Commedia dell'Arte in Paris*, 357, 360, 358–59.
73. Anne Mauduit, sieur de Fatouville, *Le Banqueroutier* (1687), in Evariste Gherardi, *Le Théâtre italien de Gherardi, ou Le Recueil général de toutes les comédies & scenes Françoises jouées par les Comediens Italiens du Roy pendant tout le temps qu'ils ont été au service de sa Majesté*, 6 vols. (Amsterdam: Michel Charles le Cene, 1721), 1:109–76.
74. Mélèse, "A propos de l'expulsion des comédiens italiens," 534.

CHAPTER THREE

1. "Pierre Mêge, Soldate de Marine, reconnu par le Parlement de Provence," in François Gayot de Pitaval, *Causes célèbres et interessantes, avec les jugements qui les ont decidées*, 22 vols. (The Hague: Jean Neaulme, 1747–51), 2:7.
2. "Pierre Mêge," 2:11.
3. "Pierre Mêge," 2:120.
4. "Pierre Mêge," 2:11–12.
5. "Pierre Mêge," 2:15.
6. Daniel Jousse, *Traité de la justice criminelle de France*, 3 vols. (Paris: Chez Debure, 1771), 2:605–6.
7. Pierre-François Muyart de Vouglans, *Les Lois criminelles de France dans leur ordre naturel* (Paris: Merigot le Jeune, 1780), 245; Guyot, *Répertoire universel et raisonné de jurisprudence civile, criminelle, canonique et bénéficielle*, 64 vols. (Paris: Visse, 1784), 24:408–9.
8. Guyot, *Répertoire universel*, 24:448, 450; Jousse, *Traité de la justice criminelle*, 3:367.
9. Pitaval, *Causes célèbres et interessantes*, 2:27.
10. Pitaval, *Causes célèbres et interessantes*, 2:18–19.
11. Depuis mes jeunes ans, j'éprouve avec constance
Les divers caprices du sort;
On me vouloit ravir l'honneur de ma naissance,
Et prouver que je suis mort;

Mais le Ciel, protecteur de la foible innocence,
Par la tempête même, enfin m'a mis au port.

12. This account of Esprit Adaoust is drawn from Hyacinthe de Boniface, *Arrests notables de la Cour de Parlement de Provence, Cour des Comptes, Aydes & Finances du mesme pays*, 2 vols. (Paris: Guignard, 1670), 2:102–20; *Dictionnaire de la noblesse*, 15 vols. (Paris: Veuve Duchesne, 1770); François Ambroise Thomas Roux-Alpheran, *Les Rues d'Aix: ou, Recherches historiques sur l'ancienne capitale*, 2 vols. (Aix: Aubin, 1846–48), 1:35–36; and *Anciennes familles de Provence. Site généologique*, http://genobco.free.fr/provence/Adaoust.htm (accessed May 25, 2021).
13. Pitaval, *Causes célébres et interessantes*, 2:109–10.
14. Pitaval, *Causes célébres et interessantes*, 2:111–12.
15. *Anciennes familles de Provence*.
16. Pitaval, *Causes célébres et interessantes* 2:120.
17. Pitaval, *Causes célébres et interessantes*, 2:23; Armand Fouquier, *Causes célèbres de tous les peuples*, 9 vols. (Paris: Lebrun, 1858–1874), 6:21.
18. Pitaval, *Causes célèbres et interessantes*, 2:39.
19. Pitaval, *Causes célébres et interessantes*, 2:162–63, 167. See also Jeffrey S. Ravel, *The Would-Be Commoner: A Tale of Deception, Murder, and Justice in 17th-Century France* (New York: Houghton Mifflin, 2008), 62–63, 93–121, 179–84.
20. Pitaval, *Causes célèbres et interessantes*, 2:61–62.
21. Pitaval, *Causes célèbres et interessantes*, 2:88–90.
22. Pitaval, *Causes célèbres et interessantes*, 2:86–87.
23. Pitaval, *Causes célèbres et interessantes*, 2:77, 89.
24. For methods of identification in early modern Europe, see Valentin Groebner, *Who Are You? Identification, Deception, and Surveillance in Early Modern Europe*, trans. Mark Kyburz and John Peck (Brooklyn: Zone Books, 1997).
25. Pitaval, *Causes célèbres*, Pitaval, *Causes célèbres et interessantes*, 2:152, 160.
26. Pitaval, *Causes célèbres et interessantes*, 2:168, 153.
27. Pitaval, *Causes célèbres et interessantes*, 2:22.
28. Pitaval, *Causes célèbres et interessantes*, 2:147–48, 104.
29. Pitaval, *Causes célèbres et interessantes*, 2:39–40, 183–88.
30. Pitaval, *Causes célèbres et interessantes*, 2:168–69.
31. Pitaval, *Causes célèbres et interessantes*, 2:166.
32. Pitaval, *Causes célèbres et interessantes*, 2:204–5.
33. Pitaval, *Causes célèbres et interessantes*, 2:205.
34. Joseph Hédouin, *De l'Usurpation de titres nobiliaires* (Paris: Arthur Rousseau, 1900), 146–47.
35. Louis Nicolas Henri Chérin, *Abrégé chronologique d'édits, déclarations, réglemens, arrêts & lettres-patentes des rois de france de la troisieme race, concernant le fait de noblesse* (Paris: Royer, 1788), 213, 255; Guyot, *Répertoire universel*, 2:315, 41:304–5.
36. Gail Bossenga, "A Divided Nobility: Status, Markets, and the Patrimonial State in the Old Regime," in *The French Nobility in the Eighteenth Century: Reassessments and New Approaches*, ed. Jay M. Smith (University Park: Pennsylvania State University Press, 2006), 60, 63; William Doyle, *Venality: The Sale of Offices in Eighteenth-Century France* (Oxford: Clarendon Press, 1996), 10, 12–13, 51; Chérin, *Abrégé chronologique*, 279–81.

37. Davis Bitton, *The French Nobility in Crisis, 1560–1640* (Stanford, CA: Stanford University Press, 1969), 97.
38. Noble indignation over venal practices was not new. Jay M. Smith records complaints from the 1560s and notes particular outrage over a 1604 edict allowing the inheritance of many such positions (Smith, *The Culture of Merit: Nobility, Royal Service, and the Making of Absolute Monarchy in France, 1600–1789* [Ann Arbor: University of Michigan Press, 1996, 11–12]).
39. Quoted in Daniel Dessert, *Argent, pouvoir et société au grand siècle* (Paris: Fayard, 1984), 82–83; Bitton, *French Nobility in Crisis*, 47, 61, 99.
40. Guyot, *Répertoire universel*, 63:10; Chérin, *Abrégé chronologique*, 97, 122–23, 134, 245.
41. Hédouin, *De l'Usurpation*, 51–55.
42. Hédouin, *De l'Usurpation*, 51–55, see also Ravel, *The Would-Be Commoner*, 102–5.
43. Chérin, *Abrégé chronologique*, 221, 240, 243; Hédouin, *De l'Usurpation*, 66; Guyot, *Répertoire universel*, 41:470–73.
44. Chérin, *Abrégé chronologique*, 237.
45. Julius-Clarus [Giulio Claro], quoted in Jousse, *Traité de la justice criminelle*, 3:366; Vouglans, *Les Lois criminelles de France*, 271.
46. Sylvie Steinberg, *La Confusion des sexes: Le travestissement de la Renaissance à la Révolution* (Paris: Fayard, 2001), 32–33, 40–49; Jousse, *Traité de la justice criminelle*, 3:367; Gabriel de Lurbe, *Chronique Bourdeloise* (Bordeaux: Simon Millnages, 1619), 45v–46r.
47. Enfin sous l'habit de fille
Est reconnu Montempuis.
C'est en vain qu'un loup s'habille,
De la peau d'une brebis.
Plus elle fit de grimaces,
Et plus on voulut savoir;
Voici, dit quelqu'un, des traces
De la barbe et du rasoir.

"L'Aventure de M. de Montempuis," E. Raunié, ed., *Chansonnier historique du XVIIIe siècle*, 10 vols. (Paris: A. Quantin, 1879–1884), 5:92–100; Edmond-Jean-François Barbier, *Chronique de la régence et du règne du Louis XV (1718–1763), ou Journal de Barbier*, 8 vols. (Paris: Charpentier, 1857), 1:250–51. Montempuis's "adventure" was in December 1726.

48. Pitaval, *Causes celebres et interessantes*, 18:288; see also Steinberg, *La Confusion des sexes*, 91–95.
49. Pitaval, *Causes celebres et interessantes*, 18:238–39.
50. Pitaval, *Causes celebres et interessantes*, 18:254.
51. Pitaval, *Causes celebres et interessantes*, 18:280–81.
52. Pitaval, *Causes celebres et interessantes*, 18:281.
53. François-Timoléon de Choisy, *Mémoires pour servir à l'histoire de Louis XIV / Mémoires de l'abbé de Choisy habillé en femme* (Paris: Mercure de France, 1966), 30–31.
54. Jean-Yves Vialleton, "La nouvelle diffamatoire dans la France de l'âge classique: le cas particulier de *La Vie de Monsieur l'abbé de Choisy*," *Cahiers d'études italiennes* 10 (2010): 163–64.

55. François-Timoléon de Choisy, *Mémoires*, 431.
56. François-Timoléon de Choisy, *Mémoires*, 476, 485, 456, 477–78.
57. François-Timoléon de Choisy, *Mémoires*, 485–86, 436.
58. Jean Le Rond d'Alembert, *Éloges lus dans les séances publiques de l'Académie française* (Paris: Panckoucke, 1779), 315; C.-A. Sainte-Beuve, "Lundi gras, 3 mars, 1851, L'abbé de Choisy," in *Causeries de lundi*, 15 vols. (Paris: Garnier Frères, 1851–1862), 3:332; Dirk Van der Cruysse, *L'Abbé de Choisy, androgyn et mandarin* (Paris: Fayard, 1995), 295, 424n39; and Vialleton, "La nouvelle diffamatoire dans la France de l'âge classique," 169n41.
59. Louis de Rouvroy, duc de Saint-Simon, *Mémoires: Additions au Journal de Dangeau*, 8 vols. (Paris: Bibliothèque de la Pléiade, 1983–1988), 6:496–98.
60. See Paul Scott, "Authenticity and Textual Transvestism in the Memoirs of the Abbé de Choisy," *French Studies: A Quarterly Review* 60 (2015): 15–21.
61. *Histoire de Madame la Comtesse des Barres, A Madame la Marquise de Lambert* (Antwerp: Van der Haye, 1735).
62. *La Vie de Monsieur l'abbé de Choisy de l'Académie française* (Lausanne and Geneva: Marc-Michel Bousquet, 1742), vi–vii, x, xiii, 238.
63. On the authorship of *La Vie de Monsieur l'abbé de Choisy de l'Académie française*, see Van der Cruysse, *L'Abbé de Choisy*, 29, 295, 424n39; and Vialleton, "La nouvelle diffamatoire dans la France de l'âge classique," 169n41.
64. The archives of the abbé de Choisy, which were left to the marquis d'Argenson, are widely disparate. They include fragments of history and biography, a miscellany of airs, poems, and songs, and the substantial manuscript *Memoirs to Serve as a History of Louis XIV*. They also include narratives recounting the lives of Mme de Sancy and the comtesse des Barres. The handwriting across the manuscripts is not consistent. That of the Sancy and Barres stories matches no other writing in the collection. The identifiable hand of Argenson, who undertook an initial organization of this material, appears throughout. It was Argenson who gave the untitled pages about Sancy and Barres a single heading: "Aventures de labbé de choisy, habilé en femme." Apart from the title added by Argenson, the name Choisy does not appear in these pages.

    In *Essays in the Style of Montaigne*, Argenson writes: "[I was] unable to refuse sharing these [manuscripts] with a woman who belonged to our family and was curious to read them. She kept them for a long time and passed them on to the abbé d'Olivet. This latter extracted a work in two small volumes, which he had published in Holland with the title *Memoirs to Serve as a History of Louis XIV*, by the late abbé de Choisy of the Académie Française. . . . One of the manuscripts left to me contains his story under the name of the comtesse des Barres. It has not yet been published, but I believe that it will be [published], as the same person who permitted the publication of *Memoirs of the Abbé de Choisy* also shared copies of this work" (*Essais dans le goût de ceux de Montaigne, Composés en 1736*, 2 vols. [Amsterdam: n.p., 1785], 2:85–86, 89–90; see also 2:96, 129).

    The following notation by Argenson appears near the beginning of the third volume of Choisy's manuscripts, which contains the stories of Mme de Sancy and the comtesse des Barres. "This volume, as well as the two preceding [volumes], are a part of several manuscripts that were left at the time of the death of the abbé de Choisy to one of his relatives, who put them in order and preserved their impression as much as he was able; however, being unable to prevent several people from reading them who had the same right as he, we have now seen the public appearance of the memoirs of the Reign of Louis 14 and a part of those that compose the present volume, but the entire first volume and half of this latter [i.e., the first-person narrative of Mme de Sancy] have eluded this Thief" (M. 3188, Bibliothèque de l'Arsenal).

The three manuscript volumes as indexed by Argenson are: "Ouvrages De Mr. L. de Choisy, qui n'ont pas été Imprimés" (Ms. 3186), "Ouvrages de M L'abbé de Choisy, qui n'ont pas été imprimés. Tome 2.—Suite des pieces continües dans ce volume / Memoires pour servir a l'histoire de Louis 14 / Fragmens d'un conversation touchant letat de la cour en Decembre 1720" (Ms. 3187), and "Ouvrages de M. L'abbé de Choisy qui n'ont point été imprimez / 1724/ Tome 3e / contenant 5. fragments des avantures de cet ecclesiastique habillé en femme" (Ms. 3188). An additional volume of manuscripts, the miscellany of airs, poems, and songs, is labeled "Sottisier ou Receuil de chansons, poësies, et autres pieces satyriques. 1er Volume" (Ms. 2935).

A curious detail concerning Choisy's history of Louis XIV suggests evidence of tampering in a way that ties the priest's life more closely to the content of the Barres manuscript. An early page of the manuscript, which was bound after Choisy's death, does not match any of its other 386 pages. It has aged to a darker shade of brown, page hinges indicate that it has been tipped into the bound volume, a half page has been glued over the verso to cover earlier text, and, most notably, there are significantly more lines of text on both the recto and verso (30 in both cases) than on most other pages of the volume, which average 22 lines each. The text on both sides starts higher on the page, and the handwriting, which differs from that of the other pages, is smaller. Both modifications would allow the addition of material while preserving end-line continuity with the previous and succeeding pages.

This page contains the work's sole reference to Choisy's supposed cross-dressing. It includes an account of his mother dressing him as a girl: "One will laugh to see me dressed as a girl until I was eighteen. My mother will not be forgiven for having wanted [original word, "suffered," crossed out] this." A passage near the beginning of the Sancy story closely resembles these sentences. The page also contains the words of a woman at court claiming that Choisy had lived as both a man and a woman, "always in extremes, plunged in either study or frivolity, admirable for a courage that would lead to great endeavor but contemptible for flirting like a little girl, and, in each of these different guises, led always by pleasure." D'Alembert quoted this passage in summing up Choisy's life in his speech before the Académie. The page also refers to "the journey to Bordeaux," which echoes a reference to "my escapades at Bordeaux" in the Barres manuscript.

If the abbé d'Olivet wished to write evidence into Choisy's *Memoirs to Serve as a History of Louis XIV* to align with details in the stories of Sancy and Barres, this would be the way to do so. The passage appears in L'abbé de Choisy, *Mémoires pour servir à l'histoire de Louis XIV suivi de Mémoires de l'abbé de Choisy habillé en femme* (Paris: Mercure de France, 1966), 32–33.

65. Argenson, *Essais*, 2:90, 85.
66. Alexis Piron, *Piron: Complément de ses oeuvres inédites* (Paris: F. Sartorius, 1866), 45, 377–78; George Louis Leclerc, comte de Buffon, *Correspondance inédite de Buffon*, 2 vols. (Paris: Hachette, 1860), 1:268.

67. Jean-Baptiste-Henri de Valincour, "Du véritable usage de l'étude des belles-lettres. Dans sa réponse au discours de réception de M. de Portail, premier président, prononcé le 28 décembre 1724, lorqu'il fut reçu à la place de M. l'abbé de Choisy," *Choix de discours de réception à l'Académie françoise*, 2 vols. (Paris: Demonville, 1808), 1:157–58.
68. Jonathan Dewald, *Aristocratic Experience and the Origins of Modern Culture: France, 1570–1715* (Berkeley: University of California Press, 1993), xii, 44.
69. Quoted in Courtine and Haroche, *Histoire du visage*, 185–86.
70. Quoted in Courtine and Haroche, *Histoire du visage*, 186–87.
71. La Chétardie, *Instructions pour un jeune seigneur*, 85–86.
72. Blaise Pascal, "Trois discours sur la condition des grands," *Opuscules*, in *Oeuvres complètes* (Paris: Bibliothèque de la Pléiade, 1954), 619.
73. René-Louis de Voyer, marquis d'Argenson, *Mémoires et journal inédit du marquis d'Argenson*, 5 vols. (Paris: P. Jannet, 1857–1858), 1:71.
74. Pascal, "Trois discours," 617.
75. Pascal, "L'Ordre de la justice véritable," *Pensées*, in *Oeuvres complètes*, 1167.

CHAPTER FOUR

1. Jean Anouilh, *Pièces brillantes: L'Invitation au château, Colombe, La Répétition ou L'Amour puni, L'École des pères* (Paris: La Table ronde, 1951), 375.
2. Marivaux, *Le Cabinet du philosophe*, in *Journaux et oeuvres diverses* (Paris: Garnier Frères, 1969), 389.
3. Marivaux, *Le Cabinet du philosophe*, 404–5, 408–9.
4. Marivaux, *Le Cabinet du philosophe*, 400–401.
5. Marivaux, *Le Cabinet du philosophe*, 417–18.
6. Marivaux, *Le Cabinet du philosophe*, 419.
7. Marivaux, *Le Spectateur français*, in *Journaux et oeuvres diverses*, 118.
8. Marivaux, *Lettres sur les habitants de Paris*, in *Journaux et oeuvres diverses*, 28.
9. Marivaux, *Le Cabinet du philosophe*, in *Journaux et oeuvres diverses*, 377–78.
10. Marivaux, *Lettres sur les habitants de Paris*, in *Journaux et oeuvres diverses*, 26–27.
11. Marivaux, *L'Indigent philosophe*, in *Journaux et oeuvres diverses*, 308, 314.
12. Marivaux, *Lettres sur les habitants de Paris*, in *Journaux et oeuvres diverses*, 26.
13. Marivaux, *Lettres sur les habitants de Paris*, 25–26; Marivaux, *La Vie de Marianne, ou les aventures de Madame la comtesse de **** (Paris: Garnier Frères, 1963), 51–52, 61–62.
14. Marivaux, *Le Paysan parvenu* (Paris: Garnier Frères, 1959), 140.
15. Marivaux, *Le Paysan parvenu*, 171–72, 187.
16. Marivaux, *Le Paysan parvenu*, 5–6.
17. Marivaux, *Le Paysan parvenu*, 265–67.
18. Marivaux, *Le Paysan parvenu*, 248–49.
19. Marivaux, *La Vie de Marianne*, 15.
20. Marivaux, *La Vie de Marianne*, 33.
21. Marivaux, *La Vie de Marianne*, 329. The critic Christopher Rivers, who has written about physiognomy and the French novel, notes that Marianne's attributes do not in themselves make her worthy of respect. Rather, in the minds of her and her companions, they "serve as a proof that she is of noble birth and *therefore* worthy

of respect" (Christopher Rivers, *Face Value: Physiognomical Thought and the Legible Body in Marivaux, Lavater, Balzac, Gautier, and Zola* [Madison: University of Wisconsin Press, 1994], 55).

22. Marivaux, *La Vie de Marianne*, 213. For an excellent discussion of the place of politeness in Marivaux's thought, see Peter France, *Politeness and Its Discontents* (Cambridge: Cambridge University Press, 1992), 67–69. A valuable study of falseness in Marivaux's work is Harold Schaad, *Le Thème de l'être et du paraître dans l'oeuvre de Marivaux* (Zurich: Juris Druck, 1969).
23. Marivaux, *L'Île de la raison*, in Pierre Carlet de Chamblain de Marivaux, *Théâtre complet* (Paris: Éditions du Seuil, 1964), 225.
24. D'Alembert, "Éloge de Marvaux," in Marivaux, *Théâtre complet*, 24.
25. Marivaux, *Le Spectateur français*, 315–16.
26. Marivaux, *Le Cabinet du philosophe*, 364.
27. Schaad, *Le Thème de l'être et du paraître*, 77.
28. *An Agreeable Criticism, of the City of Paris and the French* (London: Ben. Bragg, 1704), 43.
29. Jean Baptiste de La Salle, *Les Règles de la bienséance et de la civilité chrétienne* (Paris; François Rivière, 1708), iv; Roger Chartier, *The Cultural Uses of Print in Early Modern France*, trans. Lydia G. Cochrane (Princeton, NJ: Princeton University Press, 1987), 90–91.
30. La Salle, *Règles de la bienséance*, 154.
31. La Salle, *Règles de la bienséance*, 249–50.
32. Quoted in Jacques Revel, "The Uses of Civility," in *Passions of the Renaissance*, ed. Roger Chartier, vol. 3 of *A History of Private Life*, ed. Philippe Ariès and Georges Duby, trans. Arthur Goldhammer (Cambridge, MA: Harvard University Press, 1989), 200–201.
33. Louis-Sébastian Mercier, *Tableau de Paris*, quoted in Revel, "The Uses of Civility," 199.
34. Quoted in Chartier, *The Cultural Uses of Print*, 95.
35. "Ebauche du Portrait du Parisien," April 9, 1731, in *Le Glaneur historique, moral, litteraire & galant* (n.p.: n.p., n.d.), n.p.
36. Louis de Jaucourt, "Civilité, Politesse, Affabilité (synonymes)," in Denis Diderot, ed., *Encyclopédie, ou Dictionnaire raisonné des sciences, des arts et des métiers*, 25 vols. (Paris: Chez Briasson, 1751–1765), 3:497.
37. François-Marie Arouet de Voltaire, *Zaïre*, in *Oeuvres complètes*, 52 vols. (Paris: Garnier Frères, 1881), 2:553.
38. Quoted in Jean-Jacques Courtine and Claudine Haroche, *Histoire du visage: Exprimer et taire ses émotions (XVIe-début XIXe siècle)* (Paris: Éditions Rivages, 1988), 256.
39. Jean-François Bastide, *Dictionnaire des moeurs* (The Hague: n.p., 1773), 63.
40. Quoted in Daniel Roche, *The Culture of Clothing: Dress and Fashion in the "Ancien Régime,"* trans. Jean Birrell (Cambridge: Cambridge University Press, 1994), 49, 39.
41. Nicolas de La Mare, *Traité de la police*, 4 vols. (Paris: Chez Jean et Pierre, 1705–1738), 1:391.
42. Charles Loyseau, *A Treatise on Orders*, in *The Old Regime and the French Revolution*, ed. Keith Baker, vol. 7, *University of Chicago Readings in Western Civilization* (Chicago: University of Chicago Press, 1987), 16–17; Roche, *The Culture of*

Clothing, 40; Roland Mousnier, *La Vénalité des offices sous Henri IV et Louis XIII* (Paris: Presses Universitaires de France, 1971), 529.

43. *Ordonnance de Monsieur le Prevost de Paris au Monsieur son lieutenant General de Police* (Paris: Chez Denys Thierry, 1675); *Les Paradoxes d'état servant d'entretien aux bons esprits* (1651), quoted in Jennifer Jones, *Sexing la mode: Gender, Fashion, and Commercial Culture in Old Regime France* (New York: Berg, 2004), 205; [François de Callières], *Des Mots à la mode, et des nouvelles façons de parler* (Paris: Chez Thomas Amaulry, 1693), 9–10.
44. William H. Sewell Jr. describes the later eighteenth century's "vestimentary anonymity" that grew from a mingling of fashion across ranks in *Capitalism and the Emergence of Civic Equality in Eighteenth-Century France* (Chicago: University of Chicago Press, 2021), 134.
45. *Chronique de la Régence et du règne de Louis XV (1718–1763) ou Journal de Barbier*, February 23, 1745, quoted in Philippe Perrot, *La Travail des apparences, ou Les Transformations du corps féminin XVIIIe–XIXe siècle* (Paris: Éditions du Seuil, 1984), 38.
46. Quoted in Sewell, *Capitalism and the Emergence of Civic Equality*, 132.
47. Perrot, *La Travail des apparences*, 38; Sewell, *Capitalism and the Emergence of Civic Equality*, 133.
48. Roche, *The Culture of Clothing*, 136–48.
49. Roche, *The Culture of Clothing*, 112, 145, 174; Sewell, *Capitalism and the Emergence of Civic Equality*, 135.
50. *La Bibliothèque des Dames*, May 28, 1764, quoted in Perrot, *La Travail des apparences*, 222; Cissie Fairchilds, "The Production and Marketing of Populuxe Goods in Eighteenth-Century Paris," in *Consumption and the World of Goods*, ed. John Brewer and Roy Porter (London and New York: Routledge, 1993), 230.
51. M. de Saint-Haippy [Antoine-Prosper Lottin], *Discours contre le luxe: Il corrompt les Moeurs, & détruit les Empires* (Paris: Veuve Herissant, 1783), 10.
52. Montesquieu, *De l'Esprit des lois*, in Charles de Secondat, baron de Montesquieu, *Oeuvres complètes*, 2 vols. (Paris: Éditions Gallimard, 1949), 2:262.
53. Montesquieu, *De l'Esprit des lois*, 2:255–566, 2:263.
54. Robert Shackleton, *Montesquieu: A Critical Biography* (Oxford: Oxford University Press, 1961), 370–77.
55. Losfeld, *Politesse, moral et construction sociale*, 265.
56. Quoted in Mathieu-Guillaume-Therèse Villenave, "Notice," in Charles-Pinot Duclos, *Oeuvres de Duclos*, 3 vols. (Paris: Belin, 1821), 1:iii, xliv, x.
57. Charles-Pinot Duclos, *Considérations sur les moeurs de ce siècle* (London: n.p., 1784), 60, 65.
58. Duclos, *Considérations sur les moeurs de ce siècle*, 37, 20, 43.
59. Jay M. Smith, *Nobility Reimagined: The Patriotic Nation in Eighteenth-Century France* (Ithaca, NY: Cornell University Press, 2018), 103.
60. François Vincent Toussaint, *Les Moeurs* (Amsterdam: n.p., 1749), 197–98.
61. Toussaint, *Les Moeurs*, 147–48; Marie-Rose de Labriolle, "François Vincent Toussaint (1715–1772)," in *Dictionnaire des journalistes (1600–1789)*, ed. Jean Sgard (Oxford: Oxford University Press, 1999), 2:355–57.
62. Toussaint, *Les Moeurs*, 123.
63. Rousseau to M. de Malesherbes, January 12, 1762, in Jean-Jacques Rousseau, *Oeuvres complètes de J. J. Rousseau*, 19 vols. (Paris: Hachette, 1872), 10:300–302.

64. Rousseau to Christophe de Beaumont, quoted in Jean Starobinski, *Jean-Jacques Rousseau: Transparency and Obstruction*, trans. Arthur Goldhammer (Chicago: University of Chicago Press, 1971), 5.
65. Rousseau, *Discours sur les sciences et les arts*, in *Oeuvres complètes*, 3:8.
66. Rousseau, *Discours sur l'origine et les fondemens de l'inégalité parmi les hommes*, in *Oeuvres complètes*, 3:169–70.
67. Rousseau, *Discours sur l'origine*, 3:193.
68. Rousseau, *Émile, ou, De l'Éducation*, in *Oeuvres complètes*, 4:515.
69. Rousseau, *Émile, ou, De l'Éducation*, 4:669.
70. Starobinski, *Jean-Jacques Rousseau*, 4.
71. Rousseau, *Rousseau, Juge de Jean-Jacques*, in *Oeuvres complètes*, 2:860; Starobinski, *Jean-Jacques Rousseau*, 254.
72. Rousseau, *Les Confessions*, in *Oeuvres complètes*, 1:175; Starobinski, *Jean-Jacques Rousseau*, 182.
73. See Starobinski, *Jean-Jacques Rousseau*, 15–20.
74. Rousseau, *Julie, ou La Nouvelle Héloïse*, in *Oeuvres completes*, 2:689.
75. Rousseau, *Du Contract social*, in *Oeuvres complètes*, 3:361.
76. M. Gautier, "Réfutation d'un discours qui a remporté le prix de l'Académie de Dijon en l'année 1750," *Mercure de France*, October 1751.
77. "Sur les avantages des Sciences & des Arts, prononcé dans l'assemblée publique de l'Académie des Sciences & Belles-Lettres de Lyon, le 22 Juin 1751," *Mercure de France*, December 1751.
78. [Gabriel François Coyer], *Les Masques* (n.p., n.d.), 16.

CHAPTER FIVE

1. Victor de Riqueti, marquis de Mirabeau, *L'Ami des femmes, ou Traité de la civilisation*, unpublished manuscript quoted in Alain Pons, "Sur la notion de 'civilité,'" in *Etiquette et politesse*, ed. Alain Montandon (Clermont-Ferrand: Faculté des Lettres et Sciences Humaines, 1992), 29.
2. Jeanne-Louise-Henriette Campan, *Mémoires sur la vie privée de Marie-Antoinette*, 3 vols. (Paris: Baudouin Frères, 1822), 1:164–65.
3. "Reglement concernant la permision accordée à l'Académie Royale de Musique, de donner des Bals publics. A Paris, le 30 Décember 1715," in Jacques Bernard Durey de Noinville, *Histoire du théâtre de l'opéra en France*, 2 vols. (Paris: J. Barbu, 1753), 1:149.
4. "Reglement concernant la permision accordée à l'Académie Royale de Musique," 1:160–64; Richard Semmens, *The bals publics at the Paris Opera in the Eighteenth Century* (Hillsdale, NY: Pendragon Press, 2004), 37–43. A 1781 list of personnel and their responsibilities for balls includes a doorman who was also in charge of providing masks for the musicians ("État du payement à faire aux employés préposés de l'Académie Royale de Musique pour les 17 bals donnés depuis la dimanche 12 nov. 1780 jusqu'au mardi 27 fev. 1781"), AJ^{13} 23-VIII, A. N., Paris.
5. Semmens, *The bal publics at the Paris Opera*, 66–67, 76.
6. Jean-François Barbier, *Chronique de la régence et du règne du Louis XV (1718–1763), ou Journal de Barbier*, 8 vols. (Paris: Charpentier, 1857), 1:170.
7. Dans ce séjour fertile

L'amour offre un azile
Pour s'aimer.
Tout est utile
Pour s'exprimer,
Le secret est facile
De s'enflâmer;
Et l'on en trouve mille
Pour charmer.

"Le Bal de l'Opéra," *Mercure galant*, February 1617, 276; see also *Chansonnier historique du XVIIIe siècle*, ed. E. Raunié, 10 vols. (Paris: A. Quantin, 1879–1884), 2:3–4.

8. *Mercure galant*, February 1716, 188–93.
9. Quoted in Semmens, *The bals publics at the Paris Opera in the Eighteenth Century*, 94.
10. Quel spectacle étonnant se présente à mes yeux!
Je vois le Régent de la France
Ne s'occuper que de bals et de danse . . .
Et sans cesse avilir son rang et ses aïeux.

"Les Favoris du Régent" (1716), in Raunié, ed., *Chansonnier historique*, 2:10–11.

11. "Ordonnance de la police. 12 février 1718," in Nicolas de La Mare, *Traité de la police*. Similar versions of this ordinance, which forbids masked person from carrying swords, canes, and all other weapons, were issued in 1685, 1720, 1722, 1725, and 1729 (Ms. Fr. 21625, fols. 119–26, 195. B. N., Paris); "Reglement concernant la permision accordée à l'Académie Royale de Musique," in Durey de Noinville, *Histoire du théâtre de l'opéra en France*, 1:149.
12. November 27 and 29, 1724, Ms. 10856, f. 215, f. 222; November 3, 1724, Ms. 12479, Archives de la Bastille, Bibliothèque de l'Arsenal, Paris. I am grateful to Jeffrey S. Ravel for sharing these two documents with me.
13. Louis François Armand Du Plessis, duc de Richelieu, *Mémoires du maréchal duc de Richelieu*, 2 vols. (Paris: Firmin Didot, 1868), 1:70–74; "D'Argenson à Bernaville, 18 mai 1716" and footnote 2, Ravaisson-Mollien, *Les Archives de la Bastille*, 12:86.
14. Jean Buvat, *Journal de la Régence (1715–1723)*, 2 vols. (Paris: Henri Plon, 1865), 1:251.
15. [Louis Petit de Bachaumont and Mathieu François Pidanzat de Mairobert], *Mémoires secrets pour servir à l'histoire de la république des lettres en France, depuis MDCCLXII jusqu'à nos jours*, 21 vols. (London: John Adamson, 1777–1788), December 3, 1767, 3:261, February 7, 1771, 6:93, January 10, 1775, 7:262; *Mercure galant*, April, 1764, 2; Charlotte-Elisabeth, duchesse d'Orléans, *Corréspondance complète*, 2 vols. (Paris: Charpentier, 1855), February 27, 1721, 2:302–3; *Les Corréspondances de la marquise de Balleroy*, ed. Édouard de Barthélemy, 2 vols. (Paris: Hachette, 1883), 1:69.
16. Barbier, *Journal historique*, March 4, 1737, 2:142–43; Luynes, *Mémoires*, 1:197–201.
17. René-Louis de Voyer, marquis d'Argenson, *Journal et mémoires du marquis d'Argenson*, 9 vols. (Paris: J. Renouard, 1859–1867), 2:65.
18. Luynes, *Mémoires*, 2:361–62.

19. Campan, *Mémoires sur la vie privée*, 3:35–36.
20. Barbier, *Journal historique*, February 23, 1745, 4:16.
21. Barbier, *Journal historique*, February 25, 1745, 4:20.
22. Luynes, *Mémoires*, 5:298–300; Barbier, *Chronique de la régence*, February, 1739, 3:157.
23. Luynes, *Mémoires*, 2:344.
24. Barbier, *Chronique de la Régence*, February 25, 1745, 4:20.
25. Luynes, *Mémoires*, 6:323–24.
26. Luynes, *Mémoires*, 6:324.
27. La femme la plus sage
Dirait sans doute aussi:
Loin d'ici le scrupule,
Ce serait ridicule
De fuir le canal
Qui fait fermier général.

"Les Amours du roi," in E. Raunié, ed., *Chansonnier historique du XVIIIe siècle*, 7:52.
28. Luynes, *Mémoires*, 6:288, 6:296, 6:354, 10:97.
29. Simon-Henri Dubuisson to the marquis de Caumont, March 8, 1737, in Dubuisson, *Lettres du Commissaire Dubuisson au Marquis de Caumont, 1735–1741* (Paris: P. Arnould, 1882), 349; Argenson, *Journal et mémoires du marquis d'Argenson*, 2:65–66.
30. P. J. B. Nougaret, *Anecdotes secrètes du dix-huitième siècle*, 2 vols. (Paris: Léopold Collin, 1808), March 18, 1775, 1:82; Louis-François Métra, "Post-Scriptum au N. 13. Du 20 mars 1775," *Corréspondance littéraire secrète*, 97–98.
31. [Bachaumont and Mairobert], *Mémoires secrets*, March 4, 1778, 11:131.
32. Campan, *Mémoires sur la vie privée*, 1:164; Auguste-François de Frénilly, *Souvenirs de Baron de Frénilly* (Paris: Plon-Nourrit, 1908), 30.
33. [Bachaumont and Mairobert], *Mémoires secrets*, February 20, 1787, 34:170.
34. [Bachaumont and Mairobert], *Mémoires secrets*, June 3, 1782, 20:282; Henriette-Louise von Waldner, baronne d'Oberkirch, *Mémoires de la Baronne d'Oberkirch sur la cour de Louis XVI* (Paris: Mercure de France, 1989), 184, 198–99.
35. [Bachaumont and Mairobert], *Mémoires secrets*, February 11, 1768, 3:302.
36. Louis François Armand Du Plessis, duc de Richelieu, *Mémoires du maréchal duc de Richelieu*, 9 vols. (Paris: Chez Buisson, 1790–1793), 2:144–45; report dated February 6, 1746, Ms. 11592, f. 292, Bibliothèque de l'Arsenal: Archives de la Bastille, Paris; [Bachaumont and Mairobert], *Mémoires secrets*, February 5, 1758, 3:296; Nougaret, *Anecdotes secrètes*, February 21, 1781, 2:356.
37. Nougaret, *Anecdotes secrètes*, March 5, 1776, 2:309.
38. *Paris vu tel qu'il est* (Paris: n.p., 1781), 29.
39. Louis-Sébastien Mercier, *Tableau de Paris*, 11 vols. (Geneva: Slatkine Reprints, 1979), 3:128; *Encyclopédie méthodique*, 315; [Bachaumont and Mairobert,] *Mémoires secrets*, February 20, 1787, 34:170–71.
40. David Garrioch, *The Making of Revolutionary Paris* (Berkeley: University of California Press, 2002), 262.
41. C'est là que se rallie au cri du ridicule
Le peuple travesti qui dans nos murs circule;

C'est là qu'un vaste amas de bouffons renaissants,
En délire, en tumulte, attroupe les passants. . . .
Les sexes sont changés: l'homme endosse un corset
Dont sa large carrure a rompu le lacet;
La femme en spadassin affectant la rudesse,
De ses souples contours décèle la mollesse.

Antoine-Marin Le Mierre, *Les Fastes, ou Les Usages de l'année, poëme en seize chants* (Paris: Gueffier, 1779), 46–47.

42. Sylvie Steinberg, *La Confusion des sexes: Le travestissement de la Renaissance à la Révolution* (Paris: Fayard, 2001), 19–20.
43. Furetière's *Dictionnaire universel* includes the carnival taunt "*Il a chié au lit*" in its 1727 version but not the original edition of 1690. The designation *chie-en-lit/ chienlit* for carnival maskers first appears in the 1762 edition of the *Dictionnaire de l'Académie française*.
44. Mercier, *Tableau de Paris*, 5:245; *La Galerie des cris du carnaval: ou Sujets de plusieurs tableaux* (Paris: n.p., 1759), 4–7.
45. *Foiriana: Recueil piquant et amusant, pour les Amateurs* (n.p.: n.p., n.d.), 45; "Fragments de Caquire, Parodie de *Zaïre*," in *Foiriana*, 2–30.
46. Events of the following paragraphs are drawn from a systematic review of police reports filed during each year's carnival season. See "Plaintes, procès-verbaux et informations au Petit Criminel, 1735–91" (Y 9649A–Y 10017), A. N., Paris.
47. Jean Moutier, March 11, 1764; Jean-Louis Lefranc, March 13, 1764, Y 9695, A. N., Paris.
48. Report by Denis Girard, avocat en Parlement Conseiller du Roy, Commissaire au Châtelet de Paris, March 6, 1764, Y 9695, A. N., Paris.
49. Untitled report, March 9, 1764; Jean Baptiste d'Elfebvre, March 10, 1764; Sr. Benoist Rameau, March 6, 1764, Y 9695, A. N., Paris.
50. Claude Nicolas Le Doux, March 22, 1764; Julie Cantelou, March 21, 1764; Jean Legois, March 11, 1764; Pierre Lamy, March 6, 1764; Jean Baptise, March 11, 1764, Y 9695, A. N., Paris.
51. René-François-André, comte De la Tour du Pin, March 6, 1764, and Denis Girard, March 6, 1764, Y 9695, A. N., Paris.
52. July 21, 1764, "Parlement de Paris, Parlement criminel," X 2a 824, A. N., Paris.
53. Rétif de La Bretonne, *Les nuits de Paris, ou L'observateur nocturne*, 7 vols. (London: n.p., 1789), 1:96–97; February 3, 1761, Y 9658, A. N., Paris.
54. March 1, 1786, Y 9959, A. N., Paris.
55. March 3, 1772, Y 9790, A. N., Paris.
56. March 5, 1764, Y 9695, A. N., Paris.
57. [Bachaumont and Pidanzat de Mairobert,] *Mémoires secrets*, 17:82–83.
58. Siméon-Prosper Hardy, *Mes Loisirs, ou Journal d'Evénements, tels qu'ils parviennent à ma connaissance*, February 6, 1785, 6:58, Ms. Fr. 6685, B. N., Paris.
59. **M**auvais ami, plus mauvais citoien,
Ardent au mal, de glace pour le bien,
Vil escrément, rebut de al nature,
Paitri de fiel, d'orgueil et d'imposture,
Ennemi né des soutiens de la loi,
On reconnoit a semblable peinture,

Un traître infâme a la france, a son roi.

"Acrostiche de Maupeou," *Epigrammes, couplets, et vaudevilles. Relatifs à la révolution de 1771, et aux changements survenûs dans La Magistrature*, Y 11738, A. N., Paris.

60. C'est ainsi qu'en traçant la route
du poignard jusques a ton coeur
je veux t'abbreuver goutte a goutte,
du calice de la terreur,
[. . .]
j'insulte en paix a tes ennuis,
et, si Louis ne t'extermine,
c'est en te perçant la poitrine
que je t'apprendrai qui je suis

"Les Chancelières. Ode premiere," Y 11738, A. N., Paris.

61. Arlette Farge, *Vivre dans la rue à Paris au XVIIIe siècle* (Paris: Éditions Gallimard, 1979), 137, 101, 148, 124; Farge, *Fragile Lives: Violence, Power and Solidarity in Eighteenth-Century Paris*, trans. Carol Shelton (Cambridge, MA: Harvard University Press, 1993), 19–20.
62. La Bretonne, *Les Nuits de Paris*, 7:149.
63. La Bretonne, *Les Nuits de Paris*, 8:157, 1:100–101.
64. La Bretonne, *Les Nuits de Paris*, 7:150–51.
65. Hippolyte Taine, *Les origines de la France contemporaine* (Paris: Hachette, 1876–95), 1:200; Charles Joseph, prince de Ligne, *Lettres à Eugénie sur les spectacles* (Brussels: Chez Valade, 1774), 4–5.
66. Philippe Perrot, "La vérité des apparences ou le drame du corps bourgeois (XVIIIe–XIXe siècles)," *Cahiers internationaux de Sociologie* 76 (1984):186.
67. Guy Chaussinand-Nogaret, *La Noblesse au XVIIIe siècle. De la Féodalité aux lumières* (Paris: Hachette, 1976), 44–49; Chérin, *Abrégé chronologique d'édits*, lv.
68. Emmanuel-Joseph Sieyès, *Qu-est ce que le tiers état?* (Paris: n.p., 1789), 9n1.
69. Alexis de Tocqueville, *The Old Regime and the French Revolution*, trans. Alan S. Kahan, 2 vols. (Chicago: University of Chicago Press, 1998), 1:152; Bossenga, "A Divided Nobility," in *The French Nobility in the Eighteenth Century: Reassessments and New Approaches*, ed. Jay M. Smith (University Park: Pennsylvania State University Press, 2006), 53.
70. Pierre Serna, "The Noble," in *Enlightenment Portraits*, ed. Michel Vovelle, trans. Lydia G. Cochrane (Chicago: University of Chicago Press, 1997), 45–47; Chaussinand-Nogaret, *La Noblesse au XVIIIe siècle*, 141–42, 54.
71. Serna, "The Noble," 35; Chaussinand-Nogaret, *La Noblesse au XVIIIe siècle*, 69–70.
72. Roger Chartier contrasts the new authority of public opinion in these decades with society's pervasive insincerity. "When the concept of 'public opinion' did emerge, it effected a dual rupture. It countered the art of pretense, dissimulation, and secrecy by appealing to a transparency that was to ensure the visibility of intentions. Before the tribunal of opinion all causes were to be argued without duplicity: causes that evidently had justice and reason on their side would necessarily triumph" (Chartier, in *The Cultural Origins of the French Revolution*, trans. Lydia G. Cochrane [Durham, NC: Duke University Press, 1991], 33).

73. See Jessica Riskin, *Science in the Age of Sensibility: The Sentimental Empiricists of the French Enlightenment* (Chicago: University of Chicago Press, 2002).
74. Claude Labrosse, *Lire au XVIII*[e] *siècle* (Lyon: Presses Universitaires de Lyon, 1985), 23–32; Robert Darnton, "Readers Respond to Rousseau: The Fabrication of Romantic Sensitivity," in *The Great Cat Massacre and Other Episodes in French Cultural History* (New York: Basic Books, 1984), 245.
75. Carol Blum, *Rousseau and the Republic of Virtue: The Language of Politics in the French Revolution* (Ithaca, NY: Cornell University Press, 1986), 135–36; [François-Thomas-Marie de Baculard] d'Arnaud, *Délassements de l'homme sensible, ou anecdotes diverses*, 6 vols. (Paris: Veuve Ballard, 1783–1787).
76. See William Reddy, "Sentimentalism and Its Erasure: The Role of Emotions in the French Revolution," *Journal of Modern History* 72 (2000): 123–24.

CHAPTER SIX

1. *Chronique de Paris*, January 26 and February 14, 1790, quoted in Alexandre Tuetey, *Répertoire de l'histoire de Paris pendant la Révolution française*, 7 vols. (Paris: Imprimerie Nouvelle, 1890), 2:109, 408; *Révolutions de Paris*, February 13–20, 1790, 6; *Le Modérateur*, February 17, 1790, 192; *L'Ami du Peuple*, December 21, 1789, quoted in Antoine de Baecque, *Le Corps de l'histoire: Métaphores et politique (1770–1800)* (Paris: Calman-Lévy, 1993), 330. See also James H. Johnson, "Versailles, Meet Les Halles: Masks, Carnival, and the French Revolution," *Representations* 73 (2001): 89–116.
2. De Baecque, *Le Corps de l'histoire*, 330, 2.
3. De Baecque, *Le Corps de l'histoire*, 5.
4. Letter from Fauchet dated February 19, 1790, in *Révolutions de Paris*, March 6–13, 1790, 36–38.
5. De Baecque, *Le Corps de l'histoire*.
6. "Everything in these glorious days must remind us of liberty and equality. The people cannot simply be spectators of public pleasures, it must be the actor" (*Révolutions de Paris*, February 13–20, 1790, 20).
7. See Henry C. Clark, "Unmasking in the Political Culture of the French Revolution: A Review Essay," *Historical Reflections / Réflexions historiques* 17 (1991): 307–24.
8. *District des Récollets. Extrait du Procès verbal de l'Assemblée Générale du 21 janvier 1790*; *Extrait du registre des déliberations de l'Assemblée Générale du district des Jacobins S. Dominique. Du lundi 25 janvier 1790*.
9. Sigismond Lacroix, ed., *Actes de la Commune de Paris pendant la Révolution*, 2ème série, 8 vols. (Paris: L. Cerf, 1900), 2:326; Lacroix, ed., *Actes de la Commune de Paris pendant la Révolution*, 1ère série, 7 vols. (Paris: L. Cerf, 1894–1898), 3:636, 658; *Chronique de Paris*, February 4, 1790, 140; *Révolutions de Paris*, February 4, 1790, 139; *Moniteur universel*, February 5, 1790, 287.
10. Letter from Bailly to Lafayette, 10 February 1790, Mss. Fonds Français 11697, Fol. 36, B. N., Paris. *Jeudi gras* is Fat Thursday, the beginning of the carnival celebrations that culminate the following Tuesday, Mardi Gras.
11. Mona Ozouf, *Festivals and the French Revolution*, trans. Alan Sheridan (Cambridge: Cambridge University Press, 1988), 93.

12. Pierre-Louis Ginguéné, *De l'Autorité de Rabelais dans la Révolution présente et dans la Constitution civile du clergé, ou Institutions royales, politiques et ecclésiastiques tirées de Gargantua et de Pantagruel* (Paris: Chez Gattey, 1791), 4, 11.
13. Ginguéné, *De l'Autorité de Rabelais dans la Révolution*, 11.
14. Ginguéné, *De l'Autorité de Rabelais dans la Révolution*, 5.
15. *Révolutions de Paris*, February 18–25, 1792, 371; quoted in de Baecque, *Le Corps de l'histoire*, 314.
16. Nicole Pellegrin, *Les Vêtements de la liberté. Abécédaire des pratiques vestimentaires françaises de 1780 à 1800* (Paris: Éditions Alinea, 1989), 50–51.
17. *Révolutions de Paris*, July 16 and July 18–25, 1789, 4–5, 25–26.
18. Marie-Louise-Victoire de Donnissan, *Mémoires de la Marquise de La Rochejaquelein* (Paris: L. G. Michaud, 1817), 356, 390, 438; Pellegrin, *Les Vêtements de la liberté*, 65–66.
19. Letter from M. Challier dated January 27, 1790, in *Révolutions de Paris*, January 30–February 6, 1790, 44.
20. Quoted in de Baecque, *Le Corps de l'histoire*, 268, 271.
21. François Furet, *Interpreting the French Revolution*, trans. Elborg Forster (Cambridge: Cambridge University Press, 1981), 54; *Le Colporteur national*, October 1789, quoted in Pellegrin, *Les Vêtements de la liberté*, 67; *Le Patriote française*, June 16, 1791, quoted in Pellegrin, *Les Vêtements de la liberté*, 67.
22. *L'Ami du Peuple*, October 8, 1790, quoted in de Baecque, *Le Corps de l'histoire*, 330; *L'Ami du Peuple*, November 13, 1789, quoted in Pellegrin, *Les Vêtements de la liberté*, 67. See also Colin Lucas, "The Theory and Practice of Denunciation in the French Revolution," *Journal of Modern History* 68 (1996): 768–85.
23. François Furet, *Interpreting the French Revolution*, 46–61; Lynn Hunt, *Politics, Culture, and Class in the French Revolution* (Berkeley: University of California Press, 1984), 44–46; James H. Johnson, *Listening in Paris: A Cultural History* (Berkeley: University of California Press, 1995), 116–36; Ozouf, *Festivals and the French Revolution*; and Jean Starobinski, *Jean-Jacques Rousseau: Transparency and Obstruction*.
24. Clark, "Unmasking in the Political Culture of the French Revolution," 331.
25. Cecilia Feilla notes that the fifty most-performed plays during the revolutionary decade were not characterized by political or tragic themes but were instead overwhelmingly sentimental. "The revolutionary decade is characterized less by the infiltration of the political into all areas of public and private life, as has been the common wisdom," she writes, "than by the externalization of private affective forms and conventions into public discourse and performance." *The Sentimental Theater of the French Revolution* (London and New York: Routledge, 2016), 4, 15.
26. David Andress, "Living the Revolutionary Melodrama: Robespierre's Sensibility and the Construction of Political Commitment in the French Revolution," *Representations* 114 (Spring 2011): 109, 111–12; Robert Darnton, *The Kiss of Lamourette: Reflections in Cultural History* (New York: W. W. Norton, 1991), 3–20.
27. Andress, "Living the Revolutionary Melodrama," 116.
28. Andress, "Living the Revolutionary Melodrama," 116–17; William Reddy, "Sentimentalism and Its Erasure: The Role of Emotions in the French Revolution," *Journal of Modern History* 72 (2000):123–24; Nicole Bossut, "Terreur à Clamecy, quelques réflexions," *Annales historiques de la Révolution française* 311 (1998): 55–75.

29. Letter from abbé Mulot to *Journal de la Municipalité & des Districts de Paris*, February 5, 1790, 103.
30. *Révolutions de Paris*, January 23–29, 1790, 1–4.
31. *Journal des Clubs ou sociétés patriotiques*, March 2–10, 1791, 166.
32. *Le Publiciste de la République Française*, June 18, 1793, quoted in de Baecque, *Le Corps de l'histoire*, 281–82.
33. *Bouche de fer*, April 1791, quoted in de Baecque, *Le Corps de l'histoire*, 286.
34. *Le Carnaval de 1791. Avis au public* (n.p., n.d.), 3.
35. *Le Carnaval de 1791. Avis au public* (n.p., n.d.), 3.
36. *Actes des Apôtres*, 1790, Ch. XXIII, "Club de la Révolution," 1:119–24.
37. *Actes des Apôtres*, 1790, Ch. XXIII, "Club de la Révolution," 1:119–24.
38. *Actes des Apôtres*, 1790, Ch. XLII, "Nouvelle Conjuration Démasqué," 3:220.
39. *Le Carnaval Jacobite, ou Bal, banquet et mascarade patriotiques. Lettre d'un faux frère Jacobite, à M***, son ami à Venise* (Paris: n.p., 1791), 8, 14–15.
40. *Le Père Duchesne*, "A la Chie au Lit, ou le Tour de Carnaval du Père Duchesne à une société d'Aristocrates, et ses amours avec une ci-divant Duchesse," n.d., 5.
41. *Le Père Duchesne*, "A la Chie au Lit," 7.
42. *L'Ombre de mardi gras, ou Les Mascarades de la Cour réunies à celles du Corps législatif, & de quelques Femmes titrées; des Généraux & Officiers de la Fédérations, jointes à celles des Ecclésiastiques nouvellement fonctionnés, & définitivement celles des Juges de paix & autres membres des Tribunaux de la nouvelle organisation. Par un Fou Raisonnable* (Paris: n.p., 1791), 3–7.
43. *L'Ombre de mardi gras*, 61–62.
44. *Réimpression de l'Ancien Moniteur*, April 7, 1792, quoted in Lynn Hunt, "Freedom of Dress in Revolutionary France," in *From the Royal to the Republican Body: Incorporating the Political in Seventeenth- and Eighteenth-Century France*, ed. Sara E. Melzer and Kathryn Norbert (Berkeley: University of California Press, 1998), 230.
45. Michael Kwass, "Economics of Consumption: Political Economy and Noble Display in Eighteenth-Century France," in *The French Nobility in the Eighteenth Century: Reassessments and New Approaches*, ed. Jay M. Smith (University Park: Pennsylvania State University Press, 2006), 19; Salaville, quoted in Hunt, "Freedom of Dress in Revolutionary France," 228, 229; *Lettre d'un Provincial, député aux Etats Généraux sur le Costume de Cérémonie* (May 1, 1789), quoted in Aileen Ribeiro, *Fashion in the French Revolution* (New York: Holmes & Meier Publications, 1988), 46.
46. Ribeiro, *Fashion in the French Revolution*, 53, 70.
47. Quoted in Pellegrin, *Les Vêtements de la liberté*, 33.
48. Louis-Sebastien Mercier reports the arrest of Henri Dubois and nineteen others for wearing the "suspicious dress" of black buttons and a black collar, a potential sign of mourning for the king (Louis-Sébastien Mercier, *Tableau de Paris*, 11 vols. [Geneva: Slatkine Reprints, 1979], quoted in Pellegrin, *Les Vêtements de la liberté*, 49).
49. Pellegrin, *Les Vêtements de la liberté*, 123–24, 46, 103.
50. V. de Chastenay, *Mémoires*, quoted in Pellegrin, *Les Vêtements de la liberté*, 98.
51. *Archives parlementaires de 1787 à 1860: Recueil complet des débats législatifs et politiques des chambres françaises*, première série (1787–1799), 91 vols. (Paris: Librairie Administrative de Paul Dupont, 1867), 70:451, August 7, 1793; Sylvie Steinberg,

La Confusion des sexes: Le travestissement de la Renaissance à la Révolution (Paris: Fayard, 2001), 263–64.

52. August 9, 1793, Lombards, AA 163, f. 35; September 8, 1798, Muséum, AA 186; August 13, 1793, Butte des Moulins, f. 264, AA 91; Procès verbaux des commissaires de police des sections de Paris, Archives de la Préfecture de Police, Paris.
53. *Révolutions de Paris,* March 17–24, 1792, 537; Pellegrin, *Les Vêtements de la liberté,* 48.
54. *Chronique de Paris,* July 29, 1793.
55. The critic Roger Callois considers these differences in *Man, Play, and Games*: "In a police state, the uniform replaces the mask of a vertiginous society. The uniform is almost the exact opposite of the mask, and always symbolizes a type of authority founded on entirely opposing principles. . . . The uniform is also a disguise, but it is official, permanent, regulated, and, above all, leaves the face exposed. It makes the individual a representative and a servant of an impartial and immutable rule, rather than the delirious prey of contagious vehemence" (Callois, *Man, Play, and Games,* trans. Meyer Barash [New York: The Free Press, 1961], 131).
56. Jennifer Harris, "The Red Cap of Liberty: A Study of Dress Worn by French Revolutionary Partisans 1789–94," *Eighteenth-Century Studies* 14 (1981): 283–312.
57. "Considérations sur les avantages de changer le costume français, par le Société Populaire et Républicaine des Arts," in *La Décade Philosophique, Littéraire, et Politique,* 10 Floréal An II [April 29, 1794], 61.
58. Harris, "The Red Cap of Liberty," 299–300, 306; *Révolutions de Paris,* March 17–24, 1792, 536; *Révolutions de Paris,* March 23–30, 1793, 5.
59. Louis Antoine Léon de Saint-Just, "Sur les factions de l'étranger. Rapport fait à la Convention au nom du Comité de Salut Public 23 Ventôse An II [March 13, 1794]," in Saint-Just, *Discours et rapports* (Paris: Éditions Sociales, 1957), 159; Maximilien Robespierre, "Sur les rapports des idées religieuses et morales avec les principes républicaines et sur les fêtes nationales. Rapport présenté au nom du Salut public 18 Floréal An II [May 7, 1794]," in Robespierre, *Discours et rapports à la Convention* (Paris: Union Général d' Éditions, 1965), 254.
60. Robespierre speaking at the Jacobin Club, 28 June 1793, quoted in *Journal de la Montagne,* July 1, 1793.
61. Reddy, "Sentimentalism and Its Erasure," 143–44.
62. Saint-Just, "Sur les factions de l'étranger," 159.
63. Saint-Just, "Sur les factions de l'étranger," 161, 174.
64. Lucien Jaume, *Le Discours Jacobin et la démocratie* (Paris: Fayard, 1989), 214.
65. Robespierre, "Séance du 19 Nivose An II [January 8, 1794]," in *Oeuvres de Maximilien Robespierre,* 10 vols. (Paris: Presses Universitaires de France, 1950–1967), 10:313.
66. Pellegrin, *Les Vêtements de la liberté,* 67.
67. Pellegrin, *Les Vêtements de la liberté,* 73.
68. *Journal universel,* 11 Thermidor An II (July 29, 1794), quoted in Pellegrin, *Les Vêtements de la liberté,* 27.

CHAPTER SEVEN

1. Émile-Nicolas Massard and Gustave Dallier, *Pierre Coignard, ou Le forçat-colonel. Roman vécu sous la Restauration* (Paris: Albin Michel, 1924), is by far the best

published source about the case, with a credible presentation of sources and a judicious reluctance to fill the many gaps that remain in Coignard's biography. Most but not all of the archival sources Massard and Dallier used are in BB[18] 1039, *Archives Nationales*, Paris, and D 3 49, *Service Historique de la Défense*, Vincennes. In retelling this story, I have drawn principally from these archives, Massard and Dallier's account, the sixty-eight-page judicial summary and transcript of Coignard's trial in *Causes criminelles célèbres du XIXe siècle, rédigés par une société d'avocats*, 2 vols. (Paris: H. Longlois, 1827), and articles in the *Journal des débats* and the *Gazette de France*. Other works that tell Coignard's story include M. Froment, *La Police dévoilée depuis la Restauration* (Paris: Lemonnier, 1829), M. Alboize and A. Maquet, *Les Prisons de l'Europe*, 4 vols. (Paris: Administration de Librairie, 1850), *Vie, aventure et crimes du célèbre Pierre Coignard ou le faux Comte de Pontis St.-Hélène, et de sa bande* (Mezières: Lelaurin-Martinet, 1851), Armand Fouquier, *Causes célèbres de tous les peuples*, 8 vols. (Paris: Lebrun, 1858–67), Jules Bertaut, *L'Étonnante histoire de Pierre Coignard*, in *Les Oeuvres libres* (Paris: Arthème Fayard, 1927), Willy de Spens, *Pierre Coignard, le forçat colonel* (Paris: Éditions Gallimard, 1959), L. Mongin, *Toulon: Sa rade, son port, son arsenal, son ancien bagne* (Marseilles: Laffitte Reprints, 1978), and Bruno Roy-Henry, *Vidocq: Du bagne à la préfecture* (Paris: L'Archipel, 2001).

2. *Journal des débats*, July 4, 1818.
3. Ministère de la Guerre, November 7, 1817, D 3 49, fol. 5, S. H. D., Vincennes.
4. "Procès en identité de Pierre Coignard, se disant Pontis, comte de Sainte-Hélène," *Causes criminelles célèbres du XIXe siècle*, 2:239–40.
5. Massard and Dallier, *Pierre Coignard*, 100–101.
6. Ministère de la Guerre, December 5, 1817, D 3 49, fol. 6, S. H. D., Vincennes; *Causes criminelles célèbres du XIXe siècle*, 2:271–72.
7. A transcript of the interrogation is in D 3 49, fol. 6, S. H. D., Vincennes.
8. "État des services et campagnes de M. André-Pierre de Pontis," December 22, 1813, Massard and Dallier, *Pierre Coignard*, 81; "Rapport fait au Ministre le 14 novembre 1817," Massard and Dallier, *Pierre Coignard*, 104; Massard and Dallier, *Pierre Coignard*, 94.
9. Ministère de la Guerre, December 6, 1817, D 3 49, fols. 8–9, S. H. D., Vincennes; Baron de l'Horme de l'Ile, January 16, 1818, quoted in Massard and Dallier, *Pierre Coignard*, 130–31.
10. "Prévenu de faux en écritures publiques, d'usurpation de titres et d'état civil, en destruction du sien propre," Préfet de Police, quoted in Massard and Dallier, *Pierre Coignard*, 126.
11. Quoted in Massard and Dallier, *Pierre Coignard*, 152–53.
12. Eugène-François Vidocq, *Mémoires*, in Francis Lacassin, ed., *Mémoires; Les Voleurs* (Paris: Édition Robert Laffont, 1998), 293–94, 329–30; Lacassin, Preface, *Mémoires; Les Voleurs*, v.
13. *Causes criminelles célèbres du XIXe siècle*, 2:263–67.
14. *Registres du bagne de Toulon, an IX*, quoted in Massard and Dallier, *Pierre Coignard*, 57; *Causes criminelles célèbres du XIXe siècle*, 2:221; "Extrait d'une lettre adressée le 20 novembre 1819, au Ministre d'État, Préfet de Police, par le Commissaire du Bagne de Toulon," BB[18] 1039, fol. 260, A. N., Paris.
15. This account of Coignard's probable itinerary follows that offered by Émile-Nicolas Massard and Gustave Dallier, a reconstruction based on incomplete

records and a fair amount of speculation (Massard and Dallier, *Pierre Coignard*, 62–79).

16. Vidocq, *Mémoires*, 7–19; Lacassin, Preface, *Mémoires; Les Voleurs*, iii–iv.
17. *Vidocq à ses juges* (1843), quoted in Éric Perrin, *Vidocq* (Paris: Perrin, 1995), 50–52.
18. Vidocq, *Mémoires*, 7.
19. Lacassin, Preface, *Mémoires*; *Les Voleurs*, i; Maurice, *Vidocq*, 159.
20. Vidocq, *Mémoires*, 267, 308–10, 109–11.
21. Maurice, *Vidocq*, 175; Paul Metzner, *Crescendo of the Virtuoso: Spectacle, Skill, and Self-Promotion in Paris during the Age of Revolution* (Berkeley: University of California Press, 1998), 106.
22. Vidocq, *Mémoires*, 328–29.
23. Victor Alexis Désiré Dalloz, *Répertoire méthodique et alphabétique de législation, de doctrine et de jurisprudence*, 44 vols. (Paris: Bureau de la Jurisprudence Générale, 1845–73), 32:501–3; Adolphe Chauveau and Hélie Faustin, *Théorie du Code Pénal*, 6 vols. (Brussels: Société Typographique Belge, 1844), 2:281–82. For a comprehensive treatment of the crime of *l'escroquerie*—a word that carries connotations of fraud, swindling, and usurpation—and a history of its introduction into French law in 1791, see Cathérine Samet, *Naissance de l'escroquerie moderne du XVIIIe au début du XIXe siècle: la naissance de la notion d'escroquerie d'après la jurisprudence du Châtelet et du Parlement de Paris durant le siècle de Louis XV (1700–1790)* (Paris: L'Harmattan, 2005).
24. Massard and Dallier, *Pierre Coignard*, 216.
25. *Causes criminelles célèbres du XIXe siècle*, 2:234–36, 241–43.
26. *Causes criminelles célèbres du XIXe siècle*, 2:250–51, 279.
27. Dalloz, *Répertoire méthodique et alphabétique de législation*, 32:503.
28. Massard and Dallier, *Pierre Coignard*, 233.
29. Letter dated May 4, 1818, from *Ministre Secrétaire d'État au Département de la Police*, BB18 1039, fol. 323, A. N., Paris; undated report from the *Ministère de la Guerre*, BB18 1039, fol. 325, A. N., Paris; letter dated June 9, 1818, from *Ministère de la Justice* to the *Procureur Général de la cour Royale de Paris*, BB18 1039, fol. 332, A. N., Paris.
30. Letter dated June 16, 1818, from *Ministre Secrétaire d'État au Département de la Police*, BB18 1039, fol. 338, A. N., Paris; letter dated May 29, 1818, to M. Le Baron Pasquier, *Garde des Sceaux*, BB18 1039, fol. 330, A. N., Paris; letter dated October 6, 1819, from *Procureur Général de la Cour Royale de Paris*, BB18 1039, fol. 382, A. N., Paris; letter dated February 10, 1820, from *Cour Royale de Paris, Direction des affaires criminelles et des Grâces*, BB18 1039, fol. 383, A. N., Paris.
31. Alphonse de Beauchamp, *Le Faux Dauphin actuellement en France: histoire d'un imposteur, se disant le dernier fils de Louis XVI*, 2 vols. (Paris: Chez Le Rouge, an XI), 1:80–87, 1:180–84, 2:1–11. See also Alphonse de Beauchamp, *Histoire des deux faux Dauphins en France* (Paris: G. Mathiot, 1818), 213–14.
32. Anthelme Collet, *Mémoires d'un condamné, ou Vie de Collet, écrite par lui-même* (Paris: Melle, 1840), 85–100; Paul Ginisty, *Vie, aventures et incarnations d'Anthelme Collet* (Paris: Perrin et Cie., 1925), 162, 74.
33. Collet, *Mémoires*, 117–18; Jean-Marie Augustin, *Les Vies d'Anthelme Collet, escroc bagnard, et pédophile* (Paris: Geste, 2008), 23, 201–11.

34. Ginisty, *Vie, aventures et incarnations*, 209.
35. Augustin, *Les Vies d'Anthelme Collet*, 304, 21.
36. *Journal des débats*, August 15, 1821, November 3, 1832. See also Louis Chevalier, *Laboring Classes and Dangerous Classes in Paris During the First Half of the Nineteenth Century*, trans. Frank Jellinek (New York: Howard Fertig, 1973), 451.
37. A.-F.-V. Thomas, *Naundorff, ou Mémoire à consulter sur l'intrigue du dernier des faux Louis XVII; suivi des jugemens et condamnations d'Ervagault, sous le Consulat; de Mathurin Bruneau, sous la Restauration; et du Baron de Richemont, sous le gouvernement actuel* (Paris: Dentu, 1837), 13, 15.
38. Roy-Henry, *Vidocq*, 222–23. According to the historian Dominique Kalifa, Vidocq's original memoirs were ghostwritten by Louis-François L'Héritier and Émile Morice. See Kalifa, *Crime et culture au XIXe siècle* (Paris: Éditions Perrin, 2005), 73.
39. Vidocq, *Mémoires*, 337.
40. Vidocq, *Les Voleurs*, in Lacassin, ed., *Mémoires; Les Voleurs*, 1, 706, 719, 726, 824.
41. Vidocq, *Les Voleurs*, in Lacassin, ed., *Mémoires; Les Voleurs*, 719–20.
42. Louis Canler, *Mémoires de Canler, ancien chef du service de sureté* (Paris: Mercure de France, 1968), 299–300.
43. Maurice Alhoy, *Les Bagnes: Rochefort* (Paris: Gagniard, 1830), 46.
44. Amand Lacoste et al., *L'Auberge des Adrets, Robert Macaire* (Grenoble: Roissard, 1966), 104.
45. Frédérick Lemaître, *Souvenirs de Frédérick Lemaître* (Paris: Paul Ollendorff, 1866), 83.
46. Joseph Méry and Gautier, quoted in *Souvenirs de Frédérick Lemaître*, 194–95, 244–45.
47. Théodore de Banville, *Les Pauvres Saltimbanques* (Paris: Michel Lévy, 1853), 70, 71.
48. Catherine Coeuré, "Robert Macaire. Genèse et fortune d'un type caracaturel," in Lacoste, *L'Auberge des Adrets, Robert Macaire*, 15.
49. Coeuré, "Robert Macaire," 15, 20.
50. Lemaître, *Souvenirs*, 184, 187.
51. Joseph Méry, quoted in Lemaître, *Souvenirs*, 196–97.
52. *Robert Macaire et son ami Bertrand, contenant les vissicitudes de la vie de ces deux inséparables dans toutes les conditions où ils ont été placés par le sort, les nécessités sociales et leurs inclinations particulières; l'application des principes à la mode et des systèmes en faveur; suivies d'un chapitre des Mémoires outre tombe de ces deux célèbres contemporains* (Paris: P. Baudouin, 1839).
53. Champfleury, *Histoire de la caricature moderne* (Paris: E. Dentu, 1865), 127–28.
54. *Physiologie du Robert-Macaire*, quoted in Nathalie Priess, *Pour de rire! La Blague au XIXe siècle* (Paris: Presses Universitaires de France, 2002), 27; John McCormick, *Popular Theatres of Nineteenth-Century France* (London and New York: Routledge, 1993), 107.
55. *Physiologie du Macaire des Macaires, Par Moi* (Paris: Chez Dupin, 1842), 27.

CHAPTER EIGHT

1. Vincent Denis, *Une Histoire de l'identité: France 1715–1815* (Paris: Champ Vallon, 2008), 44–65.

2. Denis, *Une Histoire de l'identité*, 41–42, 62.
3. *La Lanterne de Diogène, ouvrage périodique, particulièrement destiné aux assemblées électorales, aux jurys, aux instituteurs, aux pères de famille & à ceux qui veulent se conduire avec quelque prudence dans la société* (n.p., 1803–1804), 1.
4. *Mercure de France*, February 1814, 340–42. "Watching others around them made it possible for Parisians to understand what distinguished elites from the *peuple* and, more important, how members of different groups related to each other," Denise Z. Davidson writes in an article on people-watching in these years. "Such awareness was essential in actually creating those distinctions. . . . As long as such structures remained vague, visibility and observation—seeing and being seen—were the primary tools used to create and strengthen new definitions of who had the right to make others defer to them and how" (Davidson, "Making Society 'Legible': People-Watching in Paris after the Revolution," *French Historical Studies* 28 [2005]: 296).
5. Quoted in Christoph Siegrist, "'Letters of the Divine Alphabet'—Lavater's Concept of Physiognomy," in *The Faces of Physiognomy: Interdisciplinary Approaches to Johann Caspar Lavater*, ed. Ellis Shookman (Columbia, SC: Camden House, 1993), 27.
6. Quoted in Ellis Shookman, "Pseudo-Science, Social Fad, Literary Wonder: Johann Caspar Lavater and The Art of Physiognomy," in *The Faces of Physiognomy*, 17; Gaspard Lavater, *L'Art de connaître les hommes par la physionomie*, 10 vols. (Paris: L. Prudhomme, 1804), 1:viii.
7. Shookman, "Pseudo-Science, Social Fad, Literary Wonder," 1:lxxxvi–xcii.
8. Christopher Rivers, *Face Value: Physiognomical Thought and the Legible Body in Marivaux, Lavater, Balzac, Gautier, and Zola* (Madison: University of Wisconsin Press, 1994), 68; Graeme Tytler, *Physiognomy in the European Novel: Faces and Fortunes* (Princeton, NJ: Princeton University Press, 1982), 82.
9. Martin S. Staum, *Labeling People: French Scholars on Society, Race, and Empire, 1815–1848* (Montreal & Kingston: McGill-Queen's University Press, 2003), 49.
10. Jan Goldstein, *The Post-Revolutionary Self: Politics and Psyche in France, 1750–1850* (Cambridge, MA: Harvard University Press, 2005), 274–77, 281–85, 291; Staum, *Labeling People*, 50–59.
11. E. H. Ackernecht, "P. M. A. Dumoutier et la collection phrénologique du Musée de l'Homme," *Bulletins et Mémoires de la Société d'Anthropologie de Paris* 7 (1956): 290; Marc Renneville, "Un musée d'anthropologie oublié: le cabinet phrénologique de Dumoutier," *Bulletins et Mémoires de la Société d'Anthropologie de Paris* 10 (1998): 479.
12. Quoted in Renneville, "Un musée d'anthropologie oublié," 482.
13. Ackernecht, "P. M. A. Dumoutier et la collection phrénologique," 294ff.
14. Staum, *Labeling People*, 52.
15. Isidore Bourdon, *La Physiognomonie et la phrénologie, ou Connaissance de l'homme* (Paris: Charles Bosselin, 1842), 165–71.
16. Bourdon, *La Physiognomonie et la phrénologie*, 74–75, 78–79, 17.
17. F.-J.-V. Broussais, *Cours de phrénologie* (Paris: J.-B. Bailliere, 1836), 128–29, iii, iv–v.
18. Félix Voisin, *De l'Homme animal* (Paris: Béchat, 1839), 49; Benjamin Appert, who devotes a chapter to phrenology in his four-volume work on criminals, crime, and the prisons of France, comes to a similar conclusion: "Once free will is

extinguished, you have no more recourse against the criminal. If you believe that an individual must inevitably, according to the form of this brain, become a thief or murderer, would you have the courage to punish him for theft or murder? If the cerebral influence on the exterior structure of the head directs the affections of a man toward a certain aim, without consulting his desires, is this not truly *fatalism*, for which it would be at once unjust and cruel to demand an account?" (Appert, *Bagnes, Prisons et Criminels*, 4 vols. [Paris: Guilbert, 1836], 4:301–2). Robert A. Nye discusses the use of phrenology in identifying and classifying criminals within the greater social, political, and medical contexts in *Crime, Madness, and Politics in Modern France: The Medical Concept of National Decline* (Princeton, NJ: Princeton University Press, 1984), 61–66.

19. Quoted in Goldstein, *The Post-Revolutionary Self*, 112.
20. Goldstein, *The Post-Revolutionary Self*, 286–87.
21. Voisin, *De l'Homme animal*, 94–99.
22. Chevalier, *Laboring Classes and Dangerous Classes*, 61.
23. Chevalier, *Laboring Classes and Dangerous Classes*, 23.
24. Honoré de Balzac, "Préface de la première édition," *Les Splendeurs et misères des courtisanes*, in *La Comédie humaine*, 12 vols. (Paris: Éditions Gallimard, 1977), 6:425. While the English translations of this novel are my own, I have relied heavily on its 1898 translation by James Waring (Balzac, *The Harlot's Progress* [Philadelphia: Gibble Press, 1898]).
25. Honoré de Balzac, *Corréspondance*, 5 vols. (Paris: Garnier Frères, 1960–66), 4:84; Lemaître, *Souvenirs*, 251–52; Léon Gozlan, *Balzac en pantoufles* (Paris: Michel Lévy Frères, 1865), 99–109.
26. Honoré de Balzac, *Vautrin*, in *Oeuvres complètes*, 20 vols. (Paris: Alexandre Houssiaux, 1855–70), 19:52.
27. Balzac, *Splendeurs et misères*, 6:430.
28. Balzac, *Lost Illusions*, trans. Herbert J. Hunt (London: Penguin Books, 1971), 650.
29. Marcel Bouteron, *Études Balzaciennes* (Paris: Jouve, 1954), 118, 133; Paul Vernière, "Balzac et la genèse de Vautrin," *Revue d'histoire littéraire de la France* 55 (1948): 53–68; Régis Messac, *"Le Detective Novel" et l'influence de la pensée scientifique* (Paris: Honoré Champion, 1929), 269–300.
30. Quoted in Philippe Perrot, *Fashioning the Bourgeoisie: A History of Clothing in the Nineteenth Century*, trans. Richard Bienvenu (Princeton, NJ: Princeton University Press, 1994), 119. The critic Jean-Claude Vareille observes that altered or disguised identities drive the plot of a number of French novels from the period 1820–1850, which, he argues, helped shape the later genre of detective fiction. "As with police novels, certain popular novels from early in the century expose the rift between essence and appearance. Their characters are feigners and dissemblers; they are not what they seem, and do not seem what they are. Scattered throughout the novels, one encounters a common metaphysics of generalized suspicion. . . . Masks abound, and the author's skill consists in pulling them off as late as possible in order to leave us in uncertainty" (Vareille, *L'Homme masqué, le justicier et le détective* [Lyon: Presses Universitaires de Lyon, 1989], 43).
31. Balzac, *Splendeurs et misères*, 6:648.
32. Balzac, *Splendeurs et misères*, 6:648.
33. Balzac, *Splendeurs et misères*, 6:648, 6:652–53.
34. Balzac, *Splendeurs et misères*, 6:648, 6:716.

35. Balzac, "Avant-Propos," *La Comédie humaine*, 1:17.
36. Rivers, *Face Value*, 105, 114–15; Honoré de Balzac, *Théorie de la démarche et autres textes* (Paris: Albin Michel, 1978), 7, 49.
37. Balzac, *Splendeurs et misères*, 6:749.
38. Balzac, *Splendeurs et misères*, 6:764.
39. Balzac, *Splendeurs et misères*, 6:898.
40. Balzac, *Splendeurs et misères*, 6:923, 925.
41. "L'air de bonté, de naïveté, la simplesse de cet homme, se confessant en termes sans âcreté, sans cette philosophie du vice qui jusqu'alors le rendait terrible à entendre, eussent fait croire à une transformation. Ce n'était plus lui" (Balzac, *Splendeurs et misères*), 6:925.
42. Balzac, *Splendeurs et misères*, 6:934.
43. Maurice Bardèche, *Une Lecture de Balzac* (Paris: Les Sept Couleurs, 1964), 150.
44. Honoré de Balzac, *Père Goriot*, trans. A. J. Krailsheimer (Oxford: Oxford University Press, 1991), 186.
45. Honoré de Balzac, "Code pénal des honnêtes gens," in *Oeuvres complètes de M. de Balzac*, 25 vols. (Paris: Les Bibliophiles de l'originale, 1965–73), 25:389, 392, 395.
46. Balzac, *Splendeurs et misères*, 6:912.
47. Francis Lacassin, "'Les Mystères de Paris' et leurs lecteurs," in Eugène Sue, *Les Mystères de Paris* (Paris: Éditions Robert Laffont, 1989), 19–27.
48. Sue, *Les Mystères de Paris*, 114.
49. Sue, *Les Mystères de Paris*, 958.
50. Victor Hugo, *Les Misérables* (Paris: Bibliothèque de la Pléiade, 1951), 96.
51. Victor Hugo, *Les Misérables*, 1460.
52. Victor Hugo, *Les Misérables*, 1287.
53. Victor Hugo, *Les Misérables*, 1410.
54. Victor Hugo, *Les Misérables*, 1420.
55. The most archaic meanings of the original Latin word *larva*—both mask and infernal spirit—reside in Hugo's use, as do its later associations with illusion, fiction, and false appearance. The naturalist Carl Linnaeus's more modern designation of larvae as insects in the grub stage is also present. In this larval state, the insect's true destiny remains masked (see James H. Johnson, *Venice Incognito: Masks in the Serene Republic* [Berkeley: University of California Press, 2011], 56–58).
56. Hugo, *Les Misérables*, 735–36.
57. Hugo, *Les Misérables*, 1238.
58. Hugo, *Les Misérables*, 1236, 1239, 1241.
59. Hugo, *Les Misérables*, 1392.

CHAPTER NINE

1. *Journal des débats*, 7 Ventôse an VIII [February 26, 1800].
2. Préfecture de police, *Ordonnance concernant les travestissements et déguisements pendant les jours dits du Carnaval*, 21 Pluviôse an IX de la République (February 3, 1803), published in *Journal des débats*, 23 Pluviôse (February 12, 1801), quoted in *Paris sous le Consulat*, ed. Alphonse Aulard, 4 vols. (Paris: Librairie Léopold Cert, 1904), 2:169–70.

3. 14 Pluviôse an XI (February 3, 1803), 5 Ventôse an XIII, DB 58 (February 24, 1805), Archives de la Préfecture de Police, Paris. In issuing instructions to those on patrol during carnival, the police prefect acknowledged the difficulty that officers were bound to face. "I cannot spell out the nuances that distinguish a joke from an insult; this is for you to discern. But I will say that in such conditions you must proceed with the greatest prudence, which I cannot recommend too strongly" (14 Pluviôse an XI).
4. *Journal de l'Empire*, 3, February 11, 1807; *Ordonnance de M. le Conseiller d'État, préfet de police*, in *Gazette de France*, January 31, 1807, quoted in *Paris sous le premier Empire*, ed. Alphonse Aulard, 3 vols. (Paris: Librairie Léopold Cerf, 1912), 3:36; *Ordonnance concernant les masques*, January 18, 1815; see also *Ordonnance concernant les masques*, January 25, 1826, DB 58, Archives de la Préfecture de Police, Paris.
5. See Victor Fournel, *Les Rues du vieux Paris* (Paris: Firmin-Didot, 1879), 249–56; Benjamin Gastineau, *Le Carnaval* (Paris: Gustave Havard, 1855), 71–77; Christiane Demeulenaere-Douyere, "Le Promenade du boeuf gras à Paris," *Gavroche: Revue bimestrielle d'histoire populaire*, no. 7 (December 1982–January 1983): 25–27.
6. *Gazette de France*, February 23, 1805; see also Aulard, ed., *Paris sous le Premier Empire*, 1:621.
7. See Aulard, *Paris sous le Premier Empire*, 3:49.
8. Reports from Préfecture de Police, quoted in Aulard, *Paris sous le Consulat*, 2:182, 2:734, 3:692, 4:655; Aulard, *Paris sous le premier Empire*, 1:611; *Journal de Paris*, February 19, 1806, Aulard, *Paris sous le premier Empire*, 2:439.
9. Report from Préfecture de Police, February 13, 1803, quoted in Aulard, *Paris sous le Consulate*, 3:660; *Journal de l'Empire*, March 4, 1808, quoted in Aulard, *Paris sous le premier Empire*, 3:553; *Courrier des spectacles*, undated clipping, R. 13033, Bibliothèque de l'Arsenal, Paris.
10. L. Montigny, *Le Provincial à Paris*, 4 vols. (Paris: Chez Ladvocat, 1825), 3:202, 204, 208; Nérée Desarbres, *Deux siècles à l'Opéra (1669–1868)* (Paris: E. Dentu, 1868), 244.
11. Victor-Joseph Étienne de Jouy, *L'Hermite de la Chaussée-d'Antin, ou Observations sur les moeurs et les usages Parisiens au commencement du XIX*[e] *siècle*, 5 vols. (Paris: chez Pillet, 1813), 2:64–65.
12. *Journal de Paris*, March 2, 1808, quoted in Aulard, *Paris sous le premier Empire*, 3:552; Alain Faure, *Paris Carême-prenant: du carnaval à Paris au XIX*[e] *siècle, 1800–1914* (Paris: Hachette, 1978), 63–64.
13. *Le Publiciste*, March 2, 1808, quoted in Aulard, *Paris sous le premier Empire*, 3:549; *Journal de l'Empire*, February 21, 1806, quoted in Aulard, *Paris sous le premier Empire*, 2:441.
14. Reports from Préfecture de Police, February 7, 1801, and March 1, 1802, quoted in Aulard, *Paris sous le Consulat*, 2:181, 760.
15. Reports from Préfecture de Police, February 17 and 18, 1801, quoted in Aulard, *Paris sous le Consulat*, 2:180, 2:182.
16. The theater journal *Vert-Vert* carried a notice of the play on January 27, 1834, that said spectators were invited to join the troupe in dancing "the famous galop of thieves and villagers."
17. *Courrier des Théâtres*, January 26, 1834; *La Quotidienne*, February 9, 1835.
18. Jules Janin, *Un Hiver à Paris* (Paris: Louis Janet, 1846), 175.

19. Heinrich Heine, *Lutèce. Lettres sur la vie politique, artistique et sociale de la France* (Paris: Slatkine Reprints, 1979), 241.
20. Taxile Delord, "Le Chicard," in Jules Janin et al., *Les Français peints par eux-mêmes*, 2 vols. (Paris: Omnibus, 2003), 1:1038; Charles Marchal, *Physiologie du Chicard* (Paris: Lachapelle, 1842), 27–28.
21. Marchal, *Physiologie du Chicard*, 60.
22. Delord, "Le Chicard," 1:1041; Balochard and Chicard, *Physiologie des bals de Paris* (Paris: Desloges, 1841), 32–34, 54.
23. "Ordonnance concernant le travestissement des femmes," November 7, 1800, DB 58, Archives de la Préfecture de Police, Paris.
24. Paul de Kock, ed., *La Grande ville. Nouveau tableau de Paris* (Paris: Bureau central des publications nouvelles, 1842–1843), 375; Louis Huart, *Le Bal Musard*, in *Les Physiologies Parisiennes* (Paris: Aubert, n.d.), 10; Maurice Alhoy, *Le Débardeur*, in *Les Physiologies Parisiennes*, 5.
25. See Judith Surkis, "Carnival Balls and Penal Codes: Body Politics in July Monarchy France," *History of the Present* 1 (2011): 59–83.
26. *Les Coulisses*, January 20, 1842, 2; Homme habillé en femme, July 11, 1846, DB 58, Archives de la Préfecture de Police, Paris.
27. Loraux, *Conservateur du Théâtre royale de l'Odéon*, January 26, 1835, F 21 1110 (Théâtre de l'Odéon), A. N., Paris; *La Mode* quoted in François Gasnault, *Guinguettes et lorettes. Bals publics et danse social à Paris entre 1830 et 1870* (Paris: Aubier, 1986), 47.
28. See Gasnault, *Guinguettes et lorettes*, 43, 53; Taxile Delord, "Le Chicard," in Jules Janin et al., *Les Français peints par eux-mêmes*, 1:1043.
29. Edmond de Lingères, comte d'Alton-Shée, *Mes mémoires (1826–1848)*, quoted in Léon Séché, *La Jeunesse dorée sous Louis-Philippe* (Paris: Mercure de France, 1910), 160.
30. From *Manuel des sergents de ville* (1831), quoted in Gasnault, *Guinguettes et lorettes*, 47.
31. See Faure, *Paris Carême-prenant*, 55; January 28, 1833, Préfecture de Police, Bulletin de Paris, F 7 3886 (1832–1833), A. N., Paris; *Gazette des Tribunaux*, January 17, 1833.
32. See Henri Gisquet, *Mémoires d'un préfet de police*, 4 vols. (Paris: Marchand, 1840), 4:225; *Le Corsaire*, February 4, 1833, quoted in Gasnault, *Guinguettes et lorettes*, 68. A journalist described watching one member of the municipal guard share in the crowd's pleasures with such exuberance that he "ended up making more noise than anyone else" (*Gazette des Tribunaux*, February 6, 1838, quoted in Gasnault, *Guinguettes et lorettes*, 52).
33. Rapport de l'Inspecteur-général du Théâtre des Variétés, A Messieurs les administrateurs Propriétaires, January 11, 1836, F 21 1133 (Théâtre des Variétés), A. N., Paris.
34. *Physiologie du Carnaval, du Cancan et de la Cachucha, par un vilain masqué* (Paris: Raymond-Bocquet, 1842), 6.
35. Gasnault, *Guinguettes et lorettes*, 172.
36. Heinrich Heine, *De la France* (Paris: Lévy Frères, 1872), 134.
37. *Gazette des Tribunaux*, March 6, 1843; Gasnault, *Guinguettes et lorettes*, 49.
38. *Gazette des Tribunaux*, January 5–6, 1846.
39. Marchal, *Physiologie du Chicard*, 61–62.

40. Séché, *La Jeunesse dorée sous Louis-Philippe*, 162; Auguste Vitu, *Les Bals d'hiver: Paris masqué* (1848), quoted in Gasnault, *Guinguettes et lorettes*, 168; Satan [Mathieu-Dairnvaell, Georges-Marie], *Le Carnaval de Paris* (Paris: Librairie Litteraire et Politique, 1848), 11.
41. "Bulletins de Police," F 7 3890, F 7 3891, F 7 3892, A. N., Paris.
42. Records of revenue for Opera balls are incomplete. The seasons of 1823, 1824, and 1826 are compared here to those of 1833–1837. These averages are based on seasonal ball totals listed in AB[XIX] 2938, A. N., Paris.
43. Faure, *Carême-prenant*, 47; Bulletins de police, February 1, 1837, January 5, 1838, F 7 3889, A. N., Paris; *Le Carnaval* (Paris: Prévot, 1840), 5, title page; Ann Ilan-Alter, "Masked and Unmasked at the Opera Balls: Parisian Women Celebrate Carnival," in *Masquerade and Identities: Essays on Gender, Sexuality, and Marginality*, ed. Efrat Tseëlon (London and New York: Routledge, 2001), 137.
44. G. Delessert, Préfet de Police, to MM. les Commissaires de Police de la ville de Paris et de la Banlieue, Decembre 13, 1844, F 21 1046, A. N., Paris.
45. See Gasnault, *Guinguettes et lorettes*, 57, 68.
46. Gasnault, *Guinguettes et lorettes*, 169; AJ[13] 1060, F 21 1011, A. N., Paris.
47. Poster for *Grand Bal Costumé, Paré, Masqué et Dansant*, 7 Février 1837, F 21 1066, A. N., Paris; poster for *Grand Bal Musard, 18 Janvier 1840*, AJ[13] 182-VI, A. N., Paris; Gasnault, *Guinguettes et lorettes*, 163; *Le Carnaval. Histoire des bals de l'Opéra, tableau des fêtes, travestissements, mascarades et carrousels qui ont eu lieu chez toutes les nations depuis leur origine jusqu'à nos jours* (Paris: Imprimerie de Ducessois, 1835), 16.
48. Satan, *Le Carnaval de Paris*, 10–11; Texier, *Tableau de Paris* (1850), quoted in Gasnault, *Guinguettes et lorettes*, 168; Huart, *Le Bal Musard*, 4.
49. Charles de Boigne, *Petits mémoires de l'Opéra* (Paris: Librairie Nouvelle, 1857), 183–84.
50. *Les Coulisses*, January 20, 1842.
51. Paul de Kock, ed., *La Grande ville*, 381.
52. *Vert-vert*, February 4, 1837.
53. *Courrier des théâtres*, February 5, 1834.
54. *Les Coulisses*, February 10, 1842.
55. Alhoy, *Le Débardeur*, 11, 5.
56. Leroy, "Le Domino de la Comtesse," in *Les Folies du Carnaval*, n.p.
57. Matéo Réo, "Une Aventure à l'Opéra," in *Le Carnaval. Histoire des bals de l'Opéra* (n.p., 1835), 21–22.
58. *Les Coulisses*, February 18, 1841.
59. Janin, *Un Hiver à Paris*, 174.
60. Letter from Henri Gisquet to the Ministre du Commerce et des Travaux Publics, January 17, 1833, F 21 1110 (Théâtre de l'Odéon), A. N., Paris. Police also discovered that the student organizers of an earlier private carnival ball had contributed proceeds to the families of political detainees (February 18, 1833, Préfecture de Police, Bulletins de Paris, F 7 3886 [1832–1833], A. N., Paris). On the political engagement of students in the Latin Quarter in 1830 and beyond, see Alan B. Spitzer, *The French Generation of 1820* (Princeton, NJ: Princeton University Press, 1987).
61. Letter from Henri Gisquet to the Ministre du Commerce et des Travaux Publics, February 3, 1833; petition from 23 merchants addressed to Louis-Philippe, February 6, 1833, F 21 1110 (Théâtre de l'Odéon), A. N., Paris.

62. Administrative correspondence, Théâtre de l'Odéon, January 26, 27, 28, 29, and February 8, 1835, F 21 1110 (Théâtre de l'Odéon), A. N., Paris.
63. *Courrier des Théâtres*, January 8 and 9, 1833.
64. *Courrier des Théâtres*, January 12, 1834; *La Quotidienne*, January 13 and February 9, 1835, and January 11, 1836.
65. For an excellent survey of Musard's career, see Gasnault, *Guinguettes et lorettes*, 95–107.
66. An example of each poster, with and without Musard's name, is preserved in the archival collection F 21 1066 (Bals masqués, Théâtre de l'Opéra), A. N., Paris.
67. Letter from Adrien Gasparin to the duc de Choiseul, Président de la Commission Spéciale des Théâtres Royaux, February 16, 1837, F 21 1066, A. N., Paris.
68. M. Bruzelin, "Copie d'un rapport adressé à Monsieur le Conseiller d'État, Préfet de Police, le 8 février 1837, par le Commissaire de Police du quartier du Roule," AJ^{13} 182-VI, A. N., Paris.
69. Émile de Girardin, *Lettres parisiennes* (Paris: Michel Lévy Frères, 1857), 40.
70. Bruzelin, "Copie d'un rapport," and Girardin, *Lettres parisiennes*, 66.
71. *La Quotidienne*, February 13, 1837.
72. Boigne, *Petits mémoires de l'Opéra*, 182.
73. See M. Gentily, "Rapport au Monsieur le Commissaire du Roi," February 8, 1837, AJ^{21} 1066, A. N., Paris.
74. *La Quotidienne*, February 13, 1837; *Le Corsaire*, February 11, 1837.
75. Adrien Gasparin to the duc de Choiseul, Président de la Commission Spéciale des Théâtres Royaux, February 11, 1837, F 21 1066; Leon Pillet, Commissaire Royale de la Commission Spéciale des Théâtres Royaux to Gasparin, February 15, 1837, F 21 1066; Gasparin to the duc de Choiseul, February 16, 1837, F 21 1066; report of Commission Spéciale des Théâtres Royaux, February 16, 1837, AJ^{13} 182-VI, A. N., Paris.
76. David Van Zanten, *Building Paris: Architectural Institutions and the Transformation of the French Capital, 1830–1870* (Cambridge: Cambridge University Press, 1994), 43.

CHAPTER TEN

1. "Le vingt-cinq de ce mois, le Comte d'Etron-mord, fut casté pour n'avoir pas mis l'épée à la main contre le Marquis de mille fleurs. . . . Le Mariage de Mr. Léche-Cul avec Mlle Soufflez-y, fut déclaré ces jours passés. . . . L'Ambassadeur Croque pets, en son Hôtel, rue de la Morellerie, donna audience au Vicomte Gobe les" (*Description des six espèces de pets, ou Six raisons pour se conserver la santé, prêchée le Mardi gras, par le Pere Barnabas, Péteur en chef, au Village des Vesses, Province des Etrons, goûtez qu'ils sont bons. Avec Le Testament de Roger-Bon-Tems, la Chanson du rendez-vous que Madame fit à son Epoux, & les petites Nouvelles que vous direz être vieilles. Nouvelle edition, Revue, corrigée, augmentée & mise dans un nouvel ordre, par Mr Chicourt, Docteur d'Archicourt, & Medecin ordinaire de l'Homme-de-fer* [Lélis: Chez Goderfe, n.d.]), 2.
2. *Description des six espèces de pets*, 3, 5–6.
3. René Rémond, *L'Anticléricalisme en France de 1815 à nos jours* (Paris: Fayard, 1976), 61–64; George Minois, *Histoire du rire et de la dérision* (Paris: Fayard, 2000),

462–67. For accounts of popular resistance to Jesuit missionaries, as well as anticlerical disturbances in theaters, broadsheets, pamphlets, and carnivalesque mockery throughout France during the Bourbon Restoration, see Sheryl Kroen, *Politics and Theater: The Crisis of Legitimacy in Restoration France, 1815–1830* (Berkeley: University of California Press, 2000).

4. "All masked, disguised, or costumed persons, as well as all others, are forbidden from insulting any other person with abuse or profane speech, or from standing in streets, alleys, pathways, public places, or promenades in order to declaim from books, most notably *Fishwife's Catechism*" (*Ordonnance concernant les masques, Paris, le 10 février 1830*, in DB 58, Préfecture de la Police, Paris).

5. *Catéchisme Poissard. Recueil indispensable pour passer gaîment le Carnaval* (Troyes: Chez Baudot, n.d.), 1–2.

6. *Catéchisme Poissard*, 33–34.

7. *Riche-en-gueule ou le Nouveau Vadé* (Paris: Poulet, 1821), *Robert-Macaire, Chansonnier grivois* (Paris: n.p., 1835), *Le Carnavaliana et Carêmiana* (Paris: n.p., n.d.), and *Nouveau Catéchisme Poissard* (Paris: Le Bailly, n.d.).

8. V'là qu'tu pleur's de rage,
Comme un vieux fromage;
N'm'ot' pas l'avantage
D'voir ta belle image,
Moule à saucisson.
Magneur' de marron,
Branleus' de bourdon,
Bouteille à poison,
Succeus' de cornichon,
Morceau de paillasson,
Grand sac à charbon,
T'es un puits sans fond,
Tonneau sans boudon,
Va t'gratter l'croupion
Plus loin de moi, grenon

Riche-en-gueule ou le Nouveau Vadé, 20–21, 22–23.

9. *Riche-en-gueule ou le Nouveau Vadé*, title page.

10. *Catéchisme Poissard*, 18–22.

11. Le récureur d'égoûts qui tombe dans la fange,
Le vidangeur qui meurt dans la merde qu'il mange,
Eprouvant des tourments moins cruels, moins affreux,
Que celui qui me trouble en voyant vos beaux yeux.
Entre un étron et vous, dieu! quelle ressemblance!

Riche-en-gueule ou le Nouveau Vadé, 147–48.

12. En la conduisant à l'église,
La merde humectait sa chemise,
Et lui battait sur ses bas blancs;
La pauvre fillette éperdue,
Serrait le cul dedans la rue
. . .
L'église sentait les latrines,

Chacun se bouchant les narines,
Reçut la bénédiction
Au milieu de l'infection.
. . .
Maintenant vous êtes ma femme,
Et je veux vous prouver ma flamme;
L'épingle saute, au même instant,
Il est couvert de dévoiement,
. . .
Fille qui lirez cette histoire,
Si jamais vous avez la foire,
Il faut vous mettre prudemment,
Un bouchon dans le fondement
Deri dera la la,
Deri dera la la

"La Mariée Foireuse," in *Le Robert-Macaire, Chansonnier grivois*, 55–57.

13. Ma mère, du matin au soir
Me cherche un tendre époux qui m'aime:
Sous prétexte de me pourvoir,
Elle se pourvoir elle même:
Censeurs, n'en dites point de mal:
Tout est permis en Carnaval

Carnavaliana et Carêmiana, 6–8.

14. Parisien, gai prolétaire,
Grisette, aux frais oripeaux,
Dansez la Robert Macaire,
Au nez des municipaux

Le Robert-Macaire, Chansonnier grivois, 96–98.

15. Regardez donc comme il est charmant
Ce bel enfant d'or et d'argent;
Il est au titre, il a l'contrôle,
. . .
C'n'est pas pour épargner ta race,
Si les charcutiers t'ont fait grâce,
On n'veut pas d'ta coine et d'ton lard
Quand tu donn'rais l'tout pour un liard,
On n'veut pas tuer un rien qui vaille;
On n'ira pas bruler d'la paille
Pour éclairer tes funérailles,
Ni t'rincer assez les entrailles
Pour faire d's andouilles d'tes tripailles;
. . .
Celui qui t'mettrait en saucisses,
Perdrait son temps et ses épices;
Il suffit de t'mettre en boudin
Pour empoisonner l'genre humain

Riche-en-gueule ou le Nouveau Vadé, 229–30.

16. Marchal, *Physiologie du Chicard*, 32; *Journal de Paris*, February 12, 1837; *Revue et gazette musicale* (1841), quoted in François Gasnault, *Guinguettes et lorettes. Bals publics et danse social à Paris entre 1830 et 1870* (Paris: Aubier, 1986), 162.
17. "Bulletin de police," February 13, 1831, F[7] 3885, A. N.; "Bulletin de police," February 11, 1834, F 7 3887, A. N.; Rodolphe Apponyi, *Vingt ans à Paris (1826–1830)*, 4 vols. (Paris: Librairie Plon, 1913), 2:151; Fournel, *Les Rues de Paris*, 246.
18. Il était gros, gras, difforme;
Il pesait un poids énorme;
A tous momens il beuglait;
Epaisse et lourde encolure,
Il avait large figure,
Et tout petit cervelet.
. . .
C'est la fin de la parade;
Bientôt ce roi de passade
Va perdre rubans et fleurs.
Cette couronne flétrie
Roulera dans la voirie
Où vont toutes nos grandeurs.
. . .
Jouis vite du seul matin
Que t'a mesuré le destin.
Roi, toi royauté d'un jour
Demain fuira sans retour!

La Caricature, March 5, 1835.

19. *Journal de Paris*, February 12, 1837; *Le Carnaval et marche burlesque du boeuf gras à Paris* (Paris: Charles Warée, 1843), 54, 51.
20. See Fournel, *Les Rues de Paris*, 259.
21. *La Descente de la Courtille* (Paris: Imprimerie Chassaignon, [1845]), n.p.
22. *La Descente de la Courtille.*
23. *La Descente de la Courtille.*
24. Eugène-François Vidocq, *Mémoires*, in *Mémoires; Les Voleurs, ed.* Francis Lacassin (Paris: Édition Robert Laffont, 1998), 796–97.
25. Auguste Luchet, "La Descente de la Courtille en 1833," *Paris, ou le livre des Cent-et-un*, 15 vols. (Paris: Chez Ladvocat, 1831–1834), 11:45, 47–48.
26. *Promenade*, quoted in Gasnault, *Guinguettes et lorettes*, 42.
27. Fournel, *Les Rues du vieux Paris*, 246.
28. Fournel, *Les Rues du vieux Paris*; Benjamin Gastineau, *Le Carnaval* (Paris: Gustave Havard, 1855), 86–87.
29. Gastineau, *Le Carnaval*, 85.
30. Luchet, "La Descente de la Courtille," 11:52; Victor Rozier, *Les Bals publics à Paris* (Paris: Gustave Havard, 1855), 85.
31. Heinrich Heine in *Gazette d'Augsbourg*, March 25, 1832, quoted in Fournel, *Les Rues de Paris*, 243; Gisquet, *Mémoires*, 4:223, 224.
32. Satan, *Le Carnaval de Paris*, 63.

33. Luchet, "La Descente de la Courtille," 11:49; on Lord Seymour, see Gastineau, *La Carnaval*, Faure, *Paris Carême-prenant*, 69–70, 58, and Fournel, *Les Rues de Paris*, 246–47; *Promenade*, quoted in Gasnault, *Guinguettes et lorettes*, 42.
34. Gisquet, *Mémoires*, 4:225. "The precise form of these promiscuous mixings and reversals—the irresponsibility of aristocrats, the sudden transgressions around femininity—was deeply threatening to the world-view of metropolitanism. It wasn't only police chiefs who were up in arms" (Nicholas Green, *The Spectacle of Nature: Landscape and Bourgeois Culture in Nineteenth-Century France* [Manchester: Manchester University Press, 1990], 79).
35. "Les Masques et les mascarades," from *Magasin pittoresque* (1840), quoted in Faure, *Paris Carême-prenant*, 56.
36. "Les Masques et les mascarades," 49; *Vert-Vert*, February 12, 1834.
37. *Courrier des théâtres*, February 10, 1837.
38. Benoist de Matougues, *Testament de Robert-Macaire. Pensées, maximes de ce célèbre personnage* (Paris: Amédée-Saintin, 1840), vi, xiii–xiv.
39. Matougues, *Testament de Robert-Macaire*, 8.
40. Matougues, *Testament de Robert-Macaire*, xii.
41. Matougues, *Testament de Robert-Macaire*, 56–57.
42. Matougues, *Testament de Robert-Macaire*, xxvi.
43. Matougues, *Testament de Robert-Macaire*, iv.
44. Matougues, *Testament de Robert-Macaire*, 30–44.
45. Matougues, *Testament de Robert-Macaire*, xi, xii.
46. Matougues, *Testament de Robert-Macaire*, 58.
47. Matougues, *Testament de Robert-Macaire*, 79–80.
48. Matougues, *Testament de Robert-Macaire*, 274, 218, 275.
49. Matougues, *Testament de Robert-Macaire*, 199–200.
50. Matougues, *Testament de Robert-Macaire*, 330–31, 335.
51. Matougues, *Testament de Robert-Macaire*, iv, v, vi.
52. Matougues, *Testament de Robert-Macaire*, xxviii.
53. Mikhail Bakhtin, *Rabelais and His World*, trans. Hélène Iswolksy (Bloomington: Indiana University Press, 1984), 10, 255.
54. Bakhtin, *Rabelais and His World*, 224.
55. Bakhtin, *Rabelais and His World*, 147.
56. Bakhtin, *Rabelais and His World*, 7, 12.
57. Bakhtin, *Rabelais and His World*, 10, 274.
58. Umberto Eco, "The Frames of Comic Freedom," in *Carnival!*, ed. Thomas A. Sebeok (Berlin: Mouton Publishers, 1984), 6.
59. Victor Turner, *The Ritual Process: Structure and Anti-Structure* (Ithaca, NY: Cornell University Press, 1969), 176–77.
60. Natalie Zemon Davis, "Women on Top: Symbolic Sexual Inversion and Political Disorder in Early Modern Europe," in *The Reversible World. Symbolic Inversion in Art and Society*, ed. Barbara A. Babcock (Ithaca, NY: Cornell University Press, 1978), 175.
61. Peter Stallybrass and Allon White, *The Politics and Poetics of Transgression* (Ithaca, NY: Cornell University Press, 1986), 14, 16.

CHAPTER ELEVEN

1. Accounts of these events appear in *Le Constitutionnel* (February 15, 16, 17, 1831), *La Gazette de France* (February 15, 16, 1831), *La Quotidienne* (February 15, 16, 18, 1831), and Alexandre Dumas, *Mes Mémoires*, 10 vols. (Paris: Michel Lévy Frères, 1865–70), 2:245–47. For reports of the duc de Berry's assassination, see *Moniteur universel*, February 15, 1820, and *Journal des débats*, February 15, 1820.
2. Louis Blanc, *Histoire de dix ans: 1830–1840*, 4 vols. (Paris: Pagnerre, 1843), 274–75.
3. Canler, *Mémoires de Canler, ancien chef du service de sureté*, 224.
4. Alexandre Dumas, *Mes Mémoires*, 2:247; Nicolas-Michel Troche, *Histoire*, quoted in Alain Faure, *Paris Carême-prenant: du carnaval à Paris au XIXe siècle, 1800–1914* (Paris: Hachette, 1978), 110.
5. M. L. Börne, *Lettres écrites de Paris pendant les années 1830 et 1831*, trans. M. F. Guiran (Paris: Paulin, 1832), 120.
6. Börne, *Lettres écrites de Paris*; Blanc, *Histoire de dix ans*, 277; *Le Constitutionnel*, February 17, 1831.
7. *La Quotidienne*, February 18, 1831.
8. *La Quotidienne*, February 16, 1831.
9. *Le Constitutionnel*, February 16, 1831.
10. *La Quotidienne*, February 16, 1831.
11. *Le Constitutionnel*, February 16, 1831.
12. *Le Constitutionnel*, February 16 and 17, 1831.
13. Arnold van Gennep, *Manuel de folklore français contemporain*, 4 vols., vol. 1, pt. 3, "Les cérémonies périodiques cycliques" (Paris: Éditions Picard, 1947), 1034–40.
14. This reconstruction of events is based on newspaper accounts from *Journal de Grenoble*, *Le Dauphinois*, and the *Gazette des Tribunaux*, testimony before the *Cour Royale de Grenoble*, and local reports and accounts published at the time, including *Rapport fait par le Maire de la ville de Grenoble sur les évènemens qui ont lieu en cette ville les 11, 12 et 13 mars 1832* (Grenoble: F. Allier, 1832), *Trois journées de Grenoble. Relation des évènemens qui se sont passés à Grenoble pendant les journées des 11, 12 et 13 mars 1832* (Grenoble: Imprimerie de L. Viallet, [1832]), and *Vengeance des Grenoblois* (Grenoble: J.-L. Barnel, [1832]). For modern assessments of the events, see David S. Kerr, *Caricature and French Political Culture, 1830–1848* (Oxford: Clarendon Press, 2000), and Charles Breunig, "Casimir Perier and the 'Troubles of Grenoble,' March 11–13, 1832," *French Historical Studies* 2 (1962): 469–89.
15. *Trois journées de Grenoble*, 6.
16. *Journal de Grenoble*, March 20, 1832, 1.
17. *Journal de Grenoble*, 2; *Trois journées de Grenoble*, 10.
18. Testimony of MM. Chépu, Nicolas, Piot, Gantillon, Riveron, Raucourt, and Guibert before the *Cour Royale de Grenoble*, July 6, 1832, transcribed in *Gazette des Tribunaux*, July 11, 1832, 905–6; *Le Dauphinois*, March 18, 28, 1832.
19. *Le Dauphinois*, March 14, 1832, 2.
20. *Rapport fait par le Maire*.
21. *Le Dauphinois*, March 14, 16, 18, 1832; *Rapport fait par le Maire*.
22. Testimony of MM. Raulier and Charpin before the *Cour Royale de Grenoble*, *Gazette des Tribunaux*, July 6, 1832, 905.

23. Testimony of MM. Raulier and Charpin before the *Cour Royale de Grenoble*; see also the testimony of M. Brès, chef de bataillon d'état major à Grenoble, before the same court, July 11, 1832, 904.
24. Maurice Duval, *Note du préfet de l'Isère, sur les événemens de Grenoble, en mars 1832*, in *Journal de Grenoble*, March 20, 1832, 1; testimony of the Baron de Saint-Clair before the *Cour Royale de Grenoble*, July 5, 1832, in *Gazette des Tribunaux*, July 11, 1832, 904. See also Breunig, "Casimir Perier and the 'Troubles of Grenoble,'" 479–80.
25. See Breunig, "Casimir Perier and the 'Troubles of Grenoble,'" 481–84.
26. *Le Dauphinois*, March 14, 1832, 3.
27. See Kerr, *Caricature and French Political Culture*, from which I have drawn much in this section.
28. Letter of July 7, 1846, to Rosalje, quoted in Kerr, *Caricature and French Political Culture*, 120.
29. See letter of July 7, 1846, to Rosalje, 81.
30. Robert Justin Goldstein, *Censorship of Political Caricature in Nineteenth-Century France* (Kent, OH: Kent State University Press, 1989), 122.
31. *Le Caricature*, November 17, 1831.
32. Kerr, *Caricature and French Political Culture*, 141–42, 90–92, 179.
33. *Le Charivari* quoted in Kerr, *Caricature and French Political Culture*, 192; see also 193, 209.
34. Charles Baudelaire, "Quelques caricaturistes français," from *Le Présent*, October 1, 1857, in *Oeuvres complètes*, 2 vols. (Paris: Bibliothèque de la Pléiade, 1976), 2:544.
35. Charles Blanc, *Dictionnaire politique, encyclopédique du langage et de la science politique*; Charles Dupont, *Procès du charivari donné à M. le baron de Talleyrand, préfet du Pas-de-Calais*, quoted in Kerr, *Caricature and French Political Culture*, 121, 195.
36. Baudelaire, "Quelques caricaturistes français," 2:526, 529, 530.
37. From *Le Journal amusant*, September 28, 1861, quoted in Kerr, *Caricature and French Political Culture*, 65. Henri Bergson's description of caricature's exaggerations builds on both natural distortions and what Philipon calls its underlying seriousness: "[The caricaturist] realizes disproportions and deformations which must have existed in Nature as mere inclinations, but which have not succeeded in coming to a head, being held in check by a higher force. . . . Certainly, it is an art that exaggerates, and yet the definition would be very far from complete were exaggeration alone alleged to be its aim and object, for there exist caricatures that are more lifelike than portraits, caricatures in which the exaggeration is scarcely noticeable, whilst, conversely, it is quite possible to exaggerate to excess without obtaining a real caricature" (Bergson, *Laughter: An Essay on the Meaning of the Comic*, trans. Cloudesley Brerton and Fred Rothwell [London: Macmillan and Co., 1913]), 26–27.
38. Champfleury, *Histoire de la caricature moderne*, vii.
39. See Kerr, *Caricature and French Political Culture*, 151–52.
40. The date in the illustration's title, 1831, is an error—or perhaps an indication that the drawing was done a year before it was published. Its title in the text of *La Caricature* is "Masques de 1832." In his 1865 *Histoire de la caricature moderne*, Champfleury attributes the work to Daumier, who signed it as "Rogelin" (Paris: E. Dentu, 1865, 49).

41. *La Caricature*, March 8, 1832.
42. *La Caricature*, August 27, 1835.
43. Judith Wechsler, *A Human Comedy: Physiognomy and Caricature in 19th Century Paris* (Chicago: University of Chicago Press, 1982), 174.
44. Baudelaire, "Quelques caricaturistes français," 2:552.
45. *La Constitutionnel*, March 19, 1832; *La Quotidienne*, March 21, 1832; testimony of M. Raucourt, *notaire et conseiller municipal* before the *Cour Royale de Grenoble* in *Gazette des Tribunaux*, July 11, 1832, 905; see also *Rapport fait par le Maire*, 3; *Journal de Grenoble*, March 20, 1832.
46. Baron Delort, *L'Ordre du Jour*, March 21, 1832, published in *Journal de Grenoble*, March 24, 1832, 2; *Ordonnance du Roi*, March 17, 1832, published in *Journal de Grenoble*; deposition recorded March 16 and published in *Journal de Grenoble*, March 20, 1832, 2; Maréchal Soult, duc de Dalmatie, *Le ministre de la guerre à l'armée*, March 22, 1832, quoted in *Journal de Grenoble*, March 27, 1832.
47. *Journal de Grenoble*, March 27, 1832, 3–4; *Le Constitutionnel*, March 21, 1832.
48. Apponyi, *Vingt-cinq ans à Paris*, 2:151.
49. *Le Constitutionnel*, March 21, 1832; *Gazette de France*, March 20, 1832.
50. Arsène Houssaye, introduction to Jules Janin, *Deburau: Histoire du théâtre à quatre sous* (Paris: Librairie des Bibliophiles, 1881), xxi–ii.
51. George Sand, *Questions d'art et de littérature* (Paris: Calmann Lévy, 1878), 218.
52. Janin, *Deburau*, 75.
53. Charles Taylor, *Sources of the Self: The Making of the Modern Identity* (Cambridge, MA: Harvard University Press, 1983), 22.
54. Stendhal [Marie-Henri Beyle], *The Life of Henry Brulard*, trans. John Sturrock (New York: New York Review Books, 2002), 83.
55. Stendhal, *Life of Henry Brulard*, 263, 197, xxxv, 309. I have slightly adjusted John Sturrock's translation regarding the bottle of ink.
56. "The word 'authenticity' comes so readily to the tongue these days and in so many connections that it may very well resist such efforts of definition as I shall later make," writes Lionel Trilling in his classic articulation. Authenticity, he goes on to say, suggests "a more strenuous moral experience than 'sincerity' does, a more exigent conception of the self and of what being true to it consists in, a wider reference to the universe and man's place in it, and a less acceptant and genial view of the social circumstances of life. . . . Much that culture traditionally condemned and sought to exclude is accorded a considerable moral authority by reason of the authenticity claimed for it, for example, disorder, violence, unreason. The concept of authenticity can deny art itself, yet at the same time it figures as the dark source of art" (Trilling, *Sincerity and Authenticity* [Cambridge, MA: Harvard University Press, 1971], 11).
57. Quoted in Kathleen Kete, *Making Way for Genius: The Aspiring Self in France from the Old Regime to the New* (New Haven, CT, and London: Yale University Press, 2012), 98.
58. James H. Johnson, "Capturing the Landscape Within: On Writing the History of Experience," in Christian Thorau and Hansjakob Ziemer, *The Oxford Handbook of Music Listening in the 19th and 20th Centuries* (Oxford: Oxford University Press, 2019), 421–39; Johnson, *Listening in Paris*, 257–80.
59. Jerrold Seigel, *The Idea of the Self: Thought and Experience in Western Europe Since the Seventeenth Century* (Cambridge: Cambridge University Press, 2005), 473.

60. Goldstein, *The Post-Revolutionary Self*, 11, 12.
61. Goldstein, *The Post-Revolutionary Self*, 180–81.
62. One Cousinian nevertheless advised against excessive introspection and warned darkly of "the sleeping chaos" that inhabited "the depths of the soul" (Goldstein, *The Post-Revolutionary Self*, 170).
63. Quoted in Goldstein, *The Post-Revolutionary Self*, 161, 166.
64. Seigel, *The Idea of the Self*, 476–77.
65. Quoted in Natalie Petiteau, *Élites et mobilités: la noblesse d'Empire au XIXe siècle (1808–1914)* (Paris: La Boutique de l'Histoire, 1997), 97; David Higgs, *Nobles in 19th-Century France: The Practice of Inegalitarianism* (Baltimore: Johns Hopkins University Press, 1987), 8. I discuss similar themes using many of the same examples in *Listening in Paris*, 228–32.
66. Adeline Daumard, *La Bourgeoisie parisienne de 1815 à 1848* (Paris: École Pratique des Hautes Études, 1963), 149.
67. Quoted in Daumard, *La Bourgeoisie parisienne de 1815 à 1848*, 244.
68. *Journal des débats*, September 13, 1830, quoted in Daumard, *La Bourgeoisie parisienne de 1815 à 1848*, 129.
69. *Journal des débats*, December 17, 1847, quoted in Daumard, *La Bourgeoisie parisienne de 1815 à 1848*, 246.
70. *Le Carnaval, ses mascarades et ses bambouches*, (Paris: n.p., 1834), 4.
71. Ann Ilan-Alter makes this point well in "Masked and Unmasked at the Opera Balls: Parisian Women Celebrate Carnival," in *Masquerade and Identities: Essays on Gender, Sexuality, and Marginality*, ed. Efrat Tseëlon (London and New York: Routledge, 2001), 135–52.

CHAPTER TWELVE

1. Cette femme, morceau vraiment miraculeux,
Divinement robuste, adorablement mince,
Est faite pour trôner sur des lits somptueux,
Et charmer les loisirs d'un pontife ou d'un prince.
. . .
Ce long regard sournois, langoureux et moqueur;
Ce visage mignard, tout encadré de gaze,
Dont chaque trait nous dit avec un air vainqueur:
"La Volupté m'appelle et l'Amour me couronne!"
À cet être doué de tant de majesté
Vois quel charme excitant la tentillesse donne!
Approchons, et tournons autour de sa beauté.
. . .
—Mais pourquoi pleure-t-elle? Elle, beauté parfaite
Qui mettrait à ses pieds le genre humain vaincu,
Quel mal mystérieux ronge son flanc d'athlète?
—Elle pleure, insensé, parce qu'elle a vécu!
Et parce qu'elle vit! Mais ce qu'elle déplore
Surtout, ce qui la fait frémir jusqu'aux genoux,
C'est que demain, hélas! il faudra vivre encore!

Demain, aprés-demain et toujours!—comme nous!

Charles Baudelaire, "Le masque. Statue allégorique dans le goût de la Renaissance," in *Oeuvres complètes*, 1:23–24.

2. "Salon de 1859," in *Oeuvres complètes*, 2:678.
3. From *Le Promontoire du songe*, quoted in Nathalie Priess, *Pour de rire! La Blague au XIXe siècle* (Paris: Presses Universitaires de France, 2002), 75.
4. Aucuns t'appelleront une caricature,
Qui ne comprennent pas, amants ivres de chair,
L'élégance sans nom de l'humaine armature.
Tu réponds, grand squelette, à mon goût le plus cher!
. . .
Pourtant, qui n'a serré dans ses bras un squelette,
Et qui ne s'est nourri des choses du tombeau?
Qu'importe le parfum, l'habit ou la toilette?
Qui fait le dégoût montre qu'il se croit beau.
. . .
"En tout climat, sous tout soleil, le Mort t'admire
En tes contorsions, risible Humanité,
Et souvent, comme toi, se parfumant de myrrhe,
Mêle son ironie à ton insanité!"

Baudelaire, "Danse macabre," in *Oeuvres complètes*, 1:96–98.

5. Christopher Prendergast, *Paris in the Nineteenth Century* (Oxford: Blackwell, 1992), 13–14; Colin Jones, *Paris: Biography of a City* (New York: Viking, 2004), 282–85.
6. David Harvey, *Paris, Capital of Modernity* (New York and London: Routledge, 2003), 108, 234–35.
7. T. J. Clark, *The Painting of Modern Life: Paris in the Art of Manet and His Followers* (Princeton, NJ: Princeton University Press, 1994), 29, 37, 39.
8. David Van Zanten, *Building Paris: Architectural Institutions and the Transformation of the French Capital, 1830–1870* (Cambridge: Cambridge University Press, 1994), 43.
9. Vanessa R. Schwartz, *Spectacular Realities: Early Mass Culture in Fin-de-Siècle France* (Berkeley: University of California Press, 1998), 1–12, 20; Georges Montorgueil, *La Vie des boulevards: Madeleine-Bastille* (Paris: Librairies-Imprimeries Réunies, 1896), 141.
10. Quoted in Clark, *The Painting of Modern Life*, 35.
11. Harvey, *Paris, Capital of Modernity*, 221; Clark, *The Painting of Modern Life*, 47.
12. Clark, *The Painting of Modern Life*, 34–35; Harvey, *Paris, Capital of Modernity*, 95, 98, 112, 221.
13. Georg Simmel, *The Sociology of Georg Simmel*, trans. Kurt H. Wolff (New York: The Free Press, 1950), 409.
14. Baudelaire, "Les Fenêtres," *Spleen de Paris*, in *Oeuvres complètes*, 1:339.
15. Baudelaire, "Les Foules," *Spleen de Paris*, in *Oeuvres complètes*, 1:291, 16–17.
16. Baudelaire, "La Peintre de la vie moderne," in *Oeuvres complètes*, 2:692.
17. Baudelaire, "La Peintre de la vie moderne," in *Oeuvres complètes*, 2:691, 693.
18. Baudelaire, "La Peintre de la vie moderne," in *Oeuvres complètes*, 2:1418–19, 2:695.
19. Fervacques (Leon Duchemin), quoted in Linda Nochlin, "A Thoroughly Modern Masked Ball," *Art in America* 71 (1983): 188.

20. Fervacques, quoted in Nochlin, “A Thoroughly Modern Masked Ball,” 188.
21. Julius Meier-Graefe, *Edouard Manet*, quoted in John Hutton, “The Clown at the Ball: Manet’s Masked Ball of the Opera and the Collapse of Monarchism in the Early Third Republic,” *Oxford Art Journal* 10 (1987): 76.
22. Baudelaire, “Salon de 1846,” in *Oeuvres complètes*, 2:494.
23. Handwritten records of revenues from the Opera’s masked balls can be found in “Opéra presse, Généralités: Bals masqués,” Bibliothèque de l’Opéra, Paris. See also *Moniteur universal*, February 9, 1875; *Liberté*, December 18, 1871; *Le Monde*, January 4, 1872; *Le Soir*, January 1870.
24. “Le Bal de l’Opéra,” *Moniteur universal*, February 9, 1875; Nérée Desarbres, *Deux siècles à l’Opéra (1669–1868)* (Paris: E. Dentu, 1868), 251–52.
25. Louis Morin, *Carnavals parisiens* (Paris: Montgrédien, 1898), 93–95.
26. “Variétés,” *Le XIXe Siècle*, January 17, 1863.
27. François Carlier, *Les Deux prostitutions* (Paris: E. Dentu, 1887), 361–62; Andrew Israel Ross, *Public City / Public Sex: Homosexuality, Prostitution, and Urban Culture in Nineteenth-Century Paris* (Philadelphia: Temple University Press, 2019), 208–9; Report from Commissaire de Police, November 25, 1872, DB 60, Archives de la Préfecture de Police, Paris.
28. *Moniteur universal*, February 9, 1875; Jean Robiquet, “Les Salons et les bals masqués,” in *La Femme d’aujourd’hui*, February 25, 1904, 55.
29. Henri de Pène, *Le Sommeil de Paris*, in *Paris guide par les principaux écrivains et artistes de la France* (Brussels: A. Lecroix, 1867), 1003–4.
30. Victor Rozier, *Les Bals publics à Paris* (Paris: Gustave Havard, 1855), 75–76.
31. Morin, *Carnavals parisiens*, 83–84.
32. “Rapport sur l’état du Théâtre,” June 10, 1848, Ministère de l’Interieur, F 21 1042, A. N., Paris; François Gasnault, *Guinguettes et lorettes: Bals publics et danse social à Paris entre 1830 et 1870* (Paris: Aubier, 1986), 217; Desarbres, *Deux siècles à l’Opéra*, 248.
33. “Les Masques et les mystifications du carnival,” in Édouard Charton, ed., *Magasin Pittoresque* (Paris: n.p., 1850), 142; Benjamin Gastineau, *Le Carnaval* (Paris: Gustave Havard, 1855), 80–81.
34. Gasnault, *Guinguettes et lorettes*, 219–20.
35. “Préfecture de police,” November 25, 1850, F 21 1066, A. N., Paris.
36. *Ordonnance concernant les mesures d’ordre à observer pendant les divertissements du Carnaval. 16 Fev. 1857*, DB 58, Archives de la Préfecture de Police, Paris.
37. *Gazette des tribunaux*, January 18, 1855, January 8, 1859, December 13, 1862; Rozier, *Les Bals publics à l’Opéra*, 80–81.
38. “Ordonnance concernant les mesmes d’order à observer pendant les divertissements du Carnaval, 26 fevrier 1852,” DB 58, Archives de la Préfecture de Police, Paris; “Ordonnance concernant les mesmes d’order à observer pendant les divertissements du Carnaval,” 16 fevrier, 1857, DB 58, Préfecture de Police, Paris; Gasnault, *Guinguettes et lorettes*, 252. A later letter from the Prefect of Police outlines these changes in dress (January 26, 1862, DB 60, Archives de la Préfecture de Police, Paris).
39. *Gazette de France*, February 8, 1853.
40. Rozier, *Les Bals publics à l’Opéra*, 82. See also Gabriel Surenne, *The French Manual and Traveller’s Companion* (Edinburgh: Oliver and Boyd, 1852), 252.
41. *La Liberté*, September 25, 1903.

42. *La Liberté*, September 25, 1903.
43. *Le Figaro*, February 21, 1903.
44. *Le Figaro*, March 5, 1905.
45. Rozier, *Les Bals publics à Paris*, 170; Fournel, *Les Rues du vieux Paris*, 280; Demeulenaere-Douyere, "Le Promenade du boeuf gras à Paris," 27.
46. Gastineau, *Le Carnaval*, 78–79.
47. Gastineau, *Le Carnaval*, 83.
48. "Masques et masquerades," *Le Peuple francais*, March 2, 1870.
49. "Variations sur le Carnaval (Elégie)," *Le Figaro*, March 1, 1870.
50. "Masques et masquerades," *Le Peuple francais*, March 2, 1870.
51. Fournel, *Les Rues du vieux Paris*, 280; "Jours gras," *Mercure de France*, March, 1899; "Ballade du triste Mardi Gras de 1904," *Le Figaro*, February 17, 1904.
52. Jean-Richard Bloch, *Carnaval est mort* (Paris: Éditions Gallimard, 1920), 120.
53. Bloch, *Carnaval est mort*, 122.
54. Fournel, *Les Rues de vieux Paris*, 260; Gastineau, *Le Carnaval*, 71–75; *La Presse*, February 9, 1869; "Avis favorable au rétablissement de la promenade du Boeuf-gras. Renvoi au Bureau d'une proposition de M. Caplain," in *Bulletin municipal officiel*, December 7, 1895, DA 408 (Carnaval, 1878–1914), 5.353, Archives de la Préfecture de Police, Paris. For a detailed three-day itinerary of the 1864 *Boeuf Gras* procession, see "Programme officiel, ordre et marche des Boeufs-Gras," DB 59, Archives de la Préfecture de Police, Paris.
55. "Les Boeufs de carnaval," *Le Constitutionnel*, March 3, 1870; *Bulletin de la Société*, November 17, 1872; Fournel, *Les Rues du vieux Paris*, 259; "Resurrexit!," *Le Journal*, February 26, 1895.
56. *Le Petit Journal*, February 12, 1896; *Rapport présenté par M. R. Bompard, au nom du Bureau, sur un proposition de MM. Caplain et Caumeau relative à la reprise de la promenade du Boeuf-gras* (Conseil municipal de Paris, November 28, 1895); *Bulletin municipal officiel*, December 7, 1895, DA 408 (Carnaval, 1878–1914), 5.353.1, Archives de la Préfecture de Police, Paris.
57. *Le Petit Journal*, February 16, 1896.
58. Ferry in a speech before the Chamber of Deputies, July 28, 1885, quoted in *Colonial Culture in France Since the Revolution*, trans. Alexis Pernsteiner, ed. Pascal Blanchard, Sandrine Lemaire, Nicolas Bancel, and Cominic Thomas (Bloomington and Indianapolis: Indiana University Press, 2014), 9–10.
59. *Le Petit Journal*, January 21, 1883, quoted in William H. Schneider, *An Empire for the Masses: The French Popular Image of Africa, 1870–1900* (Westport, CT: Greenwood Press, 1982), 62. I have slightly adjusted William H. Schneider's translation.
60. *L'Exposition de Paris*, quoted in Sandrine Lemaire and Pascal Blanchard, "Exhibitions, Expositions, Media Coverage, and the Colonies," in Blanchard et al., *Colonial Culture in France*, 90.
61. Schneider, *An Empire for the Masses*, 179–81.
62. Françoise Vergès, "Colonizing, Educating, Guiding," in Blanchard et al., *Colonial Culture in France*, 254.
63. James George Frazier, *The Golden Bough: A Study in Magic and Religion* (London: Macmillan Press, 1987), 325.
64. A. Barolo, *Folklore Montferrino* (Turin: Fratelli Bocca, 1931), 77; Richard Bernheimer, *Wild Men in the Middle Ages: A Study in Art, Sentiment, and Demonology* (New York: Octagon Books, 1970), 50–52; Cesare Poppi, "The Other Within:

Masks and Masquerades in Europe," in *Masks: The Art of Expression*, ed. John Mack (London: British Museum Press, 1994), 211; Martine Boiteux, "Carnaval annexé: Essai de lecture d'une fête romaine," *Annales E. S. C.* 32 (1977): 365; see also James H. Johnson, *Venice Incognito: Masks in the Serene Republic* (Berkeley: University of California Press, 2011), 30–34, 169–80.

65. *Le Siècle*, March 11, 1872; *Le Petit Journal*, February 12, 1896; *Le Paix*, February 25, 1897.
66. Walter Burkert, *Homo Necans: The Anthropology of Ancient Greek Sacrificial Ritual and Myth*, trans. Peter Bing (Berkeley: University of California Press, 1983).

CHAPTER THIRTEEN

1. Auguste de Villiers de l'Isle-Adam, "Le Convive des dernières fêtes," *Contes cruels* (Paris: Garnier-Flammarion 1980), 135.
2. Max Nordau, *Degeneration* (New York: Appleton and Co., 1895), 2–3.
3. Nordau, *Degeneration*, 141–42.
4. Nordau, *Degeneration*, 144–52.
5. Jean Lorrain, "L'un d'eux," in *Histoires de masques* (St.-Cyr-sur-Loire: Christian Pirot, 1987), 19.
6. Lorrain, "Chez l'une d'elles," in *Histoires de masques*, 27.
7. Lorrain, "L'homme au bracelet," in *Histoires de masques*, 78, 79, 80, 83.
8. Jean Lorrain, *Monsieur de Phocas* (Paris: La Table Ronde, 1992), 53.
9. Lorrain, *Monsieur de Phocas*, 23–24.
10. Lorrain, "L'un d'eux," in *Histoire des masques*, 18.
11. Lorrain, "Trio de masques," in *Histoire des masques*, 63.
12. See Thibaut d'Anthonay, *Jean Lorrain: Mirroir de la Belle Époque* (Paris: Fayard, 2005).
13. Henri Rivière, *Pierrot* (Paris: Hachette, 1860), 65.
14. Paul Margueritte, *Pierrot assassin de sa femme* (Paris: Paul Schmidt, 1882), 9.
15. Robert F. Storey, *Pierrots on the Stage of Desire: Nineteenth-Century French Literary Artists and the Comic Pantomime* (Princeton, NJ: Princeton University Press, 1985), 184–85.
16. Letters to Auguste Poulet-Malassis (undated) and to Edmond Picard (March 18, 1878), quoted in Bernadette Bonnier and Véronique Leblanc, *Félicien Rops: Rops Suis, Aultre ne Veulx Estre* (Paris: Éditions Complexe, 1998), 60, 135.
17. Bonnier and Leblanc, *Félicien Rops*, 113.
18. Letter to X (undated), quoted in Bonnier and Leblanc, *Félicien Rops*, 262.
19. Félicien Champsaur, *Masques modernes* (Paris: E. Dentu,1889); see also Hélène Védrine, "Félicien Rops, *Masques parisiens*, frontispiece pour *Masques modernes* de Félicien Champsaur (1889)," in Alice Ertaud and Édouard Papet, *Masques de Carpeaux à Picasso* (Paris: Hazan, 1980), 146.
20. Remy de Gourmont, *Le IIme livre des masques* (Paris: Société du Mercure de France, 1898), 8, 153. See also Gourmont, *Le Livre des masques* (Paris: Société du Mercure de France, 1896).
21. Quoted in Walter Sorell, *The Other Face: The Mask in the Arts* (Indianapolis: Bobbs-Merrill, 1973), 164, 165.
22. Ensor to André De Ridder, in *Masques de Carpeaux à Picasso*, 166.

23. Asti Hustvedt, *Medical Muses: Hysteria in Nineteenth-Century Paris* (New York: W. W. Norton & Co., 2011), 14–15.
24. "Un Bal à la Salpêtrière," *La Ville de Paris*, March 21, 1881.
25. Jean-Martin Charcot, "Cas d'hystéro-neurasthénie survenue à la suite d'une collision de train chez un employé de chemin de fer âgé de 56 ans," quoted in Bertrand Marquer, *Les Romans de la Salpêtrière* (Geneva: Libraire Droz, 2008), 74.
26. Jean-Martin Charcot, "Policlinique du 21 février 1889: Quatorzième leçons du mardi à la Salpêtrière" (Paris: Progrès médicale, 1889), 326.
27. Jean-Martin Charcot, "Sur les divers états nerveux déterminés par l'hypnotisation chez les hystériques," *Comptes rendus des séances de l'Académie des Sciences*, January–June 1882 (Paris: Gauthier-Villars, 1882), 403–5.
28. For a diagram identifying each person in the painting, see E. Broussolle et al., "Figures and Institutions of the Neurological Sciences in Paris from 1800 to 1950. Part III: Neurology," *Revue neurologique* 168 (2012): 305.
29. Hustvedt, *Medical Muses*, 104–7.
30. Claretie quoted in Marquer, *Les Romans de la Salpêtrière*, 17; Martha Evans, *Fits and Starts: A Genealogy of Hysteria in Modern France* (Ithaca, NY: Cornell University Press, 2019), 21; *Le Figaro*, August 17, 1893.
31. Daudet quoted in Marquer, *Les Romans de la Salpêtrière*, 58, 59. Jan Goldstein demonstrates the many connections between the ideological uses of positivism by leaders of the Third Republic and the diagnosis and treatment of hysteria. "If, at the fin de siècle, more Frenchwomen than ever fell ill with a condition called hysteria," Goldstein writes, "their illness was in part a political construction" (*Console and Classify: The French Psychiatric Profession in the Nineteenth Century* [Cambridge: Cambridge University Press, 1987], 377).
32. Hippolyte Bernheim, *De la suggestion dans l'état hypnotique* (Paris: Octave Doin, 1884), 5; Henri F. Ellenberger, *The Discovery of the Unconscious. The History and Evolution of Dynamic Psychiatry* (New York: Basic Books, 1970), 85–87, 111.
33. Octave Mirbeau, "Le siècle de Charcot," *L'Événement*, May 29, 1885.
34. Ellenberger, *The Discovery of the Unconscious*, 149; Pierre Janet, *L'Automatisme psychologique* (Paris: Félix Alcan, 1907), 457.
35. Trézinoik quoted in Marquer, *Les Romans de la Salpêtrière*, 382; Guy de Maupassant, *La Horla et autres contes fantastiques* (Paris: Flammarion, 1995), 81–86.
36. Paul Richer and Gilles de la Tourette, "Hypnotisme," in *Dictionnaire encyclopédique des sciences médicales* (Paris: G. Masson, 1865–1889), series 4, vol. 15, 130–31.
37. Jules Claretie, *La Vie à Paris*, 6 vols. (Paris: Havard, 1881), 2:125–26.
38. Auguste Germain, *Hystériques de Paris*, quoted in Marquer, *Les Romans de la Salpêtrière*, 238.
39. Quoted in Deborah L. Silverman, *Art Nouveau in Fin-de-Siècle France: Politics, Psychology, and Style* (Berkeley: University of California Press, 1989), 80–81.
40. Goldstein, *Console and Classify*, 327.
41. Jane Dieulafoy, *Frère Pélage*, described and quoted in Rachel Mesch, *Before Trans: Three Gender Stories from Nineteenth-Century France* (Stanford, CA: Stanford University Press, 2020), 94, 105.
42. "Ordonnance du Préfet de Police du 16 brumaire an IX" (November 7, 1800); handwritten note authorizing Catherine-Marguerite Mayer to "dress as a man," dated September 7, 1800; "Permission de travestissement" for Demoiselle Adèle

Sidonie Louis, October 28, 1862, renewed July 15, 1872, DB 58, Préfecture de Police.

43. *La Petite République Française*, April 11, 1889; *Le Temps*, September 2, 1889.
44. *La Lanterne*, November 9, 1890.
45. Mesch, *Before Trans*, 11–12.
46. Mesch, *Before Trans*, 22.
47. Rachilde [Marguerite Eymery Vallette], *Monsieur Vénus: A Materialist Novel*, trans. Melanie Hawthorne (New York: Modern Language Association Press, 2004).
48. Mesch, *Before Trans*, 146, 157–58, 176.
49. Mesch, *Before Trans*, 217, 239.
50. Mesch, *Before Trans*, 172.
51. Mesch, *Before Trans*, 6.
52. Mary Louise Roberts, *Disruptive Acts: The New Woman in Fin-de-Siècle France* (Chicago: University of Chicago Press, 2002), 6.
53. Roberts, *Disruptive Acts*, 174.
54. See Roberts, *Disruptive Acts*, 177, 179, 198.
55. Roberts, *Disruptive Acts*, 198.
56. Maurice Barrès, *Un Homme libre* (Paris: Émile-Paul, 1912), 188. For this section, I have drawn considerably from Jerrold Seigel, *The Idea of the Self: Thought and Experience in Western Europe since the Seventeenth Century* (Cambridge: Cambridge University Press, 2005). Its chapter "From Cultivated Subjectivity to the *Cult du Moi*" has helped shape the large interpretive points of this section and provided numerous particular sources and examples.
57. Blum, *La Revue Blanche*, November 15, 1897, quoted in Frederick Brown, *The Embrace of Unreason: France, 1914–1940* (New York: Anchor Books, 2014), 23.
58. Barrès, "Préface de l'édition de 1904," *Un Homme libre*, in *Le Culte du moi*, 3 vols. (Paris: Émile-Paul, 1910–1912), 2:xii.
59. Barrès, *Sous l'oeil des Barbares*, in *Le Culte du moi*, 1:32.
60. Brown, *The Embrace of Unreason*, 34–35.
61. Quoted in Brown, *The Embrace of Unreason*, 21.
62. Gustave Le Bon, *La Psychologie des foules* (Paris: F. Alkan, 1895), 16.
63. Seigel, *The Idea of the Self*, 481.
64. Jean-Marie Guyau, *Esquisse d'une morale sans obligation ni sanction* (Paris: Félix Alcan, 1885), 2; Seigel, *The Idea of the Self*, 505–7.
65. Émile Durkheim, "Preface to the Second Edition (1902)," *The Division of Labor in Society*, trans. W. D. Halls (New York: Free Press, 2014), 9; Émile Durkheim, *Suicide*, trans. John A. Spaulding and George Simpson (New York: Free Press, 1951), 258.
66. Silverman, *Art Nouveau in Fin-de-Siècle France*, 43–49.
67. Alfred Fouillée, "Les grandes conclusions de la psychologie contemporaine—La conscience et ses transformations," *Revue des deux mondes* 107 (1891): 816.
68. Arthur Rimbaud to Georges Izambard, May 13, 1871, and Arthur Rimbaud to Paul Demeny, May 15, 1871, in *Oeuvres complètes* (Paris: Bibliothèque de la Pléiade, 1934), 267–71. See also Seigel, *The Idea of the Self*, 495–97.
69. Georges Duchêne, *L'Empire industriel: Histoire critique des concessions financières et industrielles du Second Empire* (Paris: Librairie Centrale, 1869), 52, 54. See also Georges Dupeux, *La Société française* (Paris: Armand Colin, 1964), 136–39.

70. “During the Third Republic,” Patrick H. Hutton writes, “the traditional world that was passing and the modern one in the making coexisted. Each had its own social hierarchy within which there was only limited opportunity for upward mobility. Third Republic France, more than any other modernizing Western nation, was characterized by its social stability” (Hutton et al., *The Historical Dictionary of the Third French Republic*, 2 vols. [New York: Greenwood Press, 1986], 1:960–61). See also Dupeux, *La société française*, 170.

AFTERWORD

1. Anna C. Korteweg and Gökçe Yurdakul, *The Headscarf Debates: Conflicts of National Belonging* (Stanford, CA: Stanford University Press, 2014), 16, 45.
2. Marivaux, *Lettres sur les habitants de Paris*, 26; Gilles André de La Roque, *Traité de la noblesse, de ses differentes especes* (Paris: Estienne Michallet, 1678), 404.
3. Oscar Wilde, “The Critic as Artist,” in *De Profundis, The Ballad of Reading Gaol and Other Writings* (Ware, UK: Wordsworth Classics, 1999), 225.

Index